~~she~~ joined *Smash Hits* as Staff Writer ag~~e~~ i~~n~~ mid-late 80s heyday when it sold a million copies a fortnight. Life thereafter as an acclaimed freelancer has seen her sprinkle irreverence throughout *NME*, *The Face*, *Guardian Guide*, *The Observer*, *Sunday Times*, *Interview*, *The Word*, *Q* and *Glamour*. She's also the only writer to have penned sleeve-notes to the greatest hits of both Take That *and* Oasis. Because that's how she rolls (with it).

'Not to be missed ... has all the gossip you could possibly want, but what elevates this memoir is Sylvia Patterson's own personal story'
Red

'Brilliant'
Telegraph

'Hilarious ... Pop's hypocrisy and bad behaviour are revealed in glorious technicolor'
Observer Review

'I can't praise Sylvia Patterson's book highly enough; so funny, brave, sad and wise. I totally adored it'
Jenny Colgan

'Sylvia Patterson is one of the best music writers of all time, an inspiration and a genius'
David Quantick

'Fascinating ... brims with anecdotes and musings on fame'

3011780287613 2

'A hugely entertaining, gossip-fuelled insight into some of the most influential artists of recent decades'
Daily Express

'A gripping account of a golden age in music journalism'
Independent

'Brilliant anecdote after brilliant anecdote [with] tales of meeting with the likes of Prince, Madonna and Beyoncé'
i

'It is her job to be opinionated and she doesn't disappoint ... As with *H is for Hawk*, *I'm Not with the Band* hits moments of real, aching poignancy ... dazzling'
Irish Independent

'A wonderful book by one of Britain's wittiest journalists ... incisive, poignant and often very funny'
Irish Times

'All the gossip about famous people is fascinating, and Patterson does a really terrific job of giving the insider's view, but she also has a lot of important things to say about the way society has changed over the past thirty years with regards to celebrity culture and music ... hilarious and irreverent ...
A joy from start to finish'
The Big Issue

'A thrilling, must-read memoir'
Diva

I'M NOT WITH THE BAND

A writer's life lost in music

SYLVIA PATTERSON

sphere

SPHERE

First published in Great Britain in 2016 by Sphere
This paperback edition published in 2017

1 3 5 7 9 10 8 6 4 2

A CIP catalogue record for this book
is available from the British Library.

ISBN 978-0-7515-5870-8

Typeset in Caslon by M Rules
Printed and bound in Great Britain by
Clays Ltd, St Ives plc

Papers used by Sphere are from well-managed forests
and other responsible sources.

Sphere
An imprint of
Little, Brown Book Group
Carmelite House
50 Victoria Embankment
London EC4Y 0DZ

An Hachette UK Company
www.hachette.co.uk

www.littlebrown.co.uk

TO THE SPIRIT OF VER HITS

CONTENTS

'There must be more to life than this ...'

'E.S.T. (Trip To The Moon)',
Alien Sex Fiend, 1984

PROLOGUE

HARD OUT HERE (FOR A BITCH)

December 1988, the *Smash Hits* office, London's 'swinging' Carnaby Street. Tapering plumes of cigarette smoke circle overhead as electric typewriters clatter and ping. Inner City's techno-house hymnal 'Good Life' wiggles out from the record player, where the lone human being in charge of correctly identifying the Song Lyrics – Readers' Services marshal Sue Miles – is deciphering just how many 'good life … good life … good life … good life!'s beam from its vinyl grooves. Perched at his desk, rat-tat-tatting with two index fingers, there's the shaggy-haired form of writer Tom Hibbert, snout dangling from his permanently amused lips as the man he dubbed 'Uncle

Disgusting' (shambling patron of the Record & Tape Exchange in nearby Soho) hawks hessian postal sacks of promotional CDs out the door, newly exchanged for several hundred pounds by the merrily enterprising staff.

It's the last month of the year *Smash Hits* reaches its biggest-ever sales peak of one million copies a fortnight; when pop's Big Four – Kylie, Jason, Rick Astley and Bros – rule over a wonkily diverse pop landscape featuring Enya, Guns N' Roses, Big Fun, Deacon Blue, Phil Collins, Brother Beyond (forever known to us as 'The 'Yond'), the dawn of dance music's oncoming dominance (D Mob's yodelsome rave-up palaver 'We Call It Acieed') and the irksome bleatings of dreary Irish croonster Chris de Burgh (or Chris de Bleeurgh, to give him his full title).

I'm in the glass-fronted side room we call Review Nook; now the senior staff writer, aged twenty-three, sporting a fluorescent orange and green checked nylon frock, lime green leggings and black Doc Martens, a ponytailed 'spout' of hair bouncing out of a bob where a fringe would normally be. This is where 'the phoners' happen (pop stars on the blower), a tiny office with a desktop cassette recorder attached to a phone, where a centre-spread poster of Kylie Minogue has been Blu-Tacked to the wall and captioned, inevitably, 'Actual Size'. Today the ones on the blower are Rob and Fab out of Milli Vanilli, the hunky, hapless, hair-braided German synth-pop duo whose Greatest Hit, 'Girl You Know It's True', has not long boogied in its 'under-trousers' all the way to number three in the UK hit parade. (The linguistically disadvantaged pair – rumbled in years to come as models pretending to sing, which mattered not one iota to us – always described their no doubt fragrant boxer shorts as 'undertrousers').

Today's interviewing task is the *Smash Hits* Personal File, our dossier-type Q&A specialising in completely stupid questions (say, 'Have you ever grown parsnips in a gumboot?' – as a means of unearthing suburban posho tendencies) or very simple questions as a ruse for anecdotal larks. Everyone, no matter their cultural 'importance', is treated identically, whether Bono or Big Fun. On this day, in fairness to the 'Nilli's heroically enthusiastic struggles with the English tongue, only simple questions will do . . .

What's your favourite vegetable?

ROB: Ananas.

Um . . . you mean bananas?

ROB: Er . . . pineapple . . .

Um . . .?

ROB: Oh, that's a fruit!

FAB: Mice.

Mice!?

FAB: . . . I love mice. The yellow things, you know? Oh, corn! Corn on the cob!

What's the worst haircut you've ever had?

FAB: A bowler head. Er . . . bald, you know? Yes, I had the bald head because I thought maybe that would be attractive but then I lost out – no girls!

On they trooped, Rob gamely describing the shame of his childhood bicycle because it was his big sister's and therefore had 'big banana saddles', Fab confessing he liked biology best at school but only the sex education class, where he was always 'having the laughs at the back, and the teacher would have to stop for the laughings!'

Quite why this caused me such amusement at the time, and does to this day, remains as mysterious as the subjective power of mirth itself, but by the time it was over I was stumbling, cackling, out of Review Nook clutching a C60 cassette tape brimful of the absurd, affectionate silliness *Smash Hits* had come to be defined by. Only now, decades on, do I realise the bigger buffoon was me: pineapples are known as 'ananas' everywhere in the world except Britain, while Rob's love for 'mice' was American-styled 'maize'. A naively jocular exchange like this, nonetheless, was always a win-win situation: the journalists provided japes for the readers (the 'viewers' as they'd come to be known), the viewers responded by beaming ever more affection on their amusing heroes and millions of copies of both magazine and pop singles were duly sold. It seemed like we all *liked* each other. Well, apart from Jon Bon Jovi.

What there never was, certainly, was any cynical, mean, ulterior agenda whatsoever.

April 2014, alone in the living room of my council estate flat in north London. Lily Allen is on the blower, the nation's sometime favourite pop antagonist on comeback promotional duty four years on from announcing her musical 'retirement' to become a young mum living in her dream home in the country. It's hard to tell who is having the more horrible time.

The all-pervasive media was now a treacherous domain, Lily's reappearance as a public figure greeted with persistent attacks across the internet by bloggers, Twitter trolls, cross-media columnists and the mocking commentators to be found, as she'd always so winningly put it, in 'the bottom half of the internet'. She was, condemned these voices, 'racist' for casting predominantly black women in her twerking arse-quake send-up video for 'Hard Out Here (For A Bitch)', and 'anti-feminist' for wishing the word 'feminism' didn't have to exist anymore (in a truly equal world, she'd noted, it wouldn't). There'd been a damaging 'churnalism' incident after she'd bemoaned the media's tendency to credit male music producers with female artists' success (in the case of, say, Mark Ronson's production of Amy Winehouse's *Back To Black*). Describing this editorial chestnut as 'the man behind the woman piece', it was then twisted into an assertion that Lily Allen herself believed there always *was* a man-behind-the-woman while some interpreted her phrase as 'the man behind the womanpiece'. (*Womanpiece?* Nice thought, The Sisterhood.)

I wondered how she felt about this clatteringly bumpy re-entry, which had been met with incident after incident . . .

'D'you know what? I have no idea,' interrupted a clearly irked voice. 'I haven't looked at emails, I'm getting on a plane to New York, there's been a cornflake incident at breakfast with one of my babies, but that's all . . .'

There followed a crispy conversation with the then twenty-eight-year-old erstwhile Best Pop Star In Britain who felt 'betrayed by my own sex', who grimly described how 'people have their own agendas, that's the business we're in these days', how magazines needed 'scoops', editors needed 'promotion' and bloggers were deliberately twisting her intentions 'to make themselves look clever'.

This was not the Lily Allen I'd first met eight years earlier in 2006: then a fearless, twenty-one-year-old agitator in tracksuit and ponytail, circled by pizza boxes and ashtrays, describing her errant sixteen-year-old self like some middle-aged bum down the bookies. She'd smoke weed all day in bed while watching Channel 4 Racing and reading *The Racing Post*. 'I smoked a quarter of hash a day, pretty much, from sixteen to nineteen,' she announced, with a sheepish guffaw. 'Terrible! I had loads of money 'cos I'd had a record deal that came to a standstill and I took them to court, so I had this bank account full of cash. And all my dealers knew about it so I didn't even have to go to the bank, they'd come over and I'd write cheques. Dreadful! This was at my mum's and at one point she wouldn't have me there anymore so I moved in with my Godfather [original punk hero Joe Strummer from The Clash]. But they were away a lot so I had the run of this big house. To myself. And lots of mates. And a wine cellar . . .' Today, there's not a fledgling pop star alive who would confess to such unrepentant rock 'n' roll high jinks knowing the tabloids would destroy the joy of their youthful recollections in a matter of global nanoseconds.

Back on the blower in 2014, our conversation deteriorated further. I'd come that day with *Glamour* magazine's 'agenda' (to my mind the harmless girlie agenda), to explore her world of marriage, kids, fashion and 'body issues', the latter still a cultural obsession which Lily herself had pointedly addressed in the 'Hard Out Here' video with scenes of her having liposuction in hospital as an industry executive watches on.

'Sorry, Sylvia, I just don't want to talk about these body issues anymore,' she now decided when the subject inevitably arose (she'd recently lost several stone). 'It's something I've covered so much and it's boring. The more we talk about it the more it becomes an issue.'

That week she'd posted online (to her then 613,873 Instagram followers and 4.8 million Twitter followers) a beautiful photo of herself in a bikini, from the back, a shot technically known as a 'bum selfie'. Why do that?

'It's because it's an In-N-Out Burger bikini,' she replied of the US restaurant chain now with a curious sideline in swimwear. 'Oh, just no comment on that, I can't be bothered anymore . . .'

We slugged on wearily through tabloid fame ('it's all negative now, it's very seldom celebratory'), social media ('it made me what I am but it definitely brings out the worst in people'), the escalating poison of the trolls ('the trolling has definitely gotten more so in recent years'), and the permanently negative judgements of women on other women ('well, I felt that from you two minutes ago about my bum selfie, we're all guilty'). The woman the Pet Shop Boys described to me in 2013 as a 'true maverick' confirmed she compromised her music for radio plays, and allowed her 'more saccharine' songs to be picked as singles by her label: 'When "computer says yes", according to the market research department at Warner Brothers.'

The still financially plummeting music industry, she noted, like so many creative industries, had long been populated by anxious, desk-clinging yes-men-and-women in a universally 'risk averse' culture, a principal reason why unpredictable mavericks, as she had certainly once been, were neither sought nor encouraged, never mind signed. 'Well, the simple answer to it, Sylvia, is if people paid for music instead of stealing it we'd be in a position where we wouldn't have to rely on market research,' she observed. 'And people would go with their gut instincts instead of being scared of losing their job. People find it very hard to get jobs and keep jobs in this day and age.' Furthermore, the most outspoken pop star in Britain would, from now on, be censoring herself. 'I'm gonna have to button it,' she declared, disastrously. 'People are just determined. And they make me look a tit.'

How did we get *here*, then, from *there*? From journalists as sparring partners to The Stars, to smiling assassins intent on ruining lives? From absurd comedy capers to cynical clickbait sensation? From the countless creative freedoms of the once dominant music and style magazines to the singular agenda of 'mean journalism' in a merciless showbiz media? From a win-win situation to a lose-lose? From a world of 'bowler heads' to a planet-sized twerkathon of 'bum selfies'? A world where – as a protest song about fruit shortages in Brazil once had it – 'Yes! We have no ananas, today'. And, for those who weren't yet born in the eighties, *or* the nineties, what did those creative freedoms look, feel and sound like anyway?

This book is my search for the answers and my personal story from there to here. Why I had to run away with the circus. Why I believed so righteously in The Revolution. How I sought The Truth About Everything from, of all people, a pouting procession of rock 'n' roll degenerates who I somehow believed could tell me the meaning of life. How technology (and The Man) changed music, magazines and the global media forever. How I became institutionalised along the way. And how mingling with musicians has meant, most of the time, you are definitely *not with the band*.

It's a three-decade survivor's tale from childhood trauma to Child of John Peel to comedy banter with the mighty musical giants. A scenic search for elusive human happiness through music, magazines, silly jokes, stupid shoes, useless blokes, hopeless homes, booze, drugs, love, loss, A&E, disillusion, and hope – while trying to make Prince laugh, startle Beyoncé, cheer Eminem up, annoy Madonna, drink with Shaun Ryder and finish off Westlife forever (with varying degrees of success). It's a cautionary tale which makes Ed Sheeran, today, feel sorry for me. And charts the unforeseen fate of the music mags, how they all began inching, and are still inching, towards the jaws of the deadly Dumper as music journalism slides, obsolete, into history.

But before we spring onto what *Smash Hits* used to call 'rock's lost highway', I've snuck back into Review Nook and called myself up on the blower – finally finding out how it feels to chart the contours of your undulating life not only with a total stranger, but one, like me, with an indecipherable Caledonian whinny. My very own *Smash Hits* Personal File, it turned out, wasn't always a rollicking wheeze. Even if it did, as it happens, feature a pair of 'undertrousers' flying up a tree . . .

1

PERSONAL FILE

FULL NAME:
Sylvia Anne Patterson.

DATE OF BIRTH:
8 March 1965. Same day as Gary Numan, Douglas Hurd MP, Cyd Charisse and Richard out of Living In A Box (a cardboard box).

BORN:
Perth, Scotland, on my big sister Jackie's fourth birthday, with no skin. Apparently. I was literally raw, some kind of rare condition.

The only way I was able to lie in the incubator in any comfort, until I was six months old and finally grew some skin, was to have egg-white basted all over my body. So for the first six months of life I was an uncooked meringue. I also had scarred lungs, was constantly bronchial and, succumbing to double pneumonia aged eight, was once hours away from death.

An introspective, dreamy, bookish child, I was so shy that, come 8 March, whenever anybody said 'Happy birthday' I'd go knock-kneed, blurt 'Happy birthday!' back and hide behind the other, considerably more outgoing birthday girl. I had a 'thin skin' alright. And many years later, James Dean Bradfield from the Manic Street Preachers would look at me, exasperated, as I sat blubbing in a pub over the fate of Richey Edwards once again and announce conclusively: 'You've yet to develop a second skin . . . you're *worse* than Richey!'

FIRST MEMORY:

Drowning in 1969, aged four. There were five of us kids by 1969: Jackie, eight; Liz, eighteen; Ronnie, twenty (born with Down's syndrome, he was the gentlest soul I have ever known); and boisterous, black-haired Billy, twenty-one. On a family outing by the River Tay, I wobbled off for a poke at some pebbles, toddled into the river and disappeared. Jackie saw me reappear, face down, 'like a dead frog' and, shocked into silence, signalled over to Billy who dived in, a Player's No. 6 fag still wedged in his mouth, and emerged with me in his arms. Like a scene from *It's a Wonderful Life*, they saved me.

The psychologists say your first vivid memory creates the 'blueprint' for your lifelong worldview, and to this day, in my mind's eye, I see underwater bubbles clearing away to the vision of a handsome dude with ink-black hair, crooked No. 6 hanging limply from his lips, staggering through a rural idyll with a child in his arms, looking all heroic. So perhaps I was destined to be drowning forever. Or to be 'saved' by someone, or something, possibly rock 'n' roll itself. All of which suggests I was comprehensively doomed from the outset. Or, at the very least, destined to become A Massive Goth.

FIRST MUSIC LOVED:
Abba. Elton. The Eagles. High-camp seventies disco. By 1977, *Saturday Night Fever* ruled, shimmering under the global glitter ball, captivating me and my best mate since age five, Ali (Alison), who lived yards away round the corner, as robust a redhead as I was a weedy blonde. Every Saturday we skipped to John Travolta dancing lessons in a local town hall, where thirty of us would cock a hip, splay a hand and point to the sky, like a woman's man, no time to talk.

There were 'four of us' best mates from around age five. Alongside Ali strolled Evelyn and Jill – and in various combinations, into adolescence, we'd set off all the wind-up toys in the Co-op department store (mostly Ali), trawl the local funfairs ogling the Waltzer-spinning gypsy hunks (alright, that was just me) and throughout our school years smoke single fags purchased from the ice cream van parked outside the school gates while laughing like demented donkeys at nothing, forever (all of us).

HAVE YOU EVER GROWN PARSNIPS IN A GUMBOOT?
Never, but me and Ali used to throw our knickers up a tree for a laugh, a game we invented age ten called, bluntly, 'Knicker Up'. In my back garden there was a 30-foot birch tree with tantalisingly angled branches, into which we'd throw a pair of our navy blue gym knickers hoping they'd catch on a gnarly twig. For however long it took we'd attempt to unpeg the pendulous undertrousers ('breeks', to we Scots) from the lofty branch by wielding a six-foot wooden clothes pole. And if a

particularly stubborn pair refused to come undone, we'd launch the clothes pole straight at the breeks and run in the opposite direction before the pole plummeted down upon our heads like a murderously mis-tossed caber. We really *did* make our own fun in them days. Once, during a game of rounders, Ali almost knocked out all my teeth while using a clothes pole for a bat, violently swinging it back straight into my face. No wonder I was always in bed 'with a temperature'.

DID YOUR DAD POTTER AROUND A SHED LIKE PROPER DADS DO?

A lot. Especially when whittling wooden 'swords' for the Scottish country dancing lessons I took in the City Hall, aged eleven, which he painted a glam-rock seventies silver. Born in 1919, he'd been a Japanese prisoner of war, in Burma, in captivity for three and a half years of World War II, one of the men who worked on the Burma Death Railway, those ghostly spectres we see in devastating documentaries on the plight of the Japanese POWs, the men who built the bridge on the River Kwai, starved and broken beings with bodies like white papered skeletons. A six-foot, raven-haired, strikingly Egyptian-eyed twenty-six-year-old when he went to war, he returned to Scotland a shell, temporarily blind and close to death from cholera, beri beri and dysentery. In hospital, my sixteen-year-old mum nursed him back to life; the two then married in 1947, three children arriving within four years. Ronnie, the middle child, couldn't walk for years, his Down's undiagnosed until the age of seven (Mum carried him on her hip). He had two great pleasures in life: *Top Of The Pops* and shunting Curly Wurlys up the sleeve of his V-necked jumper in a bid to hide them from his sweetie-pilfering wee sisters (and Ali).

Like most World War II veterans, Dad rarely talked about The War, though we knew a few diabolical facts: how the prisoners would encourage each other to eat the maggoty rice in their mess tins because 'it's your passport back to Blighty'; how he and his Dutch cell-mate (and soon friend) would teach each other their languages to pass the time until the Dutchman, for no given reason, had his head blown off by a warder in front of Dad (occasionally, only after a few whiskies, a stream of affectionate, incomprehensible Dutch phrases would suddenly tumble forth). Dad's post-war ambition was to find as much stability as possible, becoming an insurance accountant for the General Accident in Perth. He never complained (he never complained about anything) but I always imagined he loathed it, a man who should've been uncaged, a gamekeeper maybe, free in the countryside, surrounded by dogs and fresh air.

When Mum, now a psychiatric nurse, was on night duty and asleep during the day, we'd both go home for lunch (from primary school and the GA) to his lone speciality, 'cheese 'n' egg soufflé', an egg broken over two slices of cheese in a tea plate, whisked with a fork and grilled.

Dad *loved* music and the house shook of a Saturday night to the carousing perkiness of accordion-wielding Jimmy Shand, the melodious lilt of Sydney Devine, the dramatic soaring of Welsh operatic tenor Stuart Burrows, the bossa nova swings of easy listening crooner Engelbert Humperdinck (who Dad dubbed 'Inglehump Dinglebert', which made him wheeze with laughter) and his favourite, The Man In Black, original country 'n' western outlaw Johnny Cash. He'd also play, brilliantly, the upright piano he'd inherited from his concert pianist Auntie Rose.

He took me to join Perth Library aged seven – which profoundly changed my life – and taught me the rules of snooker aged ten, *Pot Black* now a televisual staple after its introductory purpose: to showcase colour TV in 1969, a ruse invented by then BBC2 controller David Attenborough. Snooker became 'our thing', a sport which would soothingly envelop me like the folds of a cashmere blanket through the turmoil of the distant future.

Dad was a gentle, funny, musical, handsome, canyon-deep soul who called me his 'wee pal'. Until I grew up, of course, and music (and bad attitude) took over. He once charged, furiously, into my bedroom to confiscate the silver Panasonic double cassette player/radio he'd bought me for my fourteenth birthday with the words, 'That's it, I'm taking your *best friend*!' Worse, with music came boys, soon snogging insurrectionary hobos on the doorstep, at the sight of which he'd brandish his clay pigeon shooting rifle and threaten to blast them back 'from whence ye came!' (Not that he'd ever use it: he used to threaten me 'n' Jackie, when giggling into the night in the room we temporarily shared, with a weapon housed in the cupboard under the stairs, 'the green carpet beater', a threat he found even funnier than we did.) One boyfriend in '82, fanatical Elvis Costello scholar John McKeand (something of a revolutionary spirit, forever pondering running off to join anti-fascist militiamen in Nicaragua or the like), let it be known he didn't believe in God. 'What do you believe in then?' Dad wanted to know, rifle in hand. 'Communism!' blurted John, before darting off down the path.

HAVE YOU EVER KEPT A DIARY?

For two weeks, aged fourteen, during one seemingly important era in 1980 when I went to a mod revival club called St Albans every Friday night (vastly underage, wearing a four-inch miniskirt) and was obsessed with a boy called Neil. He was in a band called (yes!) ST✪B and continually made me 'seek' (sick, as in permanently romantically deflated). Here are those diary entries in full, with no indication whatsoever a professional wordsmith would someday emerge:

January 18th, 1980. Got hair cut short. It's quite nice but I found out later Neil liked it better the other way (seek). Went to St. Albs at night. Was good.

January 27th, 1980. Went down to see the ST✪B. They were crap. Neil hardly spoke to me at all – seek.

February 2nd, 1980. Went out with Neil for the very first time. Went to see The Life Of Brian. It was crap. In the pictures Neil never even put his arm round me. Later we went to Smartie's house. They never even tried anything there. Left my bag at his house – seek. Got in at quarter to 1.

February 9th, 1980. Went out with Neil to see Scum. It was really good. Neil once more never tried a thing. Got carry out and went to Neil's house. Watched darts final and snooker final. Am now going out with Neil. He tried it on tonight, so he's not as innocent as I thought. He didn't get very far though. Got in at quarter to 1.

February 16th, 1980. Was meant to meet Neil but he stood me up. Was totally seek.

Not much of a book there, eh viewers?

WERE YOU ONE OF THOSE GEEKS AT SCHOOL WHO WAS RUBBISH AT SPORTS?

I was good at the long jump, being tall. Everything else was stuffing fags down the bra for the rigours of compulsory cross-country running. Our school was average; though named Perth Grammar School it was an ordinary comprehensive, situated across from one of the town's sketchiest council estates. The Four of Us (and new pals) were always top-ish of the class and to most of the teachers enormous pains in the arse. Aged fifteen we made the new, delicate, female chemistry teacher, aged twenty-three, cry by putting gloves on our feet and laughing like donkeys, once again. I failed my Chemistry 'O' level. And Physics 'O' level. And was kicked out the maths class, any further attendance deemed 'pointless'.

FIRST RECORD BOUGHT:

'Three Times A Lady' by The Commodores, aged thirteen, a seven-inch single played on Jackie's seventies Dansette record player up to twenty-five times in a row, its brooding piano and Disney cymbal-splash fade-out promising some mythical figure, in the future, who would surely love me forever. Who I could *truly adore*. I was a *monumental* sap. I like to think merely prone to romantic reverie but my friends thought differently, ever snorting at my initials which spelled out and indeed still do spell out the word SAP.

I'd discovered Radio Luxembourg, listening under the bobbly pea-green candlewick bedspread, where I fell in love with Elton John's portentously atmospheric 'Song For Guy', believing the central lyric 'life isn't everything' to be 'life is a terrible thing' (a Massive Goth now clearly on the way). Here, The Eagles also crooned on, inspiring a lifelong urge to bawl 'Hotel California' and 'Lyin' Eyes' alongside 'Your Song' and 'Candle In The Wind' at the drop of the first three pints of cider.

Me and Ali saw *Grease* five times at 'the pictures' and I was a lot more 'sappy Sandy in her cardy' at the beginning than 'skintight hot legs Sandy with the fag' at the end. But change was a-hurtlin' down rock's lost highway and 'skin tight hot legs Sylv with a fag' was soon exactly what I'd endeavour to be, forever. In 1979 I simply moved along the radio dial to John Peel's night-time radio show and – BOOM! – overnight, on the stroke of my fourteenth birthday, became what my mother persistently described as 'a monster from outer space'. Post-punk had erupted and so had my hair. The Revolution was nigh.

DOES YOUR MOTHER PLAY GOLF?

Mum only had one hobby: knitting intricately patterned Arran cardigans, brilliantly, in a selection of vibrant pastel colours. She could also yodel, make vigorous Scotch broth, championship cheese scones and tooth-withering tablet (a hard-baked Scottish classic made from sugar, condensed milk and gum disease), and once won an award for her exceptional nursing skills. Everything else was fags and booze. She *loved* her fags. She'd sit in her armchair, elbow on the armrest, smoke twirling up through her bouffant, bottle-blonde hairdo, giving it a tobacco-coloured streak.

She was, like so many in Scotland in the 1970s, an alcoholic. The terrifying kind for whom one drink unleashes an alter ego with no 'stop' button, bottles of whisky follow and abusive screaming erupts causing the unpredictable ripple effect of inter-familial trauma. I would worry if there was even a bottle of bronchial balm Benylin in the house (and there usually was, for me) because if she drank a drop, with its tiny alcohol content, she could be triggered into The Hole. When I came home from school and she was standing at the cooker, with her back to the world, I could tell she'd been drinking just from the way she stood, completely motionless, in a loaded silence, staring at a simmering pot she was not really watching. Her eyes (green, just like mine) were fixed instead on a vanishing point maybe a foot beyond it, some kind of inner contempt, an unspoken nuclear sarcasm emanating outwards like a throbbing infrared glow in the blackness of her mood. She would turn around, in slow motion, as I backed off, fear rising, and look at me with those glassy green eyes and a watery, false smile. 'Hello,' she'd say, clipped, detached, and turn back to the unwatched pot. At these moments I was convinced she hated me. And ever since, at some point, I've been convinced anybody who ever loved me has hated me too.

In bed at 8 p.m., aged ten, I'd listen to her primal howls, screams of abuse at my beloved dad and the demonic parroting of her psychiatric patients' incomprehensible babblings. She had, the doctors eventually evaluated, both 'a high IQ' and 'psychopathic tendencies'. Aged eleven she'd send me out for whisky to the corner shop at the bottom of our road – Handy Sides it was fittingly called – with a note and some cash, saying it was alright, this wasn't for the child before the shopkeeper's eyes, but for 'Mrs Patterson at No. 49' whom everybody knew. And when she didn't send me, she sent my brother Ronnie instead.

Christmas was the worst, the now-extended family nervously navigating the meal she'd taken hours to cook, wondering what would happen when the whisky arrived. Presents were smashed against walls. Her best friend and drinking buddy ('the enabler', we'd call her today) was always there, 'Auntie Maggie' (no relation) – who laughed like Shane McGowan – 'ssscksckckskck!', who Jackie once discovered lying at the top of the stairs 'looking like police chalk had been drawn around her'. Once, ever willing to help, she boiled a can of Heinz Sponge Pudding so dry in its pot it dramatically exploded, the once-treacly content, now turned to coal, embedding itself in the ceiling. This turned out to be our funniest Christmas moment, ever.

At sixteen, seventeen, I stayed out as much as I could afford to, never wanting to go home, too scared to go home, to the shouting and the fear and the sadness. I sought parties everywhere, anywhere, too wasted sometimes to make it home anyway. At worst, post-club, I'd slope to a local park, the South Inch, choose a park bench under cover by the bowling green and sleep 'til the sun came up, in my Sisters Of Mercy T-shirt, bullet belt and long-collapsed mohican. After one such all-night stop-out, my distraught dad, on opening the front door and seeing a wasted vagrant on his doorstep, said 'You're just like her' and slapped me across the face. I didn't blame him: it was my biggest fear too.

As a righteous fifteen-year-old revolutionary I once asked

Dad why he didn't just leave her. 'Ma wee pal,' he said, as we sat on the tartan-blanketed couch. 'You don't know the woman I married.' I knew some of it: she didn't drink continuously, had a job she loved and was great at, a methodical working mother forever sticking thermometers into the mouth of her sickly youngest daughter and taking care of the calloused feet of her handicapped son. Through the early to mid-seventies she could be temporarily jolly with a drink, there were regular home parties, and at those times her favourite song, Lynn Anderson's 'Rose Garden', quivered out from the 1970s radiogram (a teak sideboard housing a record player, shaped like a coffin), its bassline thudding up through the bedroom floor.

'Ah beg yoor parduuuhn ... ah nevah promised you a rose gardeh-hen ... Along with the sunsheeeiiiine, there's gotta be a liddle raaiiin sum-taaaaams ...'

She was a libertarian in her way, teaching us not to judge the misfortunes of others – 'there but for the grace of God go I' – befriending the other town alcoholics, who were 'more to be pitied'. She'd nursed generations of the alcoholic and mentally ill herself, 'doctors, judges, no one is exempt', her mantra a positively Gandhi-esque: 'I worried about having no shoes until I met the man with no feet.'

The only TV shows she ever loved were the fantastically sentimental *This is Your Life* and, especially, David Attenborough's natural history documentaries, which we always watched together, me seated by her tartan-slippered feet, her gazing across my head towards some jungle clearing where our hushful hero framed the fate of the bounding antelope, soon to be savaged by a pouncing cheetah. 'Oh, you brute!' she'd yelp. The look of wonder on her face was bewitching to me – serene, smiling, consumed, transfixed, like a child-in-amazement herself – the happiest I'd ever see her.

But when she was drinking, and increasingly so, I was so

frightened of her I'd have all-over body seizures alone in bed at night, in my own room by age twelve, turning my body rigid, into armour, listening to the agonised baying of the alien downstairs. Then, in the morning, when nothing was said, we'd simply pretend nothing had ever happened. From the late seventies onwards, there was no social drinking whatsoever, only bottles of whisky behind the permanently closed door of what we called 'the front room', we kids having to knock for any hesitant query. Dad drank the same amount she did, yet only became either whimsically melancholy or more ready to burst into song, declaring his consumption necessary as 'the half she won't be getting'. I didn't feel like I ever knew her, not really, a spectrum of opposing personalities housed in two dominant domestic figures; either a detached, busy presence in sobriety or a volatile stranger with a bottle behind a closed door. 'There's more facets to her personality,' the psychedelically descriptive Jackie would say, 'than a pomegranate.'

I didn't know how to trust her and I never did. Which has surely, in some ways, caused psychological ruination, forever. Or at least a propensity to over-sensitivity and blubbing for very little reason, say, at the sight of a dutiful bumblebee buzzing round a single bluebell, boggled by the melancholy, fragile beauty of it all. I'd wonder, as a dreamy kid, how anyone found lasting happiness, found the answer to the meaning of it all. Because the reality in front of my eyes, and behind my eyes, didn't make any sense. I escaped from the emotional chaos into a pathological passion for almost all forms of music and it saved my life. I've been a chronic and compulsive reality-escapee ever since.

WHICH MUSICAL 'TRIBE' DID YOU BELONG TO?

All of them. 1979: Mod with a bleached blonde crop and enigmatic sixties 'shades', a sequinned, sleeveless top borrowed from Jill's mum and two-tone miniskirt made from old curtains. Me 'n' Ali danced like gibbons to Secret Affair's 'Time For Action', everything from The Specials, everything from *Quadrophenia*, especially '5:15' and its now-alarming opening holler, 'Girls of fifteen! Sexually knowing!'

All week we saved up school dinner money for fags 'n' booze at The Mod night in St Albans (two halves of cider and ten More menthol fags between us), soon hanging out with nineteen-year-old *men*, one of whom was called Rimmy, a master of absurdism and punk rock eloquence who protected we 'schoolies' from any signs of dodgy dudeness and remains the oldest male friend to The Four of Us to this day. (Whenever we can, we go on holiday together, now a gigantic extended family where we're usually, as only Rimmy could ever conclude, 'pished as three owls'.)

1981: Post-punk upstart obsessed with Iggy Pop and dancing like Adam Ant, with an imaginary whip and everything. A new club erupted, The Banana Club, where Joy Division's 'Transmission' was always played, instigating a people-on-people "77 pile up', endangering fellow revellers with my none-too-dainty bracelet fashioned from an enormous coil of pulling chain pinched from a public loo.

1982: Massive Goth, flapping around dance floors to The Cure's 'A Forest' wearing black canvas tops with buckles up the side and winklepicker shoes. Tribal warfare raged daily in the school common room, Boys vs Girls, the stinky, spotty, limp-haired boys ever-lurching towards the stereo with their hoary old vinyl 'outings' by Rush, Hawkwind and hideously perm-haired prog-shriek howlers Led bleedin' Zeppelin (*the worst*). Me and my pals stampeded in first, all the better to educate these losers with the stuff that really counted: Killing Joke, Bauhaus, Psychedelic Furs, Aztec Camera and blubsome Esperanto yodellers The Cocteau Twins.

Late 1982: Moody Art-School Dreamer in an ankle-length,

grey-reflective Echo And The Bunnymen raincoat. Me and my music-besotted school pals (now including neighbours Claire and her cousin from England, Sandra, a Pretenders devotee of bountiful rock 'n' roll fringe) were stripped of our Sixth Year right to automatically become school prefects, because we were, apparently, 'a shifty lot'. It was the first time in the school's history this demotion had ever happened. We felt more Revolutionary by the day.

1983: Indie Kid Smiths Apostle with vertical hair, a peroxide quiff held in place with wood varnish which only came out when it finally chipped out. Wearing a *really very frightening* Alien Sex Fiend T-shirt.

HAVE YOU EVER HAD A 'PROPER' JOB?
Several. Aged fourteen to eighteen: dishwasher in the Light Bite Café; dishwasher in the local police station (keep your enemies closer, etc.); raspberry/strawberry/gooseberry/potato picker across the fields of Perthshire; server behind the counter in the café at Bells Sports Centre (only in Scotland would a sports centre be sponsored by a whisky). Every penny of these teenage employment traumas was saved for indie/goth concerts across Scotland and beyond, including Leeds Futurama where Killing Joke were headlining. Bussing down with a then-boyfriend (a Glaswegian, gorgeous, brain-free late-teen who was addicted to boot-polish sniffed in a brown paper bag, who I eventually ran away from when the heroin turned up), we slumped overnight in sleeping bags deliberately outside banks, forcing The Straights to step over we gothy bums to gain access to their toils for The Man. The mugs.

HOW DID YOU BECOME A WRITER?
After joining the library I was *lost in books* (specialising in spookery, from *Grimm's Fairy Tales* to Alfred Hitchcock

mysteries), became besotted with words and was entered by the school aged fourteen into an essay competition set up by that cradle of rock 'n' roll filth, Perth Rotary Club. Its theme was 'My Chosen Career' and, not really knowing what a journalist was but it sounded like a tantalising *life*, wrote slapstick buffoonery about sports journalism, including jokes about Ian Botham (despite knowing nothing about cricket) and a sports commentator called 'Angela Ripoff'. Unfeasibly, I won.

A spark duly ignited and was further fanned by that sadly rare and incalculably important cultural hero, the teacher who inspires and encourages: in my case Mr Jim McLaren, a lanky man with 'funny' teeth, perhaps twenty-six, who wore strikingly shiny (and possibly highly flammable) pale blue suits.

In his English class, aged sixteen, we created Perth Grammar School's very own magazine – *PG Snips* (a reasonable pun on tea titans PG Tips) – the role of music editor falling to me, soon penning hyperbolic reviews of heroes (more Iggy Pop, Psychedelic Furs, The Jam) while Mr McLaren would veer off curriculum, slipping us notes with lists of essential books (which weren't the ones we were studying): *Catch-22*, *Of Mice and Men*, *Nineteen Eighty-Four*. He, too, changed my life, further politicising an already obsessive reader of the maverick-minded magazines then dominating UK youth culture: *NME*, *Sounds*, *Melody Maker*, *Record Mirror*, *Smash Hits*, *The Face*, *Blitz*. Inside these enigmatically esoteric tomes, interviews with the likes of Morrissey, the Gang Of Four and Patti Smith would steer an already burstingly ideological teenage heart to the powerful bounty of historical and contemporary literature, film, art, poetry, fashion, drugs and everything else you needed to know about sticking it to The Man.

So it's Jim McLaren, Dad, Mum, magazines and John Peel who are getting The Blame for everything.

WHAT POSTERS DID YOU HAVE ON YOUR WALLS?

Hunks. Where hunks to me, by sixteen, were Shane McGowan out of The Pogues, Nik Sex Fiend from ever-present terror-goth demons Alien Sex Fiend and the already dead Ian Curtis out of Joy Division, the band I loved with psychotic devotion, who didn't so much write songs as build towering sonic obelisks etched with the savage truths of mankind's ultimate doom. These weren't snipped-out posters, though, but full features torn mostly from *NME* and *Sounds*, often cover stories bearing the images and words from the belligerent minds of the post-punk musical cluster-bomb: Pete Murphy from Bauhaus (cover-line: 'The Alien Who Fell To Earth'), Adam Ant (the most beautiful man in the world), Police-era Sting (look, he was gorgeous in *Quadrophenia*, OK?). By the early/mid-eighties there glimmered both Roddy Frame from Aztec Camera (the only man, to this day, to have his photo Blu-Tacked above my pillow, a *Sounds* cover declaring the words 'Roddy Frame finds poetry and romance', wobble!) and Morrissey, whose interviews in The Smiths' days were as tablets of Moses appearing in utopian dreams, sculpted commandments from a peerless wit, where a riotous thrashing – or, as he would have it, a 'severe spanking with a wet plimsoll' – was meted to The Man, the Queen and the carnivores by a celibate, drug-free, teetotal librarian in National Heath spectacles with a bushel hanging out of his breeks. No wonder he called us 'apostles'. Even if we're more likely to call ourselves, today, 'increasingly mortified by the bilious haverings of his clearly unhinged mind'.

NAME ONE SONG WHICH SUMS YOU UP?

Being a reality escapee wasn't always, necessarily, a bad thing. In summer '79, a song scorched into the mainstream UK charts like a flare from the midday sun, a coronal mass ejection from France which spoke to me as much as any righteous post-punk posturing ever did or has done to this day: Patrick Hernandez's disco-insanity belter 'Born To Be Alive'. Three notes into its head-whirling vim and I am *insane*, its lyrics a manifesto for life, on never 'settling down', on never needing those stable things 'people need to justify their lives, lives, lives' (deedle-ee!). Its video, which I never saw at the time, featured a formidably ambitious young dancer from Michigan called Madonna Ciccone whom I would one day, momentarily, appal. From the teenage years onwards I had a single ambition: to live life, as Spinal Tap had it, *right up to eleven*. It wasn't even conscious. I was just *like that*. Life, to me, was euphoric. Maybe because life was also, at core, both intensely volatile and erupting with possibility. By the time I left school in 1983 life *itself* felt like The Revolution.

And the culture around me agreed.

2

I AM THE ONE IN TEN

Turning into a teenager in late seventies/early eighties Britain seared my generation with an indelible attitude, a widespread propensity for shouting 'up the revolution!', idealistic freedom fighters forever snapping gum to The Jam's toff-baiting 'Eton Rifles' with two fingers flung in the air. Unlike our sixties/seventies hippy forebears, their heads forever in a massive bong, this was less 'dropping out', more 'barging headlong into the mainstream', left-field politics and social commentary crackling throughout the mainstream atmosphere via both *Top Of The Pops* and the weekly charts, both dominated by extreme characters and their irresistible number one songs: Adam And

The Ants' 'Stand And Deliver' *and* 'Prince Charming'; The Jam's 'Going Underground', 'Start!' 'Town Called Malice' *and* 'Beat Surrender', while The Specials' 'Ghost Town' also made number one, the wiggly, trumpeting, ska-spook eulogy to the unemployed 'yoot' of boarded-up Britain always 'fighting against themselves'.

The post-punk era, roughly '78 to '83, was arguably the most richly dynamic of all musical time, an era defined by a cultural geyser of creative freedom and political indignation – all stoked, crucially, by the incendiary spark of jokes. Where so many of the young in the 1960s seemed to completely miss 'ver sixties', this was an all-pervasive pop culture impossible to avoid, a kaleidoscopically diverse landscape of principled utopian politics, planet-storming feminism, individuality against homogenous 'sheep', Fatcher-baiting alternative comedians and everyone under twenty-five looking as ludicrous as possible, with dubiously explosive and/or angular hair, especially those fright-wigged New Romantics. This was the era of sedition, dissent and wilful intent to Do The Wrong Thing, as opposed to the eternal mantra from The Man, more dominant today than ever, 'work hard, play by the rules, do the right thing'. 'Why *should* we?' we'd protest, literally on the streets, and become disobedient bohos living on the dole instead.

The world, ideologically, worked in black and white: Margaret Thatcher was The Devil, socialism ruled, the monarchy did not (even if, er, it did), women in duffel coats and CND badges camped for peace on Greenham Common, the insubordinates' bibles were *Nineteen Eighty-Four* and *The Female Eunuch* while 'studes' nationwide Blu-Tacked Che Guevara, Bob Marley and the shot-soldier-with-the-tin-hat 'WHY?' posters on their mouldering bedsit walls. From as far back as April '77 we had *Citizen Smith* on TV: the beret-sporting, Marxism-spouting urban guerrilla Wolfie shouting 'power to the people!' at the helm of the Tooting Popular Front. By '82 we had his televisual offspring, Rick from *The Young Ones*, the self-anointed 'People's Poet' in a blazer festooned with down-wiv-Fatcher badges, as played by the now greatly missed Rik Mayall. Diverse eccentrics with defiant attitudes defined the atmosphere – Orange Juice, PiL, Culture Club, The Fall, Bauhaus, Theatre Of Hate, The Cramps, Gang Of Four, Joy Division, Aztec Camera, Elvis Costello, Psychedelic Furs, Echo And The Bunnymen, New Order, Magazine, as 'indie' labels – in the increasingly influential likes of Rough Trade, Cherry Red, Postcard, Factory, Mute and 4AD – mushroomed across the UK. Music was *about* The Revolution. And so was everything else: TV, fashion, books, films ... magazines.

And everyone who wasn't at school was on the dole.

There were no jobs in Fatcher's Britain, man. Not in Scotland, not in the early eighties, not for school leavers, middle-aged builders, anyone (unless you were in the financial industries, as usual). No wonder UB40 wrote 'One In Ten' (number seven in 1981) for the dole-queue-loitering masses. With an A in Sixth Year Studies English (supposedly the equivalent of a first-year university course) I was expected and able to go to university, but I was A Revolutionary, see; a goth in green blusher with a *bad attitude*, believing students were pretentious twerps who deemed themselves superior to those who were not students, a suspicion doubtless informed by some semi-flambéd Marxist theories gleaned from the likes of the Gang Of Four (who were, ironically, political students themselves), alongside everything else pulsating nightly from the hub of all teenage knowledge, John Peel's Radio 1 show. I made a grave inner promise: whatever I did with my life, it would be in steadfast avoidance of the suffocating, grown-up ghastliness of 'mortgages, fridges and pensions'. In the month I was due to leave school, leafing no doubt contemptuously through the local newspapers, I saw an ad for An Actual Job For A Young Person In The UK Print Media.

DC Thomson was, and remains, the only publishing house in Scotland. Founded in 1905, it was an organisation so drowned in archaic ecumenical matters it refused (certainly then) to employ Catholics, an organisation famed as the creators of the epoch-defining tribunes *Jackie*, *The Beano*, *Oor Wullie*, *The Broons* and mighty pensioner's bugle *The People's Friend*. In early summer 1983 it was seeking a 'sub-editor' on one of its magazines. Not a young person's magazine but the old woman's magazine *Annabel* (deadliest rival to *The People's Friend*), whose most ubiquitous cover girl was the Queen Mother. No matter. It was a job. On a magazine. And would mean I could leave home immediately.

Dad drove me to the interview where for several hours in a windowless room I was interrogated, Orwellian style, on whether I attended a Protestant church (which of course I *did*, hem hem). I got the job.

Within weeks I'd left home, to live in a decomposing two-bedroom flat in an alley in central Perth with childhood chums Jill and Ev, sleeping in the same three-quarter-sized bed as Jill, top to tail, commuting thirty miles every day by train to Dundee, the sometime thriving industrial Tayside city famed for its 'jute, jam and journalism'. But in 1983 it was more, to me, 'heroin, hobos and humiliating drone-work hell'. The offices of *Annabel* were housed in a series of red-brick rectangles on the dual carriageway, Kingsway East, a building which looked (and certainly felt) like a maximum security prison.

I was so afraid of The Ed, a squat, balding man in a suit who never smiled, was possibly no more than thirty-seven and seemed Neolithic to me, I nervously chain-smoked rollups all day and chewed gum at the same time, peroxide blonde mohican hastily disguised by flattening down into a middle-parted bowl. To Jill's persistent exasperation I wore her neutrally coloured high street clothes because I could hardly wear my own: a selection of Alien Sex Fiend T-shirts, studded belts and shredded black drainpipe jeans. I was living a lie and bore an aura of paranoia to prove it, hunched into an ashtray even as I was given my first-ever position of editorial authority, editor of the magazine's ever-popular real-life feature, 'Crisis In My Life'. Perhaps it was the ill-disguised gothy tendencies, but this weekly saga of personal woe from the lives of *Annabel*'s permanently beleaguered readers was assumed right up my street, involving as it did dead spouses, wheelchaired children, terminal disease and cataclysmic household accidents. Each month, I'd read through a sack of missives, select the 'best' (worst) story, fix the skewed sentences and send the 'winner' their £25 writer's fee.

After a year, unsuited to the pensioners' pain, I was mercifully transferred to the main DC Thomson building in the centre of Dundee: an imposing, red-brick Victorian monolith housing the legendary teenage titles, where an allegedly cool magazine was being launched – the dubiously titled *Etcetra*, which was not only spelled wrongly but wished, impossibly, to be *The Face* magazine produced in Dundee.

As the mid-eighties approached, style, fashion and fashionable teen magazines were flourishing. DC Thomson wanted in, its original teen oracle *Jackie* now hopelessly outdated alongside its sister title *Patches*, neither of which could hope to compete with either the fashionable new influx or the now culturally dominant pop gazette *Smash Hits*, its song words and posters now the very wallpaper across Britain's teenage walls.

The weekly inky music press and glossy style mags were one thing – serious, cool, aspiring to pretension. *Smash Hits* was another – the funniest magazine on earth, the pursuit of silliness bursting from its pages like a pop-up cavalcade of infinitely bonkers jollity. I *loved* it. Here was a deeply eccentric pirate pop ship where a mysterious entity called Black Type edited the letters page sounding like a cross between P. G. Wodehouse and Vivian Stanshall from the Bonzo Dog Doo-Dah Band, permanently tipsy on 'the rock 'n' roll mouthwash'. By early 1985 he was serenading 'viewers' (and they were always viewers, apart from when they were 'listeners') with, say, a dream he'd had the other night about 'the lovely and multi-talented Anneka Rice in full combat gear' crashing through his ceiling while he brewed 'a delicious bowl of Cup-A-Soup (mushroom 'n' spring onion flavour – yum!)', his reverie ruined by the clang of his 'handy Winfield clock radio springing into action with a blast of Russ Abbot's award-winning disc "Atmosphere"'. This level of lunacy appealed to me a great deal more, by then, than Joy Division's 'Atmosphere' . . .

Moving permanently to Dundee, I worked on *Etcetra* in the city centre with no clue whatsoever how to edit a magazine section, or anything else apart from the mawkish miseries of 'Crisis In My Life'. The inevitable solution was to copy what the proper music press did while attempting to impose on the readers my catastrophically marginal musical 'taste'.

The first two issues contained interviews I'd commissioned to freelancers with drag queen colossus Divine and sprout-fringed pop elf Howard Jones, the latter huffing, petulantly, over his hair being deemed 'silly'. Soon came my professional interview debut, with Batcave-bothering 'style' pioneers Alien Sex Fiend (swoon!). Paralysed with nerves beforehand, I drank two pints of Carlsberg Special (with lime) in a pub around the corner and went to meet my heroes in a café with a push-button tape recorder and a spiral-topped Silvine notebook, which lead shrieker Nik Sex Fiend duly snatched. 'Is your flat clean?' he read aloud with a humiliating guffaw.

I was only marginally less terrified of *Etcetra*'s managing editor, the mythological Gordon Small, the man who'd launched

Jackie in 1964 and whose obituary in local paper *The Courier* in late 2011 would recall him as 'a receiver of the Paul Harris medallion (Rotary International's most prestigious accolade for services to the community)', a 'past deacon convener of the Nine Incorporated Trades of Dundee', a 'long-standing member of the Bonnet Maker Trade' and 'one of life's real characters'. He is recalled by me as an irascible, whiskery presence thundering around the floor space of our open-plan office roaring his foolproof recipe for editorial success. 'K.I.S.S.!' he would blare. 'Keep It Simple for the Stupids!'

I turned twenty and began drinking Carlsberg Special regularly, occasionally at lunchtime, blocking the reality out. Would I spend the rest of my life here, under Gordon Small's twitchy eye, a lot like being scrutinised forever by Mr Mackay in the prison sitcom *Porridge*, until I died of dissolved kidneys?

Along the corridor, a likely lad soon sauntered into view: a twinkle-eyed Dundonian called Tom Doyle with a permanent stoner's mentality. Possibly because he was permanently stoned. He soon became a pal, the pair of us giggling at the implausibility of it all, me a fright-haired goth in an Oxfam frock writing about fashionable tarts, he an old-school Beatles fanatic at just-turned-eighteen, doing his time on 'the *Patches*' writing upbeat trifles about wibbly-legged Shakin' Stevens.

Every Wednesday by 9 a.m. I'd have the new *Smash Hits* at my desk, sneakily reading its mirthsome contents under some diabolical double-page lay-out spread on the likes of pop hunk Belouis Some, having deduced Black Type's true identity, deputy editor Tom Hibbert, now something of a writerly hero. *Smash Hits*, though, was as distant a world as glamorously ringed Saturn, still earthbound as I was at *Etcetra* where an acutely fashionable feature entitled 'Men In Kilts' was presented to Gordon Small for inspection.

'Whit's this?' he twitched. 'Men in skirts? Poof's monthly!'

It was, for him, the final too-fashionable straw, *Etcetra* thereafter diluted for the young he once more deemed The Stupids, turning ever more mainstream dull. A staff member called Mairead (a sensible young woman who agreed, nonetheless, to briefly become my flatmate) presented a feature on then also-fashionable sofa beds. 'Who buys sofa beds?' Small wanted to know. 'Well, I did,' countered Mairead. To which Small stormed, 'No ye didnae!' *Etcetra* magazine folded within six months.

The staff were assigned to 'special projects' (tinkering with new ideas) while awaiting its fate, almost certainly to be sprinkled throughout the teen titles housed along the corridor, perhaps onto 'the *Patches*' to work with Tom.

That miserable winter an ex-*Etcetra* colleague named Eve slipped an advert torn from the *Guardian* onto my ash-flecked desk.

Wanted: *Smash Hits* Staff Writer.

I stared, disbelieving, and I *knew*: this was MINE. *Smash Hits* was going to save my life. And if Eve had not done this I doubt I would ever have seen it – and died from disappointed bum life in Dundee after all.

I applied like several hundred others, maximising my chances with a comically gigantic folder – nay *dossier* – of clippings from *PG Snips*, *Annabel* and *Etcetra*, including several ghoul-rock interviews (New Model Army, Killing Joke, be-kilted singing panto-Jock with a claymore above his head Jessie Rae, who was to stand in the General Election of 2015 gaining 135 votes) and a 2000-word love letter to ver *Hits*, plus a thousand-word live review of soldier-pop folk punks The Men They Couldn't Hang, who'd played the much-revered Fat Sam's venue in Dundee. A full month passed. I heard nothing.

Distraught and depressed, I was now in trouble. I hated DC Thomson, hated Dundee and probably hated myself, pressing hard on the panic button, *escape-escape-escape*. I'd taken to smuggling tins of Special Brew into work in the morning. I thought, 'I'm going to turn into my mother.' I was bound to end up, in those *Trainspotting* times in mid-eighties Scotland, a heroin addict, dead on the streets of a hard and charmless city. (Not that I'd ever taken any heroin. Not yet. Although I would do only once, in the future, 'by accident'.) Then suddenly, unexpectedly, the call: the *Smash Hits* editor's secretary inviting me to London, for an interview.

I travelled to London – where I'd never been before – on my own, twice, to be interviewed first by editor Steve Bush, a tiny giggling man and original *Smash Hits* arts editor, followed by deputy ed – gusp! – Tom Hibbert, a slight man of unfathomable age in a battered brown Fonzie leather jacket with shaggy dark hair, brown eyes ablaze with merriment behind round, wire-framed glasses. He seemed transported from a psychedelic dimension while talking like a carousing English toff in the Jeeves novels *for real*. 'I say!' he'd exclaim, 'good lawrd!' He wondered if there was anyone I'd love to interview. 'Not really,' I decided, to his astonishment. 'Madonna?' he ventured. 'Not even Prince, he *is* mad!?' I shook my head, evidently unimpressed by the eighties' most celestial stars, and bubbled over with enthusiasm, instead, for my Marxist indie hunk with the National Health specs, Stan out of The Housemartins. This somehow seemed to swing it. Where Steve Bush, I subsequently heard, hadn't been sure, the man I'd soon know only as 'Hibbs' had persuaded him otherwise. Hibbs saved me. I got the job.

Back at DC Thomson, I told twitchy Gordon Small, in his forebodingly Victorian office, I was leaving his company forever.

'Ye cannae leave,' he thundered. 'You've just been pied!' (Translation: paid.)

He changed his mind. 'You've got twenty minutes to leave the building.'

Seven minutes later I was running through central Dundee with a plastic bag of belongings, bawling on the inside: 'FREE AT LAST!'

I took with me to my new life only the essential items, sent ahead on a freight train: the three-foot-tall, laminated-wood-sided, glass-topped Sony Stack System with inbuilt turntable, cassette player and amp my folks had given me in advance for my forthcoming twenty-first birthday; a bin bag full of clothes; and one gigantic 1950s tea chest (a present from *Etcetra*'s Eve) which I'd filled with my beloved vinyl records and cassette tapes. Boarding the 9.56 a.m. to King's Cross in my Sisters Of Mercy T-shirt, sporting an outsize peroxide blonde quiff, I shouted out the window: 'I'm too young for this!'

Those were the last words I ever said as a citizen of Scotland, waving from the London-bound train as it shunted away from my damaged, deviant childhood, the vision of my hanky-flapping mum, moist-eyed dad and giggling sister fading into a vanishing point as I hurtled towards the only dream I'd ever had. Perhaps I wasn't too young, really. But I was definitely *dangerously naive*.

REVIEW SINGLES

REVIEWED BY SYLVIA PATTERSON

3

HAPPY HOUR

The spirit of *Smash Hits* in February 1986 was to be found in a tea-towel. Not just any old tea-towel with a print of a mimsy Cotswolds cottage on, but a comedy tea-towel invented by Tom Hibbert, a prize bestowed upon whichever viewer Black Type deemed had written that fortnight's best – i.e. most ludicrous – letter, possibly something about being hit on the head by a gigantic picnic table. Meticulously illustrated by Hibbs, it included his handwritten eulogy to the wonders of washing-up-wonkiness. 'WASHING UP – THE BLACK TYPE WAY!!' it declared, before a handy instructional list. 'Tap! Just twiddle the knob and – in a flash! – your sink is brimming with piping hot water!! Plug! Pop snugly into sink-hole and – voila! – sink stays full every time! No more "sinking feeling"!! Scouring pad! A short, sharp scrub and your "oh-crikey-I've-singed-the-beans-and-they're-all-stuck-to-the-bottom-of-Mum's-best-pan" problem is solved in jig time!! Lawn mower! (Not much use for washing-up, actually . . .)'

This was the planet I parachuted into from certain-death-in-Dundee, bringing the words 'jings' and 'crivvens' into every printed sentence, a planet in polar opposition to Gordon Small's K.I.S.S., a publication keeping it eternally surreal for the students and grown-ups now also reading *Smash Hits* who found in its language, irreverence and visual japes a teen-pop version of *Private Eye* edited by Spike Milligan in a particularly juvenile mood. On the first floor of 52–55 Carnaby Street (*Just 17* and *Kerrang!* were housed in the floors above) was a world free from all forms of cynical agenda, where wheezes were invented only for the sake of the wheeze, a world where U2 had finally 'taken their place in the lineage of The Greats, like the Thompson Twins'.

The staff was largely populated by indie kids, most in their early twenties, mostly Smiths 'apostles' and John Peel devotees without a trace of indie snobbery who also loved pop in all its forms. They included huge-eyed, clever and inscrutable features/reviews ed Chris 'The Toff' Heath, the first person I'd ever met who'd been Oxbridge-educated (possibly the reason he was called The Toff). Assistant design ed Jaqui Doyle was a dazzlingly fashionable Dubliner who once illustrated the lyrics to The Smiths' 'Shoplifters Of The World Unite' with a backdrop photo of a Tesco carrier bag which would've resulted, today, in a publisher-buckling lawsuit.

The Ed, Steve Bush, was an enigmatic man who seemed to view the world as if through a gigantic set of inverted commas suspended in outer space, often seen in giggling cahoots with features/design ed Vici MacDonald, a bright, intense young woman in a fetching pencil skirt and sweeping indie fringe, the staff member who found my job application 'dossier' by accident, adrift like shipwrecked flotsam under the art department desks where it had languished for a full month (while I psychologically perished five hundred miles away). She, too, had saved me; without her casual intervention I may well have been incarcerated, instead, in a Tayside prison after a Brew-led GBH incident with 'one of life's real characters'.

And right next to my staff writer's desk perched Tom 'Hibbs' Hibbert, deputy ed, rat-tat-tatting with those index fingers across a standard issue electric typewriter all day long. Hibbs was by some distance the most uniquely brilliant creative mind I had ever encountered, a man about whom I knew nothing whatsoever, neither age nor background, though he did, I'd once been told, test acid for a living in the seventies. Perhaps this had informed the sort of editorial sorcery he routinely conjured from the ether, like the cast of characters which came to dominate Black Type, the letters page now embodying the anarchy of absurdism at the heart of *Smash Hits*, its anonymous fortnightly ululations encouraging nationwide obsessions with Una Stubbs, Dickie Davis, the Eurovision Song Contest, aristocratic pop chanteuse Princess Stephanie of Monaco and the extravagantly titled 'fruit' drink 'Um Bongo, Um Bongo, They Drink It In The Congo'.

Black Type's world included officious personnel – Uncle Disgusting, Mr and Mrs Perkins, Mr Perkins' secretary Miss Pringle (who Perkins had the hots for) – Black Type himself a disembodied voice more likely to have a conversation with ver Kids about the bungled fitting of a Hotpoint washing machine than the hunky merits, or otherwise, of Huey Lewis And The News. Ironic inverted commas now floated throughout copy like exuberantly tossed confetti (Gary Glitter was forever 'fresh' off a UK tour) while the pop star nickname was an escalating sport: no longer merely the mid-eighties inventions Paul 'Fab Macca Wacky Thumbs Aloft' McCartney, Lord Frederick Lucan of Mercury and Dame David Bowie but Mark 'Horrible Headband' Knopfler out of Ver Straits, Mark Unpronounceablename out of Big Country and Morten 'Snorten Forten Horten' Harket out of A-ha. The viewers adopted these immediately, sprinkling them throughout the pen-pal service RSVP, the page where viewers listed their pop faves and looked to contact other fans – and where *Smash Hits* helpfully printed out the full names and addresses of kids as young as eleven. (Don't think that one would fly today, eh, pop pervs?)

The office itself was a riotous, open-plan explosion of Jiffy bags, cassette tapes, twelve-inch and seven-inch cardboard envelopes housing vinyl delights and those brand new, state-of-the-art silver discs called CDs which everyone associated with the dullard's favourite, Dire Straits' *Brothers In Arms* (one million CDs sold in 1985 and a format, therefore, not to be trusted). The office housed two multi-desk 'islands': writers/section editors clattered on typewriters (usually with accompanying, individual ashtrays) opposite the production/art department, whose desks were besieged by a jetsam of flat-plans, double-page spreads, coloured paper, marker pens, glue, paints, spray paints, paint-fixer spray cans and furling scrolls of printed-out proofreading galleys. That such an obvious fire hazard was not only tolerated but never questioned is made all the more boggling by the persistent strikes on boxes of Bluebell matches.

There were no health 'n' safety rules, no editorial rules and what felt like no bosses either: the publishing bigwigs we collectively knew as The Baron (publishers Emap Metro) perhaps astutely keeping their oars aloft from the editorial characteristics: a style not so much warm and friendly as blasting you upwards through a glitter cannon of jollity shouting 'piping hot!' in your earhole, its fully formed editorial personality now turning Emap from a cottage industry contender into an actual publishing empire.

I didn't have a clue what I was doing. Three months in, my very first cover story was with Mick Hucknall out of Simply Red, on whom I had an enormous crush (like several thousand other women in his unlikely, and then largely unknown, secondary career as an incorrigible crumpeteer). We spent one hour together in the offices of the mighty WEA Records, the righteous flame-haired soul brother persistently eulogising on the global success of debut album *Picture Book*, then en route to selling two million copies worldwide. Naturally, I had to steer him away from dreary sales figures, encouraging instead a stirring tirade against the dominant political force of the day. 'I think Margaret Thatcher has done more damage to this country than the Second World War,' he soon harrumphed, formidably. '*She* has *destroyed* this nation.'

Despite widespread public belief that *Smash Hits* interviews involved, primarily, favourite colours and fancy hair, it was as loud a hailer for idealism as its inky, stinky cousins on the weekly music press. Soon Hucknall began pepper-spraying opinions on the 'racist, sexist, biased right-wing media', on the aforementioned inky music press, 'a cess pit of hypocrisy', and tirades against religion, child pornography and the nuclear bomb, 'when the bomb drops people should be dancing to our records!'

Here, I wondered, as I'd wonder a thousand times throughout the forthcoming decades, if the rich, famous and successful person before me had any clue whatsoever as to The Meaning Of It All, any clue to the route to human happiness. 'Well, my first love is music,' mused a bewildered Hucknall. 'I am happy. Definitely. I fight unhappiness – you have to.' For permanently vaporising romantics like me, however, it was also LOVE I wanted to know about. 'Oh, here we go,' he cringed. 'Well, the first girlfriend I ever had was when I was eleven. I thought she was extremely wonderful. It lasted about a week. When it finished I made a pathetic attempt at killing myself! I just lay in the middle of the road and waited for a car to come. But it never did. I had to get up because I got bored! Have I ever been in love? No. In the present situation it's just impossible to make it work.'

Was he, though, romantic? 'No I'm not!' he cackled. 'I hate what romance is supposed to be – all that sending flowers and "darling, I love you" and all that smoochy stuff. What I find romantic is just being yourself and being accepted as yourself – now *that's* romance. I very rarely tell people I love them, I've only ever meant it about twice. I don't think that's sad. It makes me quite happy really – for what's to come. I'm free. Completely free and I love it.' He looked momentarily mortified. 'You're not going to write all this rubbish down are you?'

Naturally, I fell 'in love' with Mick Hucknall. And when the first copies of the new issue arrived, featuring his dreaminess on the cover, I immediately had a mentally ill person's idea: I'd take a copy to Hucknall personally, then on a UK tour with Simply Red – and on seeing this marvellous representation of himself, with the feature entitled 'I've Never Been In Love', would immediately see the folly of his romance-free ways and fall deeply in love with *me*. I found out where Simply Red were playing, which hotel they were staying in, paid for a flight to Edinburgh, booked into a B&B (single bed, floral nylon sheets, blue candlewick bedspread) and sat on a chair in a hotel foyer until Hucknall sashayed, eventually, through the door.

'Mick?' I squeaked, as he stalled, startled in his tracks. 'Uh …' he managed, no doubt with stalker-alert klaxons whooping through his mind. 'I thought you might like to see *this*?' I ventured, holding *Smash Hits* tantalisingly aloft, eyes beseeching him to see what had so obviously appeared before him: *it's me, don't you see? THE WOMAN OF YOUR DREAMS*.

'Um ... yeah ... thanks,' he mumbled and strode off, purposefully, deep inside the hotel.

Crushed, I schlepped to a pub, then back to the B&B where I curled up, alone, under the crackle of the nylon sheets and stayed awake, cringing, *for a full eight hours*. Only today, thirty years later, can we confidently assume I was the only blatantly propositioning woman the flame-topped Lothario didn't even *attempt* to seduce in the whole of the 1980s ...

Normal daily *Hits* life, thankfully, was less mortifyingly naive. Safely bunkered in Carnaby Street, I filled the news section, Bitz, with my little-known indie heroes, just as I'd gotten away with it at *Etcetra*, with fewer gothy madmen involved. Forever lurking in Review Nook, I'd be permanently on the blower with the likes of rambunctious London folk troupe The Woodentops, be-cardied Glaswegian schminders The Soup Dragons and swirling Mancunian guitar spooks The Chameleons, interviews mostly centring on their pre-'fame' lives as members of Maggie's Three Million.

'We were completely skint and on the dole,' chirruped Mark Chameleon in July '86, 'jumping up and down in front of our bedroom mirrors with guitars with no strings on. I'd rather have been doing that though and getting me £18 a week, as it was then, than getting £50 a week to pack vinegar. I never wanted a proper job. I never wanted to grow up either. In fact, I'm still sixteen in me head. Who wants to be grown up? Bills and children ... no thanks.' Hurrah!

Soon, indie heroes were everywhere, including the mighty Richard Butler out of the Psychedelic Furs, announcing he was psychologically unwell. 'When I'm by myself for any length of time late at night, I start going a bit ... round the bend,' he declared. 'I have to have other people around otherwise I lose grip really easily of what's real and what's not. I keep thinking I'm having a heart attack. I go for a run around the block and I think that if I am having a heart attack, I'll die, but if I make it back I must be alright.' Crumbs.

I'd spend a day in London with my Marxist indie-geek heroes, The Housemartins, who were none too keen on interviews, especially my beloved Stan, who agreed to speak officially only after eight hours in his company, six conversations as to whether he should or shouldn't 'do interviews' and several cans of (as ver Hits would always deem it) 'best' 'bitter'. 'Have you ever grown parsnips in a gumboot?' I inevitably wanted to know, and Stan – being a proper pop star – ran with the wheeze. 'No, but I used to grow cress in a hippopotamus,' he announced, gamely. 'Y'know those pottery hippopotamuses? I had a square yard in the back garden which my parents had given me and there I used to grow the cress in the hippopotamuses ... oh, let's waltz instead, shall we?'

Here, Stan out of The Housemartins, two years into my profound obsession with his bespectacled brilliance, waltzed me round a grassy traffic island knoll by a car park somewhere in central London while continuing to eulogise on his mossy-fingered skills, 'I also grew pansies and we had these lovely Victorian plum trees ... so as you can see I'm an incredibly boring person and I'd rather you didn't print any of this because I've got nothing to say!'

Wibble ...

The more mayhem we could muster, it seemed, the more *Smash Hits* began to sell. And sell and sell and sell ...

'Ver *Hits*', to give it its full title, was invented in 1978 by ex-*NME* editor Nick Logan, a mutineer ideas man disillusioned by *NME*'s corporate rulers IPC, a then thirty-one-year-old visionary looking to reflect the changing culture. 1978 was perfect timing, the year post-punk's sonic bomb exploded nationwide (alongside The Revolution), platoons of sometime punks now elbowing in from the shabby-togged shadows to redefine the concept of what a number one pop star could be. In November '78, Blondie were on the cover of *Smash Hits* (alongside the words 'NEW' and 'MONTHLY'), the pages within a goth/new-wave/disco-pop grotto of news, song lyrics and interviews starring Siouxsie And The Banshees, The Stranglers, Buzzcocks, The Boomtown Rats (who were, lawks, the centre-spread poster), Abba and Olivia Newton-John, alongside the words to Sylvester's 'You Make Me Feel (Mighty Real)' and The Commodores' 'Three Times A Lady' – that magnificently weedy, first-ever single I'd bought. It was the actual *definition* of the inside of my thirteen-year-old head (though I was yet to know the *Hits* existed, too distracted throwing breeks up trees).

For the first few years it was a relatively 'straight' read, friendly and informative, knowing its true power lay in full-colour posters and the words fully transcribed (sometimes hilariously) to the latest hits – in fact calling itself officially 'a song lyric magazine'. In 1981, MTV changed everything, bringing with it overnight the visually led era of dressing up, preposterous hair and huge, global hits. *Smash Hits*, too, evolved, developing a fresh, distinctive voice via its new editor and features editor, Dave Hepworth and Mark Ellen, lifelong magazine soulmates and a duo more dynamic to this day than, er ... er ... Godley and Creme (whose undulating funk-pop wobbler 'Under Your Thumb' was the fifty-first most popular song of 1981. I digress ...)

Smash Hits soon called itself 'The Most Pull-Out-And-Prise-Open Publication Of The Decade', while the words 'dreadful' and 'not much cop' were regularly spotted alongside news items titled, say, 'Extremely Silly Haircuts Department Presents: Eugene Reynolds from The Revillos' (hopeless Scottish rock ghouls whose lead singer sported a formidably backcombed mohican). Soon, such a barnet would be dubbed a 'fright wig' and a brand new *Smash Hits* lexicon emerged, enthusiastically extended by two incoming writers: theatrically amused pop scholar and future Pet Shop Boy Neil Tennant and The Legend Of Tom Hibbert. The concept of The Dumper soon arrived, the canyon-sized, metaphorical burial ground of once mighty, now ruined, pop giants. By the time I arrived in February '86, Dave Hepworth and Mark Ellen were gone (off to invent what I'd think of as hoary old bloke's magazine, *Q*), Neil Tennant was a number one pop star and Hibbs was the force behind the psychedelic lunacy now dominating the magazine, soon further encouraged by incoming ed Barry 'Banzai' McIlheney, a garrulous Northern Irishman who, during his tenure at the *Melody Maker*, had once been attacked in the street by shirtless gypsy madman Kevin Rowland.

By the time Barry arrived *Smash Hits* was Britain's Brightest Pop Gazette, a vast-selling fanzine (half a million copies a fortnight) somehow conjured between us from twelve-inch cardboard envelopes, the accompanying photographs and PR blurbs. We simply made stuff up: that summer came my inaugural Glastonbury with genial lensman Paul Rider and his equally genial wife Adele (not that one, who was not yet born), an editorial ruse erupting to pretend I'd hazardously hitchhiked to Worthy farm, up-thumbed photos of the 'stranded' *Hits* reporter duly snapped all the comfortably driven way.

I wonkily pitched a tent and in the name of 'homely' décor affixed to its interior an enormous poster of (who else?) Alien Sex Fiend. The greatest thrill that weekend was interviewing Half Man Half Biscuit – the folk-rock wits from the Wirral whose surreal-pop masterpiece *Back In The DHSS* had dominated the indie village in 1985 – in the back of their fag-fumed Transit van. The *Smash Hits* Glastonbury Team 1986 lasted one night out in the field before heading off mid-Saturday night for a delicious meal and a fluffy bed in a nearby swish hotel, photographs of which then became 'a dream sequence' printed in ver *Hits*, pretending we'd been (as if!) lying in the swamp for days.

In considerably dryer record label offices across London, larks were had with comedy goth heroes The Mission (one of whom, Craig, wore a spare make-up bag I was somehow carrying around, green and quilted, as a fetching 'cossack hat'), while indignation was doled to the newly-turned-eighteen Will Smith in his Fresh Prince guise, accused (due to the dubious lyrical content of his swaggering hip hop number 'Girls Ain't Nothing But Trouble') of being 'a vain, arrogant, conceited swine'.

'Well that's the image I'm trying to be!' he beamed, delighted, wiggling his enormous, charming ears.

And to think I was *paid* for this. An *actual* princely sum, of £10,200 a year and, certainly in comparison to DC Thomson's meagre carrots, was approaching *reasonably well off*. In the days before ATM machines existed on every high street I'd cash a £200 cheque at the bank and, being a non-believer in namby-pamby handbags for girls, £200 in notes remained wedged inside my biker jacket pocket in a rolled-up wad until I'd frittered it all away, mostly on fags 'n' booze. This was absolutely The Life. Even if I did live in the outlying south London enclave of West Norwood with a flat-owning stranger recommended via an *Etcetra* acquaintance: a formidable woman called Nicky Philbin (sister of Maggie Philbin, not only presenter of both eighties kids TV staple *Swap Shop* and soothsaying science show *Tomorrow's World* but wife of Keith 'Cheggers' Chegwin). Sidelined in Nicky's spare room more as a lodger, my wayward ways clearly made her nervous, soon leaving security-related notes around the flat: 'I am TERRIFIED of leaving you here alone.' I lived, however, mostly in the pub, possibly giving rise to Nicky's concerns as I persistently bounced into the flat at midnight to loudly fiddle with the grill.

Most nights, many of the *Smash Hits* staff would drink together either in the Coffee House round the corner on Beak Street, or in The Store round a different corner in Kingly Street, occasionally joined by the stinky-haired crew from *Kerrang!* Devilishly, they'd teach we supposedly delicate pop kids how to drink the metal-mutha staple 'Depthcharge' (a shot of tequila, in its shot glass, dropped in a pint of cider), and thus arguments were fuelled about the merits of 'hair cut' bands vs 'hair metal' bands (not so very different, after all). Routinely dressed in a black biker jacket, with bullet belt, fluorescent orange nylon dress, Doc Marten boots, vertical peroxide hair and eyebrows pencilled in like crow's wings, I was starting to be recognised. 'Oi!' I'd hear on the tube. 'It's Mary the punk off *EastEnders*!'

Of a morning, post-pub, if feeling crispy, I'd have a half-hour's snooze in the Competitions Room (sneaked in through the usually locked door by a sympathetic Sue Miles) and use the prizes as makeshift bedding: an Elvis-etched pillow for, er, a pillow, and a Black Type tea-towel for a sheet. Soon, I'd travel around Britain – and the world! – for free: off to, say, Romford, to hear how Five Star's cat was not only called 'Puppy' but the enforced wearer of a four-limbed, sparkly blue jump-suit featuring the word 'PUPPY' in silver sequins. To prove it, Doris showed me the unlikely garment pegged on their garden washing line (some years before Steadman, tragically, ran over Puppy in the family driveway). There were trips to Los Angeles, to hang out in Katrina And The Waves' tour bus, dipping my toes in the Pacific Ocean and feeling the infinite hugeness of our intoxicating planet for the very first time. And that moment would be photographed and then printed in *Smash Hits* with the caption, 'a *Smash Hits* reporter interviewing "the waves" haw haw.' The irrepressible Katrina, it turned out, was a keen UK chart watcher after being unexpectedly huge, momentarily, in Britain, with the trumpeting whistler 'Walking On Sunshine'. 'What else is in the charts right now?' she wondered. 'Is it still barking dogs and puppets and football teams and granddads and three year olds? It's a funny old chart you've got there . . .'

She *knew*: *Smash Hits*' surging success that year was made all the more satisfying in puzzling pop times. After the classic early eighties pop boom which gave us Duran Duran, Spandau Ballet, Culture Club, Frankie Goes To Hollywood, Wham! and all those faces we associate today with the Band Aid single in 1984, 1986 was a transitional period dominated by novelty pop in the likes of yodelling choir boy Aled Jones, the frothing effigies of TV's *Spitting Image* and bespectacled sitcom chambermaid Su Pollard, also the host of *It's A Royal Knock-Out*. Mere months on from the Live Aid concert in 1985, Welsh shouty-rock buffoons The Alarm were on the first *Smash Hits* cover of '86 and a pop year muddled on through the dubious thrills of cover stars Nick Kamen (Levi's-dropping simpleton 'smouldering' in a launderette), Bono and Maire Brennan (woefully windswept duet featuring The Voice of Clannad) and an indie fright-rock coup in glum-faced Glaswegian feedback pedlars the Jesus And Mary Chain, heralded by the cover-line, 'Loud, Spotty and Weird!' And still no bigwigs interfered . . .

At my staff writer's desk the madness continued daily, writing nonsensical whims for the news section, Bitz: here fizzed the magazine's crucible of editorial chaos, where the heralding of a new single by, say, The Blow Monkeys would be accompanied by a stupid poem about monkeys playing blow-football. When forced to interview 'Chris de Bleeurgh' on the occasion of his hideously humungous hit single 'The Lady In Red' (the worst song ever written), he droned on and on about his marvellous yacht and his dear friend Princess Diana, and so – in cahoots with the cackling art department – conspired to a crafty wheeze: we'd let him waffle on in print and incrementally reduce the typeface as he carried on, his dolorous dribblings soon bleeding unintelligibly off the bottom of the page. And still no bigwigs interfered.

Cocooned in Review Nook, I'd engage with The Stars in America while attempting to avoid what we called 'a Click! Brrrr ... situation' where the star would ostentatiously hang up, having failed to take amusedly to the *Smash Hits* Stupid Question which became more demented with each passing month.

Have you ever been humiliated by a conjurer?
Siouxsie Sioux hadn't, but was the kind of person who always volunteered herself to conjurers 'and was never picked' (surely too much of a liability).

Why are all budgies called Joey?
Swedish metal 'hunk' Joey Tempest out of Europe didn't have a clue. 'What's budgie? Is that another vegetable?'

Do you wear your beard in or out of the bedclothes at night?
Billy Gibbons of ZZ Top was proud and 'out'.

Sometimes, though, enquiries as to the rumoured existence of a pet goldfish (LL Cool J) or the reputed stretch of one's formidably groovy singing mouth to a full eight inches (Darryl Pandy, voice of Farley Jackmaster Funk's 'Love Can't Turn Around') did indeed produce the dread 'Click! Brrrrr ...' And *more* people bought ver *Hits*.

Occasionally, though, the unstoppable force of the japes

would come up against a more sinister immovable object. Like the moodsome, northern, childhood heroes of my inaugural goth years. The ones who used to be Joy Division and who, soon, wouldn't be my heroes anymore.

Breakfast at the Sunset Marquis. 7/11/86

4

EVERYTHING'S GONE GREEN

In 1979, part of being both teenage revolutionary and Monster From Outer Space was to voluntarily traumatise oneself with the desolation soundscapes juddering, shimmering and imploding like collapsing buildings out from the silvery cassette player via, surely, the most exquisite musical interpreters of The Horror Of Humanity the world had ever known: Joy Division.

At fourteen I was *obsessed* with Joy Division, transfixed and tormented by their sonic mortal wounds, setting myself the 'homework' of making up lyrics to their enduringly harrowing instrumental passages in my provincial bat-cave bedroom, a sombre task undertaken via scarlet lightbulbs, a purple chiffon scarf hung limply over a lampshade, while simultaneously doodling upside-down crucifixes on A4 lined paper alongside the word UNDONE. Joy Division knew The Answer, alright, and the answer was: We're All Doomed. (I was Scottish, after all.)

In the literal wake of Ian Curtis' suicide in May 1980 I'd then watched, astounded, as they emerged from the chrysalis of agonised shock into New Order, pulsating, glistening electro-rock pioneers who went dancing under disco-balls and everything.

By '86 the enigmatic Mancunians were permanently living atop unassailable ice-cliffs of cool, obstinate outsiders whose thrumming single 'Bizarre Love Triangle' became a number one classic on the 'indie' charts and a number 56 non-hit in that year's official Top 40 – which only served to make their coolness even icier. They were now a band who didn't play encores, or perform cover versions, or sign autographs, or allow any adverts or any marketing whatsoever, and very rarely gave interviews (because that's how *punk rock* they were). Not that I knew any of this when *Smash Hits* dispatched me to talk to my shadowy heroes in sunny Los Angeles in the autumn of '86. And when thirty-year-old Barney Sumner's first words to me were 'Ask us anything horrible and we'll break yor fookin' legs,' I didn't think he was being funny. I'd never met anyone from Manchester before.

New Order should never have agreed to appear in *Smash Hits* and indeed they hadn't, with no idea myself and equally naive photographer Julian Barton were arriving on their American tour. It was a profile-raising ploy invented by their Factory label boss, flamboyant mischief-maker Tony Wilson, who was also somewhere (currently missing) in Los Angeles. New Order would've deemed ver *Hits* the pamphlet of the pop weeds, its cover star on the day we arrived the dreamy-eyed *EastEnder* turned 'singer' Nick Berry (featuring the less than indie-cool cover-line, 'I can't sing for toffee').

We were alone, without a PR, a situation which was always (and remains) precarious: the public relations official is normally the single connection between reporter and artiste, their lone mission to Make Sure This Thing Happens (and keep their wallet permanently open). In the pre-digital age, when pedal-bin sized mobile phones were still the preserve of the yuppie stockbroker, your only lifeline to assistance was the landline in the hotel room you currently weren't living in. Our instructions from the *Hits* had been straightforward but minimal: meet New Order in LA (man), accompany them on-the-road to Santa Barbara, see the show, travel with them the following day to a second show in San Francisco and come home with a rollickin' tale of hilarity – despite the fact these people were New Order and indeed had once been Joy Division.

Inside a functional record label office slouched singer Barney Sumner, co-creator of some of the most life-affecting music my teenage soul had ever dissolved to, peering inside *Rolling Stone* magazine (his sort of magazine). After the leg-nobbling opening gambit, he announced he was unwell.

'Ooooh, this is my third hangover today,' he drawled, in the detached Mancunian way. 'And I've been sick.'

Me, in cheery voice: *What were you up to last night?*

'Oh, we write our lyrics in the middle of the night.'

He turned back to his journal and ignored us, exchanging derisive snorts with nearby bassist 'Hooky', instantly confirming their legendarily 'uncooperative' ways. Terry The Tour Manager informed us New Order weren't actually playing in Santa Barbara that night, it was the following night, and San Francisco was never an option 'because we haven't booked flights for you'.

Next morning, as New Order prepared to drive to Santa

Barbara, we found Barney with a breakfast bagel by the pool of our hotel, the Sunset Marquis, and duly sidled up. Accompanying him/them on the drive would, surely, be the obvious interview opportunity? 'No,' he dismissed behind his shades, 'because there's no room for you in the car.'

Minutes later, as Julian and I stepped into a cab for the hundred-mile journey (paid for by Julian's credit card, a world traveller's essential I still knew nothing about), an enormous caramel-coloured American Cadillac tyre-squealed out of the parking lot and zoomed up Sunset Strip carrying Barney in the back of it, alone. Soon, at the venue, we'd be further ignored before soundcheck, see their show (not much cop, later blamed on 'technical problems') and eventually loiter around their dressing room, which was buoyantly fizzing with an opportunistic coterie of undeniably Foxy Ladies. 'I didn't ask them back,' sniffed Barney, snatching my Sony Walkman tape recorder and switching it off. 'I don't want you going on about the girls, it's nothing to do with me, I didn't let them in.'

Eventually, around midnight, he conceded to an interview in my chalet back at the Sunset Marquis, a hush-toned, cynical affair, mostly about his aversion to fame, all hugely earnest to the chippermost kids of ver *Hits* more used to Bananarama 'refreshed' on a bottle of Tizer. After forty minutes he sloped away to a party in the chalet next door.

Around 3 a.m. your somehow genuinely startled pop reporter was stirred awake by the unmistakable sound of a rock star having sex with two groupies, as was clearly audible the moment I placed a bathroom glass to my chalet wall and strained for the very best listen. The next morning, with Barney gone, I heard the girls giggling and knocked on their door, was invited in by two gothy late teenagers, and interviewed the pair for a lark – none of which could be printed, of course, in Britain's Brightest Pop Gazette.

In October 1986 the *Smash Hits* article appeared with the headline: 'Ask us anything horrible and we'll break your legs!' Its 'highlights' included Barney Sumner's loathing of clichéd rock 'n' roll behaviour ('I could have milk bottles full of drugs, warehouses full of women, but do too much of anything and it'll do your head in'), his loathing of 'normality' ('it scares the shit out of me'), his refusal to confirm he had a girlfriend back home ('that's my private life and I'm going to keep it that way'), and a psychedelic meander on how reading a Huckleberry Hound book aged ten convinced him to never work for The Man (fair enough). The story also comprised the 'comedy' tale of the thwarted reporting the *Smash Hits* two had endured, featuring some blaring innuendo concerning our foxy young friends. 'Ten minutes later,' nudge-nudged the article, 'some very un-male-like giggling can be heard resounding through the walls – is Barney having some very restless dreams? The next morning, two American foxtresses are spotted scurrying gleefully along the hotel balcony holding aloft a pair of very horrible shorts bearing a striking resemblance to Barney's very own. How very very "strange".' In further cringing levels of unsubtlety, there was also printed a tiny photograph of the two girls, holding Barney's shorts indeed aloft, captioned with the words: 'Two American foxtresses pilfer Barney's "shorts" and have a birrova laugh!!'

Within weeks, New Order were interviewed in thunderingly righteous indie weekly *Melody Maker* and Barney had his say. If he ever saw me again he would 'kill' me. His wife was threatening to divorce him. And three years later she *did*. I did not know Barney Sumner was married and nor did I know (until I looked it up on Wikipedia in the very distant future) that the couple, in 1986, had a two-year-old son. And if I had, those cackling quips would never have been written (the *Hits* was no *News of the World*). Back in the office, Barry McIlheney now insisted I took *Smash Hits*' account cabs everywhere, 'just in case'. I was officially on Indie Death Watch.

At the time, many female colleagues congratulated me for withstanding Barney's withering attitude and outing what we'd now describe as a flagrant celebrity love cheat. Today, though, the 'great' New Order runaround fiasco of 1986 seems howlingly naive, a joyless and ill-judged one-note harrumph both on stars who refused to Play The Game and a desire to prove Barney Sumner a bounder – hardly for cheating on his wife (who I did not know existed) but for failing to turn up to a *Smash Hits* interview with an arsenal of hilarious jokes. We were always scuppered, anyway, with the realities of rock 'n' roll: to protect the youngest viewers, the majority of references to wimmin, booze 'n' drugs were merely skipped around in a riotous twinkle of euphemism, slang and innuendo, all 'rock 'n' roll mouthwash', 'foxtrels' and 'mazin' rumpo . . . speryoooo!'

In the end, as I'd relentlessly rediscover, it's often your own fault when your heroes let you down: in the up-the-Revolution eighties, certainly, the reason you loved them in the first place was because they were insolent punk-rock renegades with two fingers cocked to The Man. To them, however, some of we journos were indistinguishable from The Man, no matter the cut of our similarly 'confrontational' hairdos. Although Death Threat Issued In The *Melody Maker* was perhaps taking things a bit too far.

Almost three decades later I accidentally found the taped recordings of this saga in long-forgotten boxes and listened to them afresh, for a laugh. Hearing your own voice from three decades ago is, it turns out, a terrifying encounter with the folly of your own youth, especially if you're listening to the distant echo of yourself at your most professionally bewildered and howlingly inarticulate. And dimensions more provincial. A voice so Rab C. Nesbitt Scottish, in fact, where there's the hippie-ish 'man' today there was a clearly enunciated 'mon'. Searching for the elusive joke, here was evidence I'd asked Barney Sumner if 'Bizarre Love Triangle' was 'about a triangle?', perhaps seeking the little-known phenomenon of trigonometry-pop. 'No, I read the *News Of The World* and I thought how ridiculous it was, the headlines,' he affirmed, sounding like a sardonically stoned Professor Brian Cox. '"Saucy Vicar Caught In Bizarre Love Triangle." See, basically we're a bunch of dumb bastards from Salford.'

I not only had the Barney tape but one bearing the Biro-scratched words 'the foxtresses', their interview taped over my much-loved copy of The Men They Couldn't Hang's debut album *How Green Is My Valley* (the band I'd reviewed for my *Smash Hits* job application 'dossier' and who were, therefore, partly responsible for getting me into this mess in the first place). Midway through their lively nineteenth century Tommy-pop ('And I'll rip that shurt off you!/Oh! Your shurt of blooo!') two teenage voices piped up in the drawly Californian way. Foamy memory clouds parted and a scene re-emerged, of Julian the photographer and I sitting on the floor of a Californian hotel chalet listening to the ear-tickling recollections of two giggling LA 'rock chicks', the full details of which need not trouble us today (m'lud) but included the following telling statement: 'Oh my Gaaaahd, he was just . . . *Superman!*'

Today, I keep in the bottom of a bedroom cabinet a memento of this juvenile recklessness – Barney's beige shorts, which I can't bear to throw away. After the girls left that day, Julian and I surveyed the abandoned garment, poked in the pockets and found $123 – a fortune in 1986. So we spent it on a trip to Disneyland, where we boarded the Fantasyland boat cruise and sang through the dizzyingly twee, animatronic children-of-the-planet parade, It's A Small World. 'It's a world of laughter, a world of tears/It's a world of hope, it's a world of fear!'

On the plane home I couldn't wait to get back to the *Hits*, where the joys of surrealism would once again make sense of the confounding mores of mankind. Even though hardcore reality, soon enough, would come hurtling through the door instead.

Oh! Gumboots they surely are a full-bellied wheeze,
You can stuff them full of parsnips and feet and peas,
They're handy when you visit your farmer chum,
And the pair of you take a stroll in his field of dung.

5

HE AIN'T HEAVY

By early '87 I'd been promoted to Bitz editor and became, evidently, *mad with editorial power*. Colluding with the buoyant imaginations of the art department, the news section now indulged flights of visual lunacy, with illustrated 'theme' backdrops from aliens in outer space to underwater scenes of wonky fish and Stupid Sports of The World starring Ian 'Beefy' Botham with a toy helicopter on his head for no reason whatsoever. Interviews with marginal cult figures and personal indie heroes were now *constantly* shoehorned in; merrily bundling fame-wards The Bodines, That Petrol Emotion and Throbbing Gristle terror-dude Genesis P. Orridge (now with Psychic TV) while lobbying for, and attaining, a one-page feature for the zero-known Felt, Birmingham's single-named indie-spook luminary Lawrence, who described himself as 'horribly old' at twenty-five. The occasional 'legend' piped aboard the blower, like grandma's favourite Des O'Connor. 'I had a hit all about London in the Swinging Sixties called "Dick-A-Dum-Dum,"' recalled the golfing be-jumpered fifty-five-year-old, gamely.

In spring, I was dispatched to interview, face-to-face, my first-ever *actual legend*, Diana Ross, then aged forty-three, our differing worlds colliding in the managing director's office of her multi-million pound record label, where she sat elegantly cross-legged on a black leather settee in a cream and brown, soft woollen trouser suit. She was, it turned out, a delight, all serenades on dress-making, bringing up her three daughters and her chum Michael Jackson lying in his oxygen tent 'for fun!', a man who was 'really truly shy and music is his life'.

It was Prince, The Purple Perv, who was bonkers. The first time they met, she cooed, 'he just would *not* look me in the eye, so there was no real communication because there was no eye contact, that was *weird*'. We talked, somehow, about washing up and wearing household Marigold gloves. 'Yes I do!' she giggled. 'Ah hih hih hih! I *do* wash my dishes! Do you think people will mind if they find out I'm ordinary? Have I just come off my pedestal?'

My work, therefore, was done: transforming the world's most avowedly fabulous and notoriously pompous Original Soul Diva into a merrily domestic pot-scourer singing in a cloud of suds. Suddenly, she leaned in.

'Can I just tell you the truth here?' she shimmered.

Certainly ma'am, that's what I'm here for.

'Money does *not* bring you happiness,' she concluded, surely sensing a young person seeking The Answers. 'The things that really bring happiness don't require it. Like good friends and family. Going for a picnic. Going on a long walk. Relationships. Dancing or reading a good book. Watching a daffodil grow. I have to tell you I have a lot of sequinned gowns and jewels and I love champagne and caviar but I *also* like a hot-dog, you know?'

She autographed a press photo for Jackie – a glittering black and white photo of 'Miss Ross' singing in the seventies in a silver sequinned frock – as I had my first, psychedelic, out-of-body interview experience. Eighteen months on from certain-death-in-Dundee I now zoomed away from the face of the earth to float at the edge of space, contemplating from miles above this laughably unlikely scenario – a whimsical pop fanatic from the Scottish provinces being taught lessons-of-life by The Woman Who Embodied The History of Pop Itself. The world, now, was atomically *built* on surrealism.

Back at ver *Hits* in heady '87, the editorial language became even more preposterous as fright wigs were joined by 'perv-breeks', 'flapaway flares' and pop stars' noses forever looking 'like Bulgaria'. Ads for the following fortnight announced '*Smash Hits*: The Modern guide to parsnips and more' while concepts sprang up everywhere.

'Things In Pop Called Coal, featuring Natalie Cole, Lloyd Cole, Richard Coles (out of The Communards), Cole Porter and Arthur Scargill, "famous coalman, not much good at pop".'

'Crap Joke Corner', where the readers wrote in with a particularly hopeless joke, always positioned in a corner, usually involving a terrible pun:

Q: Which pop star can you scrub your back with in the bath?
A: Loofah Vandross.
Bitz: 'Oh dear, that so-called "quip" hardly had us a-tittering in our trousers or a-guffawing in our gumboots, did it shipmates? Indeed, when it comes to "japes" that are utterly devoid of mirth

and merriment, Julie Ford of London – the proud "donor" of this hopeless "riddle" – is clearly the tops!'

A small rumpus erupted over a review of 'Where The Streets Have No Name' by U2, the biggest-band-in-the-world and drearily po-faced windbags forever blubbing on a cactus. There were, I pointed out, 'no streets in the desert' and deemed Bono, somehow, 'a goon'. Sackfuls of hate mail arrived from U2-devoted *Smash Hits* viewers while a headline in an Irish newspaper bellowed, 'GOON BONO BLASTED BY TOP POP MAG.'

Belgium soon beckoned, an investigation into rumours of Frankie Goes To Hollywood's imminent demise, returning with my first-ever 'scoop' which had required, unexpectedly, zero gumshoe skills. Effortlessly arch frontman Holly Johnson was found luxuriating in the penthouse wing of a Brussels hotel with his boyfriend Wolfgang while the members known as 'The Lads' (Ped, Nasher and Mark O'Toole) furiously bemoaned their punter-class wing, which was undergoing massive renovations, including the replacing of the actual floor, industrial drills detonating into their hangovers at 8 a.m. This non-democratic hierarchy was further compounded by transport: The Lads (and robustly moustachioed backing singer/dancer Paul Rutherford) schlepped round Europe on a rumbling tour-bus while Holly and Wolfgang flew serenely in the friendly skies.

'I just got tired of discos and getting senselessly out of my head every night, I think I've outgrown them,' confirmed Holly, fondling the weighty biography of celebrated thirties playwright Terence Rattigan he'd been given for his twenty-seventh birthday, the soothing sounds of Peter Gabriel's *So* tinkling inside his lavishly chandeliered suite. 'I'm not *like* them,' he carried on. 'I started working with them because I was sick of working in a studio and trying to approach things intellectually.

I wanted a record deal, basically. I never really cared about the band. I only ever really cared about me.' Furthermore: 'I'm going to go off and make a solo album.'

The Lads, meanwhile, were in the hotel bar shouting 'I'm bored shitless!', drawing cocks 'n' balls all over my Silvine notebook and announcing they were all registered in the hotel under the name Bollocks. 'There's a Chris P, Airy, Archibald, Brad and Chuck,' Mark merrily declared.

Ped was philosophical. 'You get fed up with anyone when you've been with them for five years, don't you?' he mused of Holly's permanent absence. 'We've had five years, three or four with success and we've had a laugh so why should we be complaining? I was on the dole before this happened so I'm well happy. I can still play drums and nobody's ever gonna take that away from me, are they? I mean, I'm stupid but that doesn't mean I'm mad.'

When the hotel bar shut Mark raided my room's mini-bar at 2 a.m., looking for 'more bevvy!' while spelling out the truth. 'I wouldn't say the band is falling to pieces,' he announced, 'I'd say we're going to split up at the end of this tour.'

When the story was printed, it was fanfared by the dramatic but inevitable headline: 'Is This The End Of Frankie Goes To Hollywood?'

Clue: it was. (And, twenty-five years into the future, Holly Johnson would tell me exactly what he thought of my inaugural scoop in his distinctive, ice-cool way.)

Back in Carnaby Street, we discovered the joy of a single collective enemy: persistently pompous megalomaniac Jon Bon Jovi, who loathed ver Hits and its perky 'stoopid questions'. Tom Hibbert took Jon Bon Jovi on with equal persistence, now enquiring in the domain of the Personal File if the hirsute hair-metal alleged hunk (who owned a large collection of said instruments) could 'play "The Stars And Stripes" on your harmonica?' 'Ha! That's *Smash Hits*' idea of a music question, right?' he cajoled, unimpressed. 'You mean "The Star Spangled Banner", don't you? I could play it on my guitars but not my harmonicas. I'd be too busy salutin'. Ha!' Once, backstage at *Top Of The Pops*, he plucked the list of stoopid questions out of my hand and ran down the corridor towards his Jovi bandmates, reading the queries out loud. 'Do you like cats?' he sneered before providing the telling answer. 'The only good cat is a dead cat!' He then pronounced me 'some kinda kooky chick, huh?'

Soon, Hibbs had another new idea: The Bitz Book Of Life, a mini-feature almost hidden within the section which built up, fortnight by fortnight, into an 'encyclopedia of life!' starring the likes of septuagenarian scientists, eighteenth-century toffs and obscure, LSD-skewed 1970s hippies (a porthole into Hibbs' enigmatic mind). It was printed in almost illegibly tiny type, in the corner of a double-page spread, with micro-scissors drawn around its borders to illustrate its 'cut out 'n' keep' qualities. One day, after rat-tat-tatting at his typewriter with a particularly amused look on his face, he sliced the paper from his typewriter and handed me that fortnight's entry:

The History Of Rock 'N' Roll Part Three: Elvis Presley.

Born in a coal scuttle in Tucson, Arizona, Elvis Priestly, to give him his full name, was discovered wriggling his hips in a biscuit factory and soared to international stardom with his debut vinyl outing Blimey, Mum, You Should Hear My Pelvis Yodel, before donning a clip-on quiff and taking to the 'road' doing 'provocative' impersonations of a tap-dancing donkey and ending up in Hollywood, where he starred in a string of box office smashes such as Lassie Meets The Three Musketeers, in which he kissed a girl in a bikini on the lips and said, 'Aw, shucks ma'am!' quite a lot. Not much else is known about this showbiz phenomenon.

I doubt The Baron even saw it. And still *more* people bought ver *Hits* . . .

One crisp spring morning in '87, a phone rang on the art department's island, and was therefore clearly not for me. 'Sylv, it's your dad . . .' piped Jaqui Doyle, waving a receiver, motioning me over to where my dad was mistakenly on the end of the phone.

He was never on the end of the phone. I don't think he'd *ever* called me in London. His voice was barely recognisable: thin, almost inaudible.

'It's Ronnie,' he said. 'He's passed away. I think you better come home . . .'

The walls of the office billowed and rushed away as if from the effects of powerful acid. Instantaneously, here in this permanently frenzied office full of giggly voices and skittering typewriters, the sound of the world incongruously disappeared, unable to hear anything around me, only a whoosh-whoosh-whoosh coursing throughout the inside of my head. The last time I'd seen my supernaturally gentle, kind and innocent brother I was crashing out the front door of our family home shouting and swearing at my mother over the usual diabolical horrors of the family Christmas. He was probably terrified, not only of her, but of me. I never said goodbye to him and now I never would. Winded by guilt, and by regret, gentle Jaqui saved me, took me back to my flat and helped me organise a flight to Scotland.

The hour on the plane stretched to forever in a blur of outward weeping and inward anxiety – Mum would fall apart, how would Dad cope? – as a concerned air hostess took the seat beside me, offered a whisky miniature and held my hand. I had a ninety-minute compilation tape given to me by old rifle-avoiding boyfriend John McKeand and those two forty-five-minute sides of lovingly selected music finally got me back to Perth. (To this day I can't hear Fleetwood Mac's intensely sumptuous 'Dreams' without being transported back to that painful journey in the sky.)

When I walked into the living room and saw my dad's distraught face (I was used to Mum's distraught face) I had to sprint to the bathroom to copiously throw up, and did so several times over the course of the next two days. They were choosing the hymns for Ronnie's funeral and it was the first and only time I ever saw my father openly weep. I was twenty-two and my brother was, as Mum always said thereafter, 'thirty-seven and a half'. (Note to those with volatile families and anything to feel guilty about: make it better, if you possibly can, while they're still alive.)

Ronnie's coffin was the first to be lowered into the corner grave of the cemetery near the village of Luncarty, Perth, where my parents had first lived in the late 1940s, a cemetery plot where I'd eventually watch both their coffins join him. I'd had the chance to see Ronnie's body in the mortuary and didn't take it. I preferred the vision in my head, of a gently smiling soul drumming his fingers to the Dead End Kids' version of 'Have I The Right?' (which he especially loved), a Curly Wurly poking out his jumper sleeve, not-very-well-hidden-at-all from his pesky, twelve-year-old wee sister.

I'd now long moved out of (or possibly been banished from) Nicky Philbin's spare room and was living in a shabby two-bed flat-share in Brixton with a camp southern English hairdresser called Tass and his belligerent and incontinent cat, who once sneaked under the covers of my single bed and peed on the mattress while I was lying on it. Worse, without a wardrobe, I kept my clothes in a travelling case which the cat also sneaked into and actually shat in. No wonder I called it 'the bastard cat'.

In the office, meanwhile, Hibbs could no longer be contained. His genius needed in seas beyond our rudderless ship, he resigned as deputy ed in May 1987, not long after the era-defining one-off wheeze secured by *Smash Hits'* now enormous cultural reach: his interview, in No. 10 Downing Street, with Margaret Thatcher. She was a fan of Elton John, it turned out, who she deemed 'highly professional, but I'm so sad that he's having difficulty with his throat'. Hibbs presented her with a Black Type tea-towel, which she accepted – and we can only hope, to this day, it remains inside No. 10.

The autumn of '87 brought The Big Wind to Britain, the one which meteorologist Michael Fish famously described as a balmy gust and which threw a tree branch straight through the back window of the revolting Brixton bedroom. A personal storm was also approaching: I wasn't Bitz editor anymore, I was reviews editor, which I was hopeless at seeing as it required organisation, decisions, delegation and ability to decipher which singles, albums, films, videos, concerts, books and competitions were best suited to the viewers from an actual Alpine avalanche of Jiffy bags permanently engulfing the reviews desk. This was music industry boom time, *Smash Hits* its willing messenger, an appearance therein third only in cultural reach to a play on Radio 1 or a performance on *Top Of The Pops*. *Everyone* wanted in.

Pring priiiiiing!!

'Hello, Smash Hits Reviews Desk ...'

'Hi! Is that Syyyylvee-ur Padddderson ...?' came a startling voice; a man's voice, certainly, but giddy and breathless, possibly American.

He was the bass player, he was now telling me, in a band I'd never heard of and would I be interested in writing about them? This was weird: bass players in obscure indie bands did not ring ver *Hits*, their indie PRs did that for them. We had a lengthy chat about music and I found him intriguing in his infectious enthusiasm and endearingly childlike ways. He asked me out for a drink and I accepted: overnight, I was going on a Blind Date.

The following night I ambled round to the St Moritz club on Wardour Street (where Motorhead's Lemmy was usually found attached to the one-armed bandit) with no idea what this man looked like, though he said he'd know me from the Singles Page mugshot. I walked, warily, into the downstairs club where bounding towards me was An Actual Rock God From Rock 'N' Roll Valhalla Conjured By The Cackling Devils At Disney. Raven-black wavy hair undulating down and over the shoulders of his battered black leather jacket. Burnished chocolate-brown eyes and a flashlight Hollywood smile. Good nose. Six feet tall in charcoal drainpipe jeans, waspish waist, rock 'n' roll biker boots. Swarthy and girly at exactly the same time. He was half South American, half Canadian (a bit like a cheery, hair metal version of Rafael Nadal) and it was Love At First Sight.

We stayed in the St Moritz for hours and whatever we were talking about I couldn't hear any of it, transfixed as I was by the abundant bounce of his devilishly glossy hair. I took him home. He moved into the flat the very next day (I didn't tell him about the cat-pee mattress). Within weeks, though, he'd proved himself not quite as he seemed: for such a rock 'n' roll caricature, he had no corresponding rock 'n' roll character. The only alcohol he truly liked was a glass of Malibu, the coconut rum 'sensation', with milk, a concoction more befitting a twelve-year-old girl at a naughty sleepover than a twenty-three-year-old alleged Rock God.

At a party I introduced him to my writerly *Hits* pal Lola Borg. 'Blimey, Sylv,' she boggled, 'where did you find HIM?' No such compliments, mind, from soon-incoming new writerly pal and scoundrel Scouser Richard Lowe who, on hearing of my beloved's Malibu 'n' milk habit, immediately dubbed him 'Rock 'N' Roll Babylon'. Which became his official name.

During those first permanently fainting months I'd find myself with the fairly important pop reporting task of interviewing George Michael on the release of his collapsingly anticipated debut solo album, *Faith*. Emotionally berserk from the neurological frissons of loin-fizzing love, my hope that day was for high-camp gigglings from the ex-Wham! titan and ruminations on 'mazin' rumpo' (possibly without the 'speryooo!' bit). He'd written a song called 'I Want Your Sex', after all. That day, however, where the finger-clicking, shuttlecock-stuffing, twinkle-toothed dreamboat of the early eighties used to be, sat a stern-faced spectre with an over-groomed beard, wholly impervious to mirth. The first great 'important' pop interview struggle of my life was about to commence.

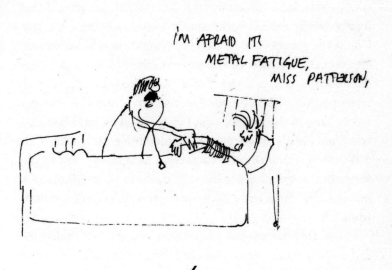

I'M AFRAID IT'S METAL FATIGUE, MISS PATTERSON,

6

JITTERBUG

Gambolling on puff-ball pillows of 'Babylonian' dreaminess into an executive office of Epic Records, my emotional heights were further enhanced by genuine pop excitement. Wham! had been *phenomenal* alright, lighting up the mid-eighties with their world-class pop euphoria, including 'Last Christmas', the greatest Christmas pop single ever written to this day. The newly solo George Michael was possessed of pop's most affecting vocal, as exquisitely proved on the solo-transitional 'Careless Whisper' single in 1984, even if his '87 solo debut, *Faith*, had been met with confused reviews over his new and dubious insistence on permanently wielding an acoustic guitar while looking all stubbly 'n' moody.

Ushered by his PR through a sturdy wooden door as if into a presidential atrium, the twenty-four-year-old George Michael coolly extended a discreetly manicured hand and settled back into a black, curved-back, gently swivelling director's seat, looking *very* stubbly 'n' moody. Nibbling daintily at salmon and cream cheese sarnies, he was expensively dressed in crisp new denim jeans, crisper white T-shirt and a long, black, collarless leather jacket. 'It's an Adolfo Dominguez,' came his measured voice. 'One of the privileges of being rich.' George Michael, it was immediately apparent, was the definition of detached. On this mellow autumn day he was feeling, he assured, 'very sedate, very calm, everything's going very much to plan'. All that was missing, evidently, was a villainously stroked, green-eyed fluffy white cat.

It was this demeanour of archness coupled with relentless earnestness which surely prompted what followed: a mercilessly blunt line of questioning from my panicking twenty-two-year-old self as a weed-tumbling chasm soon opened up where the *Hits*-shaped quips were supposed to be. I was off my rocker on lust – I couldn't do *serious* anyway. A journalistic quest soon emerged: to pinpoint a single reason behind his grim facade, believing this would perk him up, somehow, no end.

Was he so serious today, I wondered, because he'd read the less than glowing reviews of *Faith* and was permanently in the huff?

'I haven't read them yet, actually,' he coolly replied. 'What are they like?'

Mixed.

'Mixed? Hmmmn. I don't take much notice of the press over here [in the UK] anymore, it's so clouded by my success.'

Perhaps he was irked by being pipped to number one by The Bee Gees' (winningly titled) 'You Win Again'?

'I'm not at all heartbroken,' he opined. 'If you're going to be number two you might as well be number two to a record you like – I really like it! I've been singing it for the past two weeks.'

Through gritted teeth?

'Not at *all*.'

You do look like a Bee Gee.

'That's true actually. Hmmmn.'

I carried on, blithely, wondering if it was Boy George who had bothered him, his then-beleaguered Culture Club acquaintance having insisted, on Radio 1 just the other day, that George Michael was a gay man given to 'raving queen' tendencies around him. George Michael, in '87, was known to the general public as a heterosexual man with a highly visible girlfriend, Kathy Yeung, who appeared in the 'I Want Your Sex' video. It hadn't crossed my mind, being acutely naive, that George Michael might be having a colossal inner struggle with his sexuality. (We were over a decade away, still, from George outing himself in an outdoor lavvy in LA.)

'That's funny,' he replied, unamused. 'No one's told me anything about this. Hmmn. That's really weird. That's really *really* weird.'

He regained his composure, turning eerily blank.

'Well, I mean apart from the fact I hardly ever see him and I'm hardly ever with him for more than about ten seconds, I'm just *surprised* at him,' he frowned. 'I'm surprised at him for getting that *low*. Obviously things aren't going great for him' – Boy George was in the grip, at the time, of heroin addiction – 'and things have been going great for me for a long time and that's a real shame if he feels he has to snipe at me. (witheringly) Oh yeah, I really turn into a raving queen when I'm with *him*. If I was going to do that he'd be the *last* person I'd do it around, wouldn't he? I'm tempted to ring him up about it but I don't think I shall bother . . .'

Oh dear. His veil of gloom, understandably, still failing to ascend, more 'comedy' reasons were offered, now falling on stiffly humourless shoulders. He wasn't, as suggested, 'embarrassed' by perky Wham!, 'not at all ... but I'm embarrassed by "Bad Boys" – that was *such* a bad record', though he conceded life without 'musical' partner Andrew Ridgeley wasn't as much fun.

'It *isn't* as much fun anymore,' he nodded. 'And also I'm *bored* with grinning. There aren't going to be any more fun 'n' games from me because that's when I was eighteen, nineteen, twenty, twenty-one ... OK, I'm only twenty-four, I'm not exactly an old man ...'

Well indeed. That year, he'd announced he'd never play *Top Of The Pops* again: perhaps he was sad because he was missing it?

'I always hated doing it, I was a good actor!' he confessed. 'I never liked the camera work, et cetera et cetera. Just as you'd get to the best bit of your choreography they'd go to some girl waving a balloon about. Most people come to that conclusion – when they don't have to be on *Top Of The Pops* to maintain their status they don't do it.'

This was an arch reply which begged an inevitable question: did he simply take himself far too seriously?

'Aaaahm ...' came the wavering reply, 'I don't think I take myself terribly seriously. (thinks again) I've *always* taken myself seriously. And I always took the pop music I made far more seriously than most people gave me credit for. They thought it was "Wheee! Throw another one out!" and being famous was the main thing and it wasn't. Originally people thought I was a bit of an air-head and now I've set about changing that I've given myself a new problem – people think "Oooh, he's far too serious and business-like to possibly be a genuinely creative person". I *cannot* take off this professional personality that you see now – it's very protective and very professional but there's no doubt that if we met in a club we'd probably have a lot of fun, you know?'

Alright, maybe he was merely starving. Since a new exercise

and diet regime he was no longer George 'the fat Greek'. Was he, therefore, no longer fat 'n' happy?

'I've been this weight for two years – 11 stone,' he countered airily. 'I photograph like a fat pig, that's the thing. I'm fitter now, I haven't been "The 13 stone Fat George" the *Sun* knows for ages.'

Was he vain?

'Hmmn ... you see, I think vanity is not caring, just knowing that you're great-looking. Do I pluck my eyebrows? Yes, I've been doing that since I was sixteen because they join in the middle here (prods between eyebrows) and I do here a bit too (prods under end of left eyebrow) but not much. I saw someone the other day whose hairs grew all the way down here (prods halfway down nose) and he looked like a freak! Why not just take the time?'

Soon, caving in to what was most pressing on my mind, we moved onto relationships. 'I'm still very much in love with my girlfriend,' he confirmed, as thoughts of Babylon flooded my fibres, now seeking confirmation of my own feelings from the reluctant superstar before me.

What, I wondered, does being in love feel like?

'What does it *feel* like?' he scoffed. 'Well you *must* know. *Surely* you know!'

Is it ... when you feel sick all the time?

'Oh, absolutely!' he smiled, the first Mona Lisa-sized movement of his lips all day. 'Falling in love makes you feel *absolutely* sick. My sister goes to an acupuncturist and he explained to her that the knot you feel in your stomach that makes it really hard to concentrate on anything else, it's a nervous thing. When you're in love but it's not a certainty that it's reciprocated. When you feel secure, you lose that knot and you get a calmness. That's the way I feel, really calm. But I've had the knot. I've had the knot a few times. I never want it again.'

His mood appeared to plummet once more – perhaps aggrieved to have veered *off-professional* – so I hastily proffered the 'sick' question. For a year I'd persistently wondered if the famous had been sick through booze in very stupid places (in their slippers, down their cat, on a daffodil etc., as friends of mine once literally had). Had George Michael, I wondered, ever been sick on his chest?

'I've never been sick on my chest!' he balked, appalled. 'Eeuurgh! What a horrible thought. It would all congeal, wouldn't it? Usually when I'm sick, you see, it's a very forceful sick – it projects. It's a bit *Exorcist*-like but it isn't green or anything. I always manage to miss the beard as well. Who cuts it? I do it myself with a clipper every couple of days. I haven't been to a barber since I was fourteen years old. I'm not *totally* useless, you know!'

Thoughts turned to his eventual legacy, his face stonier by the second as he realised he wasn't yet . . . The Beatles?

'I think I've got a certain amount of way to go before I've established myself to the degree of The Beatles,' he declared. 'I still have to establish myself on a worldwide basis. And that's an unstoppable ambition for me. I *have* to achieve that. I want to go down in history. I want to be an historical writer as opposed to someone who was just the most successful thing of the past four or five years. I want to go down in history as someone who has done something remarkable and I think I've done quite a lot that's remarkable already, but I want to take it that much further. I'm hoping to get bored of chasing success or status. I would like to do with my career what I did with Wham! – finish it before it finishes itself. Maybe then I'll take up ballooning, who knows?'

And with this, the serenely detached George Michael slipped off his director's perch, smoothed down the crinkles in his exquisitely tailored leather jacket and disappeared into his considerably more chaotic future, full of sex in latrines with random male strangers, hip hop levels of skunk-weed addiction, political agitation via insurrectionary videos, magnificent indiscretion about every one of his fabulous peers and pranging his Range Rover into a Happy Snaps frontage in Hampstead in 2010, off his rocker on drugs. George Michael has gone down in history alright, and done *many* remarkable things. Back in 1987, though, *Smash Hits* summed him up with the following headline: 'George Michael: The Glummest Man In Pop.'

Sorry about that, George. Unlike Rock 'N' Roll Babylon, I love you to this day.

7

CAT AMONG THE PIGEONS

The second Great Eighties Pop Boom rushed towards us in striking contrast to the first, days long nostalgic already for Duran Duran and Spandau Ballet's hard-boozin', coke-snortin', model-squiring, tea-towels-on-heads-sporting world of the hell-raisin' crumpeteer. In pop's cyclical way, the new late-eighties generation was curiously 'straight', a very young, very clean Stepford Pop conveyor belt of dutiful professionalism, given punishing schedules by whip-lashing paymasters, not only avoiders of fags, booze 'n' drugs but (on the surface at least) sex-free, a generation mindful both of predominantly tweenage fans and new fans not much older than toddlers.

Kylie Minogue and Jason Donovan (refugees from *Neighbours*) successfully concealed their real-life relationship from every media outlet on earth. 'Snog up, what do you mean?' Kylie once tinkled, un-informationally, in winter '88 as 'Especially For You' made the nation's six-year-olds blub. Jason announced their true relationship had always been 'a mystery', his only confirmation of any fact being Kylie's front teeth were indeed 'quite prominent'.

Fame-shy Lancastrian Rick Astley once divulged to The Toff the title of the first song he'd ever written: 'A Ruddy Big Pig'. Its opening line declared 'A ruddy big pig went down our street . . .' and he was *never* allowed to forget it.

The female teen-pop giants we'd borrowed from ver 'States' were even soapier. Tiffany and Debbie Gibson, groomed on US shopping mall tours since '86, were gigantic in the UK in '87 and '88: flame-haired Tiffany, forever wafting in a woolly jumper, with 'I Think We're Alone Now', while Debbie gave us 'Foolish Beat' in double denim and a bowler hat (sadly, no 'bowler head' beneath).

Even Bros were oddly sexless, the Disney-faced twins Matt and Luke Goss surely bred to perfection in a Nazi eugenicist's Petri dish, with their too-ironed shirts and immaculate hair, permanently fragrant in a mist of expensive cologne. The most troubling addiction within Bros was the confectionary compulsion of the non-hunk we dubbed 'Ken', a teenager from Kirkcaldy not-particularly-battling his 'five-a-day' Boost bar habit.

As a generation this was less a thundering pop tsunami than a controlled ripple-effect in a wave-generating swimming pool – all flawless formula, zero confrontation and fixation on enormous success, the blueprint for shiny-pop 'perfection' which has endured ever since. Their supporting cast was, at least, brimful of eccentrics, a spectrum of contenders subjected to ever-increasing, conceptual, vibes-creating tomfoolery to compensate for various charisma shortcomings: our pals Brother Beyond (forever 'The 'Yond', ever keen to wear pineapples on their heads), Clark Datchler out of Johnny Hates Jazz (string of onions around his neck amid the cover-line 'Je suis un weirdo', about which he was flouncingly unamused), Chesney Hawkes (saucepan lid on his head), A-ha (comically customised T-shirts and grimaces on their faces because they were absurdly earnest and did not 'get' ver *Hits*), Wet Wet Wet (sponge cakes exploding in a food fight, a band who barely tolerated ver *Hits*, being even more earnest than A-ha, while toothsome vocalist Marti Pellow was permanently in the huff with me for insinuating in print he once fancied Kylie Minogue).

1988 belonged, though, to the unforeseen bounty of the Bros boys, who'd first appeared in *Smash Hits* back in autumn '87 with no unusual fanfare, the staff scandalously failing to make the most of this Pop Grand National-winning gift horse by treating them like anyone else, i.e. with an introductory one and a half pages in which their 'bugle' was immediately deflated by letting them address their critics, which the viewers didn't know they had.

'People think we're completely contrived,' pouted Matt. 'It's like … we have to apologise for our age! We have to apologise for the fact we look alright, too! People see you look quite good and think "what a bunch of wankers!" What can we do?'

I then described Matt as indeed 'not very ugly … and neither is the bloke standing next to him because that's his identical twin brother Luke. The other bloke looks nothing like them and that's because he comes from Scotland.' They'd been a band since the age of twelve and now their debut single 'I Owe You Nothing' had suffered an inglorious chart-free stall, unaided by my confounding review which described it as 'a very smart 'n' speedy disco fizzler and quite good for that sort of thing'.

Absolutely nowhere, outrageously, was a spotlight shone on its arresting opening couplet: 'I watch you crumble ... like a very old wall.'

By June '88 Bros were huge, their debut album *Push* containing five hit singles, Britain's girly teens now sporting Grolsch bottle tops affixed to their Doc Martens while the Bros logo – three industrial Lego-men, the central figure with his arms aloft – hovered over a spellbound Britain like a sweeping Bat Signal of pop. Their fiery fans had sprung from the already fertile landscape like Miracle-Gro triffids, calling themselves the Brosettes; one particularly aggressive microcosm known as the Peckham Posse always knew where Bros were going long before Bros did, even if the 'lads' didn't really know where they going at *any* time.

The Bros boys were harmless: cheerful, excitable, easily distracted, breathlessly ambitious and (ruinously, for them in years to come) guileless from the outset. 'This is the first time we've been on the cover of *Smash Hits* and it's really doin' it for us,' proclaimed Luke in February '88, seated in the £7,000 Suzuki jeep he'd immediately bought, aged eighteen, with Bros' label advance. Now nineteen, he intended to purchase a Porsche. They were participants in practical jokes (itching powder in each other's beds), while sharing odd superstitions (if, while driving, they saw the back of an ambulance they had to hold their collar until they saw a bird: 'we've got loads of superstitions, that's why we're successful') and a dubious secret language ('ersh, mersh, nersh').

Wherever the *Hits* went with them, the Brosettes turned up, including the Peckham Posse who claimed ownership of the band, training 'street tuff' eyes on anyone, especially female, who appeared closer to the boys than they were. Soon, I became The Bros Correspondent – the first and only time I'd be anyone's assigned correspondent – and suspicious eyes followed me around London as I leapt in and out of window-blacked people carriers with the Peckham Posse's elusive future husbands.

That summer they 'stormed' the Montreux Pop Festival in Switzerland, a rum televisual do where the pan-European pop glitterati mimed their hits in ropey nightclub The Casino. In June 1988, Bros were treated like Abba were in *ABBA: The Movie* in 1977. Every year, the paparazzi would choose their most headline-worthy quarry and circle like stealthy wolves: in '86, the disintegrating Frankie Goes To Hollywood, in '87 the VW-vandalising Beastie Boys and now, in '88, Bros, who registered in the Hyatt Hotel under the names D. Rum, P. Ano and B. Ass and had a mountainous security minder *each*. Incarcerated inside their rooms giving endless European interviews, soon, being boys aged nineteen who unfathomably did not drink, they amused themselves with a water fight, rupturing an electric security blind and soaking Craig's bed. 'We just do it 'cos we're bored!' trilled Matt. 'We've been cooped up all day [doing interviews], no fresh air, you've gotta go maaaaad!'

This, then, was 'madness' for Bros, the turny-up-jeaned trio flying back into Heathrow obsessed with the Montreux generated headlines. 'Did you see the papers this morning?' thrilled Luke. 'We've got a really big article saying something about us being the pop phenomenon of the eighties! Brilliant, innit? The whole of the eighties!' I doubt Michael Jackson agreed. They were ecstatic to find their autumn tour '88 would, apparently, be coordinated by the British police. 'There's gonna be roadblocks at motorway exits, already wherever we go in Britain the police follow us!' Then again, they had four hundred fans lingering outside their homes every day of their lives.

Once, in some spartan backstage conference room, I watched Matt eye a kettle in a kitchen area, wander into the living area and ask his PR if she would make him a cup of tea. It wasn't that the task was beneath him, he just *did not know how to make a cup of tea.* The rest of the band called him Pampers. ''Cos he has to be looked after all the time, he'll forget his glasses, forget to pack his case,' confessed Luke. 'I do tend to go off in my own world sometimes,' wobbled Matt, 'but he (Luke) is not much better, he can never decide which vest to wear!'

In a way, they were a bit like Rock 'N' Roll Babylon, as I was now increasingly becoming aware.

Back in the mouldering Brixton flat with the incontinent cat, Rock 'N' Roll Babylon was still quiveringly gorgeous and good for absolutely nothing else. I paid the rent and all the bills while he neglected to find a job, which would interfere with his 'muse'. He couldn't legally sign on the dole because he was living illegally in our flat, where he spent most days mooching around pinging on his bass guitar, usually to a new song the band had written called 'Heroine'. 'You are my heroine!' it yelped, pun intended, this being the decade when anti-AIDS and Just Say No (to heroin) ads were always on the telly.

On sunny days he took to languishing, beautifully, in his ripped jeans and capped-sleeve red-checked shirt – like a very tall Marc Bolan in 1972 – under a tree in the communal garden, individually snipping the split ends from his sumptuous locks with a pair of dainty nail scissors. By now, he had a nickname for me too: 'Cabbage'. Somehow, I was thrilled – even if an unforeseen personality trait was now creeping out from under the surface enthusiasm: jealousy. He, the Rock God, was increasingly convinced I, the Indie Weirdo, was having sex with all the stars I was interviewing. He was convinced I was having an affair with Matt Goss. Pampers, I balked, simply didn't do it for me and I most certainly wasn't *his* type. I was also, apparently, simultaneously, having sex with Wayne Hussey out of The Mission (I wished) and Carl Fysh out of Brother Beyond (definitely wasn't *his* type, being a gay man). He, the

Rock God, the one whose fans elbowed me out the way to get to his windswept tresses in some grimy-walled Camden dive, was now a steamy cauldron of insecurities as I sat at bars, with a pint of cider, like the long-suffering Rock Star Wife. But my, he was so intoxicatingly *divine*.

This, young people, is what happens when you're twenty-two and *a total schmuck*.

Spring 1988, and my old DC Thomson mucker Tom Doyle, newly nicknamed 'Tommy the D', arrived from Dundee to join us as staff writer despite having no pop bones whatsoever, being a Beatles head who knew about things like, you know, instruments, amplifiers and plugs. He was, nonetheless, persistently chosen to interview the likes of exotic pop drip Glenn Medeiros. 'I see,' he'd pipe to the hirsute Hawaiian, 'you have a hairy chest?' I made a berk of myself, meanwhile, in the presence of Aztec Camera's Roddy Frame, in a restaurant, chirpily informing him he had been the only man in my life whose image had been Blu-Tacked above my bed.

'. . . . . .' he replied with a palpable blush and immediately ended a spell on the wagon by ordering several bottles of red wine while we smoked our way through his packet of B&H. He proved adorable, remembering, as a four-year-old, asking for 'a guitar and amplifier' for Christmas; receiving a toy guitar instead, he 'ended up using it as a spaceship for ma Action Man – I took out all the strings and stuck him in the hole. Great!' Talk turned cosmic and inevitable questions arose about The Purpose of Life – soon contemplating a shack he'd recently bought in a field in Manchester. 'I lie on the roof when it's sunny,' he began, promisingly, 'and think about absolutely nothing!' *Swizz*.

'My days of contemplating the universe are over,' he carried on, tragically. 'When you get older you come to realise that' – he knocked firmly on the wooden table – 'things are what they are. Life's hard and then you die, sort of thing.' His favourite foods were the ones with 'E numbers in them', with particular fondness for crisps, especially 'Smokey Bacon, or Prawn Cocktail, or Worcester Sauce'. The only exercise he ever did, furthermore, was to 'occasionally jog round to the newsagent to get some fags'. Swoon!

By November '88, *Smash Hits* was selling one million copies a fortnight, even when Wet Wet Wet were on the cover (haw haw). Editorial meetings saw an increasingly amused Banzai McIlheney scratching his head at the where-did-it-all-go-rightness while pondering who we'd put on the cover this fortnight, if it wasn't Bros. 'Kylie? Jason? Rick? *The 'Yond?'* At that year's Brit Awards at the Albert Hall, the staff had dispersed among the stars (Wet Wet Wet, Bananarama, Alison Moyet, George Michael and – yikes! – New Order), gleaning quotable quips via some amusingly troublesome question, say, 'Are you sure you haven't left the iron on?' Banzai attempted this with U2's Adam Clayton, in the days when the bass-playing Lothario keenly liked a drink. Clayton was (and remains) a magnificent toff, with a voice as theatrical as Laurence Olivier's, and engaged with Barry's unwanted query with a swift and direct riposte. 'Clear awf!' he roared and returned to his glass of claret. Clayton, ever since, has been officially known as Adam 'Clear awf!' Clayton ...

Bitz remained dedicated to the daft. 'The Return Of The Fright Wig' (Italian Euro-pop trillster Spanga, who owned a cat called Bimbo). 'Spectacles: Their Role In The History Of Pop'. The 'Bruno Brookes Column', not written by Bruno Brookes, wherein the horrifically be-jumpered Radio 1 disc wriggler would be cut off in his gossip-peddling prime with an impudently incoming 'sniiiiiip!' Boris Becker provided the endless aside 'So do I, mate', often followed by Jason Donovan's disembodied head piping out of nowhere 'That'll do!' Our obsession with inverted commas now inevitably reached its peak, with inverted commas around inverted commas – a bit like ' " 'this ' " ' – and, once, inverted commas round a full stop ".." Crushingly for me, The Housemartins split up. 'In an age of Rick Astley, Shakin' Stevens and the Pet Shop Boys – quite simply, they weren't good enough,' parped their official statement rumly. Soon afterwards bass player Norman 'Quentin' Cook, Fatboy Slim of the future, rang the office to insist down Review Nook's blower that it was all my fault for 'turning The Housemartins into a cartoon'. One look at the plasticine dancing gonks in the 'Happy Hour' video could tell us they made a fairly good job of that themselves, eh viewers?

The cogs in pop's infinite cycle, meanwhile, were turning once more, our gleam-toothed, family-friendly chums soon blown into history by an incoming wind-rush of what was bewilderingly dubbed 'Manchestah vibes in the ae-reee-or'. Repetitive beats were surging down the M1 from all across the north (and that was just the stampede of the drug dealers, hur hur). The tectonic pop plates were shifting, dramatically, forever.

To Sylvia,
  Look after
yourself, take care,
  Love Luke + Matt
    (Bros)

8

THE PARTY'S OVER/
THE PARTY'S JUST BEGUN

After the recession of the early eighties, the late eighties was a profiteering obscenity we didn't even know we were living in. By '88 Harry Enfield's Loadsamoney was waving his bigmouthed plasterer's newly acquired enormous wad all over both *Top Of The Pops* and the cover of the *Hits*. The 'loadsamoney mentality' and 'loadsamoney economy' entered the cultural and political lexicon as the word 'yuppie' arrived, along with the first door-sized mobile phones.

The music industry was now swaggeringly drunk on CD

profits, sluicing money on journalist-wooing fancy dinners, ever more exotic foreign trips and farcically expensive parties where free booze flowed like Niagara Falls over Dover-sized cliffs of cocaine. We had Luncheon Vouchers for free lunches we could easily afford, while every two weeks 'Uncle Disgusting' from the Record & Tape Exchange arrived with his hessian postman's sacks, piling up all our unwanted CDs, vinyl and tapes and indeed exchanging the lot for hard cash, up to £250 if you were the reviews ed, which I had been for four months. Every two months, a woman called Yuko from Japanese pop tribune *Rockin' On* would fly in from Tokyo to physically gather up interview transcriptions for syndication, handing us £200 each – usually four £50 notes – in a brown envelope. The Baron knew nothing of this and Yuko's official name among we disbelieving freeloaders was Old Rope. There was an office cleaner, employed, seemingly, to merely flap a duster around our individual landline phones. *Smash Hits* had an account with 'showbiz' cab firm Addison Lee and we used it as our personal service, the staff routinely chauffeured through London from pubs to clubs and free posh dinners with the likes of EMI, putting the journeys 'on account'.

The Baron, far from complaining, now came up with its first-ever profile-expanding ruse, the money-hoovering ruse of putting the annual *Smash Hits* Readers' Poll on TV and calling it the *Smash Hits* Poll Winners' Party, in direct competition to the Brits, which was still in recovery from the Sam Fox/Mick Fleetwood-presented calamity of 1986.

Sunday 30 October 1988, they were 'all' there at the Royal Albert Hall. Philip Schofield wielded an unravelling bounty of technical wires alongside Climie Fisher (no one cared), Salt 'N' Pepa (everyone cared), Rick Astley (permanently unamused), Wet Wet Wet (Marti still in a huff), Donny Osmond (my sister Jackie's teenage hero), Yazz (in a tutu), The 'Yond (Carl wielding the possibly unwanted gift of a cuddly creature, 'an acid house octopus, a close dear friend'), Bananarama ('refreshed') and Kylie (bewildered), while Bros appeared in a pre-recorded segment, the trio now off becoming Big In Japan, explaining to Schofield how fame is 'complicated' – unless it was Ken, who deemed fame 'happening' because he deemed everything 'happening'.

Rick Astley was peeved at being voted Worst Dressed Person of '88 mainly for the brown fur-spiked 'bomber' jacket which Jean-Paul Gaultier had declared, in a Bitz interview, made him look like 'a porcupig'. A ploy was invented: we'd blow up the offending jacket – even Rick called it his 'hedgehog jacket' – on stage, but he wouldn't comply. 'I wasn't very happy with that,' he told me days afterwards, 'because I didn't want to take the piss out of the guy who made the jacket, y'know? I mean, I'm all for a piss-take, that's what the pop world's about, y'know, having fun. In the end there was so much confusion going on that I walked off without the award. Your ed's got it on his mantelpiece? And it's worth about £800? Well, I'll have it then!'

The after-show party was held in a hangar-sized warehouse in west London in the burgeoning era of the warehouse party, the sort of place films and videos were shot and where a roaring mass of showbiz humanity was now neurologically exploding on limitless free booze (and the incoming landslide of Ecstasy) to the sounds of early acid house. For a party devoted to a teen-pop cavalcade the atmosphere was intense. Bruno Brookes deliberately stood on Pete Burns from Dead Or Alive's ankle and broke off his stiletto heel, igniting the formidable Scouser's ire. Rock 'N' Roll Babylon was here, chaperoning Jackie and her husband, my extensively Scottish brother-in-law Robbie, a plumber by trade, a short man with the kind of audacious moustache we'd see on Steve Coogan's Paul Calf in the approaching future, and with equal enthusiasm for the phrase 'bag o' shite'. They were here at the awards at my surprise invitation, tickets posted in a secret envelope alongside a pre-paid hotel booking form and four £50 notes (a direct transfer from Old Rope). A rare trip away from their young children, this to them was a dazzling showbiz treat: in honour of the Donny Osmond poster my big sister used to have on our bedroom wall, many years later Jackie was jostled by the arm over to her childhood dreamboat, who I'd never met, and positioned in front of his still bonny face while I burbled on about 'sister', 'bedroom wall' and 'autograph'. She received her squiggle from Donny in real life and combusted with nostalgic joy. Robbie, meanwhile, a man with quip-Tourette's, which renders him incapable of *not* making a 'joke' with a stranger in any social situation, then asked Donny 'Whaur's Maria?' Even if his sister is called *Marie*.

Soon, we spotted Salt 'N' Pepa (with DJ Spinderella), and having recently interviewed the thrusting hip hop trio over in New York, introduced my family. 'Aw' right?' announced Robbie, Scottishly. 'Whaur's Tomatey Sauce?'

I bumped into Wayne Hussey from The Mission, sometime goth hero whom I'd interviewed in a side room in a Warner Brothers office with a plastic bat floating above the open doorway. Babylon, on viewing our lively exchange ten feet away, soon demonstrated how much he did not appreciate such animated attention on a Rock God other than himself and tipped a pint of beer over my head, drenching the hair, stinging mascaraed eyes and ruining my fancy outfit: a full pint he obviously was not drinking seeing as it was made of neither Malibu nor milk.

By midnight the party had blurred into a psychedelic matrix of booming bass, shattered glass and dance-floor discord, while shady dudes outside attempted to shunt a parked car straight through a glass wall. By 1 a.m. the atmosphere had turned sketchy and the remaining few hundred revellers were *tear-gassed* off the premises by canister-wielding security, clouds of gas tumbling across the dance floor as if to roll away the innocent exuberance of the flamboyant 1980s, replacing it overnight with a differently dazzling, potentially more lawless (and therefore even more thrilling) age.

It was the end of an era, certainly. Culturally, and personally.

'Sylv, Dad's in hospital, I think you better come home ...'

So announced Jackie in March 1989, another unexpected phone call meaning an even wobblier journey back to Scotland. The journey ended at the bottom of my dad's bed in Ninewells Hospital, Dundee, the first time we'd been in the city together since he drove me to the *Annabel* interview just six years before. It seemed a lifetime.

'What are you doing here?' he smiled. I had to lie: 'I'm here until you get better.'

This once charcoal-haired, Sean Connery-sized, huge-brown-eyed man of immense grace and stoicism now resembled those shadowy skeletons back in the war camps of Burma. Bowel cancer. Sitting on the bed I tugged at his hospital wristband, contemplating his date of birth: 17.12.1919. 'That was a long time ago,' I said. 'I know,' he said. He was only sixty-nine.

It had been a traumatic eighteen-month descent through terminal illness. Mum, unable to cope, drank sporadically but heavily, swearing constantly, as I'd hear on the few occasions I came home. At Christmas '88, she'd set fire to the Christmas savings, banknotes taken from their designated place in a bedroom drawer, before cocooning herself in bed for days. Dad handed me and Jackie all he'd managed for Christmas presents that year, a man now dying of cancer who wasn't well enough to shop anyway: to each of us a pair of tights. It was my dad's last Christmas and one of the saddest days of my life.

Mum, doubtless, had been in psychic agony, lashing out at the very thing she loved. On his deathbed, though, she became his nurse all over again, guiding him gently towards his death. 'I think,' she instructed the doctors and nurses, knowing his time was ebbing away, 'you should just make Mr Patterson comfortable.' It's how nurses talk about morphine, increasing the dosage so you slip further, under, away.

His final words to me were, 'For God's sake Sylvia, look after your health, you can't beat it.' The last sentence he ever said, a man from the Second World War generation brought up with a standard Church of Scotland religion he could never quite shake off was, 'I'll take my chance.' And his very last word, as evidently some vision, some connection, some thought or emotion or impulse rose up for the final time, was the name of his wife, my mum, whom he always loved despite everything, a loud and searching 'Rita!?' Who was right there, holding his hand.

Bros, of all people, sent me flowers and a signed message. Barry McIlheney, who wasn't even The Ed anymore (he'd now sprung up the bigwig ladder) sent me a box of cheer-up novelties from the office pals. And three weeks later, back in London, Tommy the D handed me a gift: a cassette tape of Joni Mitchell's *Hejira* album and a substantial square of dope. 'Go home,' he advised, 'listen to this, smoke that and it'll help you become a strong woman.' I did his bidding. And became a chaotic, consistent, deeply ill-suited marijuana enthusiast for the following sixteen years. It was his way, of course, of 'saving' me.

The grief I lived through in 1989 was perhaps ill-advisedly 'aided' by months of unforeseen hedonism, though *absolutely none* of it was instigated by me; the culture simply made it so. That year, with industry cash still abundant, Bros' label CBS/ Epic splashed an ocean's worth on a ludicrously lavish party in Prince's Gate, west London, in an actual embassy, over five floors. The main room was dominated by a 15 foot – *15 foot!* – ice sculpture of the word BROS and their Lego-men logo, while tables creaked under the bowlegged strain of all the national foods and all the national alcoholic drinks available to all mankind, the party's theme being an unambiguously ambitious 'The World'.

On one floor was splayed a demented spread of countless tables of pasta, sushi, curry, cheeses, fish 'n' chips, hot-dogs (and everything else), while a sweeping Hollywood staircase took you up towards equally countless tables of beer, wine, Russian vodka, sake, whisky (and everything else) in an extravagance of consumption on a Henry VIII scale with a view to permanent gout. By the time I left I could not walk (I mean, who drank free sake!?) and Tommy the D, as ever, attempted to help his beleaguered chum by flagging down the limousine of formidable global events promoter Harvey Goldsmith, who was also taking his leave. This was a man with whom I did not want to share *any* space, seeing as I didn't, at that point, even know my own name. 'I'll punch your pus, Tommy the D!' I bawled, and teetered off home instead. Years later, Tom told me he saw Andy Kershaw that night with his knob dangling out of his trousers, peeing on the red carpet. Another successful night, then, in swingorilliant eighties excess.

Soon afterwards, Babylon and I, being unsuited to each other in every way imaginable, split up. And Ken left Bros. We had a cover story about that. Under a crisp photo of the twins appeared the portentous enquiry: 'Bros without Craig – is this the end of the "road"?' Clue: yes. (Soon enough, Ken would sue the twins, who'd veer towards bankruptcy and the Ken-less Bros split up in '92.) Pop culture itself was now splitting apart, a cultural divide dramatically opening up into a Grand Canyon of diametrically opposed forces. On one side, piping over on the cliffs of perky pop, were Big Fun, Sinitta, Jason, Kylie, bendy pop Germans the London Boys and the Ken-less Bros, while throwing double-jointed shapes in their expensive trainers on the other side grooved the reticent coves of 'faceless dance music' and the Madchester madmen on *Top Of The Pops*.

Club culture now ruled, absolutely none of which suited *Smash Hits'* absurdist ways, its representatives simply *far-too-cool-for-school*: S'Express, Yazz, Bomb The Bass, Neneh Cherry, the Stone Roses, Happy Mondays, Italo House DJs and number one 'pop star' Jazzie B from Soul II Soul, whose inset photo on the cover bore the caption, inspired by his sprouting dreadlocks, 'Pipe cleaners ahoy!' That, you know, *didn't really work*. Acid house, Ecstasy and underground rave culture had hijacked the merrie pop overground and *Smash Hits* was now interviewing The Beloved inside a flotation tank, asking euphemistic questions about feeling a bit 'bendy'.

The nineties were imminent and the *Hits'* best hope for number one selling pop giants had already arrived in the form of a five-headed hydra from America. New Kids On The Block, to me, were tune-free, hunk-free piffle – as were the first sounds and sights of their cynically created UK progeny Take That. Sent to oversee their first-ever *Hits* interview, I returned with the news these northern pretenders were 'absolutely useless . . . but there's something about that Robbie'.

As proper new pop stars failed to flourish in the communal roar of The Rave Up, the cover of *Smash Hits* – once so culturally coveted and persuasive – was soon given over to whatever else, in Britain, was massive at the time, e.g. the beautiful people from *Beverly Hills 90210*, Tom Cruise, Beth from Brookside and grandma's wholesome thespo favourites Robson & Jerome. A recession was on its way. And now, *only now*, did The Baron turn up in the editorial atmosphere demanding its thousands of lost readers back, as the inevitable dilution of the sometime anarchy of absurdism began to look a lot like Gordon Small's strangulating K.I.S.S.

I interviewed Sonia, so vaporous a bubblehead I vowed I

could no longer carry on. Leaving the editorial staff in February 1990 I was given the customary leaving gift of a mocked-up *Smash Hits* cover. 'Sylvia Patterson: Spooks in her brain?' piped the cover-line, worryingly, while in-jokes were dotted around a hopeless photo where I looked like a hippy-haired goth-weed pondering some petals in a field (possibly because I was). Posters were announced for 'The Hooses!' (Housemartins), 'John Peel' and 'A bottle of Bells' (whisky, which I loathed), while song lyrics included 'I'll Punch Your Pus, Tommy the D', by The Harvey Goldsmith Fanclub. I still freelanced for the *Hits*, sporadically, while determinedly cultivating that none-more-nineties spliff habit. It wouldn't be long, surely, before I power-networked my way to other forms of freelance work. Except I didn't know how to network, had never networked, what did networking even *mean*? I smoked some more marijuana.

Within weeks I was signing on the dole.

By the time *Smash Hits* folded in 2006 it had long since capitulated to Gordon Small's K.I.S.S. ethos, a simplified, namby pop pamphlet, whose publishers had neither will nor vision to adapt its once revolutionary spirit into the revolution of the internet. Its last cover star was a tune-free TV persona known only as *Celebrity Big Brother*'s Preston ('Inside my mental mind!'), the *Smash Hits* logo seemingly made out of pink Flumps, the promise inside of '19 red carpet looks you'll love', something called 'Stars Exposed!' and 'what the stars really think about Chantelle'. Times hadn't just changed, they'd been blown up in a nuclear mushroom cloud of ideological opposition, now dominated by global showbiz entertainment and its tri-headed tyranny of reality TV, celebrity culture and talent shows.

Smash Hits at its eighties peak wouldn't be *allowed* to exist today, certainly nowhere near the mainstream, its language 'indecipherable' in Focus Group Hell, its intentions too unfathomable. We had a London pub 'wake' for the magazine the year it was finally let go, lifeless, across the slithery lip of The Dumper, a raucous riot attended by scores of the old staff, through the generations, where we cursed The Man and laughed uproariously over the most life-affirming experience, for many of us, of our entire working lives.

Not long after the *Smash Hits* wake I wrote about its downfall, girly-sap tears springing down my cheeks, pretending I still wrote for Bitz:

Revolutionary Mags In Pop Called *Smash Hits*, Part 1: *Smash Hits*. Swingorilliant pop mag invented in the hoary old Seventies, v. good in the Eighties, went a bit 'Howard out of Take That's bum' (speryoo!) in the Nineties and in 2006 went to hospital for a very long time i.e. forever. Swizzle! (Series Discontinued.) 'It's simply all too horribilis!' – The Queen. 'Look at what yer could've won!' – Jim Bowen. 'So do I, mate.' – Boris Becker.

Five years later in 2011 the world lost Tom 'Hibbs' Hibbert after years of illness, at the age of fifty-nine. At his funeral, Mark Ellen read out a passage not from any religious text but from the Bitz Book of Life: the text he'd ripped so cheerfully from his electric typewriter twenty-four years previously – The History Of Rock 'N' Roll Part Three: Elvis Presley. 'Born in a coal scuttle in Tucson, Arizona,' the irrepressible Mark read out to a suddenly giggling congregation. Soon, Hibbs would also go away for a very long time, i.e. forever, accompanied only by the soaraway psychedelics of The Byrds' 'Eight Miles High'.

9

TAKE ME INTO INSANITY (YEAH!)

Just as one piece of paper slipped onto your desk can change the content of your life, just as answering one phone call can propel you into a maelstrom of romantic trouble, opening a single door can fill the rest of your life with some of the greatest people you'll ever know and define a significant part of your fleeting existence, forever.

In March '89 I'd gotten away from the cat's pee mattress (and Rock 'N' Roll Babylon) and begun living with a PR acquaintance in a five-bedroom house-share on Stephendale Road, near Wandsworth Bridge Road, west London. We needed other flatmates and so I advertised in London's local newspaper the *Evening Standard*, including some stupid jokes about booze and larks. The doorbell duly rang.

Standing before me were two grinning visions seemingly sprung from the pages of a book of paper dolls, possibly wearing three separate outfits at once. Eventually, my eyes adjusted to the melee: the fairytale blonde one was wearing black loon pants with purple cummerbund, a petrol blue silken cape, a black wide-brimmed hat featuring an overhanging spray of marabou feathers and black Charlie Chaplin tramp shoes. The beaming brunette was similarly ravishing in a tweed 1940s wartime jacket with nipped-in waist, huge mauve silken bow tied around her neck, a tulip-shaped skirt, a sculpted Flapper Girl's cloche hat, with ribbon, and Vivienne Westwood 'rocking horse' shoes.

'We've come about the hoise!' piped a voice in a demented foreign accent. Northern Irish, it turned out, these being two likely lasses from Belfast called Tricia Kelly and Gillian Best, two fashion graduates freshly punted over on their own banana boat of naive possibility seeking a new life in ver Smoke. They'd also had a couple of drinks. This was all I needed to know: the rooms were theirs if they fancied. They moved in immediately.

Life on Stephendale Road was everything you'd hope for in a gang of exuberantly carefree young women in their early twenties – drinking, dancing, giggling, smoking, the odd E, loads of boys, loads of break-ups, rubbish meals (gigantic bowls of salted popcorn with a pound of melted cheese), stupid clothes, brilliant jokes, finding out where our edges lay and living out our communal mantra, '*carpe diem*!' (seize the day). Freelance life was fuelled by nerves and funded by John Major's government, crucially cushioned by the housing benefit I could not believe I was entitled to. Jobs came in sporadically – through *Smash Hits*, weedy London style weekly *Girl About Town* and a Spanish Hollywood gossip phone-line which paid the odd tenner for imaginative lies about the likes of Tom Cruise. Everything else was music, booze and marijuana, and the more I danced, smoked and laughed, the less I had to think about the death of my dad, or my mum's life without him, now an isolated widower, who'd retired at fifty-nine, losing herself in her early sixties in sustained years of punishing drinking. Whenever I rang she was either silent or abusive, pushing me away, a horror I had to learn to tolerate for the times she was sober and we could talk, at least, about the latest David Attenborough. Brother Billy, thankfully, was now her next-door neighbour, while my sisters also watched over her, waiting for signs of change – but as everyone knows who's been tangled up in addiction, there's no helping anyone who doesn't want to help themselves. Five hundred miles away I dealt with this the only way I'd ever known how to: music ... people ... dancing ... laughter ... seize the day ... *live forever.*

Stephendale Road was a permanent party house, skint as we were, decorating the communal rooms with the kind of spiky 'WOW!' signs you'd see on washing powder packets in the year dance music dominated the planet. Gilly B (as Irish Gill would always be known) took to dressing up in a white boiler suit with a furry hood while going boogie-berserk to A Homeboy, A Hippie & A Funki Dredd's number 56 non-hit 'Total Confusion' (TUNE).

One Saturday night a writerly pal from *Smash Hits* turned up. Sian Pattenden, a nineteen-year-old revolutionary instantly identifiable via peroxide bob, Oxfam frock and Henry Miller references, was a novice drinker who, when plied with vodka by we 'professionals', passed out on the stairs with a missing shoe and was carried off by The Toff to my fashionable futon, known as 'The Raft', which tended to attract the shipwrecked. Sian, still living at home in Twickenham, moved into our recently vacated fifth bedroom and was soon witness to a non-stop cavalcade where members of The London Musical Village randomly turned up, including our new pal (somehow) Lawrence out of Felt, The London Boys (both of whom were shockingly killed by a drunk driver in 1996), and stray members of 'vocal group' The Pasadenas, who brought with them, bizarrely, page 3 'stunna' Linda Lusardi, who sashayed up and down the stairs all night, looking all modelly. One morning, I croaked into the kitchen to find Dave Rowntree, drummer out of Blur, diligently doing the dishes despite his ongoing Ecstasy-related position as The Meltiest Man In Pop.

In May 1990 myself, Sian, Trish and Gill (fast becoming The London Four of Us) beamed up to Spike Island, the festival-sized event history would record as 'Woodstock for the baggy generation', and remembered by us as standing in a bog straining for the faintest reedy whimper of vocalist Ian Brown, as a generation of young men in paint-splattered bell-bottoms undulated limbs to the chemically-enhanced serotonin pounding through their oblivious minds.

Gilly B and I appeared, for the first and only time, in a pop video, for novelty house music belter 'Naked In The Rain' by something called Blue Pearl, Gill having made the acquaintance of a video producer looking for extras to dance like a selection of wind socks behind the alluring, unfeasibly named singer Durga McBroom. The video had 'a jungle concept' and so we found ourselves, in the early summer of 1990, wearing ripped-up sheets as loincloths (and indeed boob cloths), our unexpectedly exposed bodies smeared in chalky Aboriginal clay, limb-flailing behind the Amazonian McBroom in an abandoned car park up the back of King's Cross while being liberally hosed with a torrent of freezing water. 'Naked In The Rain' reached number four in the charts.

No wonder *Smash Hits* was still having an identity crisis, grappling with the new definition of pop throughout 1990 as a wonky-sided triangle of one-off techno-pop, newly mainstream hip hop and a selection of cultural curios, from Jesus Jones and the Rebel MC (he was street tuff), to Deee-Lite, Betty Boo, Vanilla Ice with his dangerously pistol-shaped fingers and Paul 'Gazza' Gascoigne, whose musical 'career' arose with his honking (and inevitable) Geordie tub-thumper 'Fog On The Tyne'. Three ex-*Smash Hits*/Emap staff now had a 1990 sort of idea: a dance music TV show which might even give a face to some of those faceless tunes, where coverage would be given to the likes of The Shamen years before their number one eulogy to Ecstasy, 'Ebeneezer Goode' (another TUNE).

Thus erupted, like a back-flipping homeboy down Hackney High Street, BBC2's *Dance Energy*, and through the ex-*Hits* team I was given a job as researcher. Not knowing what this meant I soon discovered it consisted almost wholly of having series producer Janet Street-Porter's boyfriend Normski, the show's presenter, persistently roosting on my office desk, smoking my snouts. Every week, the dancing studio audience was bussed in from the likes of Basildon, many of them white teenage boys sporting fluorescent knee-length American baseball shirts and consistently wailing 'I wish I was black!'

The original idea for *Dance Energy* – marginal club classics given BBC tea-time oxygen – was soon warped by the BBC bigwigs into an overly styled mainstream dance-pop show tyrannically dominated by the hyperactive Normski in a selection of oversized headgear, his catchphrase a none-too-catchy 'Respek! Is *due* ...'

The TV business was populated by weight-throwing megalomaniacs intent on belittling everyone around them in the name of gargantuan ambition, so I left, sprinting back to the music industry where the comparatively 'nice' people lived. By '91, however, a new sound was drudging over from America, made by glum-faced boys with guitars – all stinky shirts, gnarly hair and existential crises. This anti-pop, anti-fame, anti-glam ripple soon detonated outwards into the global phenomenon of American Grunge, a 'movement' fuelled by Prozac, heroin and suicidal anguish if your band sold more than three singles.

Like so many other glitter-eyed indie kids in '91 I was too old already for tormented teen spirit and far more interested in fluorescent shoes, existential jubilation and pineapples bouncing on heads, 'til dawn. The present was a foreign country so I puffed off back to another one – the past, me and the housemates soon frugging to The Faces, swooning to Scott Walker and boggling at the Bonzo Dog Doo-Dah Band, all neurologically adrift on The Raft. No wonder, via Sian's vibe-detecting ears, we discovered Pulp, finding in the shimmering Sheffield misshapes a contemporary focal point for uncannily similar retro-kitsch obsessions.

Since '91 we'd been dedicated Pulp People, their live shows now an essential glam-pop pilgrimage. In the Camden Underworld in '92 Jarvis Cocker – a human lamppost in a brown, wing-collared seventies shirt – eulogised on his emerging fame. 'This pop star business,' he mused from the stage, 'people think it's about being driven around in chauffeur-driven limousines, whereas in reality it's about starin' in a cracked mirror backstage, trying to put your contact lenses in.' The tiny Underworld featured two huge on-stage picture frames festooned with spike-heeled stilettos, the resultant 'installation' spray painted in all-over gold. (In the era of the 'shoe-gazers' – mostly sad-faced indie boys staring through fringes at feet – this was surely their anti 'shoe-gazing' statement.)

We saw them in the moist-walled venue called, well, The Venue in grimy New Cross, south London, Jarvis sporting not only a pinched brown seventies suit but a self-grown comedy moustache, holding aloft a disposable razor and announcing to a transfixed crowd, 'What d'you think, shall I shave it off or not?' The crowd roared a thunderous 'Yeeeaaah!' His moustache was hopeless, a wispy affair with sticky-up ends enlivening a motionless demeanour with the preposterous smirk of the Laughing Cavalier. He surveyed the crowd with an arched eyebrow and announced, very slowly: 'Weeeell ... I quite like me moustache, actually,' cast the razor aside and declared, 'so here's a song instead, it's called "My Legendary Girlfriend" ...'

We saw them in Cardiff, supporting the Manic Street Preachers, where they somehow didn't have anywhere to stay and so dispersed themselves among those who did. Jarvis and Pulp bassman Steve Mackay stayed with us, in a B&B twin room featuring a threadbare maroon carpet, myself and Sian in one single bed, the pop stars in the other, Jarvis soothing the assembled with goodnight cups of complimentary hot chocolate. Then, from his bed, in chocolate-brown pyjamas, specs in place, he read us a bedtime story from his on-the-road book of Russian children's fairy tales. Everything Jarvis Cocker did, said or read, it seemed, was unique.

In 1992 I was finally a working freelance journalist, long off the dole, having sought work by bombarding magazines both in the UK and the US with a host of *Smash Hits* clippings. Sporadic jobs arrived from *SKY* (the '87-launched, sex-obsessed style magazine attempting to rival *The Face*), while stylish American men's magazine *Details* dispatched me to Brighton to interview Primal Scream, one year on from their psychotropic masterpiece *Screamadelica* (by several dimensions the most singular, dazzling soundscape of the early 1990s). That day, Bobby Gillespie, a man anointed by the UK music press as 'the last great rock 'n' roll star', had taken so many drugs on their insanely narco-powered *Screamadelica* tour he ran out of his hotel room believing the carpet was on fire (merely a Quality Street wrapper glinting in the rarely seen daylight). In 1990, 'Loaded' had changed everything, their indie-schmindy '89 original 'I'm Losing More Than I'll Ever Have' melted down into an hallucinatory whirlpool of beats and horns by remix alchemist and invincible Ecstasy enthusiast Andy Weatherall. Its opening refrain perhaps *invented* the 1990s (a sample of a Peter Fonda soliloquy from the film *The Wild Angels*): 'We wanna be free ... we wanna have a party!'

Before his sudden room-bolt, Bobby Gillespie had talked that day about the power of music (a lot), about philosophy, about the 'dark side' of the human soul, fascism, racism, homophobia and 'diseased society thinking', his jaw meandering around his alarmingly grey face as the Ecstasy throbbed through his churning DNA (he could withstand up to six Es a night). 'If anyone wants to know what Ecstasy does,' he averred, 'open your mouth and throw one down. Taking a drug isn't escaping reality; it's totally real. The reality is you're feeling every single hair on your body. It's a sensual thing, an integral part of being alive. Look at most of the great writers through the ages, Byron or William Blake or Bowie or any of them. They liked to get loaded, y'know?'

He bemoaned the lack of real rock 'n' roll stars – 'where's the exoticness, where's the extraterrestrials?' he despaired, in the glam-pop wilderness of '92. 'There are no pop stars anymore, except us,' he evangelised, poetically. 'We're heavier than Guns 'N' Roses. Elvis is above me, Madonna's below. I'm alongside Jesus but swimming with Prince. We want to redeem rock 'n' roll. Our records are an orgiastic celebration of gone-ness.'

The proper pop stars, though, were already on their way, bringing with them, if not an orgiastic, at least an *unavoidable* celebration of gone-ness: Britpop. And the year before, I'd spent some time with a band who would become one of Britpop's central forces – one member of which would eventually become one of the most divisive characters in the history of British music ...

10

DAMON: THE OMEN

In 1991, three years before anything called Britpop parped into view, heralding Dick Van Dyke in a Kinks-striped blazer, the *Smash Hits* staff loved Blur. Well, we loved the tunes – 'There's No Other Way' had just become their first top ten hit – and we loved gregarious bassist Alex James who was always going on about infinity, we loved sensitive guitar-smith Graham Coxon with his indie-poet soul, and we loved drummer Dave Rowntree, an agreeable character even before he took all that Ecstasy, became The Meltiest Man In Pop and did the dishes round Stephendale Road.

Lead singer/songwriter Damon Albarn, meanwhile, was widely

acknowledged as not only Blur's but the actual *era*'s monumental pain in the arse. Where he purports today to be a shambling Man Of The People – busking around Leytonstone in east London sporting his ganja-leafed baseball hat – in '91, aged twenty-three, an air of withering superiority permanently emanated from his upturned nose in a throb of petulant boredom. Being a tyrannical musical snob, *Smash Hits* was beneath him, which didn't stop us attempting to turn Blur into proper pop stars anyway, soon requesting they spend a day out in Margate for some top pop seaside larks. Their PR was delighted and Damon was appalled, aware the Radio 1 Roadshow was also broadcasting from Margate that day. The week before, Blur had appeared on the Roadshow in Skegness. 'Bloody hell,' he muttered, dragging his trendily trainered feet onto the train. 'People'll think we're desperate. And last week they introduced us as "Blue" ...' (This was nine years before hunkin' pop tarts Blue even existed – so, you know, things could've been even worse ...)

All the way to Margate on the 9.13 a.m. train, Damon Albarn was as sullen as a huffing teen, slumped in his seat, arms crossed, up against the window, occasionally glancing at his book, Hanif Kureishi's London-set debut *The Buddha of Suburbia*, through swanky Italian shades. Dave snoozed off his hangover, Graham smoked gaspers like a sixty-year-old salty sea dog and Alex, ever the pop kid and a *Smash Hits* viewer for years, eulogised on his favourite topics: space and cheese, plus his latest literary purchase, *Gargantua and Pantagruel*, Rabelais' bawdy, scatological sixteenth-century picaresque about two warring giants, which he deemed 'absolutely hilarious!' Alex read passages aloud:

'For this cause Heraclitus was wont to say, that nothing is by dreams revealed to us that nothing ...'

Graham: 'Stop being a poser and come and have a fag!'

In Margate, everyone but Damon tried their best. Dave wore a stupid red fez and pretended to be Tommy Cooper. Alex swung a luminous toy hose which made an amusingly high-pitched 'wheeeeeeee!' sound. Graham fondled a mirror which laughed when you picked it up: 'That's very sinister.' Damon attempted to shake some scarlet tinsel cheerleader pom-poms to languidly limp effect. He decreed Margate 'crap'. To cheer himself up he had a go on a strength-gauging 'How Manly Are You?' machine, his grip on a rubber handle assessing him, triumphantly, as 'A Jungle Man'. Inspired, he then bought his first-ever copy of *Smash Hits* en route to the train home and perused a feature on the latest pop goons, Take That.

'They don't look very good, do they?' he surmised. 'Very old-fashioned. The kids don't want that do they? Now, *this*' – he waved a photo of Blur in the Bitz section, the band holding aloft the cardboard letters B-L-U-R – 'is what they need!'

That day, not a single punter had recognised them.

'We're not famous enough for that,' announced Damon. 'Yet.'

Six years later, in late April 1997 after The Britpop Wars, after Blur, Oasis and Pulp had all been the biggest bands in Britain, Damon Albarn stepped off a plane in Rome with Blur. In the year Oasis' *Be Here Now* album would arrive as a cocaine-scuppered calamity, Blur's best-known song was a seeming Nirvana pastiche which hollered (as the band bounced off sprung walls like American grunge kids) 'Whoo-hoooo! When I feel heaveeee metaaaahl!' Alex James, peering through huge, round, thick-framed, yellow-tinted 'Miami glasses', scanned the blue sky overhead and announced, to the assembled, 'Another sunny day in pop.'

Damon, standing beside him, reached in silence to the evidently offending showbiz sunnies, plucked them off Alex's face, gleefully crumpled them up in both hands and replaced them on his nose, now unwearable, buckled and lens-less. Alex merely laughed as a bemused band crew member piped: 'Who did that?!'

'Me,' smiled Damon. 'Who do you think?'

Later I mused to Alex that this wasn't, you know, a very nice thing to do. 'I know,' smiled Alex. 'Well, you know, he's a bloody ... *cunt*.'

Where Damon Albarn had consistently been an arse, I'd always liked Blur's music, even attempting to jump off the onstage speakers with Sian at their 27,000-attended Mile End stadium show in mid-1995. Oasis, however, I had *loved*, their '94 to '96 Imperial Phase responsible for the greatest surge in all-out evaporating fandom of my allegedly adult life. And, you know, taking sides in the Britpop Wars was hilarious.

In April '97 Oasis had yet to obliterate their musical reputation with the blundering *Be Here Now* and Blur's continued existence was at the very least implausible. Since *Parklife* had made them household-famous seemingly overnight in '94, Graham had been a volatile, self-loathing drunk, who called his path from oblivion to now-teetotal stability 'a miracle'. He'd become an alcoholic at the age of twenty-seven mainly through embarrassment. 'I was embarrassed about being in a pop band,' he mused in Cafe Piazza in Rome, on the coffee and fags. 'My only ambition was to get through the next tour. Alcohol helped.'

Communication between himself and Damon, his childhood friend and musical soulmate, had duly become 'horrendous' and in '97 remained strained. 'We've become,' he confirmed, 'associates instead of friends.' Pop music to him was and always had been 'fucking wank, horrible – but that's all over now, I've only just come to the conclusion I'm a musician'. Alex, he added, used to taunt him. 'Lots of things Alex said would upset me,' he noted, 'jokes like "What's fifty foot long with no pubes? The front row of a Blur gig." That would really infuriate me. And it was said to infuriate me.'

Dave, astoundingly, had also become teetotal other than the

odd 'jazz cigarette', while Alex remained permanently rollicking. Back in the early nineties, at a club called Syndrome (we were always waggishly 'going down Syndrome'), a photographer took a photo of we clubbers, a stray photograph of me then appearing in a tabloid newspaper with the caption, 'Justine, Alex's girlfriend'. A pal pointed out I could sue over this and, being skint at the time as usual, I investigated. The tabloid was duly sued and compensation awarded of £400 for the devastating slander of being wrongly accused of being the girlfriend of one of the most eligible young men in the history of indie-pop hunks. Alex himself saw the funny side and I generously bought him one pint.

In 1997 he was still, by nature, a Bolly poppin' International Playboy. 'Oh dear,' he cringed at the suggestion. 'I'm not that much of a shag athlete, I'm really not.' Nonetheless he missed his old drinking buddies. 'Me and Graham used to get drunk together, that's all we did, take acid and go on the radio and just blow raspberries because it's funny.' He contemplated why he believed, so much, in booze and narcotic oblivion, his then-favoured route to The Meaning Of It All. 'It's the chaos, the recklessness, the way everything becomes so random,' he decided. 'Suddenly you're all in a taxi going to … Belgium! It should never be the crutch, the *main thing*, but there's nothing like being drunk and irresponsible and brilliant, is there?'

People who behaved like this, he added, were merely exceptionally interested in being alive. 'Exactly that!' he levitated. 'And that's what unites people generally who are good at what they do, they've just got a fucking enthusiasm, which translates, it makes you into someone who's interested in life, who hasn't fucking given up. I know so many people who *have*. I don't know what happens to people. I'm scared of it, though.'

Three days before Rome, the day before the 1997 UK General Election and the New Labour 'new dawn', Damon Albarn was splayed on a leather sofa in a London recording studio, his gigantic blue eyes *dripping* with inner shine. At the time I concluded he must be stratospherically stoned, possibly on some powerful imported ganja. Many years later, in 2014, we finally discovered Damon had a heroin habit from 'the height of Britpop' to the early 2000s, which made him, he noted, both creatively 'free' and 'incredibly productive'. That day in 1997 he was also a conversational cloud, prone to shape-shifting thoughts across lengthy philosophical reveries, unable, or unwilling, to complete a single sentence. Now a taekwondo devotee, he was almost unrecognisable from the upright, self-conscious cynic of Margate's miserable moodiness.

'I let go of Damon the ... whatever it was I'd become,' he mused, not particularly helpfully. 'Some think ... the Devil. Maybe I was.'

Beneath the zen-state dreaminess, however, his core self still clanged with steely combat. In the dying days of Britpop, Britain's current musical output, he averred, was 'ignorant, snobbish, homogenised, class-riddled, a profoundly conservative floating ... pop factory'. No one, he harrumphed, had ever got 'the point' with Blur. They'd never celebrated Being British, more 'used caustic humour, intelligence, to highlight the staticness of everything'. The logical conclusion to Britpop's heyday, he decided, 'is that now we've got a new government' (which Britain would have four days from now), a typically old-school Damon implication that Blur were involved in bringing down the Conservative government. 'I'm not saying it changed governments,' he swerved, 'but it definitely contributed, in some convoluted way.'

Soon, his combative spirit broke free. 'I've given up being specific, slagging off bands, I've exhausted it,' he lied, before a sustained slagging of Oasis. 'I *do* like their songs,' he began, now sliding around the leather sofa, 'but they're just not very ...

bright.' Despite historical claims of loathing 'class snobbery' (and he had been 'a victor and a victim of it, I suffered at the hands of Oasis because of my class'), he dismissed both Liam and Noel Gallagher as 'thick, ignorant, stupid', seeing 'intelligence' as inherently superior to, say, human empathy, or world-class wit. 'We know how to make songs like that,' he sniffed of the mighty Oasis canon which had caused such elevational enchantment in my soul for the previous three years. 'Our first single "She's So High", if you sang that with a Manc accent it'd be an Oasis song,' he assured. 'Very simple, very driving. (witheringly) Even the lyrics are up to Oasis' standards.' He was off.

'The reality,' he judged, 'is that Oasis are the same as the Spice Girls – simple, accessible, popular music. In fact, the Spice Girls have sold more than Oasis now so they can't even hold on to being the biggest *selling* act in Britain.' A full twenty-minute anti-Gallagher tirade followed, a jeering discourse on how Oasis fans had 'given something mythical status by taking drugs to it, projecting their own altered states onto the music because it's very accessible'. On he withered, about how both John Lennon and Kurt Cobain had 'the sensitivity' to view global fame as 'a rather ugly position to be in', which Oasis, 'with their Rolls-Royces and dark glasses', completely failed to grasp. 'Oasis are the Spice Girls on drugs,' he concluded triumphantly. Furthermore, their non-appreciation of fine literature and unwillingness to explore other cultures (thus weakening The Beatles' sacred legacy) was, he finally fanfared, 'the same thing as using a Buddhist symbol and then going and killing thousands of Jews'.

Is it!?

'Well … it's not, but it's the same sort of utter kind of sort of y'know … ridiculous contradiction.'

Oasis, then, according to Damon Albarn in 1997, were the cultural equivalent of the Third Reich. And they say no one, at the time, took The Britpop Wars all that seriously.

'Well,' he smiled, satisfied, at the interview's end, sliding off the sofa, 'thanks for that, it's been good to have a more mature, adult conversation.' I'd preferred singing hosepipes and Heraclitus the Greek, to be honest, but at least he'd enjoyed himself.

Still, Damon Albarn was *never dull*. And, it would soon turn out, beyond the strains of official interview, capable of outright benevolence.

Sometime in the year 2000, renowned indie PRs Best-Est took six journalists on a trip to Iceland in an attempt to make an Icelandic pop saucestrel famous (it didn't work). While there, much Black Death vodka was imbibed. Damon Albarn, now an occasional Iceland dweller, was also there and joined us one night for a drink. Sadly, this was a night I lost my mind. 'Boo hoo hoo!' I wept in a bar, over some drama back home, possibly a boy, possibly family, possibly the lifelong, recurring, existential meltdown which had blighted me from adolescence onwards.

'Come with me,' announced Damon, unexpectedly. He crooked his arm in mine and took me for a walk, under an actual silver moon which shimmered in a still-azure summer sky, at midnight, strolling together along the stunning shore, across psychedelic purple plankton. He told me everything would be alright in the end. And eventually it was.

That night, ten years after proclaiming him the biggest arse of the early nineties, he voluntarily helped an adversarial, pesky journo, revealing some of that compassion for humanity I didn't really believe he'd finally developed. So cheers to you, Damon Albarn, I appreciate that.

Even if I still think you're a bit of a twerp and a massive weirdo, all the same.

Reviewed by
Richey James

11

THIS AIN'T ROCK 'N' ROLL – THIS IS GENOCIDE!

The Manic Street Preachers *were* (and still are) The Revolution. In 1992, when the world didn't understand them – a glam-Clash throwback shouting, confusingly, 'Bomb the past!' – some of us ferociously loved them, *Smash Hits* almost as determined as they were to turn their glittering art-rock nihilism into a multi-million-selling, indelible pop phenomenon. Young and beautiful punk-art polemicists versed in Situationist theory, they loved Kylie Minogue and loathed The Wedding Present, were repelled by mediocrity and stood Against The Cliché, fans of

Smash Hits who found their chosen pop tribune 'more effective in polluting minds than Goebbels ever was'.

To this end, we were all in Dublin in early 1992, our vodka-fuelled trip to the Irish equivalent of the Brit Awards, the Irma Milk Awards, resulting in scenes of world-class renegade disorder. Only recently signed to the Sony giant at considerable expense, they were soon riotously wrecking the Sony Music table in a hotel ballroom, a kaleidoscopic, four-man, muppet-rock vision of leopard print, fake fur, panda-eyed kohl, stencilled chiffon blouses, explosive hair and Daz-white drainpipe jeans. Nicky Wire, six foot three inch bass player/lyricist in a fuchsia feather boa, had popped all the balloons weedily affixed to the table and was fully passed out on the floor, on his back, literally under the table. Sean Moore, normally permanently mute drummer, was bawling 'Booooring!' while his cousin, intensely bristling singer/guitarist/songwriter James Dean Bradfield was frogmarched off by security after threatening to thump the onstage host, who'd jeered '*How* outrageous' at their regulation performance-ender of booting over the amps while James dived into the audience. Simultaneously, 'guitarist'/lyricist Richey James Edwards, his forearm still healing from the horrific '4 REAL' he'd carved into it with a blade ten months previously as proof of his righteous intentions, had poured several full bottles of wine into the gigantic mid-table ice bucket, heartily tapped in some salt 'n' pepper and watched it copiously overflow.

A Sony bigwig called Eleanor in a tweed jacket was appalled, bawling at her expensive new charges, 'You're SCUM! You should be THROWN out of here!', while loitering waiters deemed them 'a disgrace!' and removed the offending table from the premises. The Manics flounced from the venue as soon as they could stir their co-manager Martin Hall, found on the floor of the men's toilet gnashing to himself, 'There must be more to life than this . . .'

The following morning, only one Manic was capable of an official *Smash Hits* interview. The graceful political history graduate Richey Edwards, his fragile frame housing a powerful theoretical mind, padded into the hotel bar, huge brown eyes both Bambi-doleful and flooded with youthful life. 'I suppose I'll have to do an interview then?' he smiled, settling in a corner with a pint of Guinness, and remaining there for the next four and a half hours, occasionally sticking broken-up multicoloured twizzle sticks onto his glass and pondering the impromptu designs.

He'd just turned twenty-four, a funny, warm and acutely sensitive people's poet who said hardcore things not for effect, but because he believed them, absolutely, to be true.

'It's true!' he'd smile, coyly, and usually he was right, if unable to balance humanity's cruelty, corruption and selfishness with even a scintilla of its compassion, intelligence or happiness, other than a melancholy nostalgia for the carefree joys of childhood. If his then comically wry nihilism would become, soon enough, the calcified cynicism which killed him, he was also softly spoken, peculiarly gentle, his lilting Welsh timbre the lightness through the foreboding darkness of most everything he had to say.

'I woke up next to a Michael Jackson award for Best Video Of The Year,' was the first thing Richey announced that day, a vision of pale, dark-haired, delicate beauty in smudged eyeliner, white cheesecloth shirt and luminously matching drainpipes. We knew much of this interview would be unprintable, consisting as it did of outbursts of Marxist philosophy and sustained despair very far from the customary *Smash Hits* quips about parsnips sprouting in gumboots. Richey soon decided 'a list of books is much better', and wrote out (on a piece of hotel paper, since tragically lost) a recommended reading list specifically for the viewers including *Nineteen Eighty-Four*, *Catch-22*, *The Catcher in the Rye* and *American Psycho*. I wondered how he'd usually feel after an extreme night like the last one. Amused? Incensed? Indifferent?

'Well, the first thing I do every day is I wake up, dial nought for room service, go "Vodka and orange," put the phone down, lie there 'til it comes, put the TV on and think about our two philosophies of life: "there must be more to life than this" and "it's all fucking bollocks". Can they print that in *Smash Hits*? Can they do the f and the dash dash?!' He smiled serenely. 'Being told you're scum is just priceless, because that's what we are,' he carried on. 'We never pretended to be anything else. (shouts to Sony Music) You fucking signed us for shit loads of money! What d'you expect us to do? If you want Phil Collins, sign Phil Collins. We were never in a position of power, if they hadn't signed us we'd still be on the dole.'

Richey soon proved himself something of a pop seer, aggrieved at a shifting youth culture displacing music, at core, with TV personalities and technology. 'Pop music is dying,' he declared, here in the post-rave, pre-Britpop wilderness of 1992, 'bands are boring and drab, there's no Duran Durans anymore, that's why computer games are so massive, people want to be in control.' That day he held the human male responsible for all the abominations on Earth, 'because they're full of hate and obsessed by power and sex and ruin everything'. He thought girls, naturally, were great.

'We get loads of girls at our gigs and we get criticised for that because people think that's too poppy, "oooh, you've got girl fans", so we can't possibly be serious,' he scoffed. 'That is *soooooo* patronising, like they can't possibly like or understand the music and they're not going to have fifteen pints of lager, have a big mosh down the front and have a curry on the way home. And they should be at home reading *Jackie* and thinking about blokes. It's crap! In terms of sensitivity and intelligence, girls understand so much more than men.'

Girls, he added, didn't have the po-faced muso mindset, either.

'This bloke out of [Madchester also-rans] The High came up and started talking to me about an interview he'd just done about his guitar and equipment,' he blinked. 'When I told him I wasn't interested and that James plays my guitars on the record, he went mad. He was going, "There ought to be a union to stop people like you!"'

A strikingly attractive, charismatic young man who'd lost his virginity aged twenty-one, he'd never had a girlfriend – 'I think that's very sad and lonely' – although he didn't believe, in the first place, relationships were even possible. 'Men and women just aren't compatible,' he was certain. 'Men are too selfish. I don't think it's in human nature to be happy, because people just get bored. You sleep with somebody, you get bored, you sleep with somebody else. Everybody should just . . . fuck. They just should! There's no point, how can you have a relationship? Everyone always desires something else.'

Mankind, he carried on, was 'the worst thing that's ever happened to this planet', predicting there were 'five generations of man left' and within three generations '75 per cent of the animal species of the world will be wiped out, and it's all our fault!' Furthermore, he surmised, the Manics would eventually implode like every other band.

'Every person in a band knows they're gonna end up on the dole in south London when all the records dry up, completely forgotten about, with a big drink or drugs problem,' he was sure. 'It's the nature of fame. The excesses, it'll get us all in the end. It'll happen to Macaulay Culkin!'

(And so it would eventually come to pass for the gog-mouthed *Home Alone* tiddler.)

What is it about Fame? That so many are eventually destroyed by it?

'Well, if any student or businessman in this hotel now went up to their bedroom and smashed it up, they'd be prosecuted and might get sent to prison,' he mused, sipping another Guinness. 'If we went up and did it, the record company would pay the fine and the hotel looks good for having rock 'n' roll bands stay. (rueful chuckle) I can't believe we're so paranoid and cynical and we've had one top twenty single! What must've been going in The Beatles' minds!? They must've been so messed up.'

We talked about his tiny physique, how his normal weight was 'eight and a half stone', about his lack of violent impulse.

'I've never been violent towards anybody in my life, I've always taken out my frustration on myself,' he observed. Here, he laughed. 'There was some bloke giving me a bit of 'assle, going on about when I cut my arm and I just went, "Look, mate, I gave myself eighteen stitches on my arm, you've seen the pictures, they were pretty 'orrible, so imagine what I could do to your fucking face?" And he went really white and just ran off!'

Soon, a scorching treatise arrived on the KLF's 1992 Brit Awards performance where they threw a dead sheep on stage. 'They said, "we're gonna carve ourselves up on stage and disembowel a calf",' scoffed Richey, 'well, I could never go back on my word, I would have to do it, and I would do it!'

Things became even more alarming …

'It's the easiest thing in the world to say, "I'm so outrageous, I feel like doing this" and then not do it, fuck that!' he fumed. 'What the KLF did was easily good enough to create an impact and make people think about pop music, so why go around saying "I feel like Michael Ryan"? [In 1987, an unemployed madman in Hungerford called Michael Ryan randomly shot dead sixteen people including his own mother before killing himself.] Well, at least Michael Ryan *did it*. If they felt like Michael Ryan why didn't they just get a fucking gun and just go "boof!", die EMI, die Sony, die CBS. It's easy to do!'

I had to steer him away, sharpish, find something the *Hits* could actually print.

D'you think the so-called Revolution is ever going to happen, or is it a myth?

'Never. It's a myth. Always has been a myth.'

Nooo!

'It's true! Because human nature is so corrupt that any revolution you get, people need power and once people get power they can never get rid of it. Human beings do not want a revolution. Human beings are quite satisfied to find a little rut in life and go through it or find a way of exploiting somebody else. There's *never* gonna be a revolution. That's what always pisses me off when people think, "Manic Street Preachers think, Smash The System! Revolution!" We've never thought that for one fucking tiny second. All we've ever wanted to do was make some sense to some poor kid doing a crap job, that's all.'

What actually is your manifesto?

'Our manifesto is, don't do it kids, never get past the age of thirteen.'

Oh no.

'It's true! 'Cos once you start wanting things, once you're interested in fashion and music and impressing your friends, your lifestyle starts going really badly wrong. Before the teenage years, all you really care about is you wake up, you wanna play all day, life is excitement, it means something, no problem going to sleep. Once you start desiring things you can't get to sleep and think "I wish I had a new bike, I wish I could afford these records". Even people who have everything you can possibly expect from life, they're not content, their needs get out of control. So our manifesto is: on your thirteenth birthday, kill yourself. It's just gonna get worse and worse until you're a sixty-five-year-old wreck in an 'ospital bed. In Macclesfield. It's true! Which is why I'm going to have another Guinness ...'

On return . . .

'D'you know what I think is the best thing *Smash Hits* could ever do? In terms of promoting a massive outcry?' He sipped his Guinness, chuffed with his approaching good idea. 'Front cover of *Smash Hits*, pictures of every teen idol there's ever been and over the top in big letters, KILL YOURSELF.'

Help!

'It'd be brilliant! You'd be on the *Six O'Clock News*! The *News At Ten*, everywhere! It'd be huge! And inside you'd just have articles exploding every myth about everyone, every single bit of gossip in there. (portentous voice) "You believed the lies, now face the consequences!"'

D'you think you could explain to someone who's thirteen, perhaps on the brink of suicide, what Situationism means?

'Well it's the best political theory of all time because it realises that politics is moronic. Whatever political party is in power it's never gonna change life for the ordinary person. Who is only interested in consumption. It's tragic!'

Now traumatised, I went for the big one.

So what is it all about, Richey? What does, in fact, make us happy? What makes you happy, for example?

'Being asleep.'

Oh no!

'It's true!'

D'you think if you weren't in this group, you would in fact be dead?

He paused for several seconds. 'Yes.'

Three years later, after escalating psychological traumas with alcoholism, anorexia and depression, Richey Edwards, twenty-seven, was last seen in the Embassy Hotel, London, at 7 a.m. on 1 February 1995, the day he and James were scheduled to fly out to America for the Manics' latest tour. His Vauxhall Cavalier was found near the Severn Bridge in Wales, with a flat battery. He simply vanished.

Richey Edwards was declared officially dead on 23 November 2008.

'Not the Irma!' exclaimed Nicky Wire, six months on from the date of his best friend's official death, in spring 2009, head in hands, hearing recollections of his own excellent behaviour in Dublin. 'Well, that's what you've got to do when you're young! And in a rock 'n' roll band. We never got let in that hotel again because I came down to the lobby in my boxer shorts . . .'

Seventeen years on from Boxersgate and Nicky was in his favourite London hotel, the Langham, principally because of its elegant, pink-edged stationery, now a forty-year-old man in a shapeless, glam-free, blue hooded top. We contemplated the Richey of '92, how he had become 'more intelligent about everything but those feelings stayed the same, the bitterness and anger, that conclusion of emptiness, it just seemed to devour him'.

I wondered what made him so much less emotionally troubled than Richey, his intellectual equal. 'Simple things, like the genuine love of sport,' he concluded, which stayed with him and ebbed away from Richey. 'Little hints of normality were disappearing one by one,' he mused. 'The only interests he seriously seemed to have led nowhere really. To great art but not further on a humane level. When he stopped drinking, to try and get better, a massive piece of his life was taken away. There was definitely joy to that part of his life. Negative, but we've all got crutches. If he was around today he would be, on some level, a true in-the-public-domain star. He was a *genuine* star. In a non-showbiz, totally real way.'

Did he ever imagine, as a kid, that something like this could happen to his exceptional friend?

'When we were *kid* kids playing football, no, but as soon as we got in a band,' he surmised before an outburst of regret. 'There's not many regrets as a band, but I do really, really, really, really, *really* regret that Richey wasn't around when we were on the Brit Awards [the Manics were three-time winners in 1997]. Or playing to 66,000 people on millennium night in Cardiff. Just for him to see that scale. 'Cos we all wanted to be fucking gigantic. I remember picking up the Brit Award when we did "A Design For Life" and thinking, "There's ten million people watching this on the telly" and what would he have done? Would he have set himself alight on stage? If he could carve "4 REAL" into his arm in front of fourteen people? In *Norwich*? Imagine! Some brilliant art statement. Blank and Situationist and cryptically cutting. At the Millennium Stadium, James sang "Small Black Flowers That Grow In The Sky" [lyrics by Richey] and 66,000 people, couples, blokes, were singing (sings) "Harvest your ovaries ... dead mothers crawl!" *That* is phenomenal, *that* is fucking subversion. And *The Holy Bible* sells 5,000 albums every single year, it never stops. Much like *Closer* by Joy Division.'

Nicky had been anxious that day, feeling the 'overwhelming responsibility' of the Manics releasing their ninth album, *Journal For Plague Lovers*, featuring lyrics exclusively by Richey, words he'd personally edited from a file Richey handed him five days before he disappeared. A week later, Nicky sent a handwritten letter to my home, a list of additional statements he'd like included in an interview where, he was convinced, he hadn't articulated himself 'as well as I wanted to'.

Seventeen years after Richey wrote his reading list for *Smash Hits* viewers, here was a list written by Nicky on both sides of one piece of pink-edged Langham stationery, four Tippexed corrections throughout fourteen numbered and underlined statements in large, clear handwriting. Statements which included:

A blank page of paper and a pen is the greatest invention - it's so exciting to be confronted by possibility.

Saturday morning kids TV has been ruined by pious – pontificating – revolting chefs. We used to have the *Banana Splits, Tiswas, Swap Shop – Tarzan – Robinson Crusoe – The Singing Ringing Tree,* we had imagination. Now we have these grotesque vain people lecturing us on how to live – it's sick.

You know culture is fucked when Will Young gets a *South Bank Show.*

I love the BBC and all it stands for – but I resent paying my licence fee to subsidise U2's album campaign.

The sensitivity involved with *Journal For Plague Lovers* is crushing and inescapable. I hope we have done his words justice.

In the top left-hand corner he'd placed three stickers in a neat rectangular shape (reminiscent of the broken-up twizzle stick design on Richey's Guinness glass seventeen years before): a disembodied hand holding a black fountain pen, Andy Warhol's signature and perhaps, for him, the most fitting Warhol quote of them all: 'I never think that people die. They just go to department stores.' And tucked inside the envelope, he'd included a printed quote from George Bernard Shaw:

'A life spent making mistakes is not only more honourable, but more useful than a life spent doing nothing.'

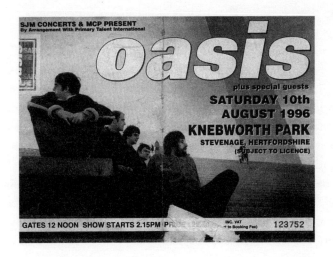

SJM CONCERTS & MCP PRESENT
By Arrangement With Primary Talent International

oasis

plus special guests
SATURDAY 10th
AUGUST 1996
KNEBWORTH PARK
STEVENAGE, HERTFORDSHIRE
(SUBJECT TO LICENCE)

GATES 12 NOON SHOW STARTS 2.15PM PRICE   INC. VAT
                                          t to Booking Fee)   123752

12

FEELING SUPERSONIC

April 1994, and I hadn't made it home, flinching awake on a Saturday morning on the couch of Tommy the D and his long-term lovely girlfriend (and soon to be wife) Karen in north London. Smoking a fag, I switched on the TV for *The Chart Show*, as everyone did on every Saturday morning in the 1990s, expecting the same old chart-bound drivel.

1994 hadn't been much of a pop year so far, because it never was back then: reggae scamps Chaka Demus and Pliers (the best name in tradesman-pop since Shovel out of M People) had given us their butt-pervin' version of 'Twist And Shout', the Crash Test Dummies had 'Mmmm'd their way into novelty-pop mythology and D:Ream had no clue they'd ostensibly invented the forthcoming concept of New Labour with 'Things Can Only Get Better'. Take That were, as they always were, number one, this time with 'Everything Changes' (and in a few weeks Wet Wet Wet would be number one with 'Love Is All Around', for approximately three decades). No wonder I was still obsessed with the past, now deep inside the spliff habit which meant in April '94 my finger was not so much on-the-musical-pulse as scratching around underneath The Raft for a pin-head of oily dope, while developing an enormous and frankly pointless crush on recently deceased Small Faces frontman Steve Marriott.

Back on Tom's couch the gasper hovered in mid-air as a black and white image of a forthcoming 'new release' thrummed into view, a song to be released two days from now on Monday, 11 April 1994: 'Supersonic', by something called Oasis. The intro immediately transfixed: a curious guitar sound like an inner-city urchin rattling a stick along an iron railing, or running a knitting needle across your own teeth. A head appeared, an undeniably attractive head festooned with a scruff-mod haircut, mouth like a dinghy and tinted circular glasses, hypnotically steady eyes staring through Elizabeth Taylor's eyelashes and through three individual screens (his glasses, the camera, the 24-inch TV) to shatter through my eyes and rearrange the contours of my neurological transmitters, forever.

'I need to be myself . . .'

Blimey.

' . . . a girl called Elsa . . . into Alka-Seltzer . . .'

Hello?

' . . . tissue . . . The Big Issue . . .'

Eh? The voice was a feline mewl wrapped around an unmistakable attitude, the one which says 'Fuck Off'.

'Alright, Sylv?' croaked Tom, padding into the living room in his tartan-checked jammies. 'Cuppa tea?'

Have you seen this, the D?

'Oasis, man. Fuckin' brilliant.'

This is Oasis? I thought they were a dance band. And who's *he*?

'That's Liam.'

Pring! Pring!

Tom answered the phone. It was his wee brother Brian, calling from Dundee.

'Yer fuckin' kiddin'!'

He turned to me, aghast.

'Fuckin' hell, Sylv. Kurt Cobain's killed himself.'

Like the lurching, veering switch-point on a railway track, this way culture shifts, sometimes in the microsecond it takes for a bullet to obliterate a brain. The early nineties – bang! – were gone, plaid shirts, Prozac and twenty-minute Parisian house music singles toppling like dominoes towards the inky depths of The Dumper. That morning, a crack appeared in the space-time continuum, letting through the first luminous shafts of musical brilliance soon to beam through a beleaguered nation: not only was Oasis' *Definitely Maybe* imminent but so were Blur's *Parklife*, Pulp's *His 'N' Hers*, Portishead's *Dummy*, Massive Attack's *Protection* and The Prodigy's *Music For The Jilted Generation*. Blur, it seemed overnight, were no longer a girlie-fringed 'indie' band fondling the hem of the charts, but Union Jack-blazered aesthetes challenging all-comers on the covers of *Select*, *NME* and *The Face*. Pulp were no longer outsider art-school underdogs for the peripheral kitsch set but had, in Jarvis Cocker, a deadpan hilarious and eminently eccentric Man Of The People who was not like any other member of The People whomsoever. And Oasis, ultimately, were The Ultimate Dreamer's Band. Which made them *my* band.

Much like being in a fantastic new band, surely, having a

favourite new band is one of life's most intoxicating thrills, a prismatic explosion of hitherto dormant energy channelled from the atmosphere directly into your soul; an atomic collision promising unknowable new possibilities of sonic beguilement, lyrical connection, dancing upside down on a dance floor with your greatest friends and talking synapse-shredded cobblers 'til three days hence at dawn. All of these things, at least, were the touchstones of Oasis fandom. It's not so very different from falling in love (even if it is in the worst possible, all-obsessional, one-directional way).

One month later, in May 1994, *NME* editor Steve Sutherland called, wondering if I'd like to come in for a meeting. Which I did, at 11 a.m. after a night spent locked in emotional combat amid copious booze with a boyfriend who I was trying, unsuccessfully, to turn into an ex-boyfriend. If I appeared to be a deranged itinerant who'd been up all night weeping, drinking and smoking fags, maybe it was the times we were living in, but he offered me a freelance job.

Thrilled for my teenage, *NME*-wallpapered self, I was also ambivalent. There was an unsavoury air of superiority and a generally suspect attitude, which I'd never encountered anywhere before, around a few of the *NME* staff and writers. One told me I was only given the job 'because you're a girl'. Another told me some were displeased because I'd had no expensive education (or any further education at all): 'They keep saying, "How did *she* get in?"'

The day I cycled into *NME*'s office in King's Reach Tower with a floppy disk containing my first-ever proper feature, with glam-ghoul psycho-billy heroes The Cramps, I confessed to the features editor it was 126 words over-length. 'Oh FUCK OFF,' he swore, loudly. 'Just fuck off and get out of my life.' To my rescue stormed sometime *Smash Hits* freelancer Johnny Dee, now also an *NME* freelancer, bolting down the corridor with a reassuring, 'Don't take it personally, Sylv, he's like that with everyone!'

NME was back then, as it always had been, a predominantly male environment, not as intimidating as mythology tells us it was in its seventies/eighties heyday, but there was nothing woman-friendly about it. As a freelancer, though, I was barely ever in the office, mostly 'out there' in the field, free, a bounty hunter working alone. The other *NME* freelancers (overwhelmingly male) were a curious crew, far from the beautiful people the public might imagine, more a coterie of socially awkward oddballs, often physically misshapen Radiohead-'style' outsiders with a selection of minor afflictions, be it excessively tall, short, overweight, psychologically unhinged or sporting a 'funny' eye: all part of the reason (like me, with a permanent inner goth) they were rock 'n' roll fantasists in the first place, in thrall to The Revolution. On the rare occasions we drank together we were a fair approximation of the boozed-up creatures babbling around the circumference of The Cantina i.e. the legend of The Star Wars Bar. But it shouldn't have been much of a surprise: outsider weirdo with a 'funny' eye is probably the definition of a music journalist (and if the Star Wars Bar had a VIP section, Radiohead would be permanently in it).

In 1995, at the *NME*'s inaugural 'Brat Awards' (insolent new cousin to the 'Brit Awards'), word seeped out that Liam Gallagher was here and a surge of expectation undulated around the room like a cosmic ripple through the multiverse. Standing next to members of Pulp (Nick, drums and Candida, keyboards), a kinetic force field dressed in double denim bowled right up beside us. It was Him. I couldn't resist it, leaping in with a jocular, 'Hello! You don't know me but ...'

Liam Gallagher, apropos of nothing: 'Man City ... fookin' ... Shed Seven ... fookin' ... cunts ...' (to infinity).

Me: 'I just wanted to tell you, you have a very charismatic over-bite, not unlike Bruce Springsteen.'

And here, the legendary two fingers sprang up from where they dangled below his knees and arranged themselves on either side of my nose. 'Fook off!' he cursed, undulated away and my life, for three seconds, was complete.

Soon, Oasis were the greatest rock 'n' roll cavalcade on earth, a permanently media-stoked soap opera starring drugs, punch-ups and the verbal obliteration of everything in culture but themselves. Whenever a new Oasis interview appeared, I'd take the day off and read it down the pub, sometimes ringing Tommy the D on the pay phone to roar out the latest quips while hoping, one day, I'd hear those quips in real life myself.

The Stephendale Road gang, meanwhile, had splintered, two off to romantic endeavours, leaving Trish and me living in a spacious, clean, three-bedroom house off Seven Sisters Road, north London, with a new housemate, *Smash Hits*' picture researcher Leesa Daniels, then beginning a relationship with the magazine's design ed turned editor, Gavin Reeve.

In my upstairs bedroom, next door to Leesa, a 'shrine' to Liam Gallagher was created, a portrait of his extraordinary face meticulously snipped from *Q* magazine, affixed to a £1.99 clip-frame and entwined in a length of fairy lights, all the better to cast a circling searchlight into the bottomless depths of those ever-unknowable eyes. Oasis songs had become my permanent soundtrack, the long-suffering Leesa enduring 3 a.m. Raft-rockin' sessions which usually began with 'Rock 'N' Roll Star', through 'Slide Away' and 'Champagne Supernova' and ended with, er, Glen Campbell's 'Rhinestone Cowboy', Gordon Lightfoot's 'If You Could Read My Mind' and the trumpeting lift-off of Barry Manilow's epic 'Could It Be Magic', the musical equivalent of rearing, untamed horses.

Sometimes, when there was no one to go out and play with, a spliff would be smoked and I'd skip aboard a north London bus, *Definitely Maybe* and *What's The Story (Morning Glory)?* on an old-school Sony Walkman and just stay on the bus for hours, pretending to live in a video, enveloped in an illusion, cocooned in a make-believe chrysalis, doing exactly what Noel Gallagher instructed me never to do: put my life in the hands of a rock 'n' roll band, who'd throw it all away.

Maine Road, Manchester, 27 April 1996. No one wanted to review it. *Of course* no one wanted to review it, everyone wanted to go to it and sing like banshees and laugh like horses and drink like Govan shipyard navvies in 1975. So *I* had to review it. Or, rather, one of the *NME* Boys did the 'proper' review and I had to do the annoying bit, the 'vox pop' section, i.e. talk to the punters, report from the frontline of The Vibes and then write it up immediately afterwards. While pished, or on drugs, at the time.

The *NME* Lot went up together from London on a Ronsway Rock Tour Bus to Maine Road, singing all the way, some on the beer, some on the spliff, me 'pacing myself' on nothing for now except forty Benson & Hedges and a crafty E hidden inside a steel-grey military jacket pocket. Sadly, we never did meet Ron, or discover his mysterious rock tour way, but alighted nonetheless at Maine Road Stadium where Moss Side had turned into a vast Oasis theme park.

We were 39,000 strong, aged five to fifty, mostly twenty-something males in the checked-shirt 'n' jeans ensemble of the-ordinary-lad, some of whom were buying tickets off touts for £300 at 2.15 p.m. The *NME* Lot piled into a boozer as beer-clutching fans outside caroused in vocal serenade – 'these could be the best days of our liiiiiiives!' – and began making up rumours. Favourite thus far: that Oasis had been soundchecking the theme tune to *Scooby Doo*, which a conflagration of twenty-two-year-olds calling themselves The Euston Posse now loudly performed: 'Scooobeee doo-beee doooo-wer! Weeear aaaah yoooo-er!'

Mike from The Euston Posse proffered a ready-rolled spliff ('Prison fag, anyone?') and wondered, 'Would you like to see our drugs set-list?' It was a work of accountancy precision, neatly drawn vertical columns next to each name detailing the revelling to come via 'Pills', 'Bag' and 'Skunk'.

'It's just like a big holiday,' chirped Mike. 'They're just that brilliant that they've taken over the world, simple as that.'

As evening approached it was sixteen-deep for the beer queues by the 'food' stalls (crisps, chocolate, chips, sausage rolls) while tambourines shimmered among the bouncing blow-up bananas and an eight-year-old announced his favourite Oasis tune ever: 'Married With Children'. Overhead, a silvery half-moon crescent began glittering directly above the stage. Was it really glittering or did I take half an E half an hour earlier? Both. (I was neurologically ecstatic anyway for another reason: I'd fallen in love, with a man we shall call The Dancer, a man I thought I would spend the rest of my life with and who came to be nicknamed 'Useless' instead.)

The gig, naturally, was QUITE LITERALLY PHENOMENAL. Afterwards, I'd gone all 'spiritual'.

'Spiritual?' choked an ordinary lad called Jamie, as delirious punters began streaming away, buoyed on rafts of euphoria. 'Bollocks! It's about real life! That lot are real fookin' kids from the street, straight down the crease, singing and talking about reality, nothing to do with ... spirituality.'

Me, wasted: 'But real life can be spiritual, man! All that stuff about living forever and people saving you and sliding away to better places down an endless corridor ...'

Jamie: 'Everyone wants to live forever, that's totally bloody normal!'

Jamie's chum, Helen: 'What you on about anyway? He wrote "Live Forever" about his mum!'

A bloke approached with a gripe: 'I'm not being funny, like, but you lot at the *NME* have always been really horrible about The Alarm and it's about time you redressed the balance . . .'

I headed off to a hotel room the size of a wardrobe with an office computer with a ball for a 'cursor' which I did not know how to use and wrote 2,500 words of reportage from the frontline of The Vibes. I can't remember writing it. But I'm glad I did, otherwise I wouldn't have remembered being there. Soon, on 11 August 1996, I wouldn't remember much about being at Knebworth, either, other than the backstage Gin Bars, The Dancer's rather attractive rust-brown suit and Noel Gallagher roaring from the stage 'This is HISTORY.'

Trish left the Seven Sisters house (more romantic endeavours), and Leesa and I now had a tantalising Room To Let. Leesa had an idea: 'Chris Abbot's looking for a place.'

Chris Abbot was the brother of Tim Abbot, one of the founders of Creation Records (home of Oasis) and soon moved in. A mercurial character looking for 'temporary' digs, he stayed in the house overnight approximately three times in six months.

It was an average Friday night when Chris wasn't in, as usual, and Leesa was away at her mum's, when I ventured out with a chum for an Indian meal, only to contract bona-fide food poisoning and return home in an acutely queasy condition. By 11 p.m., nature intervened and removed the offending poisons, the upstairs bathroom now a scene of fluorescent tandoori projectile vomiting, all the colours of a vast autumnal landscape hurled into the sink in chunks, threads and watery rivers of Babylon (there's always a Babylon, somewhere), filling the sink halfway up.

Afterwards, I was exhausted, involuntary tears of effort

splashing down cheeks through vertical streaks of sooty mascara. The headache, though, remained industrial, a throb of front-lobe pressure which meant leaving the sink as it was and retiring for the night. I had an idea: I'd retire, yes, but not to my own disarrayed domain which had no daylight-dodging curtains, but to Leesa's delightful room, with her noticeably more inviting, freshly laundered bed linen and soothing angel-festooned shrine to the still-shockingly deceased River Phoenix. And merciful rest ensued.

'Fookin' ... fookin' ... fookin' ... heheheheheheh!'

At 4 a.m., my eyes unstuck from their mascara-glued unconsciousness as a sound reverberated upwards through the living room ceiling and all the way through Leesa's carpet. Chris had come home. And he'd brought with him a man who was definitely from Manchester and definitely good at swearing and possibly even better at laughing.

It couldn't be ... could it? Could this really be the planet's foremost rock 'n' roll songwriter and mythological hero of millions in 1996, Mister Noel Gallagher? In MY living-room!?

'Fookin' ... hurghurgh!'

YES! Stunned, I slid from Leesa's bed wearing stripy purple nylon pyjamas and pressed my ear to the carpet.

' ... fookin' ... fookin' ... and wait 'til they hear who I'm fookin' shaggin' ... Patsy Kensit!'

OH MY GOD.

IT WAS LIAM.

IN MY LIVING ROOM.

What to do!? Well, I was feeling a bit better, so if I just nipped down and introduced myself ... Except I'd vomited all over my head. I'd mascara streaks down my face. My pyjamas reeked of spew and the most beautiful man in the world was laughing downstairs in my living room, a bit like having Elvis in his black leathers in 1968 in my living room while I looked like a heroin-afflicted bag-lady schlepped from a skip up the back of King's Cross. And what – *aiiieeeee!?* – if he wanted to use the bathroom? I'd better clean the revolting sink ...

Heart thumping, I sneaked out of the bedroom and into the bathroom as the sound of Paul Weller's 'The Changingman' pealed up and around the stairs. I confronted the fluorescent carnage and knew what I had to do: just batter it into the plughole with my fingers – *Pthrt! Spltt! Thttt!* – while trickling water, quietly, from the tap. But there was just too much of it.

Now squinting into the mirror, an oil painting screeched back, of Pagliacci the weepsome clown as imagined by a particularly psychotic Edvard Munch, and I knew there was no way I could meet My Hero like this. Furthermore, if Liam Gallagher knew there was a journalist lurking ten feet above where he was currently ruminating on having sex with Patsy Kensit, with whom he was not yet publicly linked in the ongoing era of the tabloids' Oasis obsession, he would've scarpered out the door a great deal faster than a cannonball walking slowly down a hall.

I sneaked back into Leesa's bedroom and hunted in the blackness for her journo's Dictaphone: if I couldn't meet My Hero, I'd at least have audio evidence of his presence in my living room waffling on about – as I could now hear, in a break from the booming music – Ian Brown.

'I mean, Ian Brown thinks he's black ... But he's not. He's white!'

See? A misunderstood genius!? The Dictaphone remained elusive, so for the next hour I sat on the carpet in the blackness and listened to the sound of two invincibly wasted twenty-something men talk incomprehensible piffle, until two words from Chris suddenly pitched into the room like a championship dart.

'Robbie Williams.'

A swift mumbling followed, a phone call was made, a cab arrived, the front door slammed and they were gone.

I crept downstairs to witness exactly the sort of scene you'd expect to see in your living room had Liam Gallagher just left it in 1996: one empty packet of Benson & Hedges, six empty cans of lager and a selection of CDs expertly scored with six-inch lines of doubtless top-quality cocaine. I sat there for a further hour, fondling the fag packet, staring at the butts he'd recently kissed, which now nestled in a girly ashtray made out of many-coloured glass pebbles.

Thank God, I thought, I didn't have my Liam Shrine on display down here . . .

On 7 April 1997, Liam Gallagher married Patsy Kensit and on 21 August 1997, Oasis released their quiveringly anticipated third album *Be Here Now*. The *NME* duly reviewed it and, in the single most conspicuous display of getting-a-bit-carried-away-with-the-vibes-of-the-times in its entire history, awarded this sonic donkey a delirious 8/10. It was up to me, four years later, to muse with Liam Gallagher, alongside Noel Gallagher, on behalf of an outraged nation, on just why it had been, in fact, undeniably shite. But as it turned out, nothing mattered less that day: it was the morning of 12 September 2001 and we'd been up all night – not taking any cocaine whatsoever, but as Noel succinctly put it, 'watching people falling out the fookin' sky'.

Back in the mid-nineties, though, everyone *still* thought they'd live forever . . .

13

EVERYONE'S GONE TO
THE MOON

Working for the *NME* throughout the mid-nineties was not only
a journalistic joy, an editorial freedom bonanza where you could
write whatever you liked with barely a trace of an editor's red
pen (long before the era of the shriekingly tabloid, headline-
seeking brief), but what amounted, at times, to getting paid
(albeit not much) for going to the pub. Once, this was a literal
commission, to replicate the immoderately refreshed lifestyle
of my now household-famous tabloid non-boyfriend, bodacious
Blur bassman Alex James, the mid-nineties spirit of the music

magazines jubilantly reflecting the extensive idiocy of the Britpop bender around them.

In a bid to *become* Alex, myself and jovial lensman Steve Double were hastened off on The Alex James Heritage Trail, required to blag our way into his widely known Soho haunts, chain-smoke his snouts and drink his drinks, seek out drugs and famous friends and generally live the heightened reality of the space 'n' cheese-bothering bon viveur 'til dawn. This involved an unlimited booze budget, one packet of individually wrapped Kraft cheese slices (for doormen bribery purposes), one copy of Stephen Hawking's *A Brief History of Time* (for chat-up line purposes) and one Duty Free Bag from Bangkok Airport for that well-travelled pop star illusion. By 3.30 a.m. we were *roaring*, drinking 'Bolly' in the street, having blagged into members-only beaneries Soho House and Blacks, been ejected from the Groucho Club (for pretending to be Alex's 'invited guests' when he wasn't yet a member – the imposter!), blagged into Stringfellows and failed to blag into members-only nightclub Browns even though I proffered a Kraft cheese slice to an impassive Kray Twins-style bouncer before howling, 'Don't you know who I am? Whigfield!' (the European pop tart with then-equally 'spouty' hair).

Arriving back at Seven Sisters having sung 'Champagne Supernova' continuously to an unimpressed cab driver, I'd spent £170.20 in total, while failing to find any drugs (this sum no doubt a pittance to Alex, who estimated years later he'd spent £1 million in the nineties on champagne alone). A party-for-one began, blaring into chums' answer phones at 4.30 a.m. the country 'n' western classic 'Crystal Chandeliers' and the theme tune to kid's TV staple *Black Beauty* before passing out with a lit fag nestling in my neck.

This was the nationwide spirit in '95, a world of permanent exuberance and party-hard high jinks, the seemingly eternal summer soundtracked daily by Supergrass' twinkle-toothed and insanely chipper 'Alright' (from the narcotically titled *I Should Coco*). History has turned anything to do with Britpop into a laughable failure, an illusion dreamt up by the music press, a musical folly with mostly risible tunes, an unfortunate blip with no lasting legacy other than Pulp's 'Common People' in a drearily retro, black and white landscape dominated by Beatles-fixated men. For me and my mates, most of us women (the London Four of Us, magazine staff, a host of exuberant PRs), it was *24 hour rock 'n' roll hysteria in excelsis*, a militant hedonism extravagantly coloured in by blue hair, amusing shoes, fluorescent yellow and pink vinyl mackintosh overcoats and, often in my case, looking as close to a Russian army stormtrooper, with dastardly boots on, as I could possibly devise. We didn't stay in for *years*, a full-on embracement of what it meant to be young with all its attendant energy and indelible belief you would *absolutely* live forever, no matter how hard you danced on the button of neurological destruction. From the gloomy grunge years wasteland, a kitsch-pop mentality had grown towards the light, London defiantly swinging against any incoming Yankee angst, a spectrum of bands, PRs, DJs, journalists, designers, artists, label personnel and a foam of freeloading chancers (sometimes exactly the same thing) permanently boozing under the electric-pink neon sign of the Astoria's Keith Moon Bar.

Hilarity and high-kitsch abandon ruled, something not lost on visitors to allegedly Cool Britannia, visitors such as kitsch-cult rock 'n' roll reality dodgers Urge Overkill from Chicago, who'd finally inched into the mainstream via their spaghetti-swing-rock cover of Neil Diamond's 'Girl, You'll Be A Woman Soon' from the *Pulp Fiction* soundtrack. 'The last time we were in Britain, it was Glastonbury all over the country,' announced lead singer Nash 'National' Kato in Los Angeles in September '95: a retro caricature in a white suit, matching white shoes, plunging dirty blond curtains of hair and enormous white oval shades, slewing an everlasting vodka cranberry. 'Something is happening that's really cool, the vibe, and it's not happening here [in America]. It's more than just a bunch of cool bands, it's a cyclical thing.'

'I think,' decided Blackie The Drummer in a Fleetwood Mac T-shirt, 'the quality of cocaine in London has improved about fifty-fold on low, *low* prices and I think that has a great deal to do with it, basically.'

'What the best British bands are also doing now is what we've always done and that's self-consciously celebrate the past, with no rules,' Nash carried on. 'We're not advancing anything here, it's a celebration of the greatest pop music. In between '91 and '92 people forgot that rock music was supposed to be fun: it went from "feel my pants" to "feel my pain" and now the guard is changing again. So, would you like to feel my pants?'

A fine cut, sir.

'From London, of course.'

If cocaine was partly responsible for the Britpop generation's capacity for oceanic levels of booze, it was never my drug of choice (although I'd given it several chances, just to make sure), finding in its neurological zippiness the introduction into an otherwise merry mood of a seizure of prolonged uptightness; a grip of anxiety which needed ten pints of cider to rectify, accompanied by six hours quacking on about, say, the majestic beauty of Gordon Lightfoot's 'If You Could Read My Mind' to the newly greatest friend you met twenty-three minutes previously.

This was surely why I was always falling over when others were not, and in the case of Urge Overkill – who absolutely *forced* me to drink sake for five hours (having learned nothing from the free sake at the Bros party episode seven years before) – sank under the table mid-interview after a rousing rendition of Oasis' mighty 'Slide Away' ('Don't know! Don't care!' etc.). That balmy

Californian evening, they informed their PR, 'The journalist is asleep!' Men who'd spent five hours intermittently shouting 'I should coco!' before pirouetting off to the loo, they ended their evening in a Jacuzzi with an unlimited champagne bar tab and three professional porn stars.

In these levitational times plane journeys were for parties, too: the Urge Overkill trip to LA beginning with myself, lively *NME* lensman Martyn Goodacre and dangerously mischievous PR Sophie Williams on the gins 'n' tonic at Heathrow Airport before the equally gin-fuelled flight, which was single-handedly powered by the crafty Goodacre, expertly stealing miniature gins off the drinks trolley before food was even served. In the name of merriment we applied 'drag queen' make-up to his dastardly face, after which – in a bout of hitherto unheard-of delinquent behaviour – he began creeping round the cabin physically lifting up the eyelids, via the eyelashes, of unconscious strangers. By the time any dozing real estate executive from Orange County awoke from a hideous nightmare where a nimble-fingered madman was attempting to pull his eyes off, Martyn was in the back row, chuckling, with me 'n' Sophie, smoking fags alongside the also-smoking air hostesses who sneaked us refill gins. (These days, of course, you'd be fined up to $5,000 or face ten days in prison for smoking on a plane, you're encouraged to 'drink sensibly', anyone approaching 'intoxication' is banned from further drinking and the days of self-amusement have long been replaced by a century's worth of DVD box sets individually gleaming in your lap. We really *did* make our own fun in them days.)

Arriving at LAX security, Martyn, in full drag queen make-up, blithely walked through nothing-to-declare while the zigzagging Sophie and I were rudely propositioned, appraised unfit to proceed, pulled over by an eye-twitching customs official and requested to open our bags. Mine, a cream 1960s Bakelite vanity case, immediately sprang open unaided, ejecting

a volley of miniature gins, fags, knickers, notebooks, Sony
Walkman and tapes into the air. Sophie and I, much amused,
sank to our knees on the floor (in the position our digital futures
would know as ROFL).

'Stand up when I'm talking to you, ladies,' barked Terrifying
Customs Dude as he inspected our juniper-based swag
(miniature gins planted in my bag, m'lud, by the thieving
Martyn Goodacre).

'Do you have a drinking problem, ladies?' he wanted to know.

'Nor 'alf!' blurted Sophie, unwisely, as I elbowed her in the ribs.

Eventually, finding no other incriminating evidence, he let us
go and we caroused our way to the Sunset Marquis – the very
hotel where, nine years previously, Barney Sumner from New
Order had lost his shorts, forever.

That year, Jarvis Cocker was beginning to rival Alex James
as Britpop's keenest reveller, musing during our *NME* cover
interview mid-1995 how mortified he was by the newly pop-
filled newspapers being scrutinised by his mum. 'I'm always
done in about it,' he cringed, glam-chic that day in an orange
and yellow-striped seventies shirt, sipping restorative tea on a
studio patio with a crushing hangover.

'Jarvis is a sex fiend,' he carried on, of the recurring headlines.
'Jarvis is hopelessly addicted to drugs. Jarvis is having sex in
public. That was a great one, a winner all round, that.'

He, too, contemplated the all-encompassing drug culture.
'I'll sound like an old fogey, but I don't think you need drugs
when you're younger 'cos there's still loads to do. You might not
have even shagged anybody yet,' he offered, brightly, then aged
thirty-two. 'During your twenties you've done quite a lot, so in
order to make them interesting again you might as well have
drugs 'cos your brain's formed, you can squish it about a bit and
you've got more chance of not going mad. So you're alright at
my age. If you start all that at fourteen you haven't even finished

growing yet. But generally people take more drugs now, people seem to need to exaggerate the normal, invent a less boring world of their own.'

Why is that, did he think?

'I blame the telly,' he mused. 'Because watching loads of telly makes everything seem dramatic. Everything has a pacey storyline and a plot and good music and then life doesn't have the pacey storyline, does it? Where's the great dialogue and the amazing sex? So you think, "Well, this ain't good enough!" Which is ironic; the telly isn't even real.'

On the very day Pulp's landmark album *Different Class* was completed, we played the silly game of Musical Questions (queries posed via song titles and lyrics). Here was my chance, then, to ask Jarvis Cocker The Meaning Of It All.

Is That All There Is? I ventured.

'Yeah, it is, I guess,' he smiled, of the concept of, you know, reality. 'And that's not particularly bad. There aren't really any new things to discover in life. The same things have obsessed people throughout the centuries. We're not going to invent a new colour now. So this *is* all there is. Everything else is your imagination. So use it well.'

By some distance, though, the most booze-berserk band of the Britpop era I failed to keep up with was that emblem of pan-dimensional narco-bombed debauchery – The Beautiful South. The genial northern quipsters, led by Paul Heaton, sometime Housemartin and invincible bon vivant, were not only connoisseurs of wry, melodic and acutely observational pop music, but the kind of band who went to the pub for breakfast. As much was witnessed via an on-the-road sojourn from Chicago to Seattle, the band arriving in the hotel bar at 7.30 a.m. for double gins followed by a 'breakfast pint', before heading off to the airport and straight to the bar.

Life with The South was like a 24-hour episode of *On The Buses* in the 1970s with a bar up the back of the bus, an endless odyssey of boozed-up buffoonery led by the boundless energy of Paul 'Heato' Heaton and his gin-flavoured cartoon reality. Throughout the twenty-strong party of men (not even co-singer Jackie Abbot was here, being eight months pregnant back in Britain) everyone had a nickname, some with a new one every three hours. Crew member Phil was 'Good-looking Phil', who looked a bit like Andre Agassi, and so became 'Andrea Gassy'. He was spotted one day with revolving eyes, weeping, 'I've never drunk so much in me life!' Unfeasibly, the more they drank, the less they succumbed to psychosis, or any hint of melancholia – they simply became funnier, and sang louder.

The only psychological drama I witnessed, in fact, was Paul Heaton's intense aversion to flying: something he quelled with even more gin. Travelling from Chicago to Seattle (flight time: four hours) I elected to sit next to Heato, hoping to begin our official interview, even if we'd been on the gin since dawn.

'I warned you,' wobbled Paul, 'you couldn't have picked a worse person to sit next to.'

As we buckled up, he unveiled a tangled bundle of talismanic effigies which would save us from otherwise certain death, then wrapping them tightly around a small, expressively womanly hand. This was the trusty and lifelong concept of Heato's Lucky Charms, which he carried with him at all times: one lucky watch, one Simon Le Bon Panini-type card, one laminated pass featuring a photo of hefty horoscope madame Russell Grant, one badge bearing the words 'No Grapes', a magic trinket box which no one knew the contents of and one Magic Pixie with fluorescent copper hair and luminously blue, forget-me-not eyes. The Magic Pixie was dangled face outwards to the window while Paul instructed the plastic totem to do its vital work, crossing himself again and again with his head bowed towards his knees as take-off rumbled forth.

'If you look into the pixie's eyes we'll crash,' he announced as I caught the gonk's neon gaze side on and prepared for the boom to oblivion.

'It's alright!' soothed Paul, 'side on doesn't count. But the last time I looked straight in its eyes we had to do an emergency landing in New York when one of the engines blew out.'

Within minutes, airborne thanks only to our Pixie pal, more gins were requested, a steady advancement of miniatures proving not steady enough for Paul so he broke out his duty free: a one-litre bottle of Gordon's. Had his hand-to-eye coordination been steadier than it currently was (i.e. not at all), he would've played his favourite in-flight game, Peanut Golf, where you attempt to land a peanut on the 'green' of an unsuspecting bald head in a row up front. He pinged down his table instead, revealing some white granules trapped from previous customers. 'Look, cocaine!' he yelped, as he expertly chopped the granules into a line before licking the lot up with a dampened finger. Salt, doubtless, from approximately 1971. As we used to say back at ver *Hits*: speryoooo ...

Paul Heaton was (and remains) a freedom fighter who believed humanity drank as much alcohol as it did (and still does) 'to break down the Berlin Wall we build around ourselves'. More gin flowed and more walls came tumbling down.

'I've never been one of the lads,' he pointed out, 'never, ever. And it's something I've resented since The Housemartins, 'cos it made me lose the plot, definitely. All these people came up to me and said "You're just like us, you just like getting a pint down the local" and I'd sit there for hours listening to that, so I ended up saying "You're right, mate, I'm just like you" and became this "alright mate" character, and it's macho bullshit. But anyone who knew me respected me for being an individual, 'cos I was different. Actually, I was a nutter. I was the bloke sat in the corner by himself with the holes in his socks and shoes. I hung around with the disruptive lads 'cos I was shit at school, but am I fuck down-to-earth. And it'll be the same for Oasis. Same with Blur. Anybody who forms a band, writes their own songs, writes their own lyrics, are they fuck just like everybody else, are they fuck one of the lads, they're *artists*. Eccentrics! They're individuals and they don't wanna be losing that. So, stay a nutter! Stay eccentric!'

Paul's own eccentricity, he added, was no hindrance to The South's ascent in America. 'In fact, it's got nothing to do with it because if I'm singing about loneliness that's the one word everybody in the entire universe understands,' he concluded. 'How the fuck can you not understand something like "Prettiest Eyes"? I put my little placard up and it's a placard for the lonely and the loved and the lost.'

Soon, I began to weep.

'Is it the gin?' wondered a sympathetic Paul.

'It's not the gin,' I croaked, 'it's you! And your unmistakable truths!'

By the time we reached baggage reclaim in Seattle, I could not walk and – in need of an immediate lie down – wiggled towards a comfy spot on a static baggage carousel and fell into deep unconsciousness. Twenty minutes later, as the carousel conveyor belt lurched into motion towards the flapping plastic slats of the baggage handler's black hole, I awoke to see the merrily marching backs of twenty men carousing towards the exit before their alarmed PR lifted me by the collar. 'Come on Patterson!' she wailed and punted me towards the taxi rank, where the invincible Paul Heaton was wondering where I'd been.

'Y'alright,' he grinned, having had, seemingly, some kind of instant post-flight blood transfusion. 'Fancy a gin?'

*

I arrived back in London insane. And immediately went out-to-lunch with unstoppable booze fiend Tim Burgess from psychedelic groovesters The Charlatans, whose undulating Hammond-led reveries had been a constant soundtrack to the 'indie-dance' rave-up since debut single 'The Only One I Know' sold 250,000 copies in 1991. Preceded by beer and followed by vodka, lunch became a four bottles of wine bonanza, during which he consumed half a bowl of his broccoli pasta and then asked four times whether we'd eaten yet or not. In a Soho pub he fell all the way down a very steep staircase where he sat momentarily dazed, a barman peering down at him and then ambling over to me. 'Ma'am?' he announced. 'Your friend. He has fallen down the stairs.' (Another night, I'd do much the same in Paris with London's chirpy melodians Dodgy: during their impromptu hotel piano rendition of Queen's 'Don't Stop Me Now', to which I'd been providing percussion, I stepped backwards onto the lip of a hitherto unnoticed spiral staircase, and plunged – to the clattering sound of a flailing tambourine – all the way down twenty-four steps, round several circular corners, coming to a halt only at the very bottom. Staring straight upwards, the concerned face of Matt from Dodgy peered 20 feet down until he shouted, seemingly satisfied with my overall condition, 'And you've still got the tambourine in yer hand!')

That day in Soho, the 'pretty bendy' Tim Burgess was also unscathed, soon giving me his fake $35 Rolex watch featuring deep sea diving countdown dials, bawling 'Champagne Supernova' while splayed on top of a stranger's car bonnet (See? It wasn't just me . . .) and couldn't remember where he lived. Not even that he lived in *London*. I had to ring Sian, who now lived near Tim (a call made on the pub payphone in those mobile-free days), to give a taxi driver his approximate address.

Years later, in 2011, Tim and I chortled over this grand day out for a feature in Mark Ellen's world-class *Word* magazine (launched in 2003, scandalously folded in 2012), returning to the pub where he'd tipped himself down the stairs. Except we couldn't remember exactly which pub it had been. 'The nineties were our seventies, really, weren't they?' he was sure, a man who used to have cocaine blown up his backside in those demented mid-nineties days (though I, mercifully for everyone, did not).

Tim Burgess, The Beautiful South and Urge Overkill were, however, narcotic amateurs in the face of Shaun Ryder and the merry men who were once the Happy Mondays. Who, in 1995, were to be found 'relaxing' in Jamaica ...

14

TWISTING MY MELON, MAN

Everywhere you've never been before, to a certain extent, always seems on arrival like some kind of psychedelic satire, your reaction to a city's searingly familiar, iconic trademarks as amusingly surreal as a trip on magic mushrooms at the age of sixteen. The steam surging up from New York streets dotted with honking yellow cabs. One thousand denim-legged, carefree students on bicycles in Amsterdam. The garish, blinking, neon-techno screen-world of bustling midtown Tokyo. The voices chirping 'calm down!' from the chipper heads of the people in the pubs of Liverpool. 'It's all true!' you roar, even as you're not entirely convinced this isn't some dastardly film director's prank.

Jamaica, though, appears to be *totally taking the piss*, all reality disappearing on touchdown like a tendril of mintiest 'erb. This is where, of all people, Black Grape were making a video in 1995, for their second single 'In The Name Of The Father' from the pointedly titled frothy-funk cauldron of their debut album *It's Great When You're Straight ... Yeah!* Not so very long ago they'd been some of the Happy Mondays – less a band, more a talismanic emblem of illegality through the late eighties/early nineties, whose tunes, unfeasibly brilliant funkadelic stunners ('Wrote For Luck', 'Step On', 'Kinky Afro'), were hewn, somehow, from the minds of chemically melting madmen. One was the laser-eyed, limb-pounding 'dancer' and percussionist Bez; another goblin-eared 'singer' and people's poet Shaun Ryder, whose lyrical imagery Factory Records' equally mythologised Tony Wilson (no help to me with runaway Barney Sumner eleven years previously) once ascribed, with his customary flair, as 'on a par with W. B. Yeats'. Though possibly not Shaun's opening musings from the Mondays' 1987 debut album: 'You see that Jesus is a cunt and never helped you with a thing that you do, or you done ...' (Certainly never had that with Coldplay, eh viewers?)

By 1993, the Mondays were finished after the great Barbados misadventure of 1992, one of rock 'n' roll's most fabled sagas, the one where Shaun Ryder was flown thousands of miles away from his heroin habit in Manchester and developed a Caribbean crack habit instead (smoking fifty rocks of crack a day – 12 grams of cocaine, suicide fans). Bedlam enthusiast Bez, meanwhile, after one beach-bound jeep-driving accident too many, had to have his arm mechanically rebuilt. They spent three months 'working' on a tambourine sound, Shaun wrote no lyrics whatsoever (Yeatsian or otherwise), the hastily hopeless *Yes Please!* album finally emerged, which sold no copies, and bankrupted Factory Records forever.

Two and a half years later Shaun and Bez were in a new band, Black Grape, with rapper Kermit – once of Manchester's Ruthless Rap Assassins, Shaun's sometime heroin dealer and possessor of a no doubt highly necessary degree in psychology. In 1995 Radioactive Records (through the Universal giant) had paid for these people to return to the Caribbean in the hope of recording a video – and I was going to visit them, with a photographer and, supposedly, a PR. Except the PR failed to turn up at the airport. We boarded the plane anyway, bound for an exotic land I'd never even contemplated going to before.

Really, you might as well have sent a toddler off with the PG Tips chimps.

We were picked up at midnight in an open-backed truck, the sort slaughtered goats would hang out the back of, by a grinning, golden-toothed Rastafarian in a towering red, gold and green knitted beanie. Bouncing alongside him (where a sensible PR should've been) was the permanently exploding Kermit, a man with the energy levels of a spindly, untrained whippet, permanently on the scent of narcotic euphoria and/or casual sex. As we jiggled along tracks in the blackness, figures lingered outside shadowy shacks which were seemingly made of crates, with corrugated iron for doors, baseball bats casually swinging from the fists of the famed Jamaican yardies.

Soon we were tipped from the truck behind a villa-dotted resort encircling a Bounty Advert beach, a navy-blue ocean visible beyond a surrounding thicket of woozily wafting palm trees. Silence, but for the crickets – *trrp! trrrp! trrrrrrrp!* – chirruping under the swirling, milky spills of the cosmos overhead. It was the kind of sublime setting which lent itself to courageous thinking: that the gigantic Jamaican spliff now being proffered by the narcotically invincible Kermit was the kind a western wimp like me could reasonably handle.

Seconds later, on a walk around the resort, Jamaica was *definitely* taking the piss. A Rasta dude, grinning (they were always grinning), sat on a wall knitting himself a new hat, in red, gold and green. A fruit stall appeared, a comically crooked shack with a straw roof 'hat', festooned with bananas, apples, avocados and a smiling Rasta proffering a freshly cut coconut shell, with jaunty straw. To check if I could still speak, I asked him what time it was.

'There is no *tiiiiiiime*,' came the none-more-leisurely reply, 'in Jah-*maaaiiii*-ca.'

Through jungly trees and into a clearing in this time-free vortex, a dreadlocked grandpa in cricket whites sat intently watching, on a twelve-inch black and white 1970s TV positioned on a wooden stool, a cricket match between England and the West Indies. It was now obvious: we were surrounded by actors, on a Jamaican version of *The Truman Show*, possibly the setting for tomorrow's video.

Confusion gripped the psyche, evolving into The Fear. I had no idea what was real, or not real. What did real mean anyway? The surrounding villas, I was convinced, were made of cardboard, the Milky Way painted overhead by an exquisitely gifted set designer. The drug-induced 'doors of perception' were, in fact, creating the opposite effect, doors slamming shut on glorious 3D reality and replacing it, instead, with a 2D plywood imposter. Kermit, seeing a traumatised face, wondered if I was alright.

'Where's the reality, man,' I blinked, 'this isn't reality … what's happened to the reality?' Soon I was convinced, somehow, I was upside down, standing on the bottom of the world, head in southern outer space. 'I don't know … which way up the world works!'

Kermit, a drugs-wise owl beneath his bounding demeanour, knew an attack of The Fear when he saw one and came up with a sensible solution: he bounced me along to the beach, helped me off with my none-more European silver platform boots and ordered my feet into the sea. 'Feel that,' he implored. 'That's the sea, below, the world's this way up!'

Stability slowly returned and I collapsed into bed in a beachside villa definitely made of bamboo, knowing tomorrow morning I'd have to pretend this had never happened and I was, instead, a professional journalist from *SKY* magazine who knew exactly what she was doing. I'd perhaps forgotten, though, the type of men I was about to encounter.

'You've got massive tits, man.'

So announced Shaun Ryder the following morning, the first words he piped on our Caribbean introduction. At least, I suppose, I was in the resort's swimming pool at the time, as was Shaun, both of us looking to becalm our crispy morning heads. The thirty-three-year-old Ryder would soon imbibe his breakfast of champions, a spliff and a bottle of Guinness, while dunking his legs in the pool, staring through palm trees and out into the steady *wooooosh* of the turquoise Caribbean ocean. All was serene. 'If I lived here, man,' he announced, dreamily, 'I just wouldn't *move*.'

Shaun was a changed man, had been on Prozac for a year, was completely off the smack and crack, even if his first bottle of 7.5 per cent Guinness was cracked open, with his teeth, at his routine rising hour of 7 a.m. (half an hour ahead of The Beautiful South), followed by a sizeable daily dent in the Jamaican ganja reserve.

Bez, however, was exactly the same as he'd always been. That night, we witnessed his 'daily' routine, the opposite to Shaun's. He rose at 7.30 p.m., announced he'd lost his shoes, hadn't seen them for days, looked for them on the patio, failed, re-entered his room via a French window he thought was an open door and smashed his head on the glass.

'I've smashed me skull in, man!'

I offered him some of my personal bounty of on-the-road codeine painkillers.

'Oh God, no,' he quaked. 'Don't tell Shaun!'

He then 'borrowed' $36, got in the band van, smashed his head once more off a light fitting, motioned to close the door, had his hand crushed in the door by Kermit's sudden door-closing gusto, attempted to eat a piece of fish, choked so badly he had to open the window and vomit it out, built a gigantic spliff, looked appeased, attempted to enter an open-air reggae club, discovered he'd 'lost' the $36 already and 'borrowed' $40 more. No wonder, in the nineties, I remained permanently skint.

Shaun and Bez, by '95, had talked almost exclusively about drugs, forever. We knew almost nothing else about these men (other than early lives funded by petty thieving). My journalistic plan, therefore, was to attempt a different approach, to delve into the wide-awake consciousness of one of Britain's greatest guerrilla minds. We all knew what Shaun Ryder *did*, but what went on in his head while he did it? And what did the meaning of existence truly mean for a reality-escapee like him? The following afternoon, he lay himself flat out on the patio sofa in his beach-side lover's chalet, and attempted to tell us all about it. With a little 'help' from his friend.

The Caribbean vibes are subdued this time . . .

'Very subdued,' agreed Shaun. 'I knew it'd be dead boring for the press, but there's some nice flowers. I always knew from when we started all this drugs stuff as young lads, nineteen, twenty, that it couldn't go on forever, so there's no great parties round here anymore and that's cool. Fucking hell, you get to thirty and you've gotta slow down a bit, haven't you?'

Did all those drugs actually teach you anything about life?

A pause the size of Colombia. 'It teaches you about *a* life. All drugs eventually make you a troubled-up, paranoid, schizophrenic fuck.'

What's the first thing you think about when you wake up these days?
'Food.'

'A shag,' piped up Bez. 'And if there's no shag, a wank.'

'That's human beings, innit,' nodded Shaun. 'Food and sex. Same as hedgehogs and pigs and fucking parrots and otters.'

Are you, Shaun William Ryder, all or any of the following ... a maverick visionary?

'Maverick was a fookin' cowboy gambler, wasn't he? Not me, man.'

Bez again. 'What are them little Irish green things? Leprechauns, that's it. Is that not a maverick vision? Dunno then.'

... a gangster?

'Nah. I'm a pop star.' Shaun rolled around the sofa. 'We're the good guys, man. We are! Always smilin'.'

... the hard man's hard man?

'People must be scared of me. I'm five foot seven.'

... a charmer?

'Well that's true, man,' decided Bez.

Your very first words to me were 'you've got massive tits, man'. You must be bloody charming, Shaun, to get away with that.

'Oh no, man, sorry about that! I didn't mean nothing bad – you won't make me sound really bad, will you? I'm not really rude, am I? I didn't mean it bad man, *honest* I didn't ...'

The band's guitarist, Wags, suddenly turned up with the evening meal: burger 'n' chips for Shaun; Grape-Nuts ice cream for Bez. Shaun asked him if he'd brought any more Guinness. 'No,' said Wags, 'but there's some gin.'

'GIN?' balked Shaun, stoned eyes finally springing wide open. 'Fook me! Oh, man, Jeez, you might as well've brought freebase back in the room! Haven't drunk gin for five month.' He now proceeded to drink some gin. 'Oh Christ! Now me brain's buzzing, it's going pingwingwingwing! I still love the buzz, knowhatImean?'

He stared at my tape recorder.

'Is that thing still on? Aw, shit, man, I'm not having that in print. That I still love having a buzz!'

Bloody hell, Shaun. That coming from you?

'I know, but if I get pissed it'll be me first night of being pissed for ages, man, I get really proper ill, 'cos I can't handle the hangover. I'd rather do cold turkey than that. I'm not a boozer, don't really like it.'

What happens?

'I wobble. Oh Christ, man, I've just smoked fucking loads of ganja and now I've gotta talk about a load o' bollocks!'

D'you ever find yourself repeating the same phrases to your children that your dad did to you? For example, a corker from my mum was, 'I worried about having no shoes until I met the man with no feet.'

'Fucking hell, man, that's heavy. Yeah, but I can't remember any of 'em. I'll tell you, I hope I won't be anything like me old man. And I'm exactly like him now. But I hope I won't be, otherwise me kids'll be like me, and I couldn't handle that, man, in case they couldn't handle it, knowhatImean? I was watching a programme the other night and, well ... no, man. No, leave it out, man.'

Here, Shaun switched the recorder off. Only then did he talk at length about his upbringing, his dad and the atmosphere in his family home. Eventually, he let me switch it back on again. Why didn't he want any of that broadcast?

'Fucking hell, man. D'you really think I'm gonna start talking about "growing up in an atmosphere of fear"? Me folks read this stuff!'

And did you?

'I was loved as well,' he said sternly. 'I always knew I was loved. But I'm not ready for talking about shit like that, man. Anyway the programme was dead funny! Heheheh!'

Soon, the gin was doing the talking for both of us.

'Fucking hell, man,' he blurted. 'I'm pissed! Fucking am, man! Oh noooooo, I really feel like getting pissed now! No, no listen man, I don't do this man, I'm a boring weed head! I like doing nothing. I do, I love it! Just like Bez! I'll tell you something about Bez, man . . .'

Go on . . .

' . . . He's totally useless, but whenever we've lived together, Bez always did the ironing. Fucking *demon* ironer.'

Jesus!

'Jesus. He was a geezer, wasn't he? He just went around getting a bit of order.'

Jesus was a . . .

'Policeman. Jesus was a Bizzy! And the Ten Commandments are basically common sense: "If you're gonna go in the desert, don't have a fookin' foreskin." I've seen the light! The Bible's just a rule book gone dolly for the primitives. It's all in there, man, from Sherlock Holmes to *Star Trek* . . .'

Momentarily, this was like being back in Review Nook, in a world of bowler heads and ananas . . .

' . . . The answers in the fookin' thing, dude,' he grinned. 'I used to laugh at that, but it's right . . . Or is it? Or have I gone completely mad? Woooooooh!'

What do you think about the phrase 'You are free to do whatever you like, you need only face the consequences?'

'I've never been free to do what I like. What I wanted to do was just live and be happy and always have nice clothes and do nothing. But I can't, 'cos I've got no dough. At the end of the day, if I was born into money, I wouldn't do a fookin' *stroke*. Not for commercial gain. I might scribble in a diary about me last ninety-seven years as a complete sail-in-the-seas opium smoking arsehole. Or I might've tried to invent penicillin, that'd be cool. But I can't do nothing, 'cos I'm a pirate.'

What's life for, Shaun?

'To explore,' he decided after a pause the size of time itself. 'Definitely. That's what it's all about, man. Go forth and explore.'

The following year, at the *NME* Brat Awards at Brixton Academy, Oasis won pretty much everything, Pulp won Best Video for 'Common People', The Prodigy won Best Dance Act, *Shooting Stars* won Best TV Show, Liam Gallagher won Most Desirable Human Being, Damon Albarn won Git Of The Year (See? It really *wasn't* just me) and Black Grape won Single Of The Year for the mighty 'Reverend Black Grape'. Prior to the event, I thought about what japes I might have, seeing my old Caribbean muckers once more for hazy reminiscences of reggae raves and the plight of Bez's shoes (while holding out zero hope for the return of any jungle-lost dollars).

In a shadowy Academy corridor that night a shape suddenly loomed over me, followed by the source of this shape – an enormous security hulk the width of a wardrobe, his face deliberately fixed to 'menacing'. Or, I *assumed* his face was menacing because I couldn't actually see it, he was pinning me up against the wall with his back, which was approximately five feet wide. Straining for oxygen behind his car-door sized shoulder blade, a finger wiggled into my face, attached to the frothing form of Shaun Ryder.

'You!' he barked, finger jabbing away. 'You! You fookin' betrayed me!'

This was terrifying, surely first-hand experience of the tactics of The Manchester Mafia.

'You said you wouldn't print it!' He jabbed on, as the realisation dawned: he'd objected to the phrase, in print, 'an atmosphere of fear', where I thought I had, at the time, protected him by not printing what he'd actually said when the recorder was switched off. But no, the phrase was enough. The kind of phrase tough guys like Shaun Ryder can never be associated with, who can never be seen as vulnerable, even if they were just kids at the time. Maybe I should've left it out, kept on pretending these things don't happen. Maybe I left it in because I empathised, knew all about growing up in an atmosphere of fear.

The finger and the wardrobe ebbed away and I sprinted off into the kindly face of fellow *NME* reporter Stuart Baillie, tears plunging down my cheeks.

'Did I ever,' soothed Stuart in his calming, Northern Irish way, 'tell you about what Paul Weller did to me?'

Rock stars, eh?

Soon, I'd have a one-off lifetime's encounter with a man who didn't just switch your recorder off, but refused to let you record his voice in the first place. Or take any notes. His name was not Prince anymore. But he was still *very* funky.

15

I ONLY WANT TO SEE
YOU LAUGHING

In autumn 1996, an epoch before Twitter invented direct communication between celebrity and fan, the thirty-eight-year-old Prince remained the definition of the unreachable, unknowable superstar. Since the 1980s he'd been one of global pop's Holy Triumvirate: only Prince, Madonna and Michael Jackson embodied the concept of the stratospherically alien superstar (Bowie, in his Tin Machine, had temporarily crashed to earth). The Purple Perv was the most enigmatic of the three, a permanently silent totem poised on a lofty plinth, a spectral entity who graciously beamed his genius towards the uplifted, grateful faces of his earthly congregation. The notion, back then, that Prince would one day join Twitter (albeit sporadically, from 2013 onwards), or play an impromptu acoustic set in the east London living room of an unknown member of the public, singer Lianne La Havas (as he did in early 2014), was as likely as the Queen herself flouncing through your living-room door for a fiddle on the fancy fretwork.

No wonder, in 1996, the global music industry exploded on contact with the sudden, startling announcement of the first fifteen-minute press conference in Prince's twenty-year career. Even if he was, now, no longer named Prince but The Artist Formerly Known As Prince, known to himself as '. . . . .', i.e. a wiggly golden Love Symbol, and therefore deciphered by the public as 'Squiggle'. Furthermore, he'd deigned to accompany this conference with a handful of face-to-face interviews, scheduled for fifteen minutes each, including the *NME*.

In expectation of a comic junket farrago, I was the chosen newshound, both thrilled and perplexed over the conversational condition: Prince's non-negotiable ban on all forms of recording equipment. Being mad, no recordings of his speaking voice were *ever* permitted because a reporter once tried to sell his voice and, besides, he believed anything important would somehow be 'remembered'. Even note-taking was forbidden and he'd been known to confiscate pens. (I should've thought myself lucky: once, he banned the asking of *questions*.)

These restrictions might seem, to the non-scribe, scant impairment to the interviewing 'trade' but, in real time, listening to what someone is saying while trying to store it in a highly stressed brain *and* attempt to steer the conversation onto a more enlightening path than the one it would no doubt currently be on (i.e. a fifteen-minute soliloquy on creative autonomy, man) is a military-level obstacle course to any conversational flow.

Then, immediately afterwards, you must accurately 'remember' everything and scribble it down in a taxi while wondering what the hell just happened. Chris Evans had reportedly also been invited for a *TFI Friday* item and, on learning the limitations, turned the invitation down, pronouncing Prince 'a purple git'. Still, that day, I'd brought along a vibes-enabling paisley-patterned notebook and quietly hoped for the best. (Tom Hibbert would've been glad to know I was *at least* as excited, now, as I had been one full decade previously over a waltz on a grassy knoll by a car park with a weedy, bespectacled Housemartin . . .)

The Paisley Park Studio complex, outside Minneapolis, was approached along the Chanhassen Freeway, where a road sign once spelled out (so legend had it) 'LIFE IS TOO SHORT TO BE LITTLE'. A huge, almost Lego-type building with many 'wings', it had been mocked in the past for its industrial blandness – more carpet warehouse than crucible of the funkin' vibes – but since The Purple Perv's marriage earlier that year to his pervy backing dancer, Mayte Garcia, twenty-four, Paisley Park was now Paisley Park On Ecstasy.

Stepping across the threshold, its once famously whitewashed interior had been transformed into a kaleidoscopic Prince-themed World of Adventures, a psychedelic makeover instigated by his wife. Its central room, a rectangular atrium, was edged with pastel-hued pillars, its walls glimmering with golden daubs and imposingly enormous murals of the purple one's gigantic Bambi eyes. The tiled floor below, as viewed from a surrounding mezzanine above (where a birdcage housed the studio dove, Divinity, aged fifteen), etched out the golden 'Symbol' sign.

Further overhead, the pastel-blue ceiling featured fluffy clouds and silvery doves fluttering downwards across one wall. Along most other walls and along the lengthy corridors gleamed gold, silver, platinum, double platinum and triple platinum discs, triumphantly tooting those pop-defining moments of the previous twenty years: *Purple Rain*, *Sign O' The Times*, *Lovesexy*, *Diamonds And Pearls*, two million sales, three million sales, five million sales . . .

Inside a purple and gold-daubed side-room, a hundred journalists and photographers newly flown in from around the planet awaited the elusive imp. That day, we knew three new facts about the man now also calling himself 'The Artist'.

1. He was creatively free, releasing music independently (that year's three-CD concept *Emancipation*), no longer in the Warner Brothers contractual straitjacket which inspired him to write 'SLAVE' across his face and ditch the name Prince 'forever'.
2. He was newly married to Mayte.
3. The couple had just had a son, reportedly born with life-threatening brain damage about which no official statement had understandably been made (providing the elephant-shaped query currently marauding throughout the room). If his appearance, today, was unlikely enough, with a child so ill it was testament to his will, surely, that this global promotional show – no doubt many months in the arranging – *must go on*.

An international gathering, there was one UK tabloid among us – The Man From The *Sun* – and, as such, the only journo to feel duty-bound to voice the dread-most query. (Being from the *NME*, I was only here for the sex, drugs, rock 'n' roll and a punt at preposterous jokes.)

Suddenly, an atomic ripple of fawn and mauve materialised through a doorway – him! – gliding as if on a moving walkway into the room to sit, alone, behind a conference table draped with expensive white linen. Like a hologram in sharp focus, he was *exquisitely* him, pixie-sized, those gigantic eyes somehow bigger than the actual man, wearing a floor-length cashmere fawn coat and slimline violet suit, with matching tie. His voice was unexpectedly low, more the grainy growl of 'Gett Off' than the soprano cuteness of 'Kiss'. Many minutes passed as he talked of freedom before proceedings were hijacked by an over-excited man from Amsterdam under the disastrous illusion he was there to be the pop star's pal.

'You are the greatest live performer of all time!' collapsed The Man From The 'Dam. 'So I have to ask, why no live alboom? I have to say now "Sorry", because I myself have many bootleg albooms!'

The Artist (definitely not to be addressed as Prince, with a huge grin): 'Security?'

Bloke in a suit with a walkie-talkie strapped to his ear: 'Last questions!'

The Man From The *Sun*, knowing this is his last chance: 'What's it like being a fath—'

The Man From The 'Dam: 'Eez so great you are talking to us! And to see you are normal because you have not spoken before and this is why we have rumours you are a crazy guy and we see now you are a nice guy!'

The Man From The *Sun*, now so desperate he fluffs his line: 'What's fff . . . father like . . .'

The Artist: 'Excuse me?'

Silence. He's on his own.

'Are you enjoying being a father, PRINCE?'

OMG. He *spoke the unspeakable*. (A collective inward gasp.)

The Artist, nonchalantly: 'Of course. That's why we do it. I had a playpen built here even before the birth.'

He then rose, stepped down from the stage and disappeared under the shoulder blades of several fast-legged handlers like an escaping caterpillar wiggling away to freedom.

Soon, he would play a show, just for us, in the cavernous Paisley Park sound-room, a catwalk snaking out across the all-white room while the global press tucked into a tantalising 'dinner' of trays of parmesan vol-au-vents, bowls of Cap'n Crunch cereal (seemingly our host's breakfast of champions) and flagons of tooth-witheringly sweet apple juice (no booze whatsoever). 'Free at last!' inspired Martin Luther King from a speaker overhead and The Artist sashayed in front of an all-white backdrop in purple velvet flared pantaloons, purple bell-sleeved silken blouse, open to the waist (six-inch span) and purple high-heeled pixie boots. His name was not Prince. And he was not chunky.

As he sashayed down the catwalk caressing his 'axe' we could literally reach out and touch him as he shot out a finger, licked it and plucked a string, the new songs from *Emancipation* pluming forth. And then 'Purple Rain'. And 'If I Was Your Girlfriend'. So his name *was* Prince after all, and he was most DEFINITELY funky.

My own private summit with The Perv was scheduled for the following day and I wore my most florid shoes – sturdy green and orange platform numbers with silver corrugated wedge heel – an act of solidarity with the most meticulously flamboyant rock 'n' roll funketeer the world had ever known.

A melee of around twenty journalists and photographers from chosen media outlets were now held in a room, awaiting The Summons (no Man From The 'Dam or Man From The *Sun*, who'd both possibly been forcibly ejected), when word arrived from a jittery PR: Prince was cancelling all photo sessions with the global photography hounds. His interviews, however, would now extend to half an hour and he granted the taking of notes. Jings! I gripped my paisley-patterned notebook and wondered how it would now be possible to scribble-scribble-scribble while staring into Prince's extravagantly eye-lashed glistening globes *right there in front of me in real life.*

Thirty minutes later I was summoned by a suited Foot Servant, and personally escorted upstairs to a small conference room where a grey office chair was positioned at the edge of a huge rectangular glass table, opposite which – six feet away – clearly glinted His rather more gilded throne.

The Foot Servant, peering down the corridor, spoke: 'He's on his way … he's coming up the stairs … he's coming along the corridor …'

I was stifling explosions of laughter, then, when Prince finally glided into the doorway, fawn coat still on, proffering a hearty, un-gloved handshake, descending into his seat and folding his hands in his lap, coat opening up to expose a tight mauve three-piece suit, skinny mauve tie, black and gold shirt and matching mauve pixie boots.

Like anyone at this extreme level of fame he was intoxicatingly familiar and yet you'd never seen him before, not like this, with no lens distortion between you, so familiar and yet so alien, like proper pop stars always are. His head was frankly stunning: paler than you'd think (liberally powdered), blackest hair slicked back, glitter-dust behind his ears, goatee beard meticulously trimmed. His enormous, brown, Disney Fantasy eyes, outlined with curling lashes, were all filled up with internal glitter, something I'd only ever seen in the eyes of the stratospherically brilliant and/or catastrophically stoned. And he spoke.

'Do you like my house?' he wondered, in a striking, unexpected baritone. For the next twenty-nine minutes, madness commenced as I scribble-scribble-scribbled while simultaneously stare-stare-staring straight into eyes surely transported directly from the Big Bang, while attempting to interject some interesting or perhaps even amusing questions into what became a single soliloquy (exactly as expected) on creative freedom or, as he described it, how he's 'not conforming to anything anymore, except the universe'.

In late 1996, mumbo-jumbo was rife, the nineties the crystal-swinging decade of Eastern philosophies and self-help books, including an outbreak of famous folk going on about publishing phenomenon *The Celestine Prophecy* and its enigmatic 'nine insights'. Prince affirmed he was something of a revolutionary, 'a punk rocker', soon turning, instead, into a hippy.

'If you put a loaf of bread on the table, it turns into medicine and to me that is incredible,' he averred, scientifically. 'The bread will eventually take care of itself. That's nature, that's the truth. Everything happens for a reason and if you know that then you will be free. That's what I had to know in order to free myself.'

Prince's secret of the universe, then – *the truth of it all* – appeared to be mould.

Nine minutes in, the door inched open and Mayte Garcia appeared, in a silvery jacket, purple-bloomed skirt skimming the top of her thigh.

'This is my wife,' beamed Prince.

'. . . . . .' beamed Mayte, silently, who left immediately after the equally beaming instruction, 'we're nearly done – I'll see you in your office.'

They'd met when she was a famously virginal seventeen and today he'd 'never been happier, now I am complete'. He'd been nuptially certain, he added, because of 'the coincidences' (something *The Celestine Prophecy* was also big on). He was christened Prince, her childhood nickname was Princess. Both dads were John. His mum was Mattie, she was Mayte. Her middle name was Janelle, his father's name was John L. Her mother's name was Nell, he was born a Nelson. They were married on Valentine's Day 1996 and he carried her across the Paisley Park threshold, laden with gifts, the last of which was a child's crib. They sat on the floor, bowed to God and wept.

'I'm so in love with love now,' he wept some more. 'And I

just wonder what kind of a life we'd all have if we did all love each other, not just one person or the family, but everyone. I believe that is the purpose and I believe it's possible. And I didn't before.'

He carried on, advocating a life of self-control and sobriety, which didn't seem very funky.

'I think it is,' he glimmered. 'See, it's all about paths. Now I know that those paths of excess, drugs, sex, alcohol – all those experiences can be funky, they can be *very* funky, but they're just paths, a diversion, not the answer, because a lot of the time people don't come back. That's the end of their road. There was no fulfilment there so the search goes on. And the search won't leave you, let me tell you, it'll hunt you down like a stalker.'

This was, however, a rather rum do. This was the man, after all, who'd built a twenty-year career as one of the most voracious advocates of sexual permissiveness in modern-day cultural history. So I told him exactly that.

'. . . . .' he replied.

You're The Purple Perv.

'. . . . .'

The Valentino of Pop!

'. . . . .'

The Errol Flynn of Funk!

'Eheheh! That may be so.'

Too right it's true! You're the man who once said, 'I never waste an erection.'

'Oh, boy. (enormous smile) Oh, man! That's right, I said, "I hate to see an erection go to waste." Heheheh! Well, I feel I've just as much sexual energy as I ever had, I just find other things sexy these days.'

What do you do with an ill-timed erection these days?

'The energy goes on other things. Look at this.'

Crushingly, he reached over and fondled a box of

Emancipation-logo embossed calendar cards counting down to release day, a cute marketing device for stores.

'That I find sexy,' he averred. 'I couldn't do that before. I find freedom so sexy I can't even explain it to you. You wake up every day and feel like you can do anything. I see now that I was searching for my freedom in sex. I was hiding from myself.'

This, then, was New Prince, one of the good guys, evolved from Old Prince, megalomaniacal bad guy who surrounded himself with yes-men, freaked people out with his silence (he never used telephones 'because I didn't have to'), and reportedly fired people who were 'telepathically unresponsive'. He'd once had, he said that day, 'a massive ego', born out of 'insecurities – and I don't have any insecurities anymore'. It was also, he added portentously, 'a great mistake to see yourself as superior to anyone else', before proclaiming himself one-of-us.

'I'm no different to anyone,' he insisted. 'Yes, I have fame and wealth and talent, but I certainly don't consider myself any better than anyone who has no fame, wealth or talent. People fascinate me. Life fascinates me!'

From here on in his life was about Mayte. There were times when he asked himself what he was running from. 'Am I lonely? Is that why I surround myself with so many friends?' And he hadn't known the answer until he decided to marry and 'make the commitment, of "I will take care of you forever."' And because of her, the thirty-six songs on *Emancipation* simply flooded out, like a free-flowing Tetley Tune Bag.

'Last questions!' barked the Foot Servant on the stroke of twenty-eight minutes. I closed my paisley-patterned notebook.

You make it very difficult for us journos, pal.

'This is my way. There are no tapes because nothing I could ever say could ever be faithful to the spirit of the music. I don't speak in the studio, y'know? The only thing I like talking about is the business and how it works against the artist and the spirit.

And against music itself. But ... (penetrating purple stare) ... we'll talk again.'

Blinded by the lightning from his luminous eyes, my mind short-circuited, couldn't conjure any 'important' questions like ... Who was taller, him or Kylie? Did he really divest early-nineties Cuban songstress Martika of her cumbersome virginity when they were both on acid (no wonder she had a funny jaw)? And what did he ever see, exactly, in Sheena Easton?

Flooding into the mind instead came the brassy bounce of '1999'. Which would be, surely, the first song played on New Year's Day 1999.

'That song was not created by me,' he cooed. 'It was a gift to me from the higher powers.'

Then again, maybe it would be played across the planet on New Year's Eve 1999, the last song played in global unison of an entire millennium. That would be a fairly big concept. Man.

'That is a fairly ... big ... concept,' he nodded. 'Well, what can I say? It wasn't me. It's only a privilege.'

A different Foot Servant humbled into the room, placed some papers under Prince's regally dusted nose as I rose to leave and headed towards the door. 'Good shoes!' announced the Footman, glancing at my stupid footwear.

Why, thank you. Shoes are important.

'Yes,' said Prince. 'They are.'

As he glanced from stupid shoes to papers and buried his head, I stepped away from his presence and Foot Servant 2 gently, but firmly, closed the door.

Prince, I think, had just liked my shoes. (This was significantly more thrilling than several billion casually bestowed Facebook 'likes', in our oncoming digital future, could *ever* be.)

Two years later Prince and Mayte separated; two years after that they divorced.

16

HEROES (JUST FOR ONE DAY)

There are very few times as a journo that you will ever meet not only the heroes of your own lifetime, like Prince, but *history*'s heroes, the ones whose contribution to humanity is the actual foundation both you and your own heroes stand on. These are the heroes from previous generations, who stayed alive long enough (against all odds) to become the faces on the Mount Rushmore of Culture Itself, whose reach is so vast they were your parents', even grandparents', heroes, too.

Growing up in Scotland in the 1970s, especially if your parents were of the war generation – insulated from the rock 'n' roll fifties by the demands of new parenthood and the new-found thrills of security – country 'n' western music spoke to the collective sensibility like no other, built as it was on the deep-down depths of damage, desolation and devils. These were the songs of agony and yearning, drunken paeans not only to heartbreak and lost love but dead dogs, random murder and Daddy-never-loved-me-anyway, the most lyrically calamitous musical oeuvre on earth.

Most Saturday nights in the early seventies Jackie and I would hear the sounds of the country greats thumping up through the floorboards of the room we shared and attempt to decipher the muffled yodelling over the unmistakable, relentless, two-note bassline – *BOOM, boom, BOOM, boom* – through all the greatest hits of Sydney Devine ('make the wuuuuurld go awaaaaaay!'), Tammy Wynette ('stai-nd baaah yooor mayin!'), Cristy Lane ('hwun day arrah taaaaaaame, sweet Jeeezus!') and the almighty Johnny Cash, whose baritone boom vibrated the very house bricks like a tunesome industrial drill through 'Ring Of Fire', 'Folsom Prison Blues', 'I Walk The Line' and the one which made my dad laugh 'til he cried, 'A Boy Named Sue'. 'How do you *do*!?' he'd wheeze, whisky in hand, as if finding it funny for the very first time, every time. It would be years before I knew Johnny Cash wasn't merely an amusing Saturday night sing-song gambit for pished and sentimental Scottish people but The Original Rock 'N' Roll Outlaw, possibly the very first punk, definitely the pioneer of rock 'n' roll rebellion and lifelong spokesman for the vulnerable, the criminalised and the misunderstood outsider. A force-of-nature who should've been, like so many of his peers, mad or dead decades before.

In the autumn of 1996, as the Britpop Massive were still shouting at each other about whose tunes were the tuniest, Johnny Cash was seated in front of me, entirely motionless, in a plush armchair in a huge, cream and gold upholstered suite of the ludicrously swish Four Seasons Hotel in Los Angeles, his hand outstretched to shake mine. This was *completely preposterous*. But there he was, really him, a bulky sixty-four-year-old seemingly made of granite, six foot two, still dressed in black (as he said he always would be, 'until world peace is declared').

I sat down on a gilded armchair next to his own, a small table between us featuring a bowl of fruit beside a compendium of infamous serial killers. When he spoke, first, his voice was so low it seemed to bubble upwards from a swamp in Alabama. He said, to my astonishment, 'I like your shoes,' exactly as Prince's Footman had said over the green and orange platform numbers with the silver heel. 'I like YOUR shoes,' I blurted back, surveying his Cuban-heeled, square-toed, alligator skin rock 'n' roll classics, size thirteen.

I lost my mind. This was like sitting next to Elvis, or a unicorn, or The Spirit Of Rock 'N' Roll Itself.

Crumbs. You're Johnny Cash. It's really you!

'Well,' he smiled, a light sparking up in his coal black eyes. 'Well, well. How 'bout that? Hmmnmn.'

Hmmnmn turned out to be closest Johnny Cash came to laughter, a low rumble in the throat of a man of few and cautious words. Who wanted, right now, to talk some more about shoes, describing how his own, aptly, had 'a real heavy sole'. His voice was now like the rumbling of an underfoot LA earthquake.

'I give 'em away to the Goodwill charity when I'm tired of 'em,' he noted of his eminently stylish footwear. 'Give 'em to other big-feet people.'

Good Lord. Do people know they're yours? Can you buy them for 'ordinary' money?

'Oh, they're not for selling, they just give 'em away.'

But they're historical artefacts!

'You're kidding. Hmnm.'

I think you'll find they are!

'Hmmn. Ehmnmnm.'

And here, in the midst of almost an *actual laugh*, he leaned over, lifted the small fruit bowl and held it directly under my nose.

'Would you like a plum?'

And so it came to pass that I was now living in a world where Johnny Cash, pals with Elvis, an architect of rock 'n' roll who embodied the very concept of The Revolution, was offering me a plum. Which I took, as he took another one, and we sat and ate our plums, me 'n' Johnny Cash, together, as if we'd been bestest pals, forever.

Throughout the fifties and sixties, Johnny Cash had hell-raised his way through America addicted to uppers and downers. He wrecked two jeeps and a campervan, turned over two tractors and a bulldozer, sank two boats and once jumped from a speeding truck just before it hurtled over a 600-foot cliff in California. He was jailed seven times (though never convicted), once at El Paso airport for stashing 688 Dexedrine and 475 Equanil tablets in a cheap Mexican guitar. He regularly wrecked hotel rooms and once burned down a whole mountainside, by accident, after the wheel of his broken campervan caught fire, becoming the first man in history to be sued by the United States Government for starting a fire deliberately, even if he hadn't, fined a then whopping $125,000. So now I was declaring him the original inventor of rock 'n' roll drug-propelled chaos.

'Who, me!?' he grinned. 'Hmmm. No! I won't accept the blame for all of it. I did my part but there were others out there doing it at the same time.'

Are you The Original Keith Richards: indestructible?

'Hmmmnnm! Well now, I didn't do as much crap out there as people said, or I wouldn't be as old as I am and feeling good. And I do feel great. Mmhergeheh!'

This, finally, *was* the sound of Johnny Cash laughing, for

three seconds, a bounder's wheeze like Muttley the dog from *Wacky Races*. We talked about his preference, like Jesus, for the human company of the dispossessed; outlaws, bums, hookers, convicts – 'I felt more at home with these people than the uptown clubbers'; about the jailbirds he personally took 'under my wing ... I believe an ex-convict should be given a chance and usually they're not.'

For a while, we tried to locate the original source of *his* evidently inherent rock 'n' roll spirit. 'Just the Devil in me, I guess,' he eventually decided. 'We'd take a pound of black gunpowder [as kids] and wrap it in twine and tape and put a fuse to it and set it in a hollow tree, out in the plains of Texas, just to watch the tree blow up.' (Maybe this was his version of Knicker Up?) 'That kind of destruction eventually turned inward and I started destroying myself. With the drugs.' (Oh no!)

What was it about amphetamines, your drug of choice? Did you feel like life just wasn't fast enough?

'I felt like it was *too* fast,' he decided (after several millennia had passed). 'And I just wanted to keep up with it, I think.'

Do you ever miss the booze?

'Never. Because I was a crazy person.'

He signed two autographs – one for me, one for my mum – and in the leafy back garden of the Four Seasons Hotel deigned to have his photograph taken for all of seven frames, in the days when photos were taken in frames, much to the photographer's professional dismay. 'That's enough,' he announced, simply, and stepped abruptly away from the lensman, slowly walking back into the hotel with the gait of a flung tombstone.

Johnny Cash only lived for another seven years.

Dad also loved Spike Milligan, especially 'The Ying Tong Song', the absurdism genius's lone contribution to history's musical canon: a 'nonsense' caper which reached number three in 1956. I was eight years old when it was re-released in 1973 (reaching number nine) and my fifty-four-year-old dad would often serenade me, usually balancing a tumbler of whisky between his delicate piano fingers, with a chuckling, mirth-eyed rendition: 'Ying tong, ying tong, ying tong, ying tong, ying tong iddle I po!!!' he'd yowl, usually followed by the joke about the man who went to a chippy and asked for a 'steak and kiddly pie' and when asked if he meant 'steak and kidney' replied, 'I said kiddly, diddle I?' This was a Spike Milligan kind of joke, the comedian who was not only my dad's generational peer but hero of *The Goon Show*, without which there would've been no *Monty Python* (as John Cleese himself has declared) and significantly less Revolution, everywhere, thereafter.

To be asked to spend an hour round Spike Milligan's house was like being asked to spend an hour with *the meaning of life* itself. Even if I was confronted with a man who appeared to be three minutes away from death.

I arrived alone, no photographer, no PR, at Spike's English homestead, in the fittingly titled Rye, where his genial wife, Shelagh, announced he was returning from the doctor's (Shelagh herself having been newly fitted with a surgical collar for an unspecified recent injury). Spike returned with apologies. 'I'm soooo sorry,' he blinked, 'I didn't have you in my diary, you're from ... the *Daily Express*?' This was the *NME*, I explained, the music paper, which ignited a memory. 'Ah yes! Adverts for trumpeters ...' he smiled fondly, a sometime trumpeting professional himself.

He shuffled into the kitchen of his enormous, plush dream-home-in-the-country, inches at a time, seemingly twenty years older than his already considerable almost seventy-eight. Stooped and frail, his white hair wisped across his forehead in no fixed direction, eyes still a striking blue but now with the pale blue transparency of a life in its wavering twilight. 'I'm getting so confused,' he announced in a thin, slow, whispery old-bean voice and soon began giggling uncontrollably, as if about to burst into tears, an infectious, endless wheeze causing his entire body to vibrate.

'Why don't you stay for dinner?' he piped, to my heart-wibbling delight. 'Stay the night! Do you have a nightdress? We can have (enormous grin) some *wine*.'

For one night only, then, I ran away to live with Spike Milligan, lifelong hero and inspiration for the gently childlike, quiet quips of my own war-upended father. This was the man who'd said, back in 1961, 'Of course I'm a rebel, a revolutionary, what else is there to be? I'm the last man alive to speak the truth.' He was also a professional dissenter, an acerbic lampoonist, an iconoclast, pessimist and dodger of death in World War II, chronicler of said war and Patron of the Manic Depressive Society, 'which I suppose means I'm the world's Number One Manic Depressive'.

He was also a film star, author, scriptwriter, playwright, poet, pioneer of idiot humour as intellectualism, seeker of Truth, subject of three editions of showbiz blubfest *This is Your Life* (my mum would've wept through them all), and the man who called the Prince of Wales 'a grovelling little bastard' on TV when picking up a Lifetime Achievement award, at which Charles laughed his ears off. Humans just do not get *any more heroic* than this.

We sat in his huge, elegant living room, dominated by a grand piano (Paul McCartney, his neighbour, was always popping by for a tinkle, as it were), featuring cosy white pile carpeting and an antique gramophone hosting a 78 rpm disc of 'The Vienna Waltz'. He folded himself into an armchair, a plate of cheese 'soldiers' on an armrest and a glass of white wine in his hand. 'Oh, I'm not a revolutionary anymore,' he scoffed, 'I've gone off the boil. But you know what it's been all about? I'm against the cliché. I *can't stand* clichés. It's the sheer bloody boredom of always knowing what's coming next.'

Like most pioneers, he had no idea he was pioneering at the time.

'Writing was the place where I escaped from myself, never mind the rest of the world,' he mused, wheezily. 'This was the world as it should be and I simply wrote it down, it was already built in me. I didn't know a thing about ... revolution. I had a wife and baby so I was just excited that I was being paid. But on reflection we must have broken the mould. We just ... threw all the clichés away and did what we liked.'

Well there you go, you knew you were a rebel.

'Oh, I was never a rebel, I was very quiet! Do you know ... I didn't give a fuck. Didn't care if anyone else thought it was hilarious, didn't give a fuck about people – fuck 'em! I just wanted to be me and do what I wanted.'

Here, he leaned in, having had enough of the olden days already.

'So, tell me honestly, what's your family name ...?'

A conversation about kilts ensued, after which he enthused, 'I'm Irish, you know!'

Spike Milligan realised very early on (mostly through the Marx Brothers) that the world was full of idiots. So he created a world of fictional idiots all of his own.

'That's right,' nodded Spike. 'I tried to precede their stupidity. I pre-empted the idiots.' We talked about his published works of hilarity. Here was a man, evidently, who had as big a laugh at his own jokes as everybody else. He'd reworked *Lady Chatterley's Lover* into a bawdy retelling featuring tea-urns falling on heads which still amused him greatly.

'It's a terrible thing I've done to it, ah-*haw*!' he guffawed. 'But then D. H. Lawrence had them screwing in a chicken house.

How could they do it with all those chickens going *buck buck buck baaaaa-buck*? I thought, these are English people, they don't do that!'

There was his mid-nineties reworking of the Bible, the mention of which ignited an extended bout of inner vibration. 'In the beginning there was darkness,' he wheezed, now weeping with mirth. 'And the Lord said, "let there be light" but owing to a fuse at Loughborough power station they said they couldn't connect 'til Thursday. And then the Lord said, "let there be grass!" and Lo, there was grass ... (more tears of mirth) ... And *lo* ... the Rastafarians smoked it ...'

After Spike was blown up in the war, 'and I should have stayed up', he felt he'd 'come to an end of myself, I didn't have any courage left, I'd gone empty'. Famously, he was given a new treatment for shell-shocked soldiers called deep narcosis and was unconscious for three weeks. This triggered the beginning of his lifelong struggle with manic depression: he suffered delusions, he'd see a raven fly in through his closed bedroom window and write passages from the Bible on the walls with its beak. Being blown up also caused him, he'd once said, 'to think for the first time'. He was the archetypal angry young man, not unlike, in fact, Richey Manic: prone to Orwellian-type statements like 'everywhere I go I see stupidity and bureaucracy and human beings being ground down into one amorphous mass of controlled actions and reactions. I hate everything, I'm against the human race.' He railed against hotels that wouldn't serve breakfast-in-bed, building societies, the nuclear bomb, washing powder and light bulbs: 'Somewhere some idiot in a bowler hat is totting up the amps. It's costing us money to bloody well sit here and *breathe*.'

We contemplated his lone chart-bothering musical contribution, my dad's all-time favourite comedy song.

'Well, I said to my friend,' he began, rascally, 'look, there's all this music going on these days, and it's crap. I said, I'll tell you what I'm going to do, I'm going to write a tune which is meaningless. With three chords: C, G, C. So I wrote the tune but I didn't have any words. So I said, well, what's words? No one understands the rock singers anyway, so I wrote the words, "Ying Tong Iddle I Po". (He began, once again, to vibrate.) And my friend said to me, "By the way, that crappy song that you wrote is number three in the charts," and I just thought, Christ! *How?* (triple-speed vibrations) And a Chinese gentlemen wrote to me, a chap called Frederick Woo and (three seconds to explosion) ... and said ... and *said* ... did I know that in China "Ying Tong Iddle I Po" means "please can I have some more petrol?" (now copiously weeping) It's *absolutely true.*'

In 1993 Spike had almost died again, on an operating table having triple heart bypass surgery which cost £30,000. 'And for that kind of money, I tried to be as ill as possible.' His greatest concern for the modern world was 'violence, the fact it's not safe, especially for women'. He'd been so appalled by the recent Dunblane school shooting (the one Wimbledon champ Andy Murray narrowly escaped) he wrote to the *Daily Mail* asking them to print his plea for all handguns to be handed over immediately. 'There's only one purpose for guns, and that's death.' The sometime suicidal natural-born pessimist was also that day a euphoric believer in life, principally for his family and the continuing joy of his jokes.

'Do you know,' he mused, now so keen to get to dinner he stood up and sat down three times in five minutes, 'I wake up every morning and think, "Thank *God,* another day." Every day I go out into a field and I lay down and I put a shovel by me and I wonder if anybody's going to bury me. And every day I come back and I say, "Guess what? I'm going to live! Yes!" Ooh, this is very nice wine ...'

He assured me he wasn't really at war with the world anymore, though he remained bamboozled by the enigma of humans, who still didn't 'make any sense'. They made little sense to me either. But maybe he knew what *did*.

Does anything make sense?

'Poetry,' he observed immediately. 'Because it excludes all the clichés. It's condensed down into just meaningful words. I'll give you an example. A poem that I wrote. I hate to say perfection, but I think this *is* perfection ...'

He cleared his throat.

> *'Last night in the twilight's gloom,*
> *A butterfly flew in my room,*
> *Oh what beauty, oh what grace*
> *Who needs visitors from outer space?'*

'I think,' he added, 'that's *perfect.*'

I wondered if this exceptional man who'd been alive for almost all of the twentieth century, since 1918 (born a year before my dad), who'd most definitely Seen It All, still had hope? For the whole of beleaguered mankind?

'Oh, there's always hope,' he smiled, wobbling to his feet. 'That's the one thing that never goes away. Hope. Yes. *Yes*. Life! Pandora's Box. So let's go and have some *dinner*. And some more *wine*.'

Soon, the gregarious Shelagh gave us our dinner on trays (pie 'n' mash), with a separate bottle of wine each, of evidently differing quality. 'You can see,' piped Spike, 'we've left you with the crappy stuff.'

We watched TV, mostly Spike's beloved boxing and rugby coverage, and talked about his latest reworking (he still wrote in longhand) of Daphne du Maurier's *Rebecca*. 'What have I done to it? I've made it *funny*.' He talked about the war and meeting Churchill, about how if he and my dad hadn't done what they did, 'we'd all be living in a bloody concentration camp'. He then excused himself, off to watch a dreadful karate film in bed, 'must be my alter ego', while back downstairs in the homely sitting room, Shelagh brought out the *boxes* of wine, soon joined by Spike's daughter Romany, a huge-hearted six-foot redhead over on holiday from Canada. At 3 a.m., Shelagh reached around the back of her neck and pinged off her surgical collar with an almighty howl of freedom. 'To hell!' Next morning, she couldn't find it. Spike, meanwhile, shuffled off to his beloved rugby after awaking, no doubt, with a smile on his face and the words, 'Thank God, another day!'

Me, I awoke in the spare room under the Milligan household's supernaturally comfortable white fluffy duvet and laughed out loud at the unlikeliness of this outrageous professional and personal privilege. I've never forgotten him, his spirit, or his astounding generosity. Who indeed needs visitors from outer space?

Spike Milligan lived for another six years.

17

WHO'S *THAT* GIRL?

Sometime in the late nineties, at booze-possessed toxin-fest T In The Park, a fledgling pop writer asked me if I was ever nervous before or during an interview with The Stars. I said something like 'not really' and her face fell like a cartoon ACME anvil off a cliff face. This was not, evidently, how she felt. 'No? *Never?*' she beseeched, all drooping disappointment. Feeling something of a terror-traitor, I offered a crumb of comfort, mumbling something about it being not so much nerves as entering into a heightened state of neurological alertness, on your toes, as you would do in a sporting endeavour. 'Maybe,' I ventured, 'a bit like being a boxer, because it's usually some kind of fight.'

Today, to any fledgling pop writer on the planet (other than suggesting you do something which pays you, with a future, instead), I can tell you this was both true and a deliberate withholding of the rest of the truth, which is that sometimes you're so atom-tremblingly nervous before talking to a Star you have considered instigating a sudden bone-breaking 'accident' en route to said Star, preferring the moulding of a leg cast in A&E to the traumatising prospect of pretending you can talk in any coherent way to, say, Madonna.

Fear of A Star is, of course, a ludicrous concept, even if they are the most stratospherically celebrated entities on earth. What is it, actually, you're afraid of? Can they stab you, rob you, throw your life in a skip? In a way, perhaps they can: because if you've been given this usually once-in-a-lifetime privileged opportunity and you muck the whole thing up – let Madonna drone on about, say, Kabbalah or how much of a 'natural progression' her new album is for your allotted forty-five minutes – you will be exposed forever – finally found out! – as a spineless weed incapable of control, wit, guile or spirit and you'll *never work in this town again*. So it's not The Stars you're afraid of. It's yourself.

NME on the blower: 'D'you want to interview Madonna?'

'Blimey, well of course I do! OK ... Two weeks on Tuesday? Right ... OK ... Cheers!'

I hung up and the inner neurotic took over.

OhmyfuckingGod! MADONNA. Impossible. I'll collapse outside the hotel room door. Be picked up off the floor in one hand by a security guard the size of a Canadian redwood, flung over his shoulder and handed to the rozzers with a weary: 'Remove the loser from the superstar's lair, Sir.' How am I going to SPEAK to HER? I'm too Scottish. She'll need an interpreter. I'll have to tell her she's a shite actress. And seeing as the idiots have had it in for her forever she's now as hard-faced and defensive-cold as the cliffs of the Yosemite Valley. I'm off to the pub, sharpish . . .

In February 1998 Madonna remained the most radiant star in pop's expanding universe, her only peers the then-chart unbothering Prince and sanity-unbothering Michael Jackson, despite her mid-nineties years of diabolical balladeering befitting Celine Dion. A mere six months on from the death of Princess Diana, global icons were not yet routinely called celebrities, Reality TV had yet to redefine the entertainment galaxy and we did not wish our heroes – the very best of whom, as David Bowie always knew, were aliens from a different dimension – to tumble from untouchable plinths into grubby mortal realms. We never wished to see, not then, the joins, the cellulite or the glimpse of bandage concealing a soon-to-be-revealed *completely new head* (as indeed Madonna appears to have today).

For eighties teenagers like me Madonna was still The Greatest, a socio-sexual pioneer and deviant antagonist, the Pope-bothering, bottle-blowing, lip-sneering renegade of 1991's *In Bed With Madonna* documentary, frozen in my mind from 1990 at her most heroically defiant and staggeringly beautiful in the indelible, black and white 'Vogue' video – still the greatest pop video ever made.

My task, though, as one of the *NME*'s few pop believers, was to view her through the prism of said *NME*. And the *NME* was, at its indie core, the so-called superficial pop star's enemy (hence the name), its default position one of skew-wigged judge to perceived crimes against 'authenticity'. Plus, the bigger the pop star, the cheekier one had to be, hurling the puncturing skewer of irreverence into the Hindenburg balloon of megalomania, and thus ensure The Truth of said star would float to the ground in sooty, coiling tatters. Or, if the Star turned out to be hilarious, charming and brimful of top-flight anecdotes, an open love letter would inevitably ensue.

The morning of the interview, I awoke early at 6 a.m. for the 11 a.m. summit, eyes springing open in the flat I now lived in with The Dancer, on Kentish Town High Street, north London, a second-floor flat above an Indian restaurant, which sported a broken bedroom window open to the wintry elements and no windows whatsoever in the irredeemably mildewed bathroom.

(Standing in the shower) *I can't believe I have to do this. If I just slip, a little bit, and merely break my ankle, I will not have to do this.*

I'd planned my outfit meticulously: fluorescent orange and brown-checked granddad's trousers from Oxfam; beautifully ironed (possibly even Bez-level) chocolate-brown shirt from Cancer Relief; the orange and green platforms which both Prince and Johnny Cash had liked (from some gothy emporium in Los Angeles, always worn on special occasions); and a brand new multi-layer wonder mascara. The hair, all special-like, was a ponytail at the back with a voluminous, lavishly hairsprayed quiff at the front, inadvertently evoking a member of an indie band with space-age-hillbilly pretensions: a bit like Yip Yip Coyote in 1984. Soon, I was wobbling along the Mayfair pavements towards Claridge's hotel.

If I just step off the kerb right now and get only slightly run over by the London bus hurtling towards me, I will not have to do this.

Outside Claridge's, a straggle of twenty Madonna fans (and three surely slightly thrilled policemen) clutched posters and CDs, waiting for a glimpse of her Madgesty. With a final lung-billowing pull on the newly invented Nicorette Inhalator cigarette substitute (my first foray into sacking off the snouts), I threw on the journalistic device I'd always called 'The Cloak' – an invisible Cloak Of Invincibility, a sort of persona which acts as both armour and inner bottle – smoothed back the quiff and boot-stomped into the foyer.

Inside, her British PR, the indomitable Barbara 'BC' Charone (from Chicago, who mythology tells us has 'Fuck It' embroidered on her wallet), escorted me to Room 312, The Piano Suite, where I hovered on one end of a sumptuous golden sofa, a highly polished black grand piano gleaming in one corner, and awaited the woman who defined my pop generation. The heartbeat slowed as The Cloak began its magic and for the next forty-five minutes I would be able to pretend this scenario was perfectly normal, I was merely doing my job.

And in walked this hippy.

'You'll have to excuse me, I'm wearing my blanket.'

Madonna slid towards me, as if on castors, around an open, stately doorway, the legendarily bony hands clutching around her shoulders a substantial length of what appeared to be an intricately embroidered rug. Enfolded in this doubtless laughably expensive ream of cloth in glimmering gold, pink and blue, she embodied the vision of a teepee-dwelling gypsy in 1973, possibly en route to a weave-your-own-wheelbarrow workshop. She wore no make-up whatsoever, her unwashed, strawberry-blonde, black-rooted hair was parted at the oily centre and pulled into plaits either side, while her hands, close up, were intricately decorated in burnt-orange Sanskrit etchings. In comparison, I felt like an over-made-up tart. This was surely an imposter: less the planet's most fabulous pop star who pioneered the conical bra, more an acid-griddled casualty staggering from the Green Fields at Glastonbury clutching stolen swag from Joe Bananas' Blanket Emporium.

Madonna, evidently, was now taking the word 'incarnation' literally, her '98 album *Ray Of Light* beamed to the planet via her suddenly omnipresent interest in 'spiritual enlightenment'. She slid elegantly onto a golden, backless, circular seat and beneath her blanket bare legs and arms poked free, alabaster white, also revealing a sober, knee-length black skirt and a clingy, sleeveless black top. She didn't shimmer with celebrity stardust and she didn't smell of anything at all, not even the patchouli oil I can still smell on my vinyl copy of the *Like A Prayer* album from 1989 (scented, nose fans, to smell like church incense).

'What does your necklace say?' came an eerily familiar voice.

It's my name in Arabic, came another eerily familiar voice.

'And what's your name in Arabic?' she enquired, and then wanted to know where I was from. I told her, instead, she didn't look anything like herself. 'Hmmmn,' she responded and the gap-toothed smile emerged. It was definitely her alright.

I wondered what she thought people saw when they looked at her?

'When people look at me,' she cooed, 'they see themselves.'

Whatever could she mean? She didn't look to me like an over-made-up tart from Yip Yip Coyote in 1984 ...

A conversation with Madonna when she was thirty-nine years old in 1998 was like having a conversation with a shoeless nineteen-year-old San Franciscan tree-fondler in 1969, a woman who had just discovered the vastness of the universe, who had finally peered through the cracked dimension of her own personally vast cosmos, a reality infinitely distorted through fame, infamy, wealth, stature and seeming cultural importance. Hers was the kind of fame, certainly, which was terminal: as she said herself, when it came to the hounds of the global paparazzi, '[Princess] Diana was the only one who had it worse than me'. After fifteen years as the planet's peerless female pop icon, the high-glam, self-propelled Material Girl who stood for power, ambition, autonomous wealth, gender equality, emancipation and sexual liberation, she'd finally found The Answer, the point of human existence and the purpose of it all. Just like so many did, in actual fact, when they had enough money, fame, infamy, wealth, stature and seeming cultural importance.

Her story that day was the oldest pop story ever told, the one invented, perhaps, by George Harrison back in 1967, the moment he pinged his first sitar in a flute-sleeved kaftan while taking 'All You Need Is Love' quite literally. By '98, the cultural concepts of oncoming Millennium Madness, already relentless consumerism and the antisocial solitudes of the still-emerging internet, were now colluding in a vague unrest, a low-level panic now propelling even mainstream minds towards New Age chicanery, Buddhism-tinged self-help books and howlingly clichéd therapy-speak as continually dribbled by the likes of Geri Halliwell. In Madonna's case, she'd Gone Kabbalah, now entrenched daily in the teachings of Eastern cultures – hence today's hennaed hands, the Sanskrit squiggle for 'Om' (which she pronounced 'ome') etched in her palm and the red string looped around her wrist, denoting kinship for the Kabbalah principles of 'friendship, spirituality and knowledge'. She'd even given up the gym (a concept as unlikely as, say, a fish giving up water) for yoga two hours a day.

This was Madonna, once again, either inventing the zeitgeist, defining the zeitgeist or outright pinching the zeitgeist for her latest self-invention, but it could've been far more obvious: when you're approaching forty, you simply go a bit What's It All About, Man? Don't you?

'It's a combination, I think,' came the steady reply, beneath the rug, 'of growing older and coming out of spending a decade or two just having a good time and searching for fun and at a certain point a lot of people do go, "Well, there must be more than this, I'm on this earth for more than making money and being successful."'

Madonna was also, then, in the year 1998, on her own quest for meaning. Prince, I ventured, had been saying something similar. Was this the conceit of the superstar? That they say 'all that I've done means nothing' only when they've done it all?

'No,' countered Madonna, 'I can't speak for other people but I can say that I've reached where I am right now because I realise I haven't done anything.'

Crikey.

'The things I've been consuming myself with is actually not doing it all. I'm just beginning to have the things that I really need, and beginning to have things that are really important, which is intimacy and love and children, those are the important things. The other things, exhibitionism, all of those things are not nothing. They're . . . fantastic expressions, manifestations of loneliness or despair or curiosity, but ultimately they never take the place of the really important things. So when you have a lot of that other stuff, fame, fortune, celebrity, whatever and you get tons and tons and tons of it and you realise ultimately that it isn't going to make you happy then you do say, "Well, there's got to be something more to this," so you go off on a search.'

Funny, though, isn't it, how people always say money doesn't matter . . .

'When they have a lot of it?'

Yes. And they say 'love is all you need' when they have literally everything else.

'Well, I disagree with that. Because I know lots of people who have very little and I consider them to be great, dignified people who are very happy with where they are.'

She was, throughout our forty-five minutes, unnervingly calm, only raising her voice once, at the half-formed question, *Do you resent . . .*

'I don't resent ANYTHING,' she dismissed, possibly in a pique of resentment. She contemplated fame, which ignited an hallucinatory reverie.

'Fame,' she explained, 'is what everybody else puts on you, it's their own fantasy, nothing to do with me at all. Fascinating, really. I mean, don't you sometimes stop and go . . . (leaning forward and hugging her legs in her arms) don't you feel hyper aware of who you are in the moment? And then think, "God, I'm me inhabiting my flesh and bones, saying my words, breathing the air that I breathe", but you're also outside of it and thinking, "But why? Why am I me? Why ... why ... what is my place here?" You know what I mean? Well, that happens to me all the time.'

Just as well you're not a stoner.

'Aha-ha-ha! Yeah, I think it's best, I must say. I don't think I would have been around for very long. A couple of cocktails is about all I can handle.'

Perhaps, though, her new-found 'spirituality' was based on something even simpler than advancing age, and even more profound: she was newly a mother, to Lourdes Maria Ciccone Leon, born on 14 October 1996. She'd been a lifelong control freak and now felt 'liberated', feeling for the first time ever 'that it's OK when you're not in control of everything – and I've been struggling with that for years'. Lourdes had changed everything.

'When you have a baby, you've got to give it up,' she mused, of the concept of control. 'Especially if you're breast feeding, it's not about your schedule, it's not about your life, it's about their life. I feel like I'm looking at life through a completely different set of eyes.'

Was the birth of Lourdes the first time someone else was controlling you?

'Definitely.'

Why has the idea of losing control always been so terrifying to you?

'Because I grew up without a mother.'

At the time, and it's an indelible memory, Madonna – this most invincible of entities – suddenly seemed to me strikingly alone. She seemed isolated, adrift in a vacuum, perhaps someone who'd spent her childhood left out, abandoned in the emotional cold. (Hey, Madonna was no stoner, but I *was*.)

'When my mother died, I felt like my world was out of control,' she carried on. 'A child always looks to their mother and suddenly I didn't have that. I had eight brothers and sisters and my father could hardly be that for all of us. I've probably spent the majority of my life trying to control every other aspect. So I became an excellent student and a really hard worker, very ambitious and success-orientated.'

A million people lose their mother in childhood, though, but there are not a million Madonnas.

'Well ... somebody had to be me! This is my karma, who I am, what I've done and everyone's here for their own lesson and their own purpose. I know that sounds very Buddhist, but it's true. I certainly don't think that I'm better than anybody else. Well ... there probably was a time in my life when I did, y'know, think I was so special. Standing in soccer stadiums with 120,000 people shouting your name. Brief, brief, brief moments. And it's a selfish perspective, it's about taking, it's not about giving, it's very surface and very deceiving. Because the important things have nothing to do with the things that you can see.'

As Madonna talked, uninterrupted for a while, as I listened on this golden couch in my stupid shoes and comedy hair and lifetime's personal perception of the woman personally talking to me now, I could feel the fourth wall begin to bend, buckle and finally crumble, bricks, joists and metaphorical ballasts crashing onto the luxuriously tapestried carpet, an imaginary golden podium toppling across the room while the final tendrils of superstar projection snaked towards the window like tapering smoke from the crack in a genie's bottle.

It was suddenly devastatingly apparent. There was no such thing as a Superstar.

Madonna was no more and no less of a human being than you, me, or anyone else who had ever lived, and that we routinely believe otherwise – that beings at this iconic level are 'other' and therefore somehow 'better' (hence our nerves) – is merely symptomatic of the ludicrous, devious, warping nature of fame. She'd done extraordinary things, of course, and everything else is our own prismatic imagination, cultural illusion and romantic, personal desire. Still, I wondered just how much of an alfalfa-foraging Earth Mother Madonna had actually become, enquiring – in this crystal-fondling age – if she'd partaken in a particularly unsavoury new trend.

Did you eat the placenta?

'. . . . . .' gasped Madonna, her face plummeting, lips pulling apart, eyes drilling into the floor, incapable of speech.

You think that's disgusting, don't you?

'I do think that's disgusting! I've heard of people doing it but I'm not one of those people!'

There was a programme on telly only the other week where a family ate the new baby's placenta in the form of paté.

'Uh!' Her hands flew to her face. 'Well, it's possible!'

And before they cooked it and pulped it, it looked like a gigantic liver.

'Ah-ha-ha-haaa! Nooooooo. Uuuh! There are certain things your body just gets RID OF!'

Madonna in 1998: not that much of an Earth Mother after all, then.

'Five minutes, my children!'

So announced the sudden presence of Madonna's formidable US publicist Liz Rosenberg, now loitering around the suite with 'BC' as the portcullis descended. We talked, inevitably in '98, about the Spice Girls. (Mere months from now, in the summer of '98, Madonna would meet Guy Ritchie and within three years be living in London.) Posh, it turned out, was her favourite. Why?

Madonna: 'She's so mysterious.'

Miserable, more like.

'Really? Well that's probably why I like her.'

'She has a really cute boyfriend,' BC joined in, 'who's a really great football player and they're engaged.'

'Good on her!' enthused Madonna. 'Well, she's got no reason to be miserable. I always think she looks the coolest. She looks like she doesn't spend as much time getting ready as everyone else.'

I would've said the opposite!

'She has great taste,' added BC. 'She said she wouldn't have a baby until Gucci do baby clothes.'

And here, one legendary Madonna arm shot vertically into the air in a different sort of spiritual recognition.

'Yessss!' she declared, triumphantly. 'Well, will you please tell Posh that Gucci *do* have baby outfits because Tom Ford sent me several.'

We parted swiftly, she disappearing back through the open door pulling her blanket closer around her shoulders, me bolting through the hotel corridors en route to the nearest pub, wondering, as you always do after summits in rarefied atmospheres, what the hell that was all about. So you had a conversation with Madonna, it seems it went quite well, you hope the readers will take something interesting from it and that is the end of that. You're only brimful of joy, ultimately, that a high-stress scenario is over and that the tape recorder definitely worked. Before you stagger back to the mildew and the broken window, possibly via some chips.

When the story was published two weeks later, BC rang the *NME*. Madonna was not amused. She didn't like 'the placenta question' and was making a formal complaint. Pointless, of course, but perhaps an example of that lingering control she was evidently still struggling to let go of.

Almost three years later, in November 2000, Madonna (much

to the chagrin of her UK fans) played a 'comeback' live show at London's Brixton Academy to a coterie of competition winners and industry liggers, a flimsy five-song affair announcing her Ali G-assisted *Music* album while flailing on a hay bale in a cowboy hat and a sparkly Kylie T-shirt from where she honked out 'Holiday' like a sea lion strapped to a trampoline. Towards the end of the show, I spotted old *Smash Hits* trouper Rick Astley, and reintroduced myself with a cheery, 'It's Sylv, from *Smash Hits* in the olden days!' Astley, memories in his mind no doubt of porcupig jackets and Ruddy Big Pigs, was also not amused. 'It's people like you,' he balked, 'who drive people like me *mad*.'

I was supposed to be reviewing the show for the *Scotsman* newspaper, but the bewildering conditions of The Wrong Madonna had meant too many ciders imbibed and no review was duly submitted, as somehow explained to a *Scotsman* copy-taker from a coin-operated pay phone in a sketchy pub in Brixton (I'd never work for the *Scotsman* again).

In 2008 *Q* magazine wondered if I might like to interview Madonna again, for their regular Cash For Questions 'readers' questions' feature (these particular enquiries submitted by The Celebrities Of The Day, meaning negligible journalistic input). Naturally, I would. But word came back.

These days, our Madonna, emblem of The Sisterhood, would only be interviewed 'by a man'.

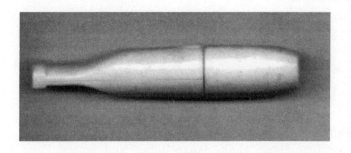

18

GRANDAD! GRANDAD!
WE LOVE YOU!

A lasting symptom of growing up through the post-punk era, with shards of the original punk mentality still lodged in your righteous convictions, meant the likes of Led Zeppelin – and everyone else the old bastards continuously called 'seminal' – were viewed into adulthood as Johnny Rotten's fossilised dinosaurs. In the mirthsome eyes of the young, such a glumly revered entity as 'ver Zep' seemed a 2D cartoon, a po-faced relic of a ludicrous age, fatted kings from the crucible of excess who'd even named themselves after a colossal hot-air balloon. To the giggling pop scribe, such gargantuan self-regard deserved only the darts of disdain – even if they remained, both to fans and to themselves, The Greatest Musicians Who Ever Lived.

To me, from the *NME* in 1998, they were defined by two ultimate sins.

1. Having no sense of humour whatsoever.
2. Only ever talking about the music, man.

I drudged off to meet them with a leaden heart.

Hello, I'm Sylvia. From the NME.

Robert Plant: 'Hello. We're Robert and Jimmy. From the 1970s.'

The lead cracked around my heart as I reeled, unexpectedly, from what you'd at least describe as a *quip*, the two rock titans – myth made real – positioned on plastic seats at the kitchen table of a tiny photographic studio in Chalk Farm, north London.

Robert Plant, known as 'Percy' to his pals, wore black leather breeches and had the largest face I'd ever seen, a huge and craggy cliff-front of a forty-nine-year-old face which looked at least ten years older. He liked to talk.

Jimmy Page sat next to him in a black leather bomber jacket, his normal-sized fifty-four-year-old face appearing at least ten years younger (the result, rumour had it, of the surgeon's trowel, or perhaps the supposedly 'preservative' properties of heroin). He only spoke when absolutely necessary. Both were puffing on endless Marlboro Lights, so I joined them with my now-permanent alternative, the Nicorette Inhalator, which looked like a cross between a tampon and a kazoo. Page and Percy goggled at its presence as Stone Age men would a television set with *Star Trek* on.

It's all your fault. Because of people like you, impressionable pink-lunged children like me grew up believing in self-destruction as a way of life. So how about an apology, hmn?

Robert Plant (puffing away, unperturbed): 'I think you should blame the Buzzcocks.'

Jimmy Page (puffing away, even less perturbed): 'My doctor told me I wasn't going to make it past thirty-five and after that I was on borrowed time.'

Robert: 'My doctor told me I'd lived a life of three men and would I like a large Scotch? When I had a major blood pressure problem about three years ago he said, "Well, Robert, you've got to face it, you've had a life three times over." But they weren't all running parallel, so I didn't consider that to be true.'

Bit greedy that, isn't it?

'Ye—' he began and then changed his mind. 'Well it wasn't intentional! (staring at tampon-kazoo) I can't believe I'm talking to a journalist sucking away on a piece of plastic. (breezily) I read the *NME* review of us at Glastonbury [in 1994]. It asked how we had the nerve to still be standing up. "God, they're still breathing. What the fuck are they doing, still here? And why is everybody enjoying it?" Apparently we played well and at the end it said "Respect." Hah! It's all just *trend*. Every generation needs its own heroes.'

Thing was, back in spring '98, the young generation had lost its collective mind, no longer with two fingers cocked to the hoary hippies but celebrating the old bastards instead. Prog rock, confoundingly, had returned. Or, at least, a-whole-lotta-noodlin' on the nonny-nonny 'axe' had returned via the likes of The Verve and the Beta Band, Britain now a psyched-out landscape of wiggy 'riffs' and bongo mayhem, the Beta Band's on-tour backdrop a projection of dusty vintage album sleeves including Emerson, Lake & Palmer and Led bleedin' Zeppelin. So now the young wanted to know all about them.

The two mythological figureheads perched before me,

though, were here to talk solely about music, specifically their marvellous new album *Walking Into Clarksdale* (since un-recalled by history). Naturally, seeing only cartoons before me, all I wanted to know about was the madness of being in ver Zep: about the private jets, the bongs, the gongs and the girlies, about life in this fabled band which, as mythology always had it, 'bestrode the world of rock 'n' roll like a colossus'. They were *defined* by the word colossal: colossal tunes, colossal shows, colossal amounts of drugs, sex, wiggly hair and on-tour earnings, affording them Lear jets, country mansions and tax-exile status. They had the colossal cheek to refuse to release singles because that's what the weedy pop kids did, and didn't bother with such trifling incidentals as album titles, interviews or appearing on telly, preferring their colossal enigma. They sold a colossal ninety million albums throughout the 1970s and were celebrated as the most colossal practitioners of rawk pig behaviour *of all time*. Behaviour which saw Jimmy Page wheeled naked on a serving trolley into a roomful of sexually ravenous nubiles eager to bend to his every 'need'. (Robert Plant referred to such people as 'friends of the family'.)

Their manager, the infamous Peter Grant, insisted ver Zep earned an unprecedented 90 per cent of gate takings for shows which, in the early seventies, sold out faster than Elvis, and furthermore insisted they receive the highest royalty rate in rock history (five times that of The Beatles, a situation said to have been achieved through the use of, er, non-negotiation at gunpoint). Their drummer, John 'Bonzo' Bonham, was fond of thirty-minute drum solos, a time delaying tactic ensuring the rest of the band could swagger backstage for a blow-job (at the very least). It was he who defined the drummer as perennial rock nutter by fatally choking on his own vomit in 1980, brimful of thirty-six measures of vodka.

All this extreme life lived, then, and all Page and Percy

wanted to talk about was the pinging reveries of African tribesmen's instruments. 'Let's talk about the music we did in the desert with the Ghawa tribe,' announced Robert Plant, disastrously. 'I had a sitar before George Harrison!' noted Jimmy Page, woefully. Worse, riff-possessed Zep fans will be distraught to know, I'd never listened, all the way through, to any of their mammoth-rock albums (not that I confessed to such a thing at the time) and was only familiar with the shrieking grandiosity of The Hits, which were never Hits because they didn't do singles. But I knew all about 'Kashmir', which was brilliant, and The Theme Tune To *Top Of The Pops*, i.e. 'Whole Lotta Love', which was mental and quite good.

'So what about the new record then, is that colossal?' Robert wanted to know.

Er, it's not as colossal.

Robert: 'Why?'

It's not as ... bludgeoning you over the head with a sledgehammer.

Robert: 'Neither was *Led Zeppelin III* ...'

(Help!)

Robert: ... only parts of *Physical Graffiti* were ...'

(Puffing hard on plastic ...)

Robert: 'And that, for me, was our finest group of moments. It wasn't just about a sledgehammer, it was about ... (suddenly remembering the new album) ... *this* is about four people in a room with Steve Albini with all the mics up playing because we love to play. When we could be on the golf course.'

Jimmy: 'Heheheheh!'

Robert: 'People a bit older than you used to talk to us and say "Why are you doing it?" As if you reach a point where you don't want to. Why would anybody ever wonder why people do something they really enjoy doing?'

Because there's some evidence to back up the theory that beyond thirty-odd, everyone goes crap?

Robert: 'Well, yes, that's true and back then we felt like that too. But we can't do much about it 'cos we're on the bus now. And we ain't competing with anybody which changes your whole approach. If you talked to Mick Jagger you'd be saying exactly the same things to him, because he's another one who you've decided has done it all, been there and is probably a hologram.'

You invented the concept of the private jet (their self-anointed 'flying brothel' The Starship): *does it all seem idiotic now?*

Jimmy: 'I don't know if we *did* invent it. The jets happened out of necessity.'

Pthrththrt!

Jimmy, ignoring outburst: 'If you were travelling around the States at the rate we were you can't rely on commercial airlines because they cancel flights. It's a logical fact that you need an aeroplane.'

Robert: 'If you put fifteen people on it and calculate how much it would cost to get from Chicago to Detroit times fifteen, you might as well take a plane that goes when you wanna go.' Here, his enormous face failed to suppress an enormous grin. 'The fact that you do cartwheels naked on take-off and have an organ playing and somebody serving exotic cocktails … well, I suppose they *were* two quid a glass! But there's no point talking it down. I'm sure any band that travels at that kind of rate, playing in one city, half an hour later you're 36,000 feet up. Everybody was in a big hurry. (to Jimmy) *You* were in an even bigger hurry than me!'

Jimmy: 'Eheheheheh!'

You two never tell anybody anything, ain't that so?

Robert: 'We've just told you why we used a private plane!'

You're sitting there smirking at each other knowingly!

Robert: 'It's at the idea of Jimmy being in a bigger hurry than me and being in the same spot at 36,000 feet! Sitting there, hurrying up!'

Would you like to accept responsibility for the rock 'n' roll excess blueprint?

Robert (now chortling head off): 'What about William Burroughs? What about Oscar Wilde? What about Caractacus? What about Hereward the Wake? I even went to see where Canute tried to turn the fucking tide back! Winchester. Went where he put his seat. Amazing! People have been zapped since time began! We can't all be shopkeepers.'

And so, that day in 1998, Robert Plant officially blamed King Canute for the 1970s. Here, the pair, now almost approaching perky, deemed their twelve years inside the world's most ludicrous rock 'n' roll band, somewhat euphemistically, 'a sensory experience'.

'It was really intense,' mused Jimmy, 'but the fact is we had the balance of coming back off the road to our home existence.'

'Yes, we had our families,' nodded Robert, chastely, 'and I was just a Black Country kid who got lucky. And I busted my balls to keep a standard of performance – and I don't mean standing in me anorak (nil-disguised disdain, here, for Oasis) looking up like that, deadpan, for an hour and a half, I mean *moving*.'

Wasn't it weird, being family men whose wives were in full knowledge of the one billion infidelities?

Robert: 'Are you from *HELLO!* magazine? Or the *Sunday Sport*? What's happened to the *NME* since we last read it? Mind you, the last time we read it Tom Jones was number one.'

Jimmy: 'I think it was termed an "open relationship" in those days.'

Robert: 'An open relationship. Hah! What did your editor say to you? Go and find out 'cos the books can't be right? Do they have a sense of humour or are they going to be miserable and sit in a corner with Dave Gilmour?'

Miserable and sit in a corner with Dave Gilmour, I'd imagined.

You're supposed to be the most serious men in the history of rock 'n' roll . . .

Robert: '*Who* said we were serious?'

Legend *says you're serious!*

Robert: 'If you came to our rehearsal room in an hour and a half, we'd frighten the pants off you! Musically speaking.'

Ooer.

In 1998, the only contemporary musicians Page and Plant bestowed their 'respect' upon were terror-rave radicals The Prodigy, based on the Essex techno-punks' intense understanding of 'adrenalin and excitement', bemoaning that day a perceived late nineties 'disenchantment with performance'. Worse, they insisted, there really *were* no heroes anymore.

'We were affected by the whole "beat" scene,' noted Robert of the drug-skewed poets/writers of the sixties/seventies (the immortal mavericks Jack Kerouac, William Burroughs, Allen Ginsberg). 'People who really did taste freedom outside of the run of society, not just pop music, a whole movement. The new rebels are either unheard of or there's some feeble new rebel that makes sure he looks pretty good in a bleached-out photograph, a coiffured, cosmetic version of rebellion. Nothing to do with the stuff that fired us up, like Howlin' Wolf roaring in some club in San Francisco, like "What the fuck is *that?*" Everything is so accessible now. Howlin' Wolf is five pounds for a double CD in Tower Records.' (We can only imagine, today, what he makes of our free-loading digital planet.)

Here, he detailed a Howlin' Wolf show at the Hammersmith Odeon, the night of 'the cold-sweat shit' when they saw James Brown ('man, that was amazing!') and how, whenever Robert had a bad throat, Janis Joplin would appear with orange juice which was six parts vodka, two parts orange. 'Everyone was in the same fan club,' swooned Robert, mistily.

Was there ever a 'spell' when you genuinely thought you were going bonkers?

'Only before we made *this* record,' retorted Robert, 'aha! You see? I'm trying to catch you out ... how *silly* of me, why should we be here talking about what we're doing now?! I mean, *really*. We'll have Nick Kent coming in in a minute asking if we've still got that gram we had off him in 1973. (ponderously) It's impossible to go bonkers when you start off bonkers.'

'I remember going out on tour in the States on two occasions with a broken, damaged finger,' announced Jimmy in something of an extended soliloquy. 'The scar's still there.' He waved, unexpectedly, an exquisitely effeminate hand.

Blimey, what extraordinarily well manicured nails you have, Mister Page.

Jimmy: '*Do* I!?'

Yes. They're artist's fingers.

Robert: 'He nearly left one of those fingers in a fence at San Diego airport.'

Jimmy: 'That's right. Got it stuck in the chain link.'

Crikey, wonder how much that would've gone for, eh?

Robert: 'How much would that've gone for!? That's the best thing I've heard all day! Next up, John Bonham's hat and Jimmy Page's finger, how much am I bid!? I better write that down, there's a song in there.'

With the level of fame and money and excess you had, you must've believed, at some point, you were actually Gods. Julian Cope, on acid, once thought he was a City Centre.

Robert (witheringly): 'Julian Cope lived in the middle of a traffic island in Wiltshire for a while, didn't he? He lives near Avebury, I believe. I proposed to somebody in Avebury Ring. I dropped on both knees in the mud. Made her hang on to the stones, man. I heard some Hawkwind in the back of my mind. (cracks up) What do you want from us? You'll get nothing!'

Here, their PR arrived to announce our time was up. 'This is the most amazing interview we've ever had!' guffawed Robert Plant to my total bamboozlement. (It seemed they really *were* never quizzed about anything other than the music.) 'And if you don't keep the tone of this interview the way it is on this tape we're going to send [Zep bass player] John Paul Jones in.'

Er ... so what do other people talk to you about then?

Robert: 'Well, some of them talk about the new record! That always comes in handy! But what you want to know about is all the ... trysts. About the friends of the family!'

Well no wonder! This is Led bleedin' Zeppelin we're talking about!

Robert: 'What are you going to do with Liam [Gallagher] when he's forty-nine!? Poor Liam will have to look back on it all and make fun of it!'

One should ruddy well think so!

Robert: 'We can't sit here and be offended by the idea we actually had a good time!'

Well, absolutely not! It would just be quite a wheeze if you talked about it, that's all!! Anyway, anyone who's 'offended' by it is probably just jealous. Though probably not about the thirty-minute drum solos ...

Robert: 'No, but they came in handy!'

Jimmy: 'They came in *very* handy!'

And what exactly were you doing?

Jimmy: 'Enjoying ourselves!'

Robert: 'I think we should pass on to the next question but they were there for a reason. Inside the gates of Eden! Hahahahah! So, when you interviewed Bob Dylan, how did that go?'

(Sadly, this was merely a quip ...)

Jimmy: 'We had a good hedonistic time, I don't see anything wrong with that, rather than going around the world whinging.'

It's been a preposterous life, hasn't it, 'boys'?

Robert: 'Steady on old girl, I can still play tennis! It's not all over yet! All it is *is* ... (pulling himself together) *we wrote a few songs*. And we were able to go out and play 'em probably more convincingly than we recorded 'em. And I hope to God we still do. That's really what we're here for. To create vehicles for us to carry on playing and looking at each other going "Yep, that's *much* better than watching the omnibus edition of *EastEnders*."'

And with that the unexpectedly chipper old boilers rose from their plastic stools, picked up their beloved cigarettes (lucky gits) and rumbled off into the London dusk.

'We're getting in our spaceship now,' honked the man called Robert from the 1970s, swinging cheerily out the door, 'with the rest of the hobgoblins.'

Two weeks later, when the interview was published, Led Zeppelin fans inundated the *NME*'s letters page to deem its contents both 'lamentable' and 'a disgrace'. Perhaps some of them had been in the common room at my school and this was their revenge for being forced to listen to the dreamy jingling of the likes of Aztec Camera in 1983.

Stinky rock boys, eh?

19

SORTED FOR E'S & WIZZ

We were somewhere backstage at Glastonbury on the edge of insanity when the drugs failed to make any difference whatsoever. 'Come on Patterson, just write any-fucking-thing!' wailed a demented James Oldham, *NME*'s normally agreeable live reviews editor, his already enormous blue eyes now expanding to electric turquoise Catherine wheels of deadline-dodged anxiety.

He was looming over me, arms folded, as I perched at a PC, hands frozen like the claws of an upturned dead parrot, failing to find a single word to adequately describe what we'd all just seen and heard: Radiohead headline the Pyramid Stage to stunningly elevational effect. It was 2 a.m. on Sunday, the copy deadline was two hours ago and I was in a state of catatonic over-refreshment – cider, bit of spliff (lessons never learned) – despite spending the day on Pyramid Stage duties believing I'd 'paced myself'. Glastonbury '97 was an apocalyptic Rainy One, the festival in peril of outright cancellation the Thursday before due to stages actually sinking. Glastonbury chieftain Michael Eavis avowed the show must go on and so, in the morning, people were *skiing* to the ever-revolting latrines. By Sunday's wee hours everyone was a bit, you know, critically Glastonburied already.

The *NME*'s normally genial gentleman Simon Williams, James's right-hand man at the makeshift backstage production department (clunky nineties desktop computers placed on foldaway garden tables in the corner of a wilting marquee), was approaching apoplexy. 'F' fuck's sake, have some of this!' he implored, wiggling a small plastic bag of white powder. I dipped a finger, licked the metallic 'whizz' and waited for words to bust through the mentally frozen dam like splinters of sharpest ice. Nothing. The paralysis was, if anything, worse, shoulders now hoisting upwards in anxiety where an amphetamine rush should've been. I couldn't *remember* why they'd been so great. *Already*. I'd scribbled notes, of course (the odd song title, the informationally barren phrase 'angels harps akimbo!') but the mind was a descriptive desert. 'Why do I have to describe what they sounded like anyway?' I squawked unreasonably. 'Everybody knows what Radiohead sound like!'

This was, ultimately, the fault of Hunter S. Thompson, the gonzo journalistic godhead who'd made malleable teenage romantics like me believe writing amid a narcotic seizure was not only possible but ultimate proof of a 'proper' rock 'n' roll scribe (and his story, of course, turned out well, i.e. fired a bullet into his own head at the age of sixty-seven).

By 3 a.m., precisely 207 words on Radiohead at Glastonbury

'97 were somehow chiselled from the cranial ice cube and my work was done, soon lying in a saggy tent listening to my whizzy heartbeat hammering in time to the Aphex Twin, who now boomed from a sound system on yonder, ghoul-possessed 'healing' fields. In 1997 everyone, everywhere, was hardcore (they knew 'the score'). Except me.

I was always hopeless at drugs. I was never psychologically robust enough for drugs, and yet I persevered like a stoic climber with one leg, no arms and spinal tuberculosis up a vertical Alpine precipice. Growing through teenhood in Scotland in the early 1980s there was no escape from drugs, permanently present in the local post-punk whirligig. There was access, everywhere, to puffs on spliffs you never paid for, in pub alleyways, in post-pub soirees with the older boys, a world where 'bathtub speed' was as common as Carlsberg Special (my drink of choice, with lime, paid for with saved-up school dinner money, as ever). I'd smoke dope aged fifteen round the house of a thirty-year-old acquaintance, telling the folks I was taking the two family dogs 'for a walk' (today, he'd be imprisoned and I'd be reported to the RSPCA).

Dope seemed harmless enough, more harmless than the Special Brew, busting open those boarded-up psychic windows to a brighter, funnier, *deeper* world, where music's inner magic shimmied into life as if a close-up time-lapse film of a rose from bud to bloom, where thoughts and ideas danced into the brain on hitherto inaccessible yellow brick roads to seemingly powerful revelation. It made the world even more astounding than it was already, turning the contrast on our cosmic existence *right up to eleven*. As well as, for a while, goblin-gigglingly hysterical and almost worth it for when The Fear descended and the incoming possibility of a paranoia-induced stroke.

It barely crossed my mind drugs were either a) illegal or

b) treacherous, because they felt neither, merely part of what it meant to be human, no different to the cavemen who first discovered fermented fruit could make the world pleasingly soft-focused and thus lessen the chill winds of Palaeolithic reality whistling through a threadbare deerskin. Not everyone has a taste for mood-altering potions, but most of us do, and I had more so than most, a believer in altered states and bending the shapes of reality. I may, of course, have inherited it. But neither drugs nor booze turned me into Someone Else Entirely the way it did my mum.

Then again, the effects of acid felt like a speedy trip straight to psychiatric hospital, inducing both the ability to literally see musical notes wafting out of speakers, sometimes in the shape of grinning skulls (especially when blaring the Banshees' 'Hong Kong Garden') and my face melting into grotesque plasticine strings. Both of which happened at my nineteenth birthday party in a pub in Perth where I was thrust, spaghetti-faced, onto the dance floor where my now ghoulish best friends were bawling the Birthday Party's terror-goth shriek-a-long, 'Sex horror vampire ... Release the bats! Release the bats!' Behaviour which is all very well, sort of, when you're nineteen and it's your birthday. Not so impressive when you're a thirty-two-year-old professional journalist in 1997, attempting to write definitive reports for the nation's allegedly most respected music publications.

These on-the-job incidents only happened, though, as a consequence of freelance life, its feast-or-famine nature meaning if you're offered work, you never turn it down. And so, in an era of plentiful job offers, I continuously worked, almost every day from 1992 to 2001, most weekends, many nights, no holidays whatsoever. A second reason was financial: mainly working for the *NME* from '94 onwards meant being paid the equivalent of a ten-year-old Dickensian urchin lodged down a tin mine in 1837.

So when the opportunity arose to 'let loose' on the job you took it – or indeed unravelled completely, like a spiralling ball of wool booted off a ten-storey tower block.

Once, in Germany, the generous gentlemen of Massive Attack enthusiastically encouraged me to smoke weed backstage, a foreign strand so potent I temporarily became insane, convinced the one who never spoke, Mushroom, a man of advanced serenity (tee-total, drug-free and vegan, *in the nineties*), held the secrets not only to human happiness but to the nature of The Universe itself. For one hour he was subjected to the question 'Why!?', as if confronted with a bothersome toddler.

'How can you come into this room and ask me "What is the purpose of life?"' he howled. 'Why ask me? Why should *I* know? I guess it's to do whatever makes you happy, it just feels good to get lost, doesn't it? In whatever you're doing.'

Mortifyingly, I began to weep before breaking into an approximation of the Gang Of Four's 1982 post-punk existential classic, 'We Live As We Dream, Alone' – 'everybody is in tooooo many pieces!' – until the 'interview' time, mercifully for all, ran out.

I should've known so much better: copious booze was enough trouble as it was. In 1997, I rose early for a flight to New York, off to interview the newly solo Gary Barlow, switching on the TV to news of Princess Diana's death. The PR for this trip, Graham, was the world's most dedicated Diana fan, a fellow bulimic whose office desk doubled as a Diana Tribute Shrine. Aboard the plane, the distraught Graham began drinking heavily, so in the spirit of solidarity I joined him. Seven hours later I was bowling towards Terrifying New York Security, fell over, bust open the same cream, 1960s Bakelite vanity case I'd carried on the Urge Overkill job two years previously (dispersing identical contents: fags, knickers, C90 tapes). Soon similarly apprehended, we could not proceed because 'Madame is intoxicated'. Quick-thinking, robust-drinking Graham appeased Security: I was, he explained, one of Princess Diana's devastated 'staff', being specially flown in for an interview tomorrow on Barbara Walters' *Today* show. Security fell for it and we lurched towards New York.

Gary Barlow, the following day, as traumatised by Diana's death as The People back in Britain, was significantly more sober than all of The People in all of Britain in 1997. He displayed signs, already, of the food obsession which plagued his creatively desolate late nineties/early 2000s and turned him into a 17-stone biffer (before the reformed Take That became the biggest band in Britain all over again). 'Ooh I do love a boiled egg 'n' soldiers,' he announced, like a seventy-eight-year-old grandpa, before a reverie over a kids' lolly from his youth, a sprinkle-topped strawberry ice treat concealing a block of chocolate within: 'Ooh,' he swooned, 'you can't beat a Lolly Gobble Choc Bomb ...' (He's been on a diet/exercise/sugar-shunning regime ever since.)

The sunny mid-nineties Britpop party quickly clouded over. During '96, Damon Albarn appeared on the cover of *Q* announcing 'there's a blizzard of cocaine and I hate it', adding, 'everyone's become so blasé, thinking they're so ironic and witty and wandering around with this stupid fucking cokey confidence. Wankers. I mean, I did it but I can't say I was a cocaine addict.' We now know he was a heroin addict instead, the drug which undid his then-girlfriend Justine Frischmann and her Elastica bandmate Donna Matthews, a once cherub-faced twenty-something who appeared in the music press seemingly made of ashes.

By '97 the drugs, for Oasis, were bigger than the music, as witnessed in the lumbering bray of *Be Here Now*, while Pulp's

This Is Hardcore was a seedy, queasy, unfathomably anxious affair. The drugs were getting druggier (ketamine and crack soon permeating warehouse raves, where guns were turning up) and the drinks drinkier. Absinthe, the green-fairy potion which once caused me to attempt to use my keys to enter a flat I'd lived in *three houses previously*, was being imported back to Britain. In '98 I lost not only my mind but my DM boots at The Verve's Haigh Hall 'homecoming show', boots recklessly ripped from my danced-out feet and punted into a ditch, saved that night by irrepressible Scottish chum and *Face* magazine assistant ed Craig McLean, who physically carried me over some swampy bog to safety ('no surprises': I didn't complete *any* kind of review for that one).

Music festivals, meanwhile, always purpose-built for oblivion, were deadly realms of zombification for those of us who were *just no good at the drugs*. In the 'high point' year of '95 I had a chemically calamitous low point, backstage at Glastonbury. There was *Melody Maker*'s force-of-nature and soon to be twenty-first-century feminist hero Caitlin Moran, on E, hat (and possibly head) set to *Wizard of Oz*, eyes the size of Kansas; there was Graham Linehan, the amenable Irishman who co-invented *Father Ted*, careening out of a Portaloo bawling 'Oooorbitaaaaal!' while sprinting towards the dance tent, even though Orbital had played the night before; there was much loved, award-winning scribe for *The Face* Gavin Hills, one of the smartest men in the media, aged twenty-nine, wearing a Mars bar smeared all over his face and breakdancing on his head, twirling upside down on the grass to some inner electro wig-out. Thus inspired, I took some drugs just like everybody else – a pill I knew nothing about. When it seemingly failed to work, I took another one.

It was twenty minutes before the first wave of nausea hit, a further ten before the contents of my large intestine (not all that much: I'd forgotten my tea as usual) projectile vomited outwards across the bottom of several strangers' trousers as I hit the ground, paralysed by the most intense wave of paranoia I'd ever known, gripping the grass, convinced I was falling off this insanely speeding, spinning world.

Through the throng, the concerned face of Gavin Hills suddenly appeared, Mars bar wiped away; a vigilant man of advanced humanity who'd won awards for war reporting, he knew a person-in-peril when he saw one. 'It's just a wave, it'll pass!' he reassured above the booming backstage drugginess. For the next six hours – *six full hours* – Gavin walked me through the fields of Glastonbury like a man who'd brought a crash-test dummy on his festival holidays (one dressed as a Russian stormtrooper), his arm steadfast round my shoulders, where my head was bobbing, feet dragging like the undead, legs in a permanent concertinaed buckle. This completely ruined his night and saved my sanity, having just accidentally taken, as I subsequently found out, cataclysmically strong Ecstasy liberally cut with heroin (they called this 'smacky E').

I'm not sure I ever thanked him enough and soon it would be too late: less than two years later on 20 May 1997, days after his thirty-first birthday, Gavin Hills slipped off a rock while fishing on the Cornish coast on holiday, and drowned. In 1997, in the ongoing era of new age hippies, crystal fiddling and 'coincidence' hokey (theories not so long ago espoused by Prince), this was the first time I can ever remember shouting to myself in a voice of profoundly shocked dismay: 'Everything happens for a reason? MY ARSE!'

In 1996, certainly, something had happened for no reason other than trouble often finds you if you hang around rock 'n' roll hobos: in Glasgow, reviewing Britpop also-rans 3 Colours Red, a party began in my Hilton Hotel room, the band also staying there alongside their PR, my friend, a twenty-two-year-old Scotswoman known as 'Susie From Creation' (Records), an indie-rock temptress (and possessor of a law degree) in a wiggy fake-fur coat. Post-show, I'd taken what's known as 'a cheeky wee half' of E and now the band's guitarist, leather-trewed Chris McCormack, who believed he was Mick Jones out of The Clash, was blowing cigarette smoke straight into the ceiling smoke detector, for a laugh. It took a microsecond for the Hilton Hotel staff to fail to see the funny side and seven minutes for three thistle-faced members of the never knowingly under-intimidating Strathclyde Police to ram-raid straight through the door, demanding to know 'Who's in charge?'

That would be Susie From Creation and so, for the next five minutes, to the heightened suspicions of my chemically enhanced mind, the two policemen and one policewoman blatantly belittled the comely Susie as if she was a visiting teenage prostitute when she was, in fact, An Actual Lawyer In Their Midst. Objecting to their jib by shouting 'bastards!' and the like, I learned a lifetime's lesson in how speedily (and painfully), should you meddle with The Filth, you will be handcuffed from behind, frog-marched off, flung horizontally like a rucksack into the back of a marked police car and flung with equal vigour, face-down, onto a concrete mattress in a subterranean police cell 'til 7.15 a.m.

The next time I saw Chris from 3 Colours Red was two weeks later, working for *The Clothes Show Magazine* in London. This involved dressing up in a nun's full habit to go shopping in Ann Summers' Perv Emporium to document the amusing results (this is what it takes, viewers, to be a reliable freelance 'all-rounder'). Seated in a café next door to Ann Summers, still fully dressed as the fugitive perv-nun, I was recognised immediately despite the crop-faced framing of the requisite tight-fit wimple. 'What the fuck,' squawked Chris, reasonably, 'are you *doing*?'

Truth is, I didn't really have a clue.

By the end of the 1990s, most of my oldest friends were

married, or having kids, or forging ahead with highly stable and even highly paid careers. Evelyn had moved to London, now a powerhouse finance executive (technically The Enemy to each other, which we both found hugely amusing) who I'd meet up with in the Slug & Lettuce near her beautiful flat in Islington: she with the *Financial Times* under her arm, me with the *NME*. Only one of The Four Of Us was *still* avoiding reality.

In 2009, twelve years after the Great Radiohead *NME* Glastonbury Review Debacle, Michael Eavis officially named Radiohead's Glastonbury 1997 appearance the greatest performance in Glastonbury's entire history. It was, he evangelised, 'the most inspiring festival gig in thirty years. Their performance that night, particularly of the song "No Surprises", was very, very moving.'

In 2015, I blew the cardigan of dust from my Glastonbury '97 edition of the *NME* and perused, for the first time since writing it, the 207-word review I eventually chipped from my icy cranium.

I was so mortified, I gave myself cramp in an ankle from a foot-contorting cringe. It contained an attempt at poetry, 'a celestial beam of atmospherics', almost the entire track-listing of *OK Computer* (possibly howled at me by James Oldham and Simon Williams), another attempt at poetry, 'prog-rock gone to heaven and impaled on the strings of Venus' harp', and included the now-legendary interruption from Thom Yorke:

'Right!' he hollers, back for the glittering, firework-fuelled encore of 'The Tourist' and 'Fade Out'. 'Turn those two blue lights at the front off fucking now. I couldn't see a fucking soul for the whole of the show. I wanna see 'em!'

I then noted, psychedelically, that the mud stretching upwards into the hilly Glastonbury horizon had all, somehow, turned purple (true) before observing guitarist Jonny Greenwood was wearing his onstage guitar-thrashing arm-brace, which he always wore to stave off recurring injury, and announced, conclusively, 'cripple-rock rules!'

Cripple-rock rules?

Cripple-rock rules!?

No wonder I'd never offer my 'services' to *NME*'s Glastonbury live desk again. Though I did offer them to the paper's Reading Festival live desk two years later and soon found myself in hospital, crippled myself, in an arm-brace considerably more substantial than anything Jonny Greenwood ever required. I'd also, by then, split up with The Dancer, been left bankrupt and seen my mother sent to prison.

Just as well I didn't believe, *anymore*, in the ways of the Karma Police . . .

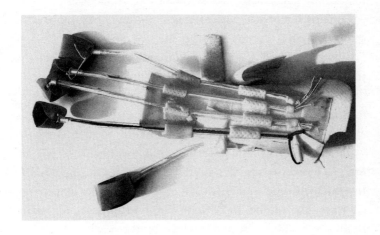

20

ONE FINGER, ONE THUMB,
KEEP MOVING

Life with The Dancer turned out to be disastrous. After six months of dazzlement by his amusing persona, cartoon sixties hairdo and really very dapper shirt-wear, the slide was agonisingly long. We lived together for eighteen months from 1996 to 1998, by which time he'd proved himself even more jealous and possessive than Rock 'N' Roll Babylon: a psychotic-level paranoiac and sinisterly effective control freak convinced I was sleeping with *every* man I met. While he danced in clubs with twinkle-toed flair (just part of his once-deceiving charm) he'd soon turn to me, sparks crackling from electric-blue eyes, and say 'You're looking at that guy,' when I was transfixed, instead, by particularly fabulous shoes.

Perhaps I mistook possessiveness for love, like some of us do (repeatedly). It was he who was the consistent cheat, as I'd discover when we split (the psychologists might call this projection), a man who, when he asked me out on our debut date to Brighton, 'borrowed' (never gave back) the money to pay for the trip from the woman he was seeing at the time. He was also a similarly Babylonian financial vampire, an alleged creative who barely worked and within months was unable to pay any rent, so I paid two rents, in north London, on a negligible *NME* freelance 'income' and ran out of money altogether by the time we were finally done. In 1997, on a train to an Essex hinterland to review a club-night performance by the newly solo Robbie Williams (then a bleach-haired, drug-possessed, psychological cyclone performing a punk rock version of 'Back For Good' alongside 'Angels'), fellow *NME* freelancer and empathic human being Barbara Ellen (a stranger) gave me a tenner so I could buy a drink, with enough money for the journey home. (I still owe her to this day.)

Why so many women who should know better – reasonably educated, defiantly independent, outwardly spirited – fall for the controllers is one of the most complex mysteries of the human psyche, but The Dancer did all the things which typifies their ilk, primarily the incremental shut-down of your independence everywhere else, certainly time spent with friends, *especially* male friends (causing so much grief you simply give up the fight).

It was famously vague tinkerbell Kylie Minogue, of all people, who once described the controllers beautifully, after she'd newly escaped from one herself: 'it's like they're drawn to the birds of paradise', she told me, 'and then they put you in a box, and your colours fade'.

When we split up, we were forced to keep staying in the Kentish Town flat, sleeping with a metaphorical Hadrian's Wall bolted through the middle of the bed, financially unable to individually move, becoming embittered old acquaintances who barely tolerated each other. I'd have rational conversations with him about how much I hated him, as if this psychological havoc was normal. Maybe, too, I didn't think I deserved any better. (In 1990, the year after my father died, seeking solace, I visited a professional astrologer – a lingering obsession from adolescence. On a busy day of clients, when she pulled out my chart the look on her face said, *'Oh no'*. She said three things I'll never forget: 'There's a big problem with your mother?' 'Your father is a disappointed man.' 'You could have everything, there's a banquet here. And you're living on beans on toast.' I wept all the way home to Stephendale Road. I probably had beans on toast that night just to prove her right and probably to spite myself.)

The year The Dancer and I split up, I was bankrupt. We had to do a runner, together, from the Kentish Town flat with the broken bedroom window (he'd put a fist through it one day in rage) having spent the day packing a minimal set of belongings for a midnight flit while crawling along the floors, the only way to avoid the bailiffs parked outside, looking upwards through the windows for signs of arrears-paying life. (I had to leave behind, to my devastation, the stack system my parents had bought me for my twenty-first birthday, which had travelled with me to London back in 1986.) That week, I'd visited a fruit and veg seller on the pavement outside, told him I had 67p and what could that buy me to make soup? Not that I knew how to make soup. I had to call Ali in Scotland to find out. I was thirty-three years old. And could not believe I had *done this to myself*.

Insanely, the only place I had to go was where The Dancer was going – I couldn't bear to burden my friends, who I hadn't seen for months anyway – to a two-bed flat-share with his friends in Camden, where he was staying in the living room, and where I also stayed for three weeks until I'd saved for a deposit on a flatshare of my own. Thus began years of moving house turmoil and erratic flatmates, including the radiophonic sound engineer who also rarely worked (a friend of The Dancer's – *fancy that*), a friendly though demented eccentric who spent his life drinking cherry beer and listening to cosmic jazz madman Sun Ra at deafening volume.

By summer 1999 I was at least solvent again, soon off to review the Reading Festival for *NME*, determined to avoid any Radiohead '97-style brain freeze incident. I stayed sober through the Friday, wrote the review as I went along, filed the words by midnight and skipped from the Review Cabin to drink three celebratory pints of cider in swift, thirsty succession. I'd forgotten, however, to have my tea. Again.

To the 'rescue' lurched a chipper chum from the *Melody Maker* proffering a tasty snack, something I'd only recently heard of called a Mitsubishi E. I took a cheeky wee half because, you know, I knew my limitations (even if this had catapulted me facedown into a Glaswegian police cell in the past). Soon, I was jaunting along the pavement away from the festival, on the way to the annual party in a Reading hotel, when a deadly combination of stupid shoes, booze, drugs and hands stuffed deep inside the pockets of my favourite jacket (fluorescent yellow imitation fireman's jacket with metal button hooks) had the inevitable effect.

A microsecond later I was on my back in the road, having simply tripped up off the kerb, now staring at my yellow-encased arm in a shape I did not recognise.

Plummeting ground-wards, the outside of my upper right arm had hit the edge of the kerb, which broke the arm clean in two, now with an extra bend – like having an extra elbow in your upper arm. As I'd hit the kerb's edge, I heard a sound in my arm, as you do on drugs, like an electrical charge running out, which is exactly what it was.

My companions were two of the greatest drugs nutters in the music industry in the 1990s (quite an accolade), a record company executive with a corking regional accent (too much of a bigwig to name here), and an *NME* buddy, Andy Capper, who was so good at drugs (and probably sex) he'd go on to become global editor of *Vice* magazine. I had an enormous crush on Andy, who was *way too tough for me*, the sort of person who, two years on from this average night, went on a personal quest for The Perfect High, which he found in a combination of coke, weed, Oxycontin, acid, MDMA powder, Ecstasy and Xanax, 'but,' as he told me at the time, 'you *are* fucked, heheheh!' This was not the sort of person to invite into his life any form of authority and yet this was the person who phoned the ambulance, stayed with me on the ground, and watched as an approximately nineteen-year-old paramedic loomed over me with a gigantic pair of industrial scissors and said, 'Is it OK if I cut your coat off?'

I was paralysed, certainly, but being on drugs could feel no searing pain (not yet), my only thought being this was some kind of public fashion test: what did I care about most? My favourite jacket? Or my arm?

'JUST CUT THE COAT OFF!'

After an audible gasp from those present at the full extent of the extra bend in the arm, our teenage lifesaver then loomed some more.

'Miss Patterson,' he announced, 'I have to inform you that you've broken your humerus bone.' I managed the quip, 'I bet you've waited your whole life to say that, son.'

'And have you been drinking, or taken any drugs?' a grown-up paramedic now wanted to know.

'Two and a half pints of cider,' I decided was all he needed to know.

Andy came with me in the ambulance, and into the hospital, where he was interviewed in a consultancy side-room as I waited for a doctor, an act of heroism I appreciate to this day considering he was so paranoid about all the drugs he had in his pockets he'd necked them all in the ambulance and was, therefore, significantly tripping in what surely felt like a CID interrogation cell. (Still tripping the next morning, he fell asleep with the bath running and flooded his hotel room. No wonder Andy, today, has long given up the drugs: he surely used up, early, any 'reasonable' lifetime's quota.) Soon a doctor actually called Dr Goodman appeared, cheerfully greeting me with 'Ah, the reveller!' and all the injury news. As well as the clean break, which he showed me on the X-ray – the bone in two, with an inch between the sections, snapped at a jaunty angle – there was extensive nerve damage, which would take several months to heal, if it healed at all. And if it *didn't* heal my arm would be rendered useless and require snipping clean off at the top.

I blinked into his matter-of-fact, doctorly face. 'You're telling me I might lose my arm?'

'You might, yes,' he nodded. 'But you might be lucky.'

I *might* be lucky? I did not consider myself a 'lucky' person. No matter that night round Spike Milligan's house, whose sense of humour in the face of medical calamity I was now urgently trying to source.

'Um ... and are you right-handed?' Dr Goodman enquired, as I stared into my future as the one-armed drummer out of Def Leppard of pop journalism, without any of his wealth. *OF COURSE I WAS RIGHT-HANDED.* The right hand on the end of the arm I was about to lose being the hand I did pretty much everything with and an essential component in the concept of, you know, typing on a keyboard, or writing in a notebook, or operating the array of no doubt professionally essential technology in my suddenly redundant future. And I was already way too old for the Paralympics and hopeless at sport anyway.

I'd have the chance, at least, to get used to the one-armed me: for as many months as it took for the nerve to prove, almost certainly, it wasn't coming back to life, my hand would remain completely paralysed, drooping off the end of my broken arm like a trowel made of dead man's flesh. The upper broken arm, meanwhile, was encased in a white, plastic, state-of-the-art orthopaedic arm-brace – pretty *Robocop* cool, as it happens – the wrist and hand in a really-very-uncool flesh-coloured plastic splint, from which sprouted five metal prongs, each with a finger-lifting sling to aid any recovering finger movement. It looked like Freddy Krueger's hand and would make kids in the street openly shriek.

It was only in the morning, all drugs worn off, I realised: this was *serious agony*, a shockingly deep, inner gnaw of savage pain. A pain only intensified via the transport back to London which Andy had now also arranged despite his neurological disarray – his mate's Del Boy Trotter-esque work van, which was fitted with zero suspension. I gripped onto my left knee with the hand that still worked throughout the forty-mile bone-shaker journey. For the next month I had to sleep upright; the pain was unbearable otherwise, despite taking painkillers so strong I was neurologically living underwater. This carried on for seven months, while still attempting to work, because I had to: being an untethered person with no sense of responsibility at the age of thirty-four, I wasn't insured for anything. So I typed for seven months with the index finger of the left hand, which made transcribing interviews as tediously time-consuming as emptying out a bath one molecule at a time.

Some other things you discover you cannot do when you've bust your arm and your hand: tie your shoelaces; wash yourself properly in the bath (because you can't get the arm-brace wet); grate cheese, prepare or cook any food that isn't a bowl of cereal or a ready-made meal-for-one; wash the dishes; change your bedclothes. A lot like watching yourself, in fact, turn into a bum. Paralympians: you are more heroic than we will *ever* know.

One day, somehow, the newly 'knitting' humerus bone suddenly split apart again, causing a rupture of pain so violent I wailed all the way to a north London A&E, alone, in a cab, and returned, exhausted, with even stronger painkillers, back to one-finger typing Hell.

Eventually, the bone knitted and the nerve *did* return to life. Even if my hand, in cold weather, still feels like a trowel made of dead man's flesh. But it *works*, and that's all I need it to do. It's the sort of experience which teaches you vital life lessons and this one was klaxon-clear: your version of physical normality is all you'll ever need. *Really*. Plus: I never took a Class A drug again.

Perhaps The Reading Arm Break Incident, I mused back then, would prove the corner I needed to turn. After this, The Dancer and the bankruptcy, maybe everything, now, was about to become OK. A whole new millennium, full of hope, was approaching. I even, by then, had a mum.

Aged thirty-four I finally had a mother/daughter relationship in my life. It was a weird one, almost like two acquaintances from different countries who hang out with each other occasionally, for some old times' sake connection they can barely remember. Unlike the lifelong relationships with my actual friends it felt like we'd no shared history: there'd been early childhood, with the constant thermometer, then late childhood with the booze and The Fear, then my teenage years where we were both as obliviously wasted as each other and then I left the country. And then my brother died. And then my dad died. And the chaos escalated.

She'd struggled badly through the nineties. There had been

a minimally-slit wrists cry-for-help incident at Christmas 1991. Abusive phone calls at Christmas 1994. But there were also spells of AA and the will to keep on living. She was, at least, financially stable, my dad had made certain of that. His pension plans were robust and she'd been mortgage-free for years. I always knew he'd look after her forever, and he did.

She was now living alone in a new, three-bedroom, semi-detached house on the outskirts of Perth. A relationship with her in the mid-nineties had been impossible: on the phone she was either deafeningly silent or venomously furious, alienating everyone around her, my siblings included, her life sinking into the static, inter-circulating oxbow lake of alcoholic depression. During one spell, we didn't talk for eighteen months. The bottom was approaching.

It was during the years of Britpop bedlam, in the year Ali was married in Scotland (the other three of The Four of Us were bridesmaids, Rimmy was there, Jackie was there, a scorching day in August '95 unfolding in sustained hysteria, in what would come to be known as the greatest wedding anyone had ever been to), that my mum finally hit the floor. After persistent calls to the ambulance service and the punching of a paramedic, she was arrested, charged, found guilty of a menace-to-society misdemeanour (obstruction of vital public services) and sent to Cornton Vale Women's Prison in Stirling, the judge assessing her with a pitiless eye, declaring her 'the authoress of your own downfall'. Her story made the local paper. My brother Billy was furious, ringing me in London: it was my duty as a journalist to expose this miscarriage of justice.

He was right: she should never have been in prison, she was *sick*, with the brutal disease of addiction. She'd become a widowed pensioner at the age of fifty-nine, and was now a broken, broken-hearted, sixty-seven-year-old woman who could barely breathe (self-inflicted as the chain smoking was), living the vast majority of her days a quiet, lonely life, rejecting the help of everyone around her. When she fell into The Hole, she turned to the ambulance service for help, knowing they'd have to respond to her calls. After a mercifully few months in prison, rehabilitation services were offered which, to her enormous credit, she accepted. With no communication between us, I'd no idea whether grudgingly or not.

In September that year, a letter arrived, wholly unexpectedly, at Seven Sisters Road addressed to Miss Sylvia Anne Patterson.

Malta House
1 Malta Terrace
Edinburgh EH4 1HR
Sunday 24th Sept.

Dearest Sylvia,

Just a 'wee' note to let you know I am thinking about you and hoping it finds you well & happy. You will see by the above address where I am.

This house is a rehabilitation house & offers a sixteen week course of intensive teaching on the horror of alcohol.

The standard of teaching Sylv in my opinion is next door to University standard and I am now sober since the 31st May + feel a lot better already. My memory is slowly returning + I find a bit more settled generally. I have gone through complete torture between one thing and another but feel when I return to Perth 23rd Dec. that I will be a bit more like the Mum you had.

I wrote to Jacqueline + received a letter back giving me all her news. She also enclosed a few snaps which were taken on her holiday. I was delighted to read all about Alison's wedding + that you yourself looked like a princess.

I feel sad that I knew so little about Alison getting married

+ that I didn't honour her day by a wedding gift but in time I
will make amends about this.

I am hoping Sylvia that you are still working away + that
you will find time to drop me a letter with all your news. Look
after yourself pet.

I love you dearly.

Meantime my

Fondest Love + Affection

Mum x

I found this letter while hunting through boxes for photos
in autumn 2015 and read it as if for the first time. I couldn't
remember seeing it ever before. Maybe I'd read it once, quickly,
and simply filed it away, unable to deal with the estrangement.
Maybe it was circumstantial: in September 1995 she might have
been sober since 31 May but I most definitely was not.

I felt a pain when I read it like some unknown chamber
collapsing inside my chest. I heard her voice again so clearly,
her writing style always so oddly detached, maybe partly a
generational characteristic. I saw, once again, her idiosyncratic
way with the word 'and'. The way she signed off every card
and letter she ever wrote throughout her life with, "Fondest
love + affection". She wasn't an emotional communicator, never
gushed in any way – I don't remember her ever saying, not once,
'I love you dearly'. Did she mean it, I wondered? I couldn't be
sure. I wondered if she believed Jackie's description of me in
the purple bridesmaid gown – 'a princess' (as if!) – or if she
always thought of me, forever, as 'the monster from outer space'.
I thought about how there was no apology for the traumas of
those particular years but then there was never any apology in
any year and her residence there in Malta House, in an alien
environment surrounded by strangers, was proof, surely, she
was sorry enough. She probably felt, as she always used to

say, 'hand-picked' – for pain, by the universe. The unspoken, in-between words, meanwhile, seemed to me louder than her matter-of-fact lines, an atmospheric sense of sadness, loneliness and regret.

It had taken me until my early thirties to see the bigger picture, of a desperately wounded woman at core, whose own dad had committed suicide, who was ten years old when World War II meant carrying a gas mask to school, every day, for years. She lost three brothers early, one in a cycling accident as a child, one a soldier killed in the war, one a brilliant academic and diagnosed schizophrenic who she personally nursed in a care home for the last ten years of his life. In the barbaric psychiatric experiments of the 1960s he'd been lobotomised and was left, as we used to describe it in the 1970s, 'a cabbage'.

After the post-prison rehabilitation she stayed sober, became a member of AA (The Serenity Prayer was framed on the wall above her armchair) and I began visiting her at home again, where I'd sit, once more, at her feet in the living room, cigarette smoke still twirling through her bouffant hairdo as we watched the documentaries of David Attenborough. She'd even started to go on holiday: to France with Jackie and family where she proved herself dangerously naive, opening up her purse to foreign shopkeepers and asking them to help themselves (possibly the result of long-term toxin damage). She travelled to Malta with a friend from AA, to South Africa to visit her big sister, Auntie Nan, who'd emigrated in the 1960s, where she accidentally, persistently, set off all the security alarms. Back in Perth she'd have the television on all day, she noted plainly, 'just for the movement', hers a mostly lonely existence day-to-day which she never complained about, not once. I think, if I was her, I would've smoked myself to death, too.

At Christmas 1999, when I came home wearing the arm-brace, the sling and the Freddy Krueger hand, she teetered out of her seat to greet me with her right hand adopting a similar 'sling' position. 'What are you doing, Mum!?' I laughed.

She looked down, unaware. 'Oh! Must be a mother's instinct!' It was certainly a mother's *empathy*. She was always a mum to me when I was sick, after all. I think I finally knew she'd been a mother to me all along. She had a merciless illness herself. She tried her best. Maybe I failed her as much as she failed me. Maybe none of the madness and the sadness was anyone's fault. And to this day, whenever I put a pair of clean, cosy, tight-fitting socks on, I can feel her professional nurse's hands rubbing confidently along the soles of my feet, making sure all the wrinkles are gone: it's a vivid, intense, indelible memory of profound comfort.

If I had become a one-armed person, the next eighteen months would've been dimensions more intolerable than they'd turn out to be, an eighteen months where I definitely *needed to carry some boxes*. The new millennium, full of hope, was now full of constant, old-school hopelessness. An extensive run of unfortunate events starring shady estate agents and criminal landlords meant I was forced to move home nine times in eighteen months from 1999 to 2001 through the perils of metropolitan renting: ceilings falling in, kitchens besieged by rats, bronchitis-inducing dampness, one freezing canal-side stone-walled hovel with bedrooms like actual prison cells and a flat not yet actually built from a hollowed-out derelict chocolate factory. This eighteen months of soul-shredding turmoil, following several years of bedlam, resulted in a single appointment with an NHS counsellor fearing I'd finally gone mad. In my mid-thirties I was living alone, working for a minimal wage, and hadn't lived in the same place for more than three months for as long as I could remember. The Irish girls of Stephendale Road were both now mothers, Ali and Jill had their second daughters, and I was living like a hobo in derelict buildings, drinking vodka to keep warm. I babbled all this to the counsellor. She asked questions about my relationship with my mother. After twenty minutes, during which she'd gleaned the 'born with no skin' information (resulting in my first six months cocooned in an incubator), she unveiled her professional conclusion: my problem was I hadn't 'been held enough as an infant'. I catapulted from my seat and bolted out the door bawling, 'I don't need a psychologist, I need a decent place to live! And a job!'

It was while living in the canal-side hovel with no heating, where I'd been placed in 'emergency accommodation' after finding on arrival that the flat I was moving into hadn't yet been built, that the *NME* called with an unexpected commission.

Four years on from Oasis playing to half a million people at Knebworth, there was a new Biggest Band In Britain. Who weren't even British.

And who were, frankly, the worst pop group in the history of recorded music.

21

THAT'S JUST THE WAY IT IS

February 2000. Four years after Underworld's 'Born Slippy' from the *Trainspotting* soundtrack reached number two, three years after The Verve's 'The Drugs Don't Work' reached number one, two years after the Manic Street Preachers also made number one with 'If You Tolerate This Your Children Will Be Next' and it was like Britpop, dance music, the-nation-on-drugs and *the entire 1990s* had never happened, already. Pop hadn't merely evolved in its cyclical way, it had looked back over its shoulder with the 'yah-boo sucks!' of a petulant runaway seven-year-old and rebuilt the world to its own Day-Glo, 2D liking. And what it liked the very *very* best was America. Which Britain now attempted to emulate.

Throughout 1999, tots' pop music had spread like measles on the torso of the global mainstream, an outbreak of vigorous commercialism for the under-tens and hormonally explosive tweens. Some of it was joyous and harmless, some class-pop tremendous, some cheese-pop atrocious with a glaze of Gordon Small's K.I.S.S. and all of it an atmospheric takeover starring Britney Spears, *NSYNC, Steps, Ricky Martin, S Club 7, Christina Aguilera, 5ive, the Backstreet Boys, solo Robbie Williams and the end days of the Spice Girls, whose unexpectedly enormous global success inspired the new American pop boom in the first place. But the biggest 'pop' group of them all by February 2000, the most successful musical entity of the contemporary age (certainly in Britain) was mimsy Irish boyband newcomers Westlife.

Boyzone had been one thing: namby-pamby teen-pop in ye olde tradition with a cherub in the middle, Ronan Keating, aged sixteen (albeit with the soul of a forty-year-old marketing executive). Westlife, however, were sculpted from an obelisk of purist cynicism, purpose-built to replace Boyzone (and co-managed by Ronan and ex-Boyzone manager Louis Walsh, in case anyone failed to realise it) with a hitherto unimaginable USP: no proper-pop qualities whatsoever.

Westlife were tune-free, sex-free, glum-faced balladeers for funerals, slumped on stools, who creaked out of their rocking chairs once per song, at the inevitable surge of the key-change. Where much of tots' pop, visually, was vibrant, Westlife dressed uniformly in grey, black or white: five dreary young men of no discernible personality, deliberately (as a ruse to cause no offence), known to me in the year of David Beckham's emergence as a floppily blond-haired divinity as three David Beckhams, a *Just 17* 'hunk' and the daft one with the big lips.

A swift ten months after the release of their debut single, they were an actual pop phenomenon about to have their fifth number one single with the greasy ballad 'Fool Again', winners of HMV's Record Of The Year 1999 with the soon-to-be-*X Factor* boyband 'standard' 'Flying Without Wings'. Inevitably, they'd been 1999's Christmas number one with withered renditions of Abba's 'I Have A Dream' and Terry Jacks' death-pop debacle 'Seasons In The Sun'. They'd already sold two million albums, needed no help selling kerzillions more and yet felt it in their unstoppable interests to talk to the *NME*. So it was up to me – in the old 'gunslinging' *NME* tradition – to finish them off forever. And seeing as I lived in a derelict building and was in no way bitter (hem hem), I was up for an old-school joust . . .

There were three of them in the bedroom of Suite 621 of a semi-posh London hotel, relaxed and breezy as they draped themselves around the room: Bryan McFadden, nineteen, one of the three David Beckhams, a former McDonald's security guard slouched on a chair; Shane Filan, twenty, the *Just 17* 'hunk' and ex-trainee accountant on an opposite chair; and Kian Egan, nineteen, another David Beckham and ex-kissogram who was once in a rock band called Pyromania, strewn across a king-size bed with his face clearly set to 'suspicious'.

Westlife were talking to the *NME* because they wished to 'expand our audience', were certain the readers loved them on the inside but were 'too cool' to confess. 'There is,' noted Kian, gravely, 'some great rock guitar on our ballads.'

They proved themselves, immediately, impervious to cheek.

'A lot of people probably do think we're shite,' agreed Bryan, merrily, 'the same as a lot of people like us.'

'Everybody's got their own opinion at the end of the day,' nodded Shane, 'and if people wanna think we're crap and a waste of time, that's fine.'

(Not much of a fight so far, eh viewers?)

Westlife were *inevitable*, a true 'product' of their time. They were the progeny of the Spice Girls, who'd pioneered the aggressively marketed 'band as brand' (still an emerging phrase), whose images had been seared on lollipops and lunch boxes since 1997 as pop became ever more image-led, shiny and superficial, as uber-consumerism not only hijacked culture but *became* culture itself.

The Man, in 2000, seemingly on the stroke of millennial midnight, was now running every show on earth, corporate-speak infiltrating the everyday office with its ululations on blue skies, leverage and calibrated expectations. Money was now the only game in the global entertainment town. Westlife were less a pop group, more a marketing idea, the first enormous new group of the twenty-first century to represent pop's incoming new values: not only the perennial lures of money, success and fame, but purposely conservative personas, the lawless ideologies of the rock 'n' roll nineties crunched underfoot by the choreographed dance routines of Steps in Britain and then-Bible-fondling, no-sex-before-marriage-advocating Britney Spears in America.

Westlife were the *straightest* of them all, five innately conventional young men to whom the world, society and culture operated beyond their control. Exactly twenty-three times that day Westlife justified themselves with the phrases 'that's just the way it is' and/or 'that's the way life is'. And, once, bawled, 'It's just this age now and that's the way it is!' They were, they piped proudly, 'a modern-day boyband' and as such were the face of modern-day pop. So there was nothing else for it.

Come on then Westlife, who wants a fight!?

Westlife: '.........'

Shane: 'Men don't fight women, that's unfair.'

What's The Point of you, do you think?

Kian: 'We like to sing.'

Shane: 'And to make a lot of people happy. And we do, definitely.'

D'you think people would be equally happy with a Topic and a packet of crisps?

Shane: 'Our ballads, they're meaningful, they relate to people's lives, cross over to a lot of topics.'

(Help!) How far are you reaching into people's souls, d'you think?

Bryan: 'I think you know when your song's reached the people when you hear things back, like, that your song's been used at a funeral. (chuffed) Our first single, "Swear It Again", in Ireland, was voted The Most Popular Funeral Song!'

Pthrthrhth! Funeral pop! Westdeath! Ghostlife!

Bryan (remaining chuffed): 'And Most Popular Wedding Song. That's weird, like. That's, like, black and white, y'knowhatImean?'

You don't feel pop music should be about youth, celebration, escapism and life? As opposed to death?

Kian: 'But the youth still buy it! And for the older audience it's bringing out their youth again.'

Here, we had a verbal duel over the all-pervasive concept of karaoke-pop and the vocal giftage (or otherwise) of Celine Dion, where I was reduced to declaring the conclusive fact, 'she's *definitely* shite'.

Bryan (annoyed): 'You can't say her singing talent is shite.'

It's technically proficient yodelling for dead people!

Bryan: 'You can't say she's shite if people love her! People don't buy a shite song.'

Kian: 'You can't brand something as shite because it's not to your personal taste!'

And so, in forty-five swift seconds, Westlife had deftly binned the entire history of cultural critique, forever. I tried to be reasonable, discussing the perils of the era of aggressive marketing only to be assured this was 'a good thing'.

'I understand what you're saying,' mused Shane. 'Especially now, most pop groups kind of know their destiny as soon as they sign a record deal and it's all because of how good your record company is, the whole circle moves together. Before, if it was a rock group and they were good they'd do well. But, if you took all that away, all the marketing, you wouldn't see the songwriters of today who are writing for us and Celine Dion and Mariah Carey. There are so many good songs out there *because* of marketing, a lorra, lorra good songs now because songwriters that haven't got the talent to sing are getting a chance to get their songs out there through a marketed band. It's good, because at the end of the day, it's about good music and keeping the people happy.'

Aha! 'Keeping the people happy.' Is that the same thing as 'keeping the people sedated'?

Westlife: ' . . . . '

I shouldn't have expected, really, any Richey Manic-style minds. We discussed, instead, the death of any kind of cultural revolution, as I wept at the sky, 'We're doomed!'

'Yeah,' agreed Shane, 'it's not allowed anymore is it? I think the bottle's gone. The bottle's gone to what The Beatles used to do, the Sex Pistols. And U2.'

Perhaps you'd like to take some of the blame for that?

Shane: 'Well it's a very small minority of people that are complainin' that rock is gone, because it's the kids of the nineties that love pop.'

'If you want to buy a rock song,' snorted Kian, 'go into the music shop and buy it. It's not gone, it's just not slapped all over the TV like pop is.'

What's the difference between you and Boyzone?

Shane: 'About ten years. Heheheh!'

Nicky looks a lot like Ronan, for a start. Aren't you crying out for the faintest, flimsiest sense of yourselves?

Bryan: 'But we try to be as different as we can from each other! I'm the tall, fat one, he's the small one ... there's only however many different colours of hair so it's gonna be blond or black.'

I'm talking about individuality as a band! What about personality?

Shane (becoming more Irish by the second): 'That's you! *You're* getting caught up in marketin'! We're not about havin' a Ginger Spice, a Posh Spice, we're about singin'!'

But even that, at least, would be FUN, don't you see?!

Shane: 'But that's not what we're here for!'

Well, indeed!

Bryan (incredulously): 'Nicky looks like Ronan? He's born that way! We didn't market him to look like Ronan. We didn't market me or Kian or Nicky to look like David Beckham.'

Yes you did. You're the Dolly The Sheep of boy bands!

Shane (appalled): 'Have you actually listened to our CD?'

'Seasons In The Sun' is the worst song ever written. (Er, apart from Chris de Bleeurgh's 'The Lady In Red'.) *And it's now a soaraway Christmas tune about cancer. Cheers!*

Bryan: 'Well, we actually said at the start we were never gonna do a cover, ever, that was our one thing.'

Pthrht!

Bryan: 'But then Louis Walsh, our manager, had been sayin' for the last ten years, if that record was released it would be a massive hit. And it was our biggest selling single. But I personally don't like it.'

(Pummelling self in face to make sure this is not a 'dream') You're saying you sing songs even YOU don't like in the name of 'success'?

Shane: 'Well, I didn't like the original. I must be honest. I only remember it as a football anthem (arms aloft) "We had joy! We had fun! We're off to the USA!"'

Kian: 'It sold seven million records worldwide regardless whether you like it or not. I thought the original was crap, myself. But we'll never not try anything, so we tried it and ours made it better. And 75 per cent of people agree!'

You're not even camp, explain yourselves.

Bryan and Kian: 'Because we're not gay.' (Except, it turned out, for the daft one with the big lips, Mark Feehily, who finally came out in 2005.)

Kian: 'We don't want to be camp, we are what we are.'

But it's your duty, don't you see? It's pop fantasticness! It's magical, liberational fun!

Kian: 'So? We're not takin' the piss here. That's the difference, we're doing this as a serious job.'

What about SEX? What about EXCITEMENT?

Shane: 'Sexy, exciting? As in a bit mad, like? A bit wild? Well, a lot of older women come to our concerts.'

Oh. God.

Shane: 'It's true! And that's a good thing in itself. We've covered that area! (bemused) What do you mean by ... sex?'

(Throws self out of sixth-floor window)

Shane: 'D'you mean, like, lots of women hanging around in short skirts in our videos?'

As in YOU being SEXY!

Shane (bewildered): 'Us being sexy?'

'Cos it's all so bloody serious!

Shane: 'Well, it is. Maybe that's the way we are.'

Kian: 'Maybe that's what people like about us!'

It was no use. Westlife were the least insultable band in history, the easiest target we knew turned chillingly invincible, protected by the conclusive evidence of the almighty majority vote. Everything I specifically hated about them they found their greatest asset. And they were absolutely right.

Don't you ever wake up gripped by the icy fear that all you are to RCA (their major label) *is a mountain of cash, that you exist purely to be exploited?*

Kian: 'But we're making a living out of it for ourselves as well!'

Shane: 'We can't make our music without a record company! If you're a good footballer you're out there every day running and running, goin' mad, the rich chairman just sitting there, that's the way life is.'

Don't you think big business is inherently evil? And therefore, so are you? You've never thought, 'I am The Devil'? Don't you THINK about these things?

Shane: 'I definitely think about it. But that's the way things are in this . . .' (sniiip!)

And it's wasting your time thinking you can change that?

Kian: 'Yeah, there's no point, what can you do?'

Bryan: 'No, 'cos it's not us, we're only a tool at the end of the day. (begins chuckling) Sex symbol tools! Naaah, that's gettin' way too deep! That's like saying, "Well, I better not go to McDonald's now, 'cos that's a huge money machine." And without the record company we'd probably still be back working in McDonald's, so we'd still be working for a big company anyway.'

Alright, forget 'deep'. Who wants a big, fat line of cocaine?

Westlife: 'Tssss! Mmnn.'

Kian: 'I, personally, have never had anything like that offered to me. And if I was, I'd turn a blind eye to it.'

What's wrong with you boys? Why aren't you out in a club on E, like every other nineteen-year-old in Britain? What about (then uber-cool hip hop visionaries beloved of young Britain) *the Wu-Tang-Clan?*

Shane: 'The only different kind of music I've listened to lately has been a couple of Puff Daddy songs.'

Never fancied an E then? You must've done. Teenage intrigue at least!

Shane (deep earnestness): 'Only teenage interest to sing.'

Kian (witheringly): 'Teenage intrigue to see how other people die from it.'

How long d'you think you've got?

Kian: 'I think we could do ten years. We could be The Bee Gees.'

'There will never be another Beatles,' Shane now averred, gravely. 'Elvis, Abba, they were the greats, we can only try and add to it, maybe be one of the biggest boybands. Even the Backstreet Boys, who've sold sixty million albums, they can never touch The Beatles.'

Does the word 'revolution' mean anything to you at all?

Shane (suddenly vastly amused): 'There'll be a hundred revolutions! I guarantee there'll be somebody along soon to make you happy!'

Here, Westlife declared I was living in some sepia-tinted memory of a long-gone rock 'n' roll fantasy. And in February 2000, they were right about that too. 'I actually feel very sorry for you,' smiled Kian, 'because you're very sad there with the whole rock aspect.'

Bryan: 'You're sad because everything's moved from rock to pop! We'll write a rock song for you!'

Shane: 'That'll make yer sad alroight.'

Then again, maybe you're the last of your kind.

Kian: 'I seriously doubt it.'

Maybe you've taken it to the end of its natural life. The bubble has to burst. Maybe you're about to explode, maybe you're, as we speak, slaying The Beast, singing the songs blaring from the pews at your own funeral!

Shane: 'Maybe it's true!'

Kian: 'Like a bomb! (sings) "Gonna start a revolution from moi bed"!'

Bryan: 'Well, we are Irishmen, look at moi socks!'

And so I found myself, defeated, staring at the jauntily fleur-de-lys-patterned sock of an invincible Irish teenage millionaire who'd just merrily called me 'sad'.

In 2000 they didn't know the half of it, as I packed up my tape recorder and headed back to my derelict 'home'. If the nineties had faded to a yellowing parchment already, a new phrase was now defining pop culture as we knew it, and still know it, to this day.

'Celebrity Culture.'

THE BRITISH LIBRARY

133177PAT

EXPIRES
24 SEP 1999

PATTERSON
S A, MISS

22

SINGLE LADY (PUT A SOCK IN IT)

As the year 2000 twinkled on in fantastical illusion, the term Celebrity Culture embedded deeply into our distraction-seeking psyches as the fabulous Americans began aggressively taking over: where we had skip-along innocents Billie Piper and Samantha Mumba, they had the sexually risqué peak years of both Britney Spears and Christina Aguilera. Where we were thrilled enough with the petulant teenage Sugababes, they had the stunningly invincible Destiny's Child, led by the none-more-fabulous, nineteen-year-old Beyoncé Knowles, whose millennium year gave us 'Jumpin', Jumpin'', 'Say My Name', 'Bills Bills Bills' and the peerless fem-pop anthem 'Independent

Woman Part 1' (which spent eleven weeks atop the US *Billboard* chart).

In such a mainstream atmosphere *The Face* magazine was struggling, its once-thrilling, pioneering, zeitgeist-creating eighties/early nineties heyday ruthlessly crushed by incoming cultural forces, an edge-seeking entity which could do very little with a concept like the classic Destiny's Child line-up – Beyoncé, Kelly Rowland, nineteen, and Michelle Williams, twenty – a three-woman headline-avoiding hydra renowned for their hermetically sealed private lives, gee-shucks politeness and steadfast Christian values. *The Face* also knew, however, as did the rest of planet pop, the group held in its midst a solo superpower of the future. My pop reporting duty, then, was to encourage into the public domain the hitherto hidden personality of Beyoncé Knowles and elevate her, somehow, into a discernibly strident character, perhaps even one with an actual opinion and everything.

In the year 2000 the eight-million-album-selling, global No. 1 R&B-pop phenomenon Destiny's Child were on the M40 heading towards Birmingham. That year's shimmeringly dominant pop force, they were travelling as the locals did, in a standard British coach more befitting the ferrying of pensioners to an Aylesbury awayday than the most glamorous pop stars alive (in the same month the Backstreet Boys were spanning the planet in a million-dollar private jet, which housed a vibrating bed). We travelled together for four full days of punishing promotional bedlam, from *CD:UK* to the *National Lottery Live* to countless phone interviews (some nights averaging forty minutes' sleep), while performing each evening in Manchester, Birmingham, London and Dublin. The three (often in golden sequins) were permanently fabulous, talked in irresistibly charming shucks-y'all Texan, didn't drink, smoke or swear (even once), were toothsome, polite and permanently 'blessed' other than when they were 'truly blessed!' (and carried bibles with them everywhere to prove it).

Beyoncé's 'mom', Tina Knowles, was there, too. The girls' stylist and on-the-road moral guardian (friendly yet formidable, wearing an eyebrow ring), who (alongside then-manager dad, Matthew Knowles) had set out rules years ago for producers or anyone else wishing to work with the wholesome prodigies: no drugs, booze, cigarettes, 'profanity' or the playing of hardcore rap or hip hop. At one photo shoot in Dublin, muthafuckin' NWA was vetoed for the photographer's choice of The Andrews Sisters' forces knees-up 'Chattanooga Boogie'.

Beyoncé, it turned out, even thought her eyebrow was too rock 'n' roll, its naturally high-camp arch seeing her dubbed at school The Girl With The Eyebrow. 'And I was too young to arch my eyebrow,' she cringed, confessing she now trimmed its apex and attempted to comb it straight. No wonder, to the average British teenager, she was (then as now) an intoxicatingly alien enigma. She was also, in conversation, more hologram than human, possibly the greatest master of the muted personality gambit in showbiz history, a skilful avoider of any dangerous proximity to the personal or even minutely controversial, lest a glossy loose lip unleash a tsunami of foaming negativity and threaten to sink the buoyant mothership of her global brand forever (even if artistes as brands was still an emerging concept). And the only way the pesky pop journo could break through the lead-lined barrier was stupid jokes, shock tactics and outright barefaced cheek.

For well over a decade British youth culture had been a throbbing landscape lit from within by recreational drugs, via Ecstasy-charged rave culture and cocaine-bedevilled Britpop but Destiny's Child had not only never taken any drugs, they'd never *seen* anyone take drugs. Chugging up the M40 on our pensioners' coach, Beyoncé and Michelle were in the seats

directly in front of me, Kelly leaning across the gangway, my
tape recorder poked between the backs of the seats. Tina
Knowles was 'asleep' behind me (listening to every word) while
all of Destiny's Child proved themselves deft deflectors of the
even mildly inflammatory query. They 'never' went to parties,
chirped Michelle, 'we hardly ever go out, we're hardly ever seen
in public.' When asked what she thought of Ecstasy, her voice
dropped to a whisper.

'You might get raped or something,' she hushed, 'there's
thousands of people that go to these things, next thing you know
you dance an' all, you don' know 'em from a can of beans.'

'I have a question,' interjected Beyoncé, boldly. 'Everybody
knows what goes on in raves and when you find out – and this
is off the record – why don't police officers or somethin' come?'

Here, Kelly switched the tape recorder off.

I switched it back on again.

*People have always been interested in oblivion. You don't think
Ecstasy could merely be the new vodka?*

Beyoncé humphed. 'Well I just hope young people become
more aware. But until somethin' happens, until one day young
people realise it's not gonna help you, it's just something that you
have to go through.'

You have no natural curiosity?

Together: 'No.'

'Never,' Beyoncé confirmed. 'Ever. Ever. Because I'm fulfilled
with life and I'm fulfilled with being on stage, I don't think
there's a better feeling than that.'

'We also feel good knowing that when we get off stage and go
home to the hotel we gonna wake up in that same bed the next
day,' added Michelle. 'We ain't like, "what in the world!?" You
can't enjoy your life if you can't *remember* it.'

Approaching defeat already, I edged towards sex, wondering if
they were aware of their worldwide 'dream girl' status.

'That's wonderful,' mused Beyoncé. 'Overwhelming. But weird.'

Michelle: 'We ain't tryna be a dream woman or . . . hopefully this will never come but (whispers) sex symbols, y'knowhatImean?'

A discourse was then attempted on the seeming dichotomy between Christianity and their magnificently displayed cleavages.

'Here, they're totally confused,' Beyoncé began. 'For some reason it doesn't compute. I think they don't understand American Christianity. We wear whatever we want because it's not about how you look, to God. God is *in* you. But we've never been in underwears and bras and lingerie. Yeah, we have our legs out but we won't have boobs hangin' all out and cleavage hangin' all out with legs and thighs hangin' all out. I do think there's an appropriate way of dressin'. If we feel like anyone's jus' gonna be starin' straight at our boobs or butts, then, no.'

Back then, unlike the Obama-schmoozer Beyoncé would eventually become, the girls declined to confess how they voted – 'That's personal, a sacred thing!' scolded Kelly – while the Britney-inspired query as to whether these conservative Texans believed in no-sex-before-marriage was given the dismissal it doubtless deserved.

'Well, we don't talk about . . . um, sexuality,' balked Beyoncé. 'We think that's private. Everybody has their own preference and we're not trying to put our beliefs on anybody. If you say this, there's a lot of people that have had sex before marriage and who are we to tell them that's wrong? Or right? That's their business. And what we do is our business. So.'

So there's no temptation there either?

'It's kinda easy for us to be how we are, 'cos that's how we were taught,' Beyoncé now concluded. 'But sometimes you do get temptations to do the wrong things, you do get the splurges to do young, dumb, teenage things, just go out to a party, get drunk, go crazy, but there might be press there. And that might go on the internet and some people that might do everything that you do might go and do it afterwards. And they might get in trouble or get into a bad situation. So we think about that kinda stuff.'

Kelly, suddenly inspired: 'And hopefully, as role models, that's the way that we can possibly change the world!'

By the time we arrived in wintry Dublin – the three hunched together for warmth in the back of a black cab – a glimmer of just what it took to become an eight-million-album selling global colossus (aside from those still glorious fem-pop classics) was beginning to emerge. Their scorched-earth attitude finally rose to the surface, confessing a belief in some sort of God's Own Voodoo wherein anyone who dared do them wrong would be somehow spirited away. The three sometime original Destiny's Child members were cited, two of whom had recently left amid threats to sue Beyoncé's father (who had managed Destiny's Child since Beyoncé formed the band at a jaw-wobbling nine years of age).

'Anything that's getting in the way of us becomin' mega-superstars?' boomed Beyoncé. 'They always remove *themselves* from us. So we don't have to deal with it. They get sick. They walk out. Anybody that we had a funny feeling about? *Anybody* negative? They're just . . .'

All three: 'Outta there!'

The other three, now, must feel very foolish indeed.

'Only they know where their true hearts lie,' intoned Beyoncé. 'I can't imagine leavin' a group and then a month after I leave that group, that group becomes number one. I couldn't imagine tryna fire somebody that helped me get there and then me partin' from that group and then a month later havin' three more number one singles and sellin' eight million records. I would be *embarrassed*, I would feel *stoopid*, I would feel like a made a *dumb* decision.'

Kelly, clutching stomach: 'I feel sick!'

This was Destiny's Child at their most tempestuous, an emboldened outburst of indignation and powerhouse ambition made all the more glorious on the way to the Dublin venue by their shimmering golden frocks. Beyoncé now clenched a fist, exquisitely manicured nails digging into her palm, buoyed by a tangible fury.

'A lotta groups woulda broke up then, right before they got their big success,' she declared. 'Destiny's Child didn't break up. If we woulda stopped back then, we woulda been at two million records and we woulda been in the past, but now we're at eight million records and we're ... (the clenched fist slammed into her oncoming left palm) 'number one! (punch!) And we are *not* gonna let the haters and the people that have negative things to say get in our way, because we have a dream! (bigger punch!) My dad had a vision! (biff!) *We* have a vision! (splatt!) We have music inside of us and when we get on a stage it's magical and there's nothin' that any *critic* (blam!), or any *hater* (wallop!) or any *negative person*, there's nothing they can *say* (splatt!) or *do* (oof!) to stop that magic comin' through!' (Hallelujah!)

Three years later, in the gilded restaurant of the Four Seasons Hotel in New York, Beyoncé was now a world-class solo artist, newly conjoined to the Jay Z juggernaut in both music (the newly released 'Crazy In Love') and relationship (something she'd yet to officially confirm), the rules over her proximity to hardcore hip hop having been, evidently, seriously relaxed. That day she was eerily calm and even more informationally barren, mindful no doubt of her emerging 'megasuperstar' status, now a solo star on the cover of *The Face*. Over a cheese omelette (no carbs), she deigned, at least, to perform a slo-mo rendition of the instantly mythologised 'Crazy In Love' side-on booty-quake. 'You just have to practise isolation,' she glimmered, saucily. Today, aged twenty-two, she was one week away from her first fortnight off work since she was nine years old. 'I've kind of paid my due,' she noted, fairly.

Why do you work this hard?

'Because I wanna be remembered. And I wanna be respected. And I wanna be an icon.'

What's your message, ultimately?

'I just want women to accept themselves. And their imperfections. I try to take everything that happens to me, every bad experience, and make it something positive.'

Soon, I was frantically trawling for Jay Z-related info.

How many times have you been in love?

'Uh ... I dunno.'

Yes you do.

'No, I don't. I'm not sure! I have been in love.'

And right now?

'Right now? (nibbling some omelette) Yoooo're funny. I'm happy. I'll say that.'

When did you last see Jay Z?

She failed to suppress a glossy grin. After an enormous pause: 'On television today. On the ["Crazy In Love"] video.'

And how did you feel?

'I've seen it a hundred times. Huh-huh-huh!'

Did you feel a flutter in your heart?

'Yoooo're funny.'

Why all the mystery? Is it because you believe in the fascination of enigma?

'Well. Ohm. The older I get, the more I feel I have to protect certain things. Not only my relationships, my personal relationships, but ... the inside of my house. Or what kinda car I drive. Or what I spend my money on. Or *if* I spend my money. Any question that you wouldn't ask a stranger.'

Two and a half years ago you implied to me that you didn't believe in sex before marriage.

Her forkful of omelette froze in mid-air.

'I never said it. I've never talked about that. Because I don't think that would be smart. For one, it's no one's business. For two, people never forget certain things that you said. And they don't allow you, once you say anything, to change. Y'know? So I've never talked about any sexual experiences. Or any lack of. Because that's private.'

Incidentally, if you ever get married to someone called Mr Castle that would be a mistake.

'Uh . . . oooooh kaaaay! Awl-right! Thank you!'

I talked to your mum about The Rules: no cursing, drinking, smoking or playing of hardcore hip hop, and now you're (at the very least) working with Jay Z and loads of tough guys. You're hanging out with ex-drug dealers now!

'Uuuuum!' Her fork pranged on her plate. 'Well, the morals and the way I treat people and handle myself is always in me. Me working in the studio with . . . people, everybody I work with, they're professionals. And they're very talented.'

How does your mum feel about Jay Z's background?

'My family is, like I said, anyone that I'm around, they know are good people.'

And here, her famed eyebrow leapt off her forehead and she laughed hysterically for several seconds.

I see. So now you're down the studio cussin 'n' drinkin' and smoking a gigantic blunt to NWA?

'Nuh-huh-huh! Noooo . . . not quite.'

By 2003, Celebrity Culture's dominance was rooting firmly into an actual era, one defined then, as now, by illusion, control, protection, distraction and brand damage limitation. Media training, for the biggest stars, was now a widely-used PR gambit. With careers often hugely augmented by global corporate sponsorship, there was simply way too much money at stake. That year, Madonna and Missy Elliott appeared in a Gap ad together, while Beyoncé was sponsored by both L'Oréal and Pepsi. I'd never understood it, not really, why these multi-millionaires cheapened (to me) their own often magnificent brands by endorsing other people's (often significantly less magnificent).

Why do you do these things when you clearly don't need the money?

She blinked at me, genuinely bewildered. 'It's an honour to do a Pepsi commercial. Michael Jackson. For one it's a historical thing, especially Pepsi, that's huge.'

It's a part of culture you actively want to be involved with?

'Yeah. L'Oréal, the pictures are beautiful. It's just a cool thing to do. I go to Japan, France, I have L'Oréal ads all different places, so I'm able to be exp … y'know people can see me there. It just makes you … a bigger star. And who's to say that people don't like the cash? Or need it? Huh-huh-huh!'

Does it bother you that the world runs on money?

(enormous pause, Westlife-shaped answer approaching) 'It's way the world is. Yep.'

Every day, via entertainment culture, The Young are fed concepts of colossal fame, wealth and success: are these aspirations unrealistic?

'Hmn. I know what you're saying. It is sad, somedays. You think "what is reality?"'

What indeed!?

'You have to really think about what you love and what you want, out of life, know the difference between reality and superficial things. You can't blame people on TV. The people around you, your family, it's up to them to instil certain things. Success to me does not mean a lotta money. I wanna be happy. This album, I didn't write it to make money, I wrote it to make quality music. To make history, more so.'

A few months later we were talking again, this time on the phone, this time for a stop-clocked half hour as the screws turned ever tighter on her now inarguable global powers. She was calling from a recording studio where Oprah Winfrey had just wandered in for a chat, where she'd been working with Bono for an African AIDS benefit CD and accompanying show where she'd perform for Nelson Mandela. Important, worthy stuff, but by now our gossipy celebrity pop world was after – finally – some confirmation (or any facts at all) on her relationship with Jay Z.

So ... where did you actually meet Jay Z for the first time?

'Ohm, I don't wanna talk about that, because then the interview will become about that, but probably a long, long time ago. We started the same year, '96. So, a while ago.'

Was this as a new friend, or a working colleague?

'See!?' she scoffed. 'That's why I didn't wanna answer that question, because after that question, there's more!'

What are his finest qualities as a man?

'Well, I'm not gonna talk about him! 'Cos I just *know*. But in terms of just friendships, female, male, people that are around me, I really respect people that are honest with me. Because I need that. Someone that I could trust. And someone who I can learn from, y'know? And now you might as well go to the next section! Ah-huh-huh!'

From here, a random volley of enquiry ensued, seeking some kind, any kind, of emotional, human response.

What did you get picked on for as a kid?

(expertly avoiding an emotional reply) 'My ears. They were really big and they stuck out. People would put objects like cinnamon rolls up to their ears to tease me.'

So many pop stars dress like lap dancers and strippers now, is pop culture too sexualised?

(expertly avoiding an opinion) 'Y'know, I feel like whatever a person individually feels like they're comfortable doing, that's their business.'

When did you last go somewhere alone?

'Good question. I haven't ever taken a trip anywhere alone. And I haven't been alone anywhere in a while 'cos I usually have security or someone with me, 'cos it's not very safe.'

As the stop-clock clanged towards twenty-five minutes, desperation arrived, now frantically fishing for the first known sighting in the public domain of a funny remark from the more-fabulous-than-ever Beyoncé. I wondered when she'd last made a complete fool of herself, and a lengthy anecdote ensued about falling over on stage in Dallas, a stiletto catching in the lace of her dress. 'And I fell down at least fifteen stairs,' she cringed. 'I was like, sliding, so my head was just bobbing, bob-bob-bob, all the way down the stairs and the worst thing is I tried to keep singing! I musta been thinkin', "The show! The show! I'm just gonna play it off as I bob downstairs!"' With Beyoncé, evidently, in a comedy frame of mind I let go of the reins altogether, with an old-school *Hits*-type completely stupid question.

Have you ever been sick all down your cleavage?

'In my *cleavage*!?' she roared, incredulously. 'Nooooo ... what are you *sayin'*? With drink? Been *sick all in my cleavage*, awl-*right*! I have *never* been sick and all vomiting and all that, no!'

This, then, was my final exchange with Beyoncé and will surely be my last, out of reach as she is today, her interviews hand-picked, rare and controlled (if given at all, which looks increasingly unlikely). She's more inclined, certainly, to self-direct her own HBO documentaries as she did in 2013 than endure, say, a stranger's reasonable query on her staggeringly nonchalant reaction to her sister's attempted stiletto-skewering of her husband's bollocks, in a lift, in 2014.

It's an on-going vocal reticence which made her Superbowl performance of 2016, of course, all the more unexpected; Beyoncé, of all people, the sometime headline-avoiding hologram, exploding into real life via her African-American rally-call 'Formation', affixing her considerable cultural clout to the BlackLivesMatter movement, the activist organisation created in 2013 in the wake of several fatal police shootings of young black men. Whether this courageous artistic statement inspires a new era of long-gone protest in music, or was merely a shrewd and timely contribution to today's global conversation on diversity, remains to be seen. Either way, Beyoncé that night, once again, made sure she'd be remembered, and respected, as an icon, who made history, more so.

She remains a global entertainment superpower. And there's nothing any pesky pop journo can do (boof!) or say (wowsa!) to stop that magic comin' through.

23

THE FUTURE'S SO BRIGHT,
I GOTTA WEAR SHADES

'Revolution,' announced Bono, promisingly, seated in a restaurant in Dublin in the year 2000, his ludicrous specs for once not on his face but placed by his steak-filled dinner plate, 'is always about throwing off the thing that is most oppressive in an era. Whether that was royalty at one time, the church, government, communism, capitalism. And the thing that's most oppressive in our era is celebrity. And that's why people want to burn my house down.'

'I think I understand that,' he carried on. 'Celebrity is ugly.

What it does is belittle real life, which is where actual heroism is. And it magnifies the foibles and the soap opera of people who already are the selfish. In which I include myself. And there's got to be something just completely wrong about that.'

If people feel diminished by celebrity, then how come, simultaneously, they worship it?

'I think they *hate* it,' decided Bono. 'You know the person that you don't like, is often the one you're most interested in? It's that sort of thing. I think it's a deep, deep resentment. And, unfortunately, it creates an awful atmosphere where they can't believe in anyone. And that's sad. But it's the way of the world right now.'

Almost one full generation on from this heartfelt statement, Celebrity Culture has shown no signs of a revolutionary overthrowing and Bono remains surrounded, perhaps more so than ever, by a metaphorical mob of incensed detractors waving flaming torches at the foundations of his house. The more famous someone becomes, the bigger a target they become and there's been times when Bono (frontman of the still-biggest band in the world since 1983) has seemed permanently locked in figurative medieval stocks, specs stuck to his irksomely familiar face, being pelted by the cabbages of The Critics. And long before 2007, when implications arrived that Bono and his pious U2 pals were tax-avoiding schemers after all; dodgy purveyors of hypocrisy and self-interest, just like everybody else (global financial arrangements they rigorously defend to this day). And long, *long* before they forcibly thrust their thirteenth album *Songs Of Innocence* into half a billion iTunes users' inboxes in 2014, for free, prompting incensed calls for Bono's scalp to dangle, once again, from the sweeping scythe of global indignation.

An interview with U2 today, then, would be a weighty affair: a combative, agenda-driven, investigative endeavour possibly best carried out by the corporate business editor of the *Financial Times*.

Back in 2000, an interview with U2 was barely contentious at all, other than finding out if Bono really was a billowing windbag of grandiose pomposity, or the irresistibly charming raconteur most everyone who ever met him insisted him to be. And, either way, would he like to apologise for all those idiotic specs?

Not that I knew if he could take this sort of jovial jibe, or if this was a one-way ticket to a security heavy throwing me through a wall. Whichever way, I was happy for a trip out of London, now living in a mouldering basement flat in then crack-bedevilled Clapton, east London, the kitchen besieged by a raccoon-sized rat, where police ticker-tape fluttered at the end of the road most weekends announcing yet another drive-by shooting. And Bono, surely, of all people, would be kind to a citizen of the world in peril ...

U2's Dublin studios were housed (and still are) on an industrial quayside, in a two-storey building next to breezily-titled parcel couriers Go Easy. Inside, all was wooden and homely, low-slung sofas and ashtrays. The four men of U2 ambled towards me, proving themselves unexpectedly Comedy Irish (to the cartoon level of the Jamaicans, as if *surely* taking the piss): twinkling, direct, overwhelmingly genial and hypnotically slow-talking – apart from Bono, who blah-blah-blabbed in the 'grand' tradition of the Irish compulsive talker. (As the similarly blathersome Sinead O'Connor once said: 'You can tell an Irishman, but you can't tell him much.')

Here was The Edge, 'ethereal' guitarist, in his signature clamped-on woolly hat, wondering, unfeasibly, with the voice of Terry Wogan, 'What's happening in London, apart from UK Garage?' There was bassman Adam 'Clear awf!' Clayton, U2's celebrated sometime playboy, wearing two items of all-purpose rainwear, seemingly disguised as a camping guru on a windy hike in Donegal. Here was Larry Mullen Jr, the most hunkin' drummer the planet had ever known, with the hopeful enquiry, 'Have you ever interviewed Eminem?' And here was Bono looking, frankly, like a decrepit old punk dude down on his luck: short, dyed black hair springing backwards, no specs, revealing deep and well-earned lines below fluorescent blue eyes, epaulette-shouldered Clash-era black shirt bunching up at the buttons, 'distressed' grey drainpipe jeans and scuff-heeled DM shoes. Possessed of a supernatural energy, he was physically more domineering than you'd think, a man of five foot six who could give you, as the Dubliners might have it, 'a serious hidin''. He wanted to know how I got along with 'Ben'.

Ben?

'Your editor!' he chortled, of the *NME*'s newly installed Ben Knowles. 'Met him the other day.' Ben wasn't the only man in a position of 'power' Bono had met that week (some of whom addressed him as 'Bonio'), including infamously hard-nosed right-wing US Congressman Jesse Helms, reasoning with him in Washington about 'economic redemption' until Helms was in tears (they'd been 'rolling down his face', it was all over CNN). The Republican powerhouse had personally agreed, in public, to give back $435 million in cancelled debt to the third world countries currently being obliterated through starvation and, withered Bono, 'something *stupid* like malaria'. He added, relieved, of the promised cancelled debt, 'and it looks like we're going to get it'.

'So that,' added hunky Larry, 'is what Bono does in his spare time. No fish farmin' for Bono.'

Yeah, where's your trout farm? Call yourself a rock star?

Bono: 'Hmmn, looking after the *hungry trout* ...'

It must be a nightmare, being Rock's Conscience.

Bono: 'Oh, I'm not *rock's* conscience, it's just *having* a conscience. What's hard is not conscience, it's just how *un-hip* that makes you. Hahahargh!'

It was, it turned out, *impossible* not to be charmed as a nightingale out of a singing ringing tree by Bono's bonhomie. We were seated in the downstairs lounge, strewn across sofas, wooden table in the middle, where Bono, then forty, proved himself one of the world's true, singular eccentrics. Attempting to engage him in discussion over U2's latest album *All That You Can't Leave Behind* was futile. He was too busy railing here, jesting there, wandering out of his seat, leaping into exceptional impersonations of Keith Richards, his dad, political figureheads, Johnny Cash (so rumblingly accurate, it was as if The Man In Black was back in the room), a man who was evidently Born To Speak. For the first time in history I resorted to bawling, 'Anyway! The album!' (And if Page and Percy had also been in the room they would've keeled off their stools in astonishment.)

The album's title was inspired by a passage from the Scriptures, about 'the fire you pass through and all the straw and wood and bollocks is burned away and you're left with the eternal things, like friendship and like love and like laughter'. (Years later, I dubbed this speech 'The Burn Away The Bollocks Speech', which, if you say it loudly enough, and Irishly enough, highly amuses any otherwise U2-oblivious teenager anywhere on the planet. Even as it remains, behind its Bono-shaped bluster, as true a musing on The Meaning of It All as I've ever heard.) There was no quip, aside, or questioning of his motive and/or integrity which Bono hadn't thought of himself, his generosity extending to a sudden invitation to dinner, Larry Mullen Jr driving me into town in his posh jeep, alone, much to the inner wibbliness of my immortal seventeen-year-old self. This was the man, after all, who inspired Bono's earlier quip: 'Y'know *The Picture of Dorian Gray*? Larry's got one of them in his attic. And it's *me*.'

At 10.30 p.m. we were in a restaurant called Eden witnessing more of the famed Bono charm offensive.

A wine-only establishment, he was after a pint of Guinness. A waitress approached our table.

'Any chance you could get us a *point* of Guinness in the pub across the road?' Bono lilted to the deeply tickled waitress. 'Y'know, in an emergency. You wouldn't *believe* the week I've had. And I'm a free man of the city!'

Ten minutes later, good things in pint glasses came to those who waited, to the kind of man who used to have barrels of Guinness flown over for U2 shows in Italy. Well you would, wouldn't you? If you *could*.

I'd never truly had it in for Bono, or U2. In 1980 I'd loved their debut album *Boy* with an incendiary passion, the brightest flare in Ireland's post-punk uprising, the faintest peal of the opening notes from 'I Will Follow' igniting a sequence of involuntary movements on a dance floor akin to a sprinting, electrocuted octopus. By *The Joshua Tree* in '87, however, U2 had not only gone all religious (which would never do in my Godless heart), but become the most earnest band on earth, all 'important' cacti, leathery breeks and going on and on about America, hence the Goon Bono Blasted By Top Pop Mag incident back at ver *Hits*. Through U2's baffling nineties I'd found Bono a sometimes misguided but often emboldened prankster attempting ambitious onstage stunts: calls to the White House, to a sex phone-line, ordering 10,000 pizzas. A preposterous rock star attempting to Save The World, meanwhile, was surely more productive (if less Spinal Tap) than doing nothing whatsoever with your planet-sized influence except cocaine, women and houses the size of Ohio. And if he did all these things because of Catholic Guilt, so be it.

We were seated around a tiny table, elbows-to-elbows, attempting to make sense of one of the most ridiculous rock 'n' roll groups the world had ever witnessed, Bono proffering a personal ethos: 'If your version of being true to yourself is making an eejit out of yourself, then I think you just have to go there.' When U2 seemingly discovered humour, irony and looking like gonks fallen out of a cereal packet throughout the 1990s (stage production concepts including the 40-foot onstage lemon of 1997's gigantic *PopMart* circus) it was a way, he added, to 'disguise' what they really still were, interminably earnest, 'so we didn't just *bleed* all over everybody'.

But there was no need, surely, to go as far as the PopMart *cavalcade?*

'It was experimenting with Pop Art, it was that simple,' justified Bono. 'Having fun with size, no bad seats, but I must confess we did reach an end there. Woody Allen referred to us as, "Isn't that the group that gets out of a citrus fruit during their show?" And maybe you don't want that on your gravestone! But if you ever get the chance, and it sounds like *purgatory* for you, check out *PopMart: Live From Mexico City.*'

Er ... watched it last night, actually. It looked like three Robbie Williams and James Dean on drums.

The rest of U2: 'Murghurgh!'

'*Ooooof,*' Bono suddenly exclaimed, screeching his seat back and rising from the table. My fork froze in mid-air. Was *this* the moment I was thrown through a wall?

'I'm just going to have to walk around the table,' he carried on, as mirth began dancing across his face (and my fork was safely lowered). 'I love Robbie for all those reasons, for the colour,' he announced and circled the table for a second time muttering under his breath, 'gettin' a *tongue-lashin'* here!'

Bono was, in fact, *encouraging* a tongue-lashin', something he saw as tremendous sport. 'I take it as a compliment, I really do!' he decided, settling back in his seat. 'I think Robbie's better than *he* thinks he is.'

D'you think your colossal fame has happened in inverse proportion to the strength of The Classics?

Bono: 'I would've subscribed to the idea that U2 were crap and *then* got it together and *then* went off into the ether!'

Maybe U2 are just massive and that's really all *they are?*

'Well! (brightly) That *is* disappointing.'

Is there anything you'd like to apologise for?

'The mullet. And ... and ... em ... em ...'

What about some of them specs?

'Heheheh! I better come up with something real quick or you're gonna keep helpin', aren't yer? I needed a place to ... go! Seriously! (spot-on impersonation of Jerry Lee Lewis) Ah was awl shook up out there in the lahm-laht! I've *slept* in my sunglasses on occasion. On a big one.'

Which ones did you give to the Pope (on the occasion of his personal blessing of the Jubilee 2000 campaign)?

'The blue ones.'

Did they look better on him than they did on you?

'Well *you* would tink so. Put it *that* way! I can just hear you at the back of the Vatican, "Whatever you do, don't give them back!"'

You're always surrounded by supermodels. How come?

Bono: 'Adam.'

At the risk of an incoming 'clear awf!', I wondered whether Adam was still friends with his ex-fiancée, Naomi Campbell?

'Yes, we still talk,' confirmed Adam, theatrically as ever. 'What a whirlwind! Yes, yes, quite a year.'

You, Adam, would never in a billion years have posed naked on the sleeve of Achtung Baby *if you weren't substantially endowed, would you?*

Adam: '.........' (enormous grin)

Edge (to the rescue): 'He was *magnificent.*'

Bono (to Adam): 'And you thought it was just *me* that was gonna get it, didn't yer! (nods to Larry) Have a go at *him.*'

Well, there is one thing; Larry, did you really have no qualms about calling your son Elvis?

Larry: 'He's happy!'

Bono (joining in): 'But what about later on, when he gets complexes?'

Larry: 'He's gonna get complexes anyway. He's my kid!'

Bono: 'The amazing thing is, if you see Elvis, the question is over.'

Larry: 'It's the make-up and the silver suit.'

Maybe it's an Irish thing. U2 were even more impervious to cheek than Westlife. And *even more Irish*.

Bono was acquainted with many of the richest, most famous, most powerful, beautiful and possibly bonkers people on the planet. He was chums with hell-raisin' wordsmith Charles Bukowski before his death, while two of his closest friends, Michael Hutchence and Paula Yates, had died in the previous three years. At Paula's funeral he sang Willie Nelson's 'Blue Skies', and was still devastated for her daughters. 'It's their tragedy more than anyone's, it *breaks your heart*.' He'd lost his own mother at fourteen and sung about 'the hole' this leaves, forever. 'I don't know many singers whose mother is alive.' He had 'healing' nights on the town with his dad, a man who still slept with an iron bar under his pillow, as he had done since Bono was Paul Hewson, the lad. 'And [the iron bar] wasn't for burglars, it was for *me*.'

In America, Bono regularly gave tramps on the streets $200 handouts and didn't tell anybody (but people, you know, found out). He had two young daughters who liked The Sugababes 'and all the girl groups, 'cos they're girls'. ('So do I,' added Adam, inevitably.) He was a strange, funny, serious, bright, melancholy and formidably optimistic man who no longer felt compelled to act out the 'eejit' within. The 'cackle of unintelligent derision' that once followed him around and bothered him, 'no longer gets through, it means nothing to me, I'm not messin''.

Why did Bono, in the end, do all the things Bono did? 'God' knows, he didn't have to.

'I often think Catholic Guilt but I don't know if it is,' he mused, now slewing a post-meal coffee. 'That's what I *tell* people. But I know what it is. Punk rock. Exactly that. Because people who have that year, 1976, tattooed on their psyche, it's just in us.'

We talked about the obscene money spent on their live spectaculars and how this was a 'classic contradiction', but without being irredeemably branded into the earth's atmosphere the way U2 were he wouldn't have 'the ear of the powerful'. This way, he had the chance to turn ideology into change.

'I don't believe in ideals that you can't live by,' he stated, firmly, 'I don't think they're useful. The only ideals worth having are the ones you can apply to your daily life. And apply to the world.'

The fact it took someone like himself, or specifically himself, to be a mouthpiece for 'issues' made him even more nauseous than it made everybody else.

'It's *sick*,' he agreed. 'SICK. But it's just access. We have access other people don't have. You're one of us that became one of them, is the truth.'

People expected him to hand his house over to the homeless, give all his money away and go off into the desert with his sandals on his head, didn't they?

'Like some Sadhu, with your hand up like that for a year,' he nodded, a Hindu palm aloft. 'I have thought about stuff like that. Early on, I found it very difficult to live in ... what felt like privilege. But, in the end, I like the life too much. I actually love it. It's sad to say this, but I am actually your definition of a champagne socialist. I am *actually that*. I admit it. I'm not an ostentatious person, but I like the life. I like to go out.'

So in order to justify the life, he had to do good with it?

'Maybe.'

Otherwise he'd be destroyed by guilt?

'Whether it's Catholic or punk rock? Maybe. I am the easiest target in the world. I know that. It's a sucker punch. Absolutely. But I've certainly found a place where I can face myself. It would be very hard for somebody to get me in a corner and have that argument with me. But I probably have the argument with myself.'

Five years on from his supposed 'tongue-lashin'' in Dublin, Bono was named *Time* magazine's Person Of The Year 2005, alongside Bill and Melinda Gates, for services to (generally) Saving The World. Two years later, he received an honorary knighthood from the Queen, the KBE (Knight Commander of the Most Excellent Order of the British Empire). The following year, 2008, the Nobel Peace Laureates awarded Bono their annual Man Of Peace prize for two decades of activism tackling African debt, poverty and disease. And in 2012, U2 headlined Glastonbury for the first time, proved themselves ingloriously hopeless at rock 'n' roll's most coveted live slot (Bono's leather breeks were particularly unsavoury) and the natural order of everything was suddenly resumed. Cabbages rained upon the enormous U2 target and everyone, everywhere, had a jolly good laugh, once again, about what an eejit Bono must be.

'It's bonkers being you, innit, Bonio?' I'd chirped back in Dublin.

'I've had some mad times alright,' grinned the multimillionaire rock 'n' roll tramp. '*Mad* times. There's mad times to come.'

Part of the madness, maybe, was that by the year 2000, Bono and U2's lifelong notion of what rock 'n' roll was, wasn't rock 'n' roll anymore. There was a new rock 'n' roll. Called hip hop.

24

INSANE IN THE BRAIN

'Rock'n' roll is hip hop now. Hip hop has infiltrated everything, every form of pop culture, movies , television, clothes and rock music – it's just taken over. Who the fuck would ever've thought that ten years ago, y'knowhumsayin'?'

So announced DJ Muggs from twelve million album-selling, Latino rap-rock pioneers Cypress Hill in 2000, two years after hip hop officially outsold country 'n' western music (the States' eternally top-selling genre) in America for the first time, with collective CD album sales alone of eighty-one million. Globally, it was exactly the same: hip hop/gangsta rap/conscience rap/pop rap (even-the-bloody-Spice-Girls-rapped) had now comprehensively ruptured through the deepest underground sweatbox ceilings to carpet the crust of the earth.

The hip hop titans of America were our global pop stars now and were therefore treated as such: scowling from the covers of the international music press, a media primarily run by middle-class white men and mostly read by suburban white boys, both increasingly transfixed by the beguiling music made, overwhelmingly, by the black and Hispanic American male from 'the ghetto' – a seventies-born, eighties-raised hardcore generation of predominantly ex-drug dealers and firearms offenders, many of whom had been in prison.

In the month of DJ Mugg's speech I was no longer living in the derelict canal-side building (a few months before the rat-besieged basement and the drive-by shootings), now given (what would become habitual) 'emergency' accommodation in a one-bedroom conversion in Hackney, once again with no heating (a decade before any hipster gentrification). A toxically porous environment it turned out to have deadly damp, which gave me permanent bronchitis, soon twining fairy lights around curtains and shelves for the illusion of comfort and warmth. Despite already poisoned lungs, I puffed away the existential gloom with determinedly-smoked weed. It was hardly 'the ghetto' but I felt a scintilla of affinity with the disrupted lives of the planet's hip hop massive.

Not for these reasons, though, did I unexpectedly become A Hip Hop Correspondent through the late nineties and early 2000s, despite knowing almost nothing about hip hop other than The Greatest Hits, including every word of the smashing rappy bit at the beginning of The Sugarhill Gang's 'Rapper's Delight' ('I said a-hip, a-hop, a-hippy . . .'). A lack of fanzine-level knowledge had one huge advantage: lack of intimidation by these formidable characters. An *NME* staffer claimed some of the Serious Hip Hop Boys on the paper were somehow 'too scared' to engage with their hard-men heroes and so the task fell to me, the pop-loving, nature-blubbing, vegetarian Smiths apostle with an accent so provincial I might as well have been from Nizhny Novgorod, Russia, to the lesser-travelled tough guys of crack-bedevilled South Central LA. Plus! In an overwhelmingly male environment, as hip hop was back then, a female interviewer was a disorientating novelty for the 'ho'-fixated rappers and more likely, therefore, to swerve away from their belligerent macho stereotypes. Maybe even, you know, have a birrova laugh?

Cypress Hill were hardcore. Cripes, they were *tough*. Three thirty-ish, Latino wise-guy heavyweights whose opening speech in a Manhattan parking lot let me know, immediately, how much they hated interviews and having their picture taken at the exact moment they were about to be interviewed and have their picture taken. Looking on was the almighty presence of the Hill's equally hardcore manager, Paul Rosenberg: a towering, bearded, tattooed figure with terrifyingly languid eyes, the sort of eyes you'd associate with the Mafia and the phrase, 'you think I'm funny, funny how?' He was also a sometime personal injuries lawyer, a graduate from the Mercy School of Law at the University of Detroit. No wonder his management company was called Goliath Artists Inc.

In 1993, Cypress Hill's irresistible, berserkoid single 'Insane In The Brain' had sprung them overnight to global fame. Which sent them, indeed, 'insane in the membrane', retreating thereafter into deliberately chart-unfriendly musical terrain. As DJ Muggs put it, the follow-up album had 'no singles on it' and was 'the murkiest record we could make', all of which was deliberate since 'we didn't like the attention'. By 2000 they were prepared to re-engage with the media game, the original Godfathers of the rap-rock hybrid now seeing their exceptional soundclash outright stolen by the likes of metal-hop numbskulls Limp Bizkit. Besides, they'd returned with a song with 'a message'; 'Rock Superstar', a portentous treatise on the all-pervasive, throwaway consumerism which now inarguably ran the planet. Here was a song, in the year 2000, about materialism gone berserk, vacuous celebrity, empty desires, creative rip-offs, fame as the new self-esteem and the worthless values of a surface culture where all ver Kids wanted was, as the lyrics mewled, 'a big house, with five cars . . .' (Unwittingly predicting, it seems, the way the world would work ever after.)

Cypress Hill, spoken to individually, turned out to be engaging, thoughtful men. B Real, the one with the nasal rap style, as if a wiggly, sarcastic worm lived inside his sinuses, was in a car hurtling towards JFK airport clutching a swing-bin sized bag of marijuana 'bud' as big as a two-foot Christmas tree, though what they intended to do with it come Hardcore NY Security Interface was never divulged (these men were official spokesmen for America's National Organisation For The Reform of Marijuana Laws, NORML).

'Back in the day,' mused the measured B Real (as all hip hop people must), 'when a lotta artists were starting they were only doing it for the love of the music and if the music was right the fame and the limelight and the money would come. Kids these days, they don't love what they're doing. They know it's a way to make money and be a star. That's the motivation. They're attention seekin', egotistical, greedy sons of bitches. A lot of kids' mentality these days, it's pathetic.'

Who did he blame?

'The record companies, obviously.'

At thirty, B Real sounded like a granddad already, son of a Mexican dad and Cuban mum, a South Central LA-raised sometime cocaine dealer and Crips gang member who'd once been shot in the lung. 'It felt like being punched by a fist, some other places it's gonna be a lot more painful.' Plenty of his friends had been murdered. 'You become immune to death.' Music was The Only Way Out, as had been the case for most of the hip hop pioneers, the art form Public Enemy's Chuck D had once deemed 'black America's CNN' now long become mainstream news itself.

Since Tupac Shakur's fatal shooting in Las Vegas in 1996 (aged twenty-five) and Notorious B.I.G.'s fatal shooting in LA in 1997 (aged twenty-four), the late nineties East Coast/West Coast wars had seen several more 'beef' related murders. In 2000 the twenty-eight-year-old Jay Z, worth an estimated $25–50 million even then, was facing twenty-two years in prison if convicted for the near-fatal stabbing of record label executive Lance Riviera (he was acquitted). By 2000, DMX had been cleared of rape, the Wu Tang Clan's Ol' Dirty Bastard had been arrested four times in a six-month period, Busta Rhymes and Coolio had had their collars fondled for gun possession, and the increasingly erratic Puff Daddy was indicted on several weapons charges (he was later aquitted).

'We're all cursed, man,' swore B Real, back in the speeding cab. 'We come from that generation of hip hop that will always get in trouble. We came from fucked-up backgrounds, y'know? But a lot of the times it's not the actual artist that does anything to get himself in trouble, it's the people they're affiliated with. I truly believe that's what happened with Tupac. I don't think he raped and sodomised any woman, I think the people around him did some shit and he got caught up. He was set up. Because he was the famous guy.'

He despaired some more. 'Nobody really gives a shit about what happens to anybody, hell, not even themselves, that's the way most people think these days, unfortunately,' he announced, astonishingly bleakly. He also lamented the lack of 'the message' anywhere in popular culture (even then). ''Cos there's just too much out there,' he decided. 'So much shit you don't know what's real and what's not.'

DJ Muggs was an enormous Italian Noo-Yoiker, a man who attended high school for one year only and was so hard, so steely of eye, so bullshit-free and fuck-you fearless, it was hard to stifle the laughter. Especially when you spotted, under his NY-motived baseball hat, what appeared to be a pair of tights pulled over his head (shade: American Tan).

Why are you wearing a pair of tights on your head, 'Sir'?

'It's a stocking,' he said nonchalantly, peering down at me through a veil of semi-amused, stoner suspicion. 'Keeps ma hair flat,' he deigned to add, but didn't also add, though his face said it anyway, 'what *are* you, NUTS?'

He was standing upright in Paul Rosenberg's Goliath Inc. management office (a cluttered box-room featuring mounted magazine covers of Cypress Hill, Kid Rock and Eminem), all the easier to peg it sharpish should a pesky question arise. Like Harvey Keitel's Mr Wolf in *Pulp Fiction* you half expected him to say: 'If self-preservation is an instinct you possess, you better fuckin' do it and do it quick, if I'm curt with you it's because time is a factor . . .'

Unlike B Real, he didn't give 'two fucks' about the state of the world, or even music, a comically self-assured hard-man with a catchphrase – 'puh-*lease* believe it!' – who loved Phil Collins (especially 'In The Air Tonight') and dancing, especially to Ricky Martin's high-camp calypso beezer 'Livin' La Vida Loca'. 'I'll dance to anything, d'you think I give two fucks?' he scoffed. 'I like to go out, rub some butts, puh-*lease* believe it!' Music, he opined, is merely 'entertainment, fun'.

Shouldn't it, though, be something more important than that?

'My *family* should mean something important to me. Music's just music. I'd let it all go tomorrow for my friends. Just walk away and close my eyes. Music's like skateboardin', entertainment, gives us something to do in-between, y'knowhatImean?'

But hadn't he always been about, you know, cultural revolution? Even as I wondered, his eyebrows lifted in a knot of amusement, maybe even pity.

'When I started it was about music and it was no bigger than my neighbourhood,' he shrugged. 'I didn't understand cultural revolution, I just knew I wanted to make some bangin' music that my peers respected.'

Here, an impassioned speech followed on how Cypress Hill's incendiary sneer-rap was in no way therapy, merely 'music which makes you wanna do push ups, and fight, it's fun and its fun-eeeee'. He was no spokesman for a generation.

'Don't give a shit!' he honked, 'I'm not yo' mommy and yo' daddy!'

Tights on his head, then, and the coolest man alive.

Sen Dog, the Cuban-born third member, gave several fucks and a lorryload of shits about *everything*: a thirty-four-year-old who'd seen two friends murdered as a teenager and fled gang life for 'hard work' via a warehouse job before music took over. Sitting in TGI Friday at JFK airport he came with a reputation: a volatile character who'd, finally, ten years into his rapper's career, 'learned to control my temper'. He loathed being famous, at its height had 'hated my life' and behaved 'like a dick, to everyone . . . but I'm a lot more comfortable now'.

Was he still, though, a loose cannon?

'I don't know about a loose cannon but definitely, y'know, don't piss me off.'

Sen Dog was old-school, a strident believer in a steadfast work ethic, even in a job you loathed. 'F'real, because you're contributing to life, you wanna sell drugs and kill people you're contributing to the genocide.' He had old-school family values, despaired of the weed 'n' gun possessed kids of urban America. 'There's no respect,' he fumed. 'Kids are killin' their moms, foul shit goin' on, family life is too brief. The kids are lost now, they're lost.' One year on from the Columbine school killings, he blamed the materialistic middle-class parents for the murderers' warped minds. 'All they do is work, kids in an empty house, watching fuckin' porno movies, give 'em a BMW when they're sixteen years old and they're smokin' coke and doin' crystal and they're losin' their fuckin' brains. Kids need to strive.'

An intense, deep thinking man-of-the-world, towards the end of our wide-ranging if relentlessly bleak conversation, Sen Dog's eye wandered towards a blonde waitress in denims who he described as 'the Statue of Liberty in hot-pants!' He leaned over the table conspiratorially, evidently now seeing me as some kind of ally.

'We were talking about drugs and honestly the strongest, most powerful reel-you-in-and-make-you-kiss-it drug there is, is pussy,' he whispered, while loudly thumping the table. 'It is pooh-seee! I can't understand how there's fags. I can't. 'Cos once you've had poooh-seee!?'

I was crushed. Here was an insightful man who'd just lost his rational mind. He was old school in less productive ways and so I found myself spelling out gay sexuality as if addressing a nine-year-old boy.

Well, Mr Dog, the gays just aren't interested in the opposite sex, you see?

'How can you not be?'

What you're saying forms the basis for all homophobic thought on earth.

'OK. No, no, no.' He gripped the table, again leaned into the tape recorder. 'First and foremost, I have no problem with homosexual people, I'm just saying I don't understand the shit out of it 'cos that [waitress] is beautiful to me.'

Gay people find someone sexually attractive in exactly the same way you do. Exactly *the same way.*

'OK. That's cool.'

But you do think they're 'missing out', don't you?

'They're making more opportunities for me! Neheheheh! I can't disrespect anybody for their preference, y'knowhatImean? I had an uncle that was like that, he passed away from cancer in '79 and if I'd shown dislike for my own uncle that would be wrong. So to anybody that's gay and digs Cypress Hill, keep on diggin' it man, I'll shake your hand, just like anybody else's.'

Here, he told the story of a Mexican fellow in a club one night who was following him around, 'in my face the whole night, "Wanna blow job?"' Sen's friend grabbed him and shoved him out the way. There was, I told him gravely, a thin line between that and killing somebody for being gay.

'I understand that,' he mused. 'But it wasn't about being violent, it was "On your way, he's not interested." But I just don't think you should walk up to a person and be like that if you don't know the person. One thing I must say, though, straight people, they don't make an issue out of it, walking around having parades 'cos they're straight, it's a normal, everyday thing.'

With Sen Dog now sounding like a grandpa in a village backwater in 1937, I found myself in the farcical position of spelling out to a black man of West Indian origin in a Latino hip hop band from South Central LA the nature of 'oppression'.

'OK, I believe it,' he decided. 'Be gay, be proud. But you don't need to hit nobody over the head with it.'

He stood up to leave and leaned down into the microphone one last time.

'I just wanna say this has been the most mentally challenging interview I've ever done and I totally dug it.'

That's ridiculous!

'People don't ask me to speak on these subjects and I hope

people can see from this that I'm not a racist, I don't hate anyone for their sexual preference, I don't hate ... I don't *hate*. Y'knowhumsayin'? I'm too old to be hatin' on anyone. I just want everybody to know that life is what you make of it and if you make the best that you can of it, life will give you the best that it has. And if you put yourself in a fucked-up situation, that's on you.'

Really, I should've left it there. Hip hop culture, everything he'd been brought up with, had informed his mindset up to then. Only time and experience would change him (and surely has by now). Instead, back home, I reassessed a Sen Dog-penned track from the Hill's latest album called 'A Man': an almost comically aggressive diatribe announcing he didn't 'suck cock' and how he was 'everything you ever want to be/A fuuuuckin' maaaan!' The *NME*'s Cypress Hill cover story was duly printed with the observation that this particular song was 'easily construed as the most sinister anti-gay statement the Hill have ever made', further dramatising our exchange. Woozy on the moral high ground, after quoting his 'fucked up situation ... that's on you' speech, I'd written: 'And this one's on him. Believe that. No "please" involved.'

Even as I wrote these things, as I felt I must, exposing the wrong, I felt heavy-handed, and personally responsible for any potential repercussions. Sen Dog was not The Enemy. He was open enough to offer his opinion, speaking as many of his generation of men did, wearily misguided as they still were. Tolerance works both ways.

When the story was published, the *NME*'s still-new editor (and new 'friend' of Bono's) Ben Knowles had decided to make his mark with an all-new comic tone, and so the hardcore hard-men of Cypress Hill were featured on the cover with three speech bubbles wiggling out from their faces.

B Real, holding a bushel of grass to his nose: 'Hmm ... weed.'

DJ Muggs: 'I love Phil Collins.'

Sen Dog: 'Hmm ... the gay issue.'

Three weeks later, a very fucked-up situation should've been on Ben Knowles. Instead, it would be on *me*. A rape threat, followed by a hammer-in-the-head threat. From the biggest and most controversial hip hop star on the planet.

HOME SWEET HOME 2000

25

WILL THE REAL SLIM SHADY PLEASE STAND UP?

Paul Rosenberg was furious. It was a quiet fury, which made it somehow even more furious as his heavy footfall – the speed and sound of an approaching, say, Tyrannosaurus Rex – boomed along a corridor and swung into his New York office. Exactly the same office I'd been in three weeks previously, with the mounted magazine covers of Cypress Hill and Eminem. Naivety, once again, had placed me in peril: until arriving in New York that morning I'd failed to deduce the vital information that Cypress Hill's manager was also Eminem's manager, indeed CEO of Shady Records and Eminem's right-hand businessman. And I was here to interview Eminem, currently not only hip hop's brand new superstar but the most cavalier enthusiast of the word 'faggot' in contemporary entertainment.

Rosenberg was still gigantic, still with huge, Mafioso-languid eyes, and was holding in his hand the most overtly obvious piss-take of Cypress Hill's otherwise edgily cool career: the *NME* cover with the speech bubbles: 'Hmm … grass', 'I love Phil Collins' and 'The gay issue'.

He stared at the cover, which he'd seen for the first time that morning, stared at myself and *NME* photographer Kevin Westenberg, the very person who'd taken the offending photographs of Cypress Hill three weeks previously, and (his being the highly developed mind of a criminal lawyer) spelled out his conclusion: Westenberg and I were hip hop hunt saboteurs come to identically expose Eminem as a homophobic berk. And that's *exactly what it looked like.* And he must've thought the *NME* run by imbecilic schmucks to send the same pair again, to exactly the same place, *as if he wouldn't notice.*

'Can I have a word?' intoned the most intimidating man on earth, shuffling me into Eminem's own small office housing a red boxing punch-bag, a sofa and a five foot wide TV. 'This is a mocking tone,' he declared, jabbing at the speech bubbles, demanding an explanation.

I attempted to appease him, told him this was a new ed's way of bringing fresh young eyes to a newly amusing and therefore newly accessible Cypress Hill.

Eventually, five hours after we were initially informed he'd 'freaked out' over this 'fucked up shit', and fully expecting to be punted back to Britain on a plane with no access to the most thrilling pop persona on the planet that year, Rosenberg relented. The interview would go ahead on two conditions: there would be no talk today of 'faggots', he commanded, as 'Eminem has his opinions and from now on they stay on the album.' There would be no talk, either, about his 'personal life'. He'd only talk 'about the music'.

And then I met Eminem. And everything turned *even worse . . .*

I *loved* Eminem. I had his debut *Rolling Stone* magazine cover in 1999 exquisitely framed on Hero's Wall, a procession of the all-time greats I hung in every flat I lived in (a *lot* of time was spent hanging new walls); heroes from Johnny Cash to Joe Strummer and Liam Gallagher, still framed in his twinkling, fairy-light shrine. Eminem's face, on that now-iconic cover – stoner's ice blue eyes perving out from an angular face – was *defined* by sexual filth, as the cover-line understood: 'Low Down And Dirty White Boy Rap'.

By the year 2000 Eminem/Marshall Mathers/Slim Shady, the three-headed virtuoso Concept MC, was both the most controversial musical entity on earth and its greatest unique pop star, a luminous beacon in a millennial pop world overrun by disinfected boy/girl bands, maybe even a genuine creative genius come among us *at last*. Even if I did have to meet him in appalling physical condition, bronchially wrecked by the toxic Hackney flat and permanently sipping on a bottle of my childhood staple: Benylin.

'They're gonna get me on a stage and dress me up like a fuckin' chicken!' squawked Eminem, blasting through the back door of the theatre located in the back of the John Jay College For Criminal Justice. 'What the fuckin' Backstreet Boys is fuckin' goin' AWN in here!?'

Eminem was *loud*, wearing a silvery-grey tracksuit and white backwards baseball cap, even if you could barely see him for the posse surrounding him, six in number, including his D12 hip hop bandmate MC Proof. A physically compact twenty-six-year-old with those all-perving, almond, crystalline blue eyes, this wasn't actually Eminem at all: this was the gun totin', bitch rapin', girlfriend murderin', drug munchin', living embodiment of Bad Attitude that was and remains Slim Shady, the vessel for, as he always noted, 'my sick psychotic thoughts', who was not be taken literally. Faced with Slim Shady in 'real life', though, it was impossible not to. Pacing the theatre stage, suspiciously, he was either belligerently shouting, unnervingly silent, or playing to the gallery of his constantly snickering pals.

This was his reaction, it seemed, to three days spent with the British media, a constant influx of varying magazines who all believed he *was* Slim Shady anyway. They'd asked him to be photographed thus: with a chainsaw, switched on (which he did, fake blood splattered all over his face), smoking dope with fourteen-year-old Puerto Ricans (which he did, although drew the line at the request for 'smoking crack'), with a selection of pornographic 'bitches' in hotel rooms and up the back of limos (which he did, although drew the line at the request for 'actual fucking'). Starved for years of a real-deal satirical anti-hero, the Eminem phenomenon inspired open season on wilfully offensive/illegal high jinks and the lensmen hadn't had this much fun since the Beastie Boys, the Happy Mondays and Liam Gallagher in their inaugural madferrit years.

The first of his dubious *NME* tasks today was a brief video Q&A for the newly 'important' nme.com website, easy and timeless questions from a standard stockpile. 'Slim' found this pathetic, strewn on a low, scarlet, imperially plush theatre couch as his loitering chums egged him on.

'Why do I have to answer stoopid fuckin' questions,' he blared. 'Why can't anyone be angry anymore!?'

He began an overview of every interview he'd ever known.

'Which Spice Girl do I wanna impregnate? What's it like working with Dr Dre? How big is my DICK? Eleven and a half centimetres.'

MC Proof, giggling, chipping in: 'What's it like being a white rapper?'

Slim Shady spied my notebook.

'That's a question on there, ain't it?'

Yes, it's the first one.

MC Proof, aghast. 'Are you *serious*?'

No. Haw haw! OK, let's get this done and remember I'm not in it (Neither heard nor seen on camera).

'You will be,' assured Slim. 'I will pull you in. What is that accent?'

Scottish.

Here he attempted a Scottish accent, possibly inspired by The Simpsons' Groundskeeper Willie. 'Scoh-iiiish! Lih-uh bit uva Scoh-iiish accent!'

Which song, out of all the songs in the world, describes you the best? And why?

'What is this, trivia?' He began fondling the couch, singing '"I'm too sexy for this chair ..."' (changing mind) I don't know which fucking song describes me the best! "I Just Don't Give A Fuck", my song, describes me the best, 'cos I wrote it and it's about me and it's basically talkin' about people like *you*.'

What's the worst trouble you've been in?

'The worst trouble I've been in, besides from my VD, herpes, syphilis, AIDS, complex 12 ...' He told a lengthy story about himself, Proof and a friend called Champ shooting paint balls at bums, hookers and skateboarders and being put in the cells for it. 'We were up for, like, felonious assault, the cops whupped our ass, they beat me and Champ up worse than Proof, they stood on the back of my friend's neck. Why am I telling you this?' He grinned. 'Why do you people deserve to know this about me? I dunno if that was bad, or when I raped six twelve-year-old girls. Those are the top two things I've been in trouble for.'

At least you got away with one of them, eh?

'I got away with all of 'em. I'm here! Right now. About to rape *you*.'

You temptress. (I know, I was always hopeless at sarcasm.)

'Take a look at this lady for a minute! Get a good look at this lady. Would I rape her? Would I rape this innocent . . .'

Innocent? Me!?

'OK, I *would* rape you. Y'want me to rape you right now? We can get that. How about, *fuck* the boring questions, let's get raping you!'

I pressed on, regardless. *What would you do if you were invisible for the day?*

'I'd jack off in front of everybody. This is like grade school questions. What if red was blue?'

How do you react when you see a nun?

'YAAAAAAARGHGHGHGH!'

Aiiieeeee!

Posse: 'Heheheh!'

Which song would you have played at your funeral?

'A Backstreet Boys song. I don't know any songs by 'em, they're all so corny. Are we done? OK! My name is Marshall Mathers and I'm signing out, I hope you're watching this at home, fuckin' murderin' people right now as you watch. Marshall Mathers. My name's Marshall. From D12. Dirty Dozen.'

Thank you, Marshall, for sharing that with the class . . .

'. . . . .'

Frankly, I didn't have a clue how to deal with any of this.

Paul Rosenberg escorted me into his office and played four songs from Eminem's new album, *The Marshall Mathers LP*. Perhaps it was the menacing man looming over me, but my ears turned into Brussels sprouts, the notes I took spelling out a 'sonically thin', 'wearily self-conscious', 'gloomy', 'grave' and 'mirth-free disappointment'. Even his masterpiece 'Stan' (soon to be number one across the planet) was somehow 'watery'. Some hours later, Slim Shady once again blasted through a door, this time into Goliath Artists' management offices, this time shouting 'What the fuckin' Backstreet Boys, *NSYNC, Britney Spears is fuckin' goin' AWN in here!?' before booting over three chairs, sending them tumbling across the room.

Suddenly, he was wielding a very large hammer in the direction of my head. Not content with the 'raping', he was now, evidently, going to kill me. 'This,' he announced, 'is for the journalist who asks the WRONG question. Usually I just punch the punching bag.' He attacked the punch-bag and an almighty roar went up – 'AAARRGHGH!' – at which I leapt a foot in the air.

'I'm sorry!' he now screamed. 'SORRY! I'M SO! FUCKIN'! SOH-RAAAAY.'

He leaned out of an open window and hollered diabolically loudly.

'I'M SOOO ... FUCKIN' ... SOH-RAAAAAY!!'

An alarmed Paul Rosenberg bowled in from his office next door.

'It's all over, Paul,' I said. 'I've had a hammer in my head and he's throwing himself out the window ...'

'I'll take this away ...' sighed Paul, confiscating the hammer as if from an errant toddler, and disappeared back to his office.

During the next ten minutes, our interview time rapidly evaporating, Slim kicked over an entire can of Coke. 'Maid service!' he roared, clicking his fingers. 'Paul!?'

Paul arrived back with an armful of paper towels and one of his still loitering posse. '*She* did it!' pouted Slim, pointing to me.

Nothing to do with me, I can assure you.

'I can ashoooor-yih!' he scoffed, Scottish accent even worse than before. 'Ashoooor-yeeeh!'

Aye. And wur doomed.

'Wur dommed! Rrrrrr! Rrrrrrrrrr!'

Here, his chum joined in, the pair now apparently doing impersonations of a rabid Scottish terrier: 'Arrrr! Rrrrrr! Arrrrrrrr!'

Slim went to the loo and MC Proof wandered in. 'I like your jacket,' he announced of my pea-green waist-cropped army jacket with military epaulettes. 'You know how it is, Proof,' I ventured, having a quick sip on the Benylin, 'every day is a battle.'

'Heheheh!' he guffawed. *'True.'*

Eminem's was a shady story alright: born in 1974 to a seventeen-year-old girl called Debbie, he'd never met his dad, was raised in trailers all over Detroit's mostly black underclass neighbourhoods, lived on welfare, moved school four times every year while she popped pills (Tylenol: she 'introduced' him to it), and discovered hip hop aged nine through his Uncle Ronnie, who was Marshall's age. By twelve he was helping raise his half-brother Nathan, was bullied and beaten up continually, usually by black kids, once so badly, aged fifteen, he sustained a brain haemorrhage and was hospitalised in a coma for nine days. The same year, he failed the ninth grade three times and dropped out, his mother telling him to 'get a fucking job' while she played bingo all day. He'd been shot at, held at gunpoint, known suicide (his beloved Uncle Ronnie, aged nineteen), murder (his Uncle Todd fatally shot his brother-in-law), and all the while became a unique and exceptional MC while simultaneously being booed off stages by the overwhelmingly black Detroit hip hop scenesters and told to give it up, white boy, and move into rock 'n' roll. He worked as a minimum-wage cook from age sixteen, had a long-standing on-off relationship with his girlfriend Kim, saw the birth of his daughter Hailie Jade on Christmas Day 1996 and was duly sacked from his job.

Something snapped and Eminem effectively did kill himself, replacing his rap persona with the venomous alter ego Slim Shady while living with Kim in crack-house neighbourhoods with bullets flying through the trailer windows. He was 'discovered' in '97 by Dr Dre via the Rap Olympics, signed to Dre's Aftermath label on Interscope, recorded *The Slim Shady LP* in twelve days, start to finish, much of the time on Ecstasy. On its release, Debbie duly filed a $10 million lawsuit for defamation over the most infamous line in its global anthem, 'My Name Is': 'I just found out my mom does more dope 'n I do.' This suit remained in litigation, the 'crazy bitch' Debbie insisting, from the outset, 'Marshall was raised in an alcohol and drug free environment.'

You'd think there'd be much to talk about, but Slim Shady minus his posse did not become hip hop art-terrorist Eminem but reality-pummelled Marshall Mathers instead: a disastrous interviewee who loathed the process and treated every query with ice-blue, swivel-eyed suspicion. Contemplating his turbulent life, he didn't blame: not his family, his country or The World. He merely accepted, over and over again, 'I been through a lotta shit.'

Where I'd hoped for a sweeping discourse on poverty, politics and The Meaning Of It All, his only enemy, in 2000, was the gleam-toothed tyranny of the 'boy/girl bands' he found 'fuckin' phoney', as if he'd just discovered the existence of superficial pop. Maybe he had. Then again, it had never been quite this dominant. The gripe was also personal: a good-looking, blond, blue-eyed white boy, most of the planet's twelve-year-old girls couldn't have cared less if he was hip hop's greatest-ever superhero or a member of *NSYNC.

'Right,' he furrowed. 'People might confuse me with that. I think it's the blond hair thing.'

And you're terribly good-looking as well, you see.

'Uh ...' He flinched, mortified. Then, a microscopic smile. 'Thank you. But, um ... I just wanna make sure that people don't put me in that category.' He returned to annoyed. ''Cos every time I turn on a fuckin' TV, I'm seein' a fuckin' boy/girl group, this shit is so fuckin' corny, this shit is fake, horrible.' He began shouting. 'Life is not that happy! *Fuck* *NSYNC, *fuck* Backstreet Boys, *fuck* Britney Spears, *fuck* Christine Aguilera, *fuck* all that bullshit, that shit is *trash* to me.'

How come you've referred to all the boybands as 'faggots'? And we're going to talk about this once and talk about it fast, OK?

'Faggot to me,' began Eminem, wearily, 'doesn't necessarily mean gay person. Faggot to me means pussy, sissy. If you're a man, be a man, knowhumsayin'? That's the worst thing you can say to a man, it's like callin' 'em a girl. Growing up, faggot was a common word. I don't give a shit about *gay*, if they wanna be gay then that's their fuckin' business.' His hand sprang into the air. 'Don't try that shit on *me* but, hey, as long as they ain't hurtin' nobody, ain't hurtin' me, whatever. Be gay, do your thing, if you take it in the ass, you take it in the ass, you suck dick, whatever, that's your business, knowhumsayin'?'

Why would that freak you out so much anyway?

He was now addressing an alien. 'Why would it freak me out? A man suckin' another man's *dick*!? I just said it! I don't get it.'

That's it, I give up. What is it with you hip hop geezers?

'In hip hop it's just not cool to be gay. It's just not.'

But why go on about it all the time? This obsession?

'It's because hip hop is all about manhood, about competition, about bein' macho, it goes with the territory. And I'd rather we go on to something else, if we may.'

The interview disintegrated further, attempts to cheer him

up with flirty comments on how much girls now loved him received like a hammer of damnation pranging off his head.

'I wasn't cute before,' he seethed, 'and suddenly girls are throwing themselves at you, literally, it's extremely fucking weird to me.'

He slid further down the back of the couch.

'To tell you the truth, fame is not all it's cracked up to be,' he frowned, 'it's a lotta bullshit. My life ... story, is like, for the public to view now. And that shit don't make me happy. I've had to deal with racism, critics, reporters askin' stoopid fuckin' questions, being too personal, about my life, or my daughter. I gotta keep some sense of privacy about me, some shit just ain't people's business. I can't say I enjoy it 24/7. I'm not gonna lie.'

The Eminem Phenomenon, remarkable enough in itself, was even more so as a microcosm of nu-celebrity. In the year 2000 this was a still-burgeoning new world, where you did become, literally overnight, an actual global superstar, from the moment you woke up after your first gigantic hit single supersonically propelled you around the multi-media superhighway. The Machine, from this day on, put you to work on an equator-sized conveyor belt to burnout oblivion, a vast, multi-layered, internationally agreed conspiracy to exploit your Moment for maximum profit, no matter the cost to your mind, soul, body or relationships, even your music or your future. If you were Westlife you went mad, you toed the line, you grinned and you bore it. If you were Graham out of Blur/Richey Manic you went mad and took it out on yourself. If you were Eminem, you went mad, got madder and madder and took it out on the immediate world around you.

After twelve months and one global anthem ('My Name Is') Eminem had had enough already, bearing the cynicism and suspicion of a three-album veteran. The speed of nu-celebrity was insane enough if you came from Normality and really wanted it: he wanted to be An Artist and came from Hell. He said he watched himself on TV and saw a stranger. 'It's like I don't know who I am,' he blinked, 'you absolutely lose your identity.' His '24/7' workload had led to 'total confusion', no longer able to view life outside the entertainment industry. In one year he'd gone from no money whatsoever to incalculable wealth. 'To tell you the truth, I have more money than I know what to do with,' he nodded, 'I went from not being able to afford nothing to ... limitless money, almost.' The only thing money was good for, he added, was security for his daughter. 'She's gonna be able to go to college and be something.'

The first Hip Hop Superstar of Self-Loathing also showed signs of the bullied becoming the bully. 'That's the one part I do love about it,' he eventually smiled. 'I sit back and wait for people to diss me. And if someone does diss me I will fuckin' demolish your self-esteem. I will fuckin' say everything I can in my fuckin' power to hurt you and make you wanna jump off a bridge. Y'knowhumsayin'?' He tapped his temple. 'I think I was given this ability to put words together like I do, in order to do this. That's how I came up, in the hip hop circles, in battles, MC-ing, and through arguments with my mother, fights with my girl, period. That's just how I am. I'm a very spiteful person if you do me wrong.'

Do you run on vengeance?

'Yeah,' he answered, immediately.

That's your main motivation?

'Probably.'

Has being famous made you like yourself any more?

'No. It's the same.'

Seeing as you're three people now – Marshall, Eminem, Slim Shady – if those three were walking down the street together how would you describe them?

'Marshall Mathers would be a regular person,' he mused.

'Eminem would be a nice guy and Slim Shady would be a fuckin' asshole, a complete dick.'

Which one d'you want for a friend?

'Marshall.'

Which one d'you most admire?

'Slim Shady.'

Who'd win in a fight?

'Slim Shady.'

Who's the smartest?

'Eminem.'

Who's the loser?

'Marshall.'

Who's the winner?

'Slim Shady.'

And he sloped off out of his office with his head down and his hood up, back into the shadows of a waiting, sleek black car.

Eminem continued to go though 'a lotta shit', becoming severely addicted to prescription drugs (up to sixty Valium and thirty Vicodin pills a day), entered rehab in 2005, relapsed, almost overdosed on methadone in 2007 and was two hours away from death as his vital organs began shutting down. *The Marshall Mathers LP* went on to become acknowledged as a hip hop classic, a work of supreme guile, originality and hilarity – even by me, through a column in *The Face* magazine titled 'Eminem, An Apology'. I'd made the mistake, again, of being disappointed when a hero turned out to be, you know, *not a particularly nice person*. And why should he have been? He's EMINEM. Who remains to this day, to some, the greatest rapper of all time.

Arriving back in London after the Eminem trip, I walked into the bedroom of the heater-less flat in Hackney and the bedroom ceiling had fallen in, the damp finally proving structurally fatal, collapsed segments of plasterboard and painted panels now scattered across a mouldy green-streaked duvet. My clothes, on a free-standing, damp-exposed rail, were also ruined. I coughed ruefully, once again.

Every day was a battle alright, but dramatically more so for MC Proof. On 11 April 2006, six years on from admiring the benign vision of a pea-green military jacket, he was fatally gunned down in a Detroit nightclub. He was thirty-two years old.

Back in 2001, though, just like the splintering, mouldy ceiling in my Hackney hovel, the spirit of the once inspirationally subversive *NME* began collapsing in on itself, too ...

26

THE MAN DON'T GIVE A FUCK
(ABOUT ANYBODY ELSE)

Walking into a newsagent's in April 2001, the new *NME* proudly shimmered from shelves, its cover image so alien to me it caused an involuntary out-loud shriek. Busting out from the front of the magazine which had once been my foamingly important teenage wallpaper, fount of all ideological fervour and crucible of The Revolution, was a pair of bikini-clad breasts, without the apparently irrelevant accompaniment of a head, the word 'MIAMI' written in several lines of cocaine across the cleavage.

The previous December, the ongoing disintegration of the

music press had seen *NME*'s weekly rival *Melody Maker* topple into The Dumper. This latest *NME* cover 'star' was a woefully crude attempt at luring in the readership of the more steadily successful dance music magazines of the early noughties (*Mixmag*, *Muzik*), the inside non-story a gaudy report on the annual sex 'n' drugs fest of the music industry's Miami Music Conference. Most gallingly of all, it didn't even look out of place.

In 2001 the culture, everywhere, was warping. The past twelve months had ushered in not only bands-as-brands (soon *everything* would be a brand) but newly appointed Brand Managers now ubiquitous throughout publishing. Since the rollicking dramas of the mid-nineties Britpop Wars, the tabloids had become obsessively pop fixated, showbiz columnists now in every redtop newspaper, outré 'goss' on personal lives routinely swapped for coverage in unspoken, symbiotic deals between celebs and their media hosts. Gossip mags were shooting upwards throughout an eerily shiny pop landscape like toxic toadstools, the 1999-launched *Heat* magazine soon finding its voice via *Big Brother* and *Pop Idol* in UK Reality TV year zero. Most dominantly, though, The Internet had changed everything, not only wrecking the mags' already tenuous claim to 'exclusivity' but creating in the celebs a default position of paranoia as all public figures became aware, for the first time, any lone journo's microphone was actually a radioactive global megaphone just one careless (interesting) quip away from a hollering tabloid headline. The result (as we'd seen so effectively in Destiny's Child): the emergence of guarded personalities, suppressed opinion and avoidance of the controversial (years before the exposing pitfalls of Twitter even existed).

The media was now run on a cold, corporate philosophy, 'the needs of the market' met at the expense of absolutely everything else (say, in-depth quality, an original idea, even a comedy joust with the world's worst boyband). A gleaming entertainment landscape was now sculpted by focus groups, redesigns and 'rebrands' in search of all-important 'growth', often butchering the brand while they were at it. It seemed DC Thomson's Gordon Small was some kind of zeitgeist guru after all. His Keep It Simple For The Stupids ethos was now taking global root, the phrase 'dumbing down' entering everyday use amid escalating corporate sales-speak, all 'rightsizing' here, 'incentivising' there and 'blamestorming' absolutely everywhere as creative freedom was eclipsed by lowest common denominator commercialism and continuous use of the word 'product'. Everything, now, was a commodity.

Globalisation brought us homogenised high streets and the beginning of Everyone Looking Exactly The Same, while the word 'bling' bounced into the mainstream, rap's original political idealism now morphing into the era where hip hop dudes in America, as I had witnessed, were reading newly published best-seller *Think Yourself Rich* (first line: 'It is your God-given birthright to be rich.')

Loaded magazine, once a hub of world-class wit, was ruined overnight by its latest redesign, another attempt to chase the readership of best-selling rivals *FHM* and *Maxim*. Its new direction, imposed by a new editor (arriving from gossip mag *Chat*), comprised caught-out wanking stories, guides to removing bras 'without her knowing' and stories on the 'twenty-five-year-old male virgin laid by a porn star'. Its first Showbusiness Editor was also appointed, transported in from the *News Of The World*. The magazine's managing editor John Aldred resigned in protest, while *Loaded* creator James Brown declared the men's magazine sector 'pathetic'.

So emerged the risk-averse culture Lily Allen would identify over a decade later as all-encompassing – the fear, primarily, of losing your highly coveted job (and so capitulating to those market needs), without which you'd be forced down the corporate ladder into the flat earth world of, say, David Brent. No wonder *The Office* first aired in 2001, with its low-level sales meeting miseries, Slough's Wernham Hogg paper company the place where, as the company slogan had it, 'life is stationery'.

That year, *The Face* was still in trouble, its greatest editorial coup an interview with newly appointed England Captain David Beckham, the cover image seeing him splattered in blood-like soya sauce in the name of looking all sinisterly hunky. An image enhanced by the first public sighting of his close-cropped mohican, Brian Clough was inspired to the world-class quip, 'looks more like a bloody convict than an England captain'. Given this insanely zeitgeist-tickling interview task, I asked the editor what he wanted to know about the newly iconic Becks. 'I want to know,' he announced, 'what he's going to say that I can put on the cover of this magazine so it'll sell some fucking copies.' No wonder, in this environment, the gossip mags, those experts in the field of K.I.S.S., were taking over the planet. Still, with the nation besotted with Becks (mere weeks before his free kick against Greece took England into the 2002 World Cup finals), I seized the opportunity to ask The Zeitgeist why The Zeitgeist was now as it was, an emerging brand himself, a full year before he defined the also-emerging concept of the 'metrosexual'.

In 2001 David Beckham was both the cultural equivalent of Miss World in 1974 – a 100 per cent sexually objectified figure of intellectual ridicule – and the perfect study in contemporary fame, he and his wife now the love/hate media-stoked obsession of the unstoppable celebrity age. He'd seen a recent documentary featuring a girl who 'hated' Posh 'n' Becks yet bought every publication they appeared in, 'to find out,' as Becks put it, 'what we're doing – it's a strange fascination'.

We were in a tiny dressing room in a photo studio in

Manchester, his tanned arm stretched tantalisingly along the back of the sofa we were both rather cosily sitting on. I'd just begun wearing reading glasses, which I now took off, so *nothing would come between us.* I had a chance, too, to have another go at Westlife and their floppy fringes.

Did you shave your head initially in 2000 because Westlife were at their peak with 'three David Beckhams' and were the worst band in the world?

'Neuh! Neurgh, heurgh!' came the sound of David Beckham's unexpectedly infectious laugh, as he picked up a pen and pinged it – ting! – off the back of a nearby chrome chair. 'Aw, I can't answer that,' he smiled, dreamily. 'I shaved my hair initially 'cos there were so many people ... with my sort of hairstyle.'

So it was them. It was! It was! It's written all over your face!

'No no no, it was people in general.'

You had your trademark pinched. And trademarks are really important to you, aren't they?

'Yeah, definitely.'

That's very canny you know.

'Yeah?'

Because you're not just a footballer, you're an entity, a phenomenon and a brand.

'Hmn. Never looked at it that way.'

Why did you want to be the face of Police sunglasses?

'I thought it was cool.'

You obviously don't need the money.

'No I don't but I like doing it, I enjoy it.'

Is it because you fancy yourself as a bit of a model?

'Oh no. No no no! I definitely don't fancy meself as a model, definitely not. I'm not good looking enough for that. (much protesting from me) I'm not!'

Well, why then?

'I just like it! I think you've always gotta have sumfink outside of your job. Shoots like this I enjoy, its a nonna [translation: an honour] even though I'm all soy sauce.'

Is it because you always wanted to be much more than just a great football player? A contemporary icon?

'Well you don't see the possibilities that you get coming. At a young age I wanted to be the best footballer in the world. Well, see . . . people say icon and it's a bit embarrassing for me to talk about.'

I always thought you were at ease with it all.

'I am in a way. So many people have talked about it I have got used to it. But I don't turn round to Victoria and say "Good morning, I am an icon".'

And she says, 'good morning, so am I'.

'Exactly!'

And then you say, 'my icon's bigger than your icon'.

'Yeah. And then we explain to each other what icons we are. And then I say "I'm a gay icon".'

And that's definitely a football first. A real barrier obliterated.

'I think it is. Because footballers have always had that label of drinking and being macho and I think it's definitely changing.'

Is it because it's the nature of the world? It's a big, gay modern world out there and you want to represent it?

'Well it's the nature of my world. So I'm happy with it, I'm comfortable, it's never been a problem, ever, and why should it? It's just the way I am. It's the way I was brought up, I'm not prejudiced against anyone.'

D'you think it's really funny that the football geezers have to give you your due because of your talent when, in their minds, they cannot get over the fact you're The Perfumed Ponce?

'Yeah. Neuh heuh!' he chortled, delighted. 'I do. I fink it's *hilarious*. Deep down I don't give a monkey's. Before the Finland game we was staying at a hotel and I got a phone call from the press person in London saying "Have you just had a manicure?" And I said "Well, yeah," and she said, "Well, one of the papers has got hold of it.' And I was like "Well, what's the big story? I have had it done, but tell 'em I haven't had it done." They didn't run it in the end: England Captain Gets His Nails Done . . .'

We talked about his lifelong love for clothes, about how, aged seven, his hairdresser mum Sandra took him to find a pageboy outfit for a family wedding and he insisted on the one with white socks up to the knees, velvet maroon knickerbockers, white ballet shoes, a frilly Spanish shirt and matching maroon waistcoat. Mum told him he'd be laughed at and he didn't care, began wearing it round the house. The only thing he was interested in at school was art and if football hadn't existed he might have gone to art college. He liked clothes so much because he didn't want to be 'a sheep' and because they made him feel 'artistic'. The infamous Beckham sarong (Gaultier) wasn't Victoria's idea, it was his own, bought while shopping with Mel B's ex-husband Jimmy Gulzar in Paris. He thought it 'so cool' he bought several in different colours. Ever since, the assumption was born, as he noted himself, 'she's wearing the trousers and she's got him wearing a skirt'.

What d'you think your clothes say about you?

'That I'm relaxed in whatever I wear. I'm not afraid to wear sumfink different. (The Smile.) What d'you think they say about me?'

(momentarily blinded) I'm not telling you that . . .

He giggled his head off. 'You're supposed to say "You look like a tart"!'

Curses! Outwitted by the allegedly stupidest man in the universe. Soon, I'd have the chance to ask David Beckham what 'it' was all about.

Here's a quote for you, from Brad Pitt: 'I'm the man who has everything, right? Well, let me tell you, as the guy who has everything,

*when you get everything, all you're left with is yourself.' D'you think
that's true?*

An enormous pause: 'Yeah. I do think that's true.'

Why?

'Because I was happy before. I was happy when I didn't have
anything. I was happy anyway.'

Back on earth, *NME* acquaintance Andy Crysell, in an attempt
to forge new creative pathways, invented a music/arts website
called Ammo City, for which I wrote a weekly column, 'Slant'.
The rebranded *Loaded* and the Great *NME* Cocaine Tits scandal
of 2001 became topical material around a wider rumination on
the woefully changing mores of Britain's sometime best-loved
magazines.

That year had seen several dreadful *NME* covers: an overview
of the alleged hip hop explosion (a cultural constant since
the 1980s, visualised via illustrations on the cover rather than
photos of the black artists so revered inside), a celebration of
New York City (featuring a guide to scoring crack) and a report
citing British teenagers as 'the worst in Europe', claiming they
imbibed more fags, booze and drugs than any other nation,
which it responded to with the teen-text cover-line: 'BRTNS
YTH: 2 FCKD 2CARE'. The story inside implied education
didn't matter, having no politicised worldview didn't matter
and selling drugs on the streets of Brixton 'ain't a bad thing,
it's a good income' in the words of nineteen-year-old Neutrino
from techno tiddlers Oxide & Neutrino, a pull-out quote which
didn't exist in the main text, having evidently been edited out.
This was a message telling *NME* readers education counted for
nothing, from an editorial staff of university graduates with the
young folks' dream jobs in the media.

Around this time I was told by an *NME* staffer there'd be
no one on the cover again who had a 'visual drawback' and,

furthermore, they were planning a cover interview with Janet Jackson, who clearly had no visual drawbacks whatsoever.

I was, you might say, on the brink.

That month I'd been in San Francisco with instrumental 'orchestrated rock' visionaries Mogwai, from Glasgow, who *were* appearing on the cover, albeit with instruction from the *NME* that they must somehow be caricatured – maybe a straitjacket here, a bucket of blood over their heads there – all the better to distract from their evidently hideous 'visual drawbacks'. A band of abundantly sane, prodigiously smart and stand-up-comedian-level wits, these twenty-five-year-old, *NME* heartland musicians were mortified. They refused to dress up, as lead musician/spokesman, the gloriously uncompromising Stuart Braithwaite had it, 'like cunts'. Being the *NME*'s representative I too was mortified, and after many hours in the pub began to blub, soon carried out of a bar in the arms of their pragmatic PR man, John, and punted off to bed.

San Francisco had proved a catalyst for these persistent indignations, the home of what we once called the counterculture still a haven for outsider thought, a city where leaflets found on the subway implored 'Do Not Trust The Corporate Media'. In a free arts 'n' music city guide found in a café, a writer commented on the most potent force field sculpting our thoughts today, the worldwide mainstream media and its creation of a whitewash of fleeting, entertainment idiocy while people, the planet and everything else literally burned. 'We need to save the present,' it concluded, dramatically, 'from a future without memory.'

Mogwai were inherently outsiders, the kind of creative minds whose very oxygen was robust opinion, for whom U2 were 'as evil a corporation as Sony'. A band whose merchandising T-shirt once announced 'Blur: are shite' (plans to create the follow-up, 'Gorillaz: even worse', were sadly shelved). Concerned I'd been 'upset' on the trip, they suggested we meet again for a less fraught follow-up interview. We did, back in London – on the very day the Cocaine Tits cover appeared.

'You pick up the *NME* and there's a pair of exposed breasts with Miami written in cocaine, that really sums up modern culture in Britain,' observed Stuart. 'I like breasts but let's not be stupid here. I think that some really, really, *really* vulgar ideology crept in a few years ago, some really fucking nasty sexist ideas and anti-thought devices and they got largely ignored by anyone with any intelligence or integrity. But since then, they've been so omnipresent that a lot of young people and people who actually have a bit of say, don't think anything of them. A pair of breasts on the cover of *NME* would've been seen as abhorrent eight years ago. Even *one* year ago, but eight years ago *unthinkable*. But breasts are now the selling point of almost every magazine in every shop.'

'We have no relevance to that one-dimensional view of culture,' continued Stuart, evenly. 'The *NME*'s meant to be the alternative and now it's the Indie *Heat*. What is a young person who's into music gonna learn from Janet Jackson and her publicity machine? Music as a cultural force is a way of life. And to move the goalposts to the point music isn't a cultural force anymore, but actually a commodity, is the sad, sad fact of what's happening. I just ... *pity the young*. Even when they bring in hip hop, it's in a really embarrassing, patronising way.'

'With cartoons,' noted drummer Martin Bulloch. 'Too scared to put a black person on the cover.' (This was a reference not only to the hip hop 'Explosion' illustrated cover, but the Wu Tang Clan's recent cover image, the Batman-homage Wu Tang logo, despite photos specifically taken to accompany several interviews I'd completed in New York with the supposedly terrifying Clan, who'd proved positively adorable.)

The young might tell you this is what they wanted all along.

'What the people want and what the people need are often

very different,' decided Stuart, with a rueful snort. 'But from getting into music, you can get from that source so many different cultural things. For a lot of people it doesn't come from anywhere else. And it's depressing when people are patronising, it's depressing when people are sneered at. Because a lot of the people we're talking about here went to Oxford University, and they should know better.'

When I sent this interview in, the new features editor, Alex Needham, was (understandably) furious. Alex was a sometime *Smash Hits* contributor, *Face* team staffer and friend of mine who clearly thought I'd gone insane, sending an email declaring it obviously unprintable, insisting I tone it down, likening my right-on indignations to the lyrics of po-faced UK grunge troupe My Vitriol.

On receiving it, I battered out a reply and was reading it one last time before pressing 'send' when Alex suddenly rang up. We argued for twenty minutes – about my Ammo City column, Cocaine Tits, Mogwai, the New York/hip hop covers, Janet Jackson – and I never did press 'send'. But I never pressed 'delete' either, and found this email recently, by accident, on one of my old semi-conscious laptops. Reading it back, hand clasped to face, the ghost of my former, vibratingly righteous self was rebooted into electrical life like Frankenstein's monster fizzing upwards on the laboratory table. (Note to Alex, old chum of the Um Bongo ways: Let's hope we can both laugh about it now – but, as a beloved old song once said, at the time it was terrible . . .)

> Alex
>
> First of all, I would've appreciated having a 'real' conversation but seeing as that appears to be impossible, we'll have to do it the 21st Century way.
>
> I was asked to write about the new *Loaded* for Ammo

City and suitably appalled I did. This was the very week the *NME* tits 'n' cocaine cover left me feeling literally sick in the newsagents. I suppose it's this more than anything that marked what I considered The End, the end of any notion of the *NME* I've ever had. I don't care it was a last-minute decision, someone there thought this was a marvellous wheeze and it went ahead with everyone's blessing and, quite frankly, it's unforgivable. I was ashamed of 'my' paper and angry. I always thought, as Spike Milligan once said, *NME* was 'against the cliché' and I don't think it can be justified on any level. What the drug-riddled music industry on its vastly expensive holidays has to tell any *NME* reader is 100% beyond me.

You're free to believe I 'led' Mogwai into a discussion of the state of everything if you so choose. We did an interview in San Francisco and it was strained because of the way the band were being asked to be represented. There's been a good few years' history now of making Mogwai feel they're just too damn ugly to appear on the cover of the *NME* and, once again, *NME* had come up with some schemes to turn them into something more acceptable i.e. wear straitjackets or pyjamas or fake blood and look like, in their estimation, a bunch of cunts. The band told me they felt 'humiliated'. So I felt humiliated. And even more angry.

They asked to meet me again because they were 'concerned' that I was 'upset' and I did and there the tirade began, on the very day the tits 'n' cocaine cover appeared on the shelves. I had absolutely no idea 'The Indie *Heat*' was an office in-joke. There's been plenty people who've mentioned that very phrase to me these last few weeks, people who've nothing to do with the media as well as the ones who are everything to do with it. It's not the smartest joke in the world but it looks like it's the most obvious. I can only assume it's a 'major problem' because it's true.

Yes, I told them *NME* was doing a Janet Jackson interview, because it seems to me another indication of the direction *NME*'s going in. It's a 'celebrity' interview, no more, no less, and as you said yourself it's all about sex. She's been going on about sex for the last 10 years. Are you seriously trying to tell me it's because of her 'contribution to R&B'? And the single's absolute arse.

The 'great' *NME* debate about not putting black people on the cover has been running for years and years. For a lot of people, the Wu Tang logo cover and the 'cartoon' hip hop cover was yet more confirmation of the traditionally perceived conspiracy. It's nothing new. I liked the Wu Tang logo myself but the whole idea of a hip hop issue announcing its 'arrival' a hundred years after its inception is howlingly pathetic and we all know it. Furthermore, the first person who ever said to me exactly what Martin Bulloch did was a black hip hop guru himself only two months before. Furthermore, it wasn't any of you lot who had to put up with apologising to the 395 foot tall manager of Cypress Hill for the puerile and wholly unnecessary cartoonisation of the band last year, it was me, in a room, on my own, being told *NME*'s visual representation of Cypress Hill was 'insulting'. I stuck up for the paper 100% and inside I was dying. Without which flannel, I was on the next plane home and *NME* would've had no interview with Eminem, as crap as it was.

Personally, I don't give a flying fuck where anyone went to university. All Mogwai are saying is the people who have always run *NME* are highly educated people who know how important education is. For people like Mogwai, and people like me, the NME has always been the well-spring of an alternative reality, free from conventional confines, even when I barely knew what anyone was writing about. The pages of the NME were my actual wall-paper when I was a bairn. It meant everything to me. And that's specifically why I do what I do. And then came Smash Hits and it was the same thing except it was free from the uptight wordiness and the funniest thing I'd ever read in my life. Don't forget, Alex, how many it sold. Why people think only the crap sells is also beyond me. Then again, maybe I was spoiled. But I still believe in it and I always will. Then again, exactly the same 'powers that be' are doing exactly the same thing to the NME now as they did to Smash Hits 12 years ago. Maybe I just can't take it anymore.

Mogwai are on the cover, or perhaps were, for reasons of tokenism. It was you that said to me you'd quite a few 'glamorous' or was it 'big-name' covers around then, 'so we need some quality ... well not quality ... um' ... what exactly did you mean? And you wonder why I can't talk to you properly anymore. There'll be no accusations of giving up on the indie heartland as long as you've got Mogwai there. And I can't believe I've just written something so obvious.

I could also never in a million years think you were an 'absolute cunt' or a 'handmaiden of Satan'. I'm not that shallow and I'm not [the late furious NME polemicist] Steven Wells. I know you wouldn't have taken this job on if you didn't mean it, I know you think it's making things better, I just don't agree. Now, if you'd had a photo of the exceptionally good-looking and not bad Strokes on the cover (even though they're still The New

York Gene), I might've enjoyed buying it, guiltily, as a pervy aunt, instead of feeling my entire lifetime's belief in music media was being hollowed out in front of my eyes. Again.

I also think the NY cover looks like a bunch of crap. From ten years ago. It took me 20 minutes to read the whole thing and I was really trying. The overwhelming 'idea' I get from this week's issue is that it's a really good idea to go to New York and score loads of crack. And here's where and how. Yeah, crack's a really funny joke.

Every single week now the *NME*'s identity crisis becomes more and more apparent. Sex surveys more puerile than anything even *SKY* magazine could muster. 'Tune' into nme.com and there's competitions to meet Westlife. It's *Front* Magazine, *Kerrang!*, *Mixmag*, *Time Out* … I don't know what 'you' are supposed to do Alex, I'm not in your business. All I know is sex, drugs, shite tunes and vacuous bollocks are everywhere and nowhere is there any suggestion of love or poetry or art or depth or compassion.

Just in case you didn't know, *NME* pays its freelance writers less than any other established music publication in Britain. There's been no pay rise certainly in the last seven years since I've been there. It's still 10p a word. No one, of course, gives a fuck about that.

I deeply resent the 'My Vitriol' comment. I deeply resent the email you sent me.

Obviously, I resign.

Sylvia Patterson

3 May 2001

On finishing reading this for the first time in well over a decade, I laughed like a donkey for a full three minutes (even if

I was *still right*). I wrote that email having just turned thirty-six and shouldn't so much as have left *NME* years before as neither known nor cared if it still existed. But I didn't just care, I cared *way too much*.

I'd been in music journalism, of some sort, since the age of fourteen, penning Psychedelic Furs reviews for school magazine *PG Snips*. Twenty-two years later, like a long-term inmate in *The Shawshank Redemption* unable to make the transition to outside society, I was institutionalised, feeling like a knackered, coughing, flimsy echo of the mighty Lester Bangs, the most righteous music writer of them all. 'Don't ask me why I obsessively look to rock 'n' roll bands for some kind of model for a better society,' he wrote in 1977, obsessed that year by The Clash. 'I guess it's just that I glimpsed something beautiful in a flashbulb moment once, and perhaps mistaking it for prophecy have been seeking its fulfilment ever since. And perhaps that nothing else in the world ever seemed to hold even that much promise.' By 1982, aged thirty-three, he was dead, from an accidental drugs overdose, his record player locked into a groove of the Human League album *Dare*. This was not, you know, rock 'n' roll, a good look, or anything you'd hope to emulate.

I might have lived three years longer than Lester already but that year, in the midst of profound professional disillusion, after The Dancer, the 67p soup budget and eighteen demoralising months of moving-home-hell I was more insane than even Alex had surely imagined. But one important progression, at least, had been made: an old boyfriend and now pal had rescued me from the derelict buildings, renting me out a room in his fourth floor, two-bedroom flat in an ex-council block near King's Cross. (A man who must remain nameless, seeing as he once told me, cheerily, 'If you ever write about me, I will hunt you down and burn your fucking house down.') It was here where I was reading a tower of Oasis press cuttings – preparing to finally interview the Gallaghers, for the *NME*, which I would not be doing had I pressed 'send' on an email four months previously – when Radio 1 announced its hourly news bulletin, unusually from America. A passenger plane had flown straight into the World Trade Center and the building was ablaze, in what appeared to be a devastating one-off accident. And then a second plane struck.

Abandoning the rock 'n' roll high jinks I lurched into the living room and switched on the TV as the phone rang. It was a stunned Gilly B (ex-Stephendale Roader), also alone in her new home, and together we watched the twin towers collapse on live TV.

By midnight the images were indelible through constant repetition: the planes, the fireballs, the doomed 'jumpers', the moments of collapse, the spiky, twisted, remnant ground floor girders of the buildings hazily visible through the debris and ash, in a world now seen through a filter of grey, like the world's first photograph of the entry gates to Hell.

In the morning, after three hours' sleep, the images on TV were exactly the same. Someone got the ironing board out, it must've been me, the banalities of everyday life blithely carrying on, now ironing a shirt I could not see for the constant splash of tears as the mind fired off hopeless thoughts: Well that's it, then. We Are Fucked. Why did we ever bother crawling out the sea in the first place? Mankind, this time, was comprehensively rumbled as a dubious blip, a hideous mistake, a DNA experiment too successful for its own good, and the quicker we all blew ourselves up and gave the planet back to the algae, the better. And now I had to board a bus to meet my nineties heroes and ask them why *Be Here Now* was rubbish, and other queries of no consequence whatsoever. And to think, four months previously, I'd wept over a cleavage on the cover of a rock 'n' roll magazine.

27

ROLL WITH IT

September 12th 2001, 11 a.m.
'I've been up all night watching people falling out the fookin' sky . . .'

Seven years' wait to meet Noel Gallagher properly and he strode, with formidable purpose, into a white-walled photographic studio in Kentish Town, north London, exactly on time, perfectly proportioned, dressed in regulation black, three feet tall, fired up about everything *but* rock 'n' roll high jinks.

' . . . you know what they're like in the Midwest,' he carried on, pacing around the floor, 'old Chip polishing his fucking M16 he uses to kill deer sat watching it thinking "Right! (claps hands) Where's the nearest fucking Arab?" Well, it's the end of the world, innit?'

For the next fifteen minutes Noel Gallagher, thirty-four, proved impressively knowledgeable on Middle Eastern politics, most of us only hearing the words 'Osama bin Laden' for the first time yesterday afternoon. The kitchen door then detonated off its hinges as Liam Gallagher shattered through it, thumping down on a sofa adjacent to his brother. My, he was still beautiful. But it was never a sex thing, for me, with Liam, I just wanted to look at him, and marvel, as you would at an intoxicating visitor from an intergalactic dimension.

What d'you reckon, Liam?

Liam, puffing on a snout, just as he had been in my living room five years previously: 'It's too good. It's bullseye. (puff puff) Nostradamus. Apparently, New York will be flattened by a geezer wearin' a cloth on his 'ead. Before the year 2010. Pretty much on its fookin' way, innit?'

Noel: 'Anyway! "Roll With It", what a fucking song . . .'

It was surely the heightened emotions of the day, and the sleep deprivation, and the feeling we were living at The End of Time, that lent seventy-five minutes with the Gallaghers that morning an acutely ironic atmosphere of comic hysteria, the kind you need for release at a particularly devastating funeral. Positioned around the sofas we addressed the suddenly insanely inconsequential 'Oasis issues' of the day, beginning with the nationwide consensus that they had, by then, already turned into this generation's Rolling Stones, an endless, lumbering nostalgia machine.

'Nah nah nah, there's none of that, man!' blared Liam, wound up already, a peg-fresh shiny blue cagoule zipped up to his chin, the light from his enormous 'Liz Taylor' eyes beaming like lasers straight through his John Lennon shades. 'There's no way I'll be turning like the fookin' Rolling Stones,' he assured, 'I don't go on the road to make money, it just so happens we do, but I go on the road to have a laugh an' play me rock 'n' roll and that's the fookin' end of it, and if anyone tries to tell me different they're off their fookin' tits. I don't wanna be the biggest band in the world anymore, I wanna be the best, and we *are* the fookin' best, he's the best songwriter in the world, end of story and that's all I can say . . . so I'll see yous all later!'

He leapt up, attempted to stifle a grin, thundered over to a fridge, swiped a water and bowled back to his seat.

You broke my heart with Be Here Now.

Noel: 'Well, I don't know what people expected.'

Some more brilliance, of course.

Noel: 'Well, I apologise.'

Well, good. Because the spirit went. And the spirit was everything.

Liam: 'What, like, with the music? Oh yeah, completely!'

Noel: 'That was my fault.'

I listened to that album pished, stoned, tried it in the morning, in the night, on a hill, trying to find the soul.

Noel: 'You should've tried it on nine grams of charlie, 'cos that's what it was written on.'

Liam: 'Eheheheh!'

Noel: 'Well, everybody has a shit period and hopefully we've had ours. And this new album . . . is fucking mega! I'm not a drug addict anymore. So it's not just "well, fuck it, that'll do" which is what *Be Here Now* should've been called.'

Soon, the pace began accelerating, Noel leading an increasingly spirited obliteration of everything in contemporary culture (apart from The Strokes, who had 'the tunes, man'); scorching derision for the rise of Coldplay and the 'sensitive' guitar weeds, the posturing of the US nu-metal gonks (Limp Bizkit, Slipknot) and the continuation of the tot's pop jamboree dominating the atmosphere, still. All Noel listened to was 'the television, 'cos everything that comes out the radio's pish, basically'. Liam deemed the likes of Chris Martin 'Christian Rock', now exuberantly chain-smoking his brother's snouts. 'And they're all dead nice, scared of saying anything that's remotely fookin' interesting, it's embarrassing,' he thundered on, describing a cultural shift which was only just beginning.

'There's too many polite people and too many clever people making music these days. And if they weren't in a band they'd have a great fookin' job anyway, y'knowhatImean? It's different for people like us, it's the band or nothing, it's life or death. 'Cos I can't do anything else.'

Equally hopeless was panto-villain rock from Marilyn Manson, which caused Noel to furiously pace the floor, imagining Manson's band in rehearsals, in jeans and trainers. 'Hey, so uh, Mar-i-lyn? What am I doing at this point?' he roared, impersonating the crutch-wielding ghouls. '"Well, I'm gonna pretend to decapitate you man! But you have to understand man, you're gonna be wearing stilts!" People set their standards too low in their fucking icons these days.'

Fame, added Liam, was the new generation's No. 1 priority, 'the pop lot, right, their goal in life is to have their picture took', while the boot was also stuck into football. 'Where's the fucking balls!?' balked Noel, comparing Michael Owen and Alan Shearer to 'fucking coppers. Alan Shearer looks like CID and Michael Owen looks like trainee CID, I've been busted by Alan Shearer so many times it's unbelievable.' Money, fumed Noel, had kicked the rock 'n' roll out of football too.

'They're groomed now aren't they? *Groomed*,' he despaired. 'David Beckham went into media training for three weeks before he went on *Parkinson*. Fookin' trainin' for what!? Just answer the fookin' question! Football is the same as music, it's TV, but it's not just a business, it's now a system. They're put in the system. And they're put in the system by people to perpetuate the system, otherwise it's "we'll send you back to the gutter". The Man has taken over the world! All the kids look up to now are bland, faceless fucking trainee police officers! He [Liam] should be given a knighthood! A *knighthood*! You couldn't imagine Chris Martin from Coldplay laying out a photographer for takin' a picture of his kid! It's all gone. Gone! Who's the biggest icon in the country? David Beckham. He gets a mohican and everybody writes column inches in the paper? He got a fookin' mohican! It's not even a proper Exploited one!'

Noel was now apoplectic, his cackling brother joining in when he could find a sliver of an entry point. Liam announced he didn't care if he sounded like a grandpa already, ''cos at the end of the day, shite's shite, I don't give a fuck, I'm a moaning cunt and I'm twenty-eight', while Noel was steadfast in his old-school spirit.

'Too right!' he blared. 'I'm glad to be old-school. I'm glad I've got ideals and they were taught to me by Bob Marley and John Lennon and John Lydon and Paul Weller and Morrissey and Marr. And now people start bands for a *career*. Careerism! We never started this band as a career move, we did it 'cos we were bored shitless and we were all on the dole and this is our life. We never asked for a record deal, somebody gave us one. We never asked for fucking twenty million record sales, it just came, y'knowhatImean?'

He sprang from the sofa once more and circled round the back of it, twice, just as Bono had done in indignation the year before.

'The people who are sat in the offices of fucking Sony, who I'm signed to, they're a bunch of fucking cunts,' he boomed. 'And the rest of 'em in Virgin and all the rest of it, they're fucking killing it, they're stealthily taking away extremism and talent. Alternative music is now like fucking Val Doonican to me, same with football. If they were to find George Best on a playing field right now on Hackney Marshes, they'd sign him up, tell him to stop drinking, stop smoking . . .'

Liam: 'Stop shagging birds . . .'

Noel: ' . . . get your fucking sponsorship deal, get married immediately. The last two, great, working-class things, football and music, they're coaching all the talent out of people. Music should be spontaneous! *And* football. And *all* the arts. I just find it really sinister. And it's the faceless people who are responsible. And we're *all* responsible. The bands are responsible. If people are selling 250,000 records every six months, they don't care, it's "get me the money, get me it now". And ten years later it'll be your Greatest Hits. And ten years later it'll be your Greatest Hits Remastered and ten years later it's your Greatest Hits Remastered and Repackaged and then when one of you dies it'll be your Greatest Hits all over again with sleeve-notes by some fucking geezer who walked your dog once. It's all up its own fucking arse, man! And I have actually worked myself up into a bit of a fookin' state!'

It's alright lads, Bob The Builder's number one!

Noel: 'I remember when there were good fookin' novelty records and nobody gave a fuck. Now, Bob The Builder's number one and Mel C's phoning him up wanting to do a duet. A fucking builder and a joiner. All you need is Ronan Keating and you've got a builder, a joiner and a fookin' plasterer! They'd be better off starting their own firm . . .'

Reaching a crescendo, he blazed through fledgling musicians with managers before they even had a record deal, and musicians who took A level Music, as old foe Damon Albarn had confessed he did (and failed it), on a recent *South Bank Show*.

'Is there an A level Music?' scoffed Noel. 'How d'you do that!? (solemnly) "I got my Bach mixed up with my Beethoven." Fucking *Bach-hoven*. Music's in your fucking *bones* man, it's in your fingernails, you play one chord on a fookin' guitar you're a musician, end of fookin' story. People slag us off for it, but it's a proper emotional thing, it's a human playing a tree. Three chords on a guitar, go write a song. I only know eleven. But I tell you what, God *help* you when I find the twelfth! I'm tellin' yer! And if I ever start reading fookin' *books*!? I'll take over the fookin' world! It'll be *me* crashing into the fookin' Trade Towers!'

Here, he took off in flight across the studio, arms out like a Spitfire, 'flying' around the sofa, hollering how music should make you levitate off the floor.

'When we played "Roll With It" at Wembley, and I hate that song, you saw 76,000 people leaving the floor, *that's* what it's all about,' he serenaded before an impersonation of a jazz toff. 'It's not about "that was an *amaaaazing* suspended eighth you just played there man and I really like the direction of the new rekkid and that gong man was out there". Fucking shurrup man! And *you* drum faster and *you* sing louder and *you* tear up your fookin' amp! Fuck's sake, there's a war going on! The world's gonna fookin' end!'

Maybe there's never been a better time to 'fookin' 'ave it', then, after all . . .

'Actually,' decided Noel, now indeed levitating off the floor, 'fookin' *respect* to the fookin' Islamic Jihad fookin' Hamas fookin' whatsisname Binliner fella! Fookin' set the tone for the fookin' tour! We're all dyin'! Scud missiles are on their way!'

Liam: 'So mine's a fookin' triple . . .'

Noel: '. . . an' fookin' *roll with iiiiiit!* And on that fookin' bombshell let's go'n rehearse rock 'n' roll history. I'm outta here! And d'you know what? That was actually a fookin' pleasure!'

He bolted out the door and didn't look back in anger or anything else as Liam surveyed the empty space where a vibrating Noel Gallagher had just been. 'Our kid's a cracker again,' he beamed, his face (for once) all lit up with genuine, brotherly love.

*

Five weeks after 9/11, I took my first holiday in ten years, invited to join childhood chum Jill (from The Four Of Us back in Perth), her husband Phil (you could tell he was an Irishman but you *certainly* couldn't tell him much) and their two young kids, then eleven months and almost four. Jill was a midwife and had lived in Abu Dhabi in the Middle East for over a decade. Aghast at global events, she was defying humanity's horrors via a beachside villa in Ko Samui, Thailand, for *one full month* and would I like to join them? Just as The Three Of Them had always done, she saved me, once again.

In Thailand, there were significantly more profound things to think about than whether the *NME* was ideologically finished or whether Noel Gallagher would ever write another classic song. The world was now a white-sand, shore-lapping, palm-wafting panorama lit up with neon fireflies, a world populated by the gentlest people on earth, where the pace of life slowed to hitherto unimaginable serenity. After an actual lifetime of emotional, psychological, neurological and professional pandemonium, I didn't just relax. Three weeks in, I finally *stopped*. And thought *this* is what life is for. Friendship. Extended families. Sharing your life with the people you love. I didn't need to ask Mushroom out of Massive Attack anymore. Maybe I'd finally, as Bono had it, burned away the bollocks. To the eternal stuff, like friendship and like love and like laughter.

I had the best friends on earth, the same friends forever, who'd been there for me for a lifetime, the most stabilising forces I'd ever known. All those Oasis songs I'd loved so much, the best ones anyway, were all *about* friendship. And the very purpose of Oasis' music was, as Noel Gallagher once said, 'a celebration of the euphoria of life'.

The world was on fire, bombs were now raining on Afghanistan, but the world was also *burstingly* beautiful. This was a new millennium. There were other worlds to explore.

The possibilities, surely, were endless. Weren't they? I felt like a long-term inmate in *The Shawshank Redemption* once again, but this time Red, who made parole after forty years, who made the journey of hope to find his buddy Andy painting his boat on the edge of the Pacific Ocean.

'I find I'm so excited that I can barely sit still or hold a thought in my head,' concludes Red, setting out on that journey, at the close of one of the most inspirational films ever made. 'I think it's the excitement only a free man can feel. A free man at a start of a long journey whose conclusion is uncertain. I hope I can make it across the border. I hope to see my friend and shake his hand. I hope the Pacific is as blue as it has been in my dreams. I *hope*.'

KYLIE MINOGUE
SMASH HITS

28

BETTER THE DEVIL YOU 'KNOW'

'How old are you now, Sylvie?'
Thirty-seven.
'Oh, *Sylvie . . .*'
The ninth of March 2002, the morning after my thirty-seventh birthday party and Kylie Minogue, almost thirty-four, felt sorry for me, proffering a nice (china) cup of tea, smiling sympathetically, those famed teeth remaining, as Jason Donovan had once observed, *quite prominent.* Since the previous year and the great Cocaine Tits/Mogwai Huff Scandal of 2001, I'd edged away from the *NME*, now more a glossy pamphlet for twelve-year-olds, to work for a glossy monthly for

twenty-eight-year-olds. *Glamour* magazine, launched in the UK in 2001, beautifully reflected our shiny, aspirational, consumerist new millennium, its tag-line famously fanfaring 'Fits in your life as well as your handbag'.

Post Thailand I'd firmly gripped my hopeful new perspective and faced economic reality: The Revolution was an unreliable paymaster currently sending me to debtor's prison and the only way to earn a living was to take the coin of the culture now shimmering unstoppably towards me. And *Glamour* magazine was, unlike so many of the allegedly maverick titles, exuberantly honest. It was also, crucially, beneath its lip-glossed, hobble-heeled, fragrant facade, dedicated at its core to The Sisterhood (with some eye-twitching articles on sex). The inaugural issue, in April 2001, set out its fabulous stall: sumptuous cover star Kate Winslet ('Why my man is one in a million', a few months, it turned out, before her first divorce) alongside tips from Victoria Beckham ('My 10 unbreakable style rules'), 'Oscar-Worthy Hair (Hollywood style to inspire your new look)', 'His 121 Secret Sex Thoughts (The details racing through his mind right now)', '839 Luxury Fashion & Beauty Looks (You'll love them and so will your wallet)' and something not-so-glamorous entitled 'Why did a nice girl help her boyfriend to commit murder?'

By October 2001 I'd become their music correspondent and the ed, winningly wry Australian Jo Elvin, not only liked but encouraged ludicrous jokes, which, after the tone-it-down directives of a confused *NME*, felt like the open door of freedom. Working for *Glamour*, from the off, was a pleasure: encouraging staff, overwhelmingly positive profiles and matey probings defined by sisterly friendliness. *Glamour* UK proved an immediate success, selling half a million copies a month, the biggest-selling women's magazine in Britain.

In spring 2002 came *Glamour*'s summit with Kylie Minogue, the sixth in our simultaneous careers (hers a *soupçon* more fabulous than mine). We were where we usually were, on a vast, spongy orange sofa in The Bluebird Club, a private members' beanerie near her Chelsea home, at precisely 11 a.m. She wore a soft-wool golden jumper, hair up in a pony, flawless skin, fittingly glamorous, while I was formidably hungover, fitfully dressed in an Oxfam floral shirt from 1982 and no doubt horrifying to her permanently elegant self. There'd been no point in birthday sobriety in the name of a hangover-free encounter. I *knew*: the very lovely Kylie never told you anything about anything, ever.

Kylie was, and remains, the definition of the-blank-canvas-upon-which-we-project-our-fantasies, a punishingly hard-working, old-school showbiz trooper who fills a room with translucent light and, er, that's about it. To sustain this mercurial canvas, summits with Kylie were (and remain) brief affairs – mostly twenty minutes – a PR control ruse in operation since the *Smash Hits* days. The Completely Futile Kylie Minogue Interview Caper, then, was something we'd both been enduring since the late eighties (to this day the person I've interviewed more times than any other), something we both knew was a pointless formality where I fished for jokes, found none, poked around The Hologram, sought The Soul, emerged none the wiser and we both went home relieved it was swiftly over.

That morning in The Bluebird in 2002 she was, as ever, delightfully polite and breathily inarticulate – 'um ... I ... ahoo ... hnnn!' she flustered (she was always flustered). Back then magazines were yet to persistently equate 'female' with 'tragic' (as the celeb mags do today), a future landscape which would demand of Kylie show-me-your-pain profiles covering heartbreak, Botox, childlessness and cancer. That year, though, both the golden hot-pants of 'Spinning Around' (which her former duet partner and my acid-crocked teenage Birthday Party tormentor Nick Cave had stupendously dubbed 'Australia's Turin Shroud') and the strategically slit white jumpsuit of

'Can't Get You Out Of My Head' (one of the greatest pop songs ever written) meant the focus on Kylie was aimed like a scientific laser on her exquisitely squishy yet minuscule derriere. Ludicrously high-camp exchanges were the only game in this shimmering showbiz town.

Congratulations! With 'Can't Get You Out Of My Head' you've become the nation's undisputed number one pop perv.

'Pop perv?' she cooed, famed eyebrow arching towards the ceiling. 'Did you just make that up!? Hihihih! With a per-vee video.'

You're getting pervier and pervier . . .

'Hmn, yes, but so are most things. I must admit when I first saw the video, I actually found myself just watching that white dress and going (several sharp intakes of breath) "uh . . . uuuh . . . uuuh! Woah, she's gonna *go* . . ."'

D'you think you might be, even slightly, a sexual exhibitionist?

'Part of me, yeah. I just am. But there's the other side of me that is a *complete prude*. And I literally want a game of Scrabble. But I'm well aware, as is everyone else by now, that there is that other side to me. And perhaps it's because there's some protection in it, I'm playing a role.'

She'd been playing a role forever, wondering who she was underneath, describing herself as 'an average girl' from an average family (her dad, like mine, an accountant), who'd been famous since teendom and a millionaire for most of her adult life (no similarities *there*).

We'd met twice in her early nineties Sex Kylie phase (nervy, flirty, waffly, impenetrable), Indie Kylie in '97 (nervy, self-deprecating, given to apologising for 'my past'), Camp Kylie in 2000 (self-belief emerging, 'I've become myself') and twice in the previous five months where she'd now become just Kylie. Finally, it seemed, she'd shed her Russian Doll personas to find the high-kitsch pop figurine she'd always been at core, the kind of showgirl personality who'd owned a tiara for years. During the nineties she'd asked herself, 'Am I just pretend? Actually I'm not, I *am* like that.'

She was, she once confessed, 'not the best talker', finding discussing herself 'incredibly boring, because I talk about it in such a way that ... it's just blah-blah-blah really. Well it is to me!' I'd go on to meet her five more times after 2002, and by 2012 realised one statement throughout all those summits probably best described the elusive soul of 'our' Kylie.

'There's definitely a lot that I do keep to myself, but I don't think it's terrible things I have to hide,' she mused, genuinely. 'Perhaps people think there's more than there is to know.'

It took Kylie to fully fail in public to realise who she really was, her professional nadir coming in '97 with her brief, doomed sojourn into Indie Kylie, seeing her single with the Manic Street Preachers, 'Some Kind Of Bliss' (which sounded like Texas) limp to a bliss-free number twenty-two. That year Kylie wasn't in The Bluebird Club but in a basement restaurant in central London, meticulously tearing up a napkin, mirroring her shredding nerves, aged twenty-nine. 'I just want to be myself, and that's a never ending quest,' she wobbled (perhaps alternative lyrics to Oasis' 'Supersonic'). 'I can't profess to say I do [know who I am], so how could anyone else?'

We played a quiz game to ascertain, at least, how 'indie' or 'pop' she truly was, during which she kept the scores on fists-up fingers as we went along. Thus we discovered she owned no Smiths albums, had never slept in a ditch and failed to complete what was always known as the indie-saddo ethos: 'I just do what I do and if anyone else likes it, it's a bonus.' ('I just do what I do and ... be?' she hoped, wrongly.) Eventually, she gave up. 'I'm just not *designed* for indie,' she wailed, 'not a sparkle in sight!'

I told her a fact about the Manic Street Preachers' Nicky

Wire: at the infamous Irma Awards fiasco in Dublin five years earlier, he'd been wearing a 1987-era Kylie badge on the lapel of his leather jacket. 'Nooo!' she screamed, head buried in her hands. 'No! I might cry! Those things leave me ... speechless. *Speechless*.' She pointed to her eyes, which brimmed with tears, proving she was no hologram after all. 'I was supposed to be a one-hit wonder, let's face it, one smash hit and be gone,' she blubbed. 'Like [Stock, Aitken and Waterman 'contenders'] the Reynolds Girls, Big Fun, that's where I came from. So now to still be here after ten years and have someone like him ... I'm just *touched*.'

By 2000 and the 'Spinning Around' comeback corker, she was identifying herself as 'a very short drag queen trapped in a woman's body'. That year, back on the Bluebird sofa, we had an excellent rumour to discuss.

Did you really have sex with Michael Hutchence on a plane directly behind the Australian prime minister?

'Ladies and gentlemen, she's wagging her finger at me! Nooo! Noooooo!'

It's true, it's true, that one's true!

'I'll say it's *almost* true! They haven't got their facts quite right and I'm not gonna clarify them for you! Michael would've told that story with absolute *glee* ...'

In 2001, she confessed she'd had, aged nineteen back in the late eighties, 'a little breakdown' after her teenage pop years were mocked by the tabloids: her songs were useless, she couldn't sing, she was anorexic, 'an alien'. 'That was responsible for me losing it for a bit,' she nodded. 'I wouldn't have the life that I like without the press but I remember feeling helpless. There was a rage, an anger I don't really express. But my silence is *deafening*.'

By 2002 she was an insecure workaholic. 'You've got to strike while the iron's hot, I'm sure all performers are ... entirely insecure!'

And by 2004, now thirty-four, she was so jet-lagged she could barely speak, 'um, sorry, I'm so nnn . . .' she managed, tongue in her bottom lip. I wondered if she sometimes awoke, in the blur of the showbiz conveyor belt, and thought: My life is a vacuous illusion, populated by idiots?

'I wish,' replied Kylie, eyebrow shooting north, 'I was that articulate!'

With her pop life now at its creative peak, in a long-term relationship with actor-hunk Olivier Martinez she was the happiest she'd ever been. 'I'm content,' she smiled, toothily.

Less than one year later, in May 2005, Kylie was diagnosed with a particularly aggressive form of breast cancer and disappeared from public view.

Two years on from 2005, Kylie told me she'd truly believed she would die. 'Was I thinking, "that's it, I'm going to fall off my perch"? Oh yes. Yeah, yeah, yeah,' she nodded, now aged thirty-nine, serenely seated in the wooden church conversion of her then-manager's office. 'I was *really* scared. Upset. Angry.' Ever since, people had behaved differently towards her. 'People know that I'm human now,' she noted wryly. We contemplated a phrase I thought she'd like: 'camp is the lie that tells the truth'.

'I think,' she decided, 'it's akin to "never a truer word spoken in jest". There's something there about not being afraid, of being who you really are.'

Looking for levity in our understandably sombre conversation I wondered if she'd actually approved her new Madame Tussauds waxwork, of Kylie on all fours, backside in the air. 'I absolutely did not!' she yelped, mortified. I had a new, perv-related theory: that her visual self was so hyper-stylised and hyper-sexualised people assumed it was all a pretender's facade. But, actually, it's a double bluff and in real life she's a volcanically sexual perv. Just like her sister, Dannii, once told me.

'What did she say!?'

She said, 'They think Kylie's the pure one and I'm the dirty bird . . .'

Here, Kylie's faux-indignation cracked into peals of mirth.

'. . . and it's actually the other way around. It's just the characters we play. She's absolutely The Filth. She plays the good girl very well though. Pop Princess? Filthy Queen!'

'Well!' Kylie pursed her lips theatrically, drummed her fingers on the table. 'You can choose your friends . . . I won't comment on that! But I'm really pleased she's now on the *X Factor* and everyone's loving her . . .'

You're skilfully avoiding talking about being a perv!

'I told you I wasn't answering that question! My sister's wild thoughts and accusations . . .' She held up her tiny palm. 'Talk to the hand!'

The greatest life change since her illness, meanwhile, was the reduction of her hours to 'office': after a daytime photo session say, she'd now announce, 'You've got it? Right, I'm off,' no longer keeping going 'til she was 'shaking in the corner'. This was tremendous news, I enthused, she was becoming a proper diva at last. At this, she collapsed head first onto the table, thumping it twice with her negligible fist. 'I think something like that has happened actually, I think you've hit on something!'

Everyone knows you're a fundamentally nice person, but maybe you'll now start calling people cunts to their faces.

She clapped a hand across her mouth, eyes a-twirl.

'Hnnn!'

To be honest, it felt like swearing in front of the Queen. Kylie turned deafeningly silent.

Er, sorry about that, possibly took it a bit too far there.

'Oh no Sylvie, go right ahead. I wouldn't want *you* to hold back.'

And so, after twenty years of conversational meanderings, Kylie Minogue had finally issued me a withering broadside. And I felt like a chump.

Two years on from the disease she thought would kill her, and still I was looking for the gags. She'd changed, alright, for the better. Me, in this climate, for the worse.

At that year's annual *Q* magazine awards, she won the Q Idol gong. Stepping from a sleek black vehicle outside the courtyard of the Grosvenor House Hotel, she was attempting to be fearless once again, facing a wall of frenzied photographers bawling 'Kylie! Kylie!' as their flashbulbs crackled in a curtain of silvery light. 'Overwhelming!' she puffed, escaping inside.

The next day, she rang from a car. 'Idol speaking,' came her high-camp quip. I told her what an over-refreshed Damon Albarn had observed the day before. 'Kylie looks like a woman now,' announced my old plankton-walking pal (if still a bit of a twerp). 'As opposed to something Mattel made.'

'I take that as a huge compliment,' was Kylie's delighted response. 'Well, I'm not Mattel-made and I never was.'

After two decades in pop, what did she think she represented?

'Sparkle, joy, dreams,' came the certain reply. 'I think that's my purpose.'

In 2012 Kylie celebrated her twenty-fifth year in showbiz. Now forty-three and actively encouraging 'my past', which no longer embarrassed her, she announced her guest appearance on the forthcoming PWL (Pete Waterman Ltd) tots' nostalgia tour singing 'Especially For You' with Jason Donovan. 'I'm sure the audience all went through the *Neighbours* wedding,' she noted, happily. 'It's gonna bring the house down!' She sipped water from a sparkly blue promotional 'Kylie' glass and announced, camply, 'Water, dahling, is all I need ... hydration!' She'd never been more 'Kylie' in her life.

That year she also won *Glamour* magazine's Outstanding Contribution Award. She wasn't, she noted, 'objective enough' to analyse what her outstanding contribution might be but Rufus

Wainwright may have said it best a few years earlier: 'Kylie is the gay shorthand for joy.'

'He's a poet,' she smiled. 'So I'll accept that.'

Still a punishingly hard worker, she'd invented a new line of bed linen, which she swore she used herself – 'Oh yes, they're good, I've one that's less embellished, with a silky top' – occasionally worrying her life was consumed with work. 'Actually, when I've been a bit down that's one of the things I say, "I don't even have a *hobby*",' she mock-wailed. 'And then I'm reminded, "What you do is pretty much your hobby." If I couldn't be creative, I'd wither away. That's what floats my boat.'

She was also completely free from cancer, 'but I have memories every day of it, you're physically and mentally scarred'. Her life perspective was permanently changed. 'Because now and then I will think, "God, I might not even be here."' I told her I'd had a fantasy on the way to meet her that day – 'should you be telling me this!?' she cackled – that when she was sixty, she'd have a Dolly Parton-style theme park, her very own Kyliewood. Maybe a glorious representation of those things she'd once said define her, without which any human life would be significantly poorer: sparkle, joy, dreams.

'Can you imagine!?' she giggled. 'Kyliewood! Kylie-would-what!? Well, myself, my tour manager and my assistant, we've joked for ten years about The Kylie Caff. We're gonna end up in Byron Bay. Shaun [tour manager] will be making coffees, I'll appear, "So, which cocktail would you like? The Showgirl ... the Spinning Around ... or the *Sloooow*?" And you've got, naturally, really hot waiters – let's call a spade a spade! Maybe I could wrestle the gold hot-pants back from the museum they're in for a special appearance ... But I dunno what I'll be doing in ... sixteen years. Time ticks along. And unless you decide to make a big change or you're forced to make a big change, things will probably just keep going, if I'm lucky enough. So let's just keep going. I feel very fortunate that I'm not going, "Oh, I've been doing this job for twenty-five years that I hate". Which is the case for so many people. So I'm just grateful for that.'

When she stood up to leave, all two feet of her, she announced, for the very first time, that we'd had 'a good chat' – probably because, by then, I'd abandoned the pointless gags. The next day, her lifelong PR, Murray Chalmers, sent me an email: Kylie was inviting me to choose a sumptuous set of bed linen from her latest range, for free.

To this day, I sleep under a coral and chocolate-piped duvet cover which indeed has a silky top. This, then, had been the culmination of a quarter of a century in conversation with the shimmering Kylie Minogue.

Free showbiz sheets.

29

I KNOW WHY THE
CAGED BIRD SINGS

Where Kylie is now the gay shorthand for joy, Britney Spears is surely the gay shorthand for contemporary showbiz ruin. Britney is also, more than any other single pop entity, the one who best illustrates the beginning of the collapse of mainstream pop journalism at the dawn of the second millennium. Or, at the very least, she's the one most surrounded by paranoid corporate robo-PRs sporting 'important' ear-to-mouth headsets, intent on suffocating the very joy from life itself, never mind the now ironically titled Entertainment Industry.

In the autumn of 2001, Britney Spears was already the multi-million-album-selling teen-pop phenomenon of her era, the sex-pop siren whose second album *Oops! ... I Did It Again* was number one in fifteen countries and sold thirty-seven million copies worldwide. A purposelessly visual construct, custom-built by business-pop alchemists in the lab of teenage fantasy, brilliantly, she was sponsored by Pepsi (and Listerine) and aggressively marketed as the perfect pop brand, a 2D hologram projected onto the international skyline for captivated fans to colour in with the crayons of their own imagination. With pulsing sexual charisma and some of the greatest pop tunes, and videos, of the modern age, Britney Spears Inc., therefore, was a towering mountain of golden doubloons shielded from the global media by any means necessary, the first line of defence being PR sniper-beings pointing the rifles of banned questions to your head at point-blank range.

Britney, from the outset, was a trained exponent of the inoffensive interview gambit, the damage-limitation ruse which knew boring wouldn't dent your sales, but controversial might. Especially in America, where the Christians, conservatives and, especially three weeks after 9/11, the gun-toters lived.

Brrring! Brrrring!

It was The Man From Jive Records, about to connect my landline to nineteen-year-old Britney Spears, currently on tour in Australia.

'Hi ... um ...' came a nervy voice. 'So, um, you're gonna have thirty minutes to do the interview? And, um, I just wanna make sure that you don't focus on, like, what's happening in the States right now? 'Cos this is really just an ennertainment interview and she's not prepared to talk about, like, world politics and stuff like that? And if you could just not broach any questions about, like, virginity? And sexually explicit questions, I would appreciate that as well. Because she's not prepared to talk about that either.'

Blimey. She's very protected, our Britney, isn't she?

'Yes.'

(No wonder, two months later, she released the single 'Overprotected' ...)

Talking to Britney Spears for exactly thirty minutes on the blower in October 2001, she'd presented a fair impersonation of a regular teenager, albeit substantially 'God'. The first thing she said (after I'd ignored the directives from The Man From Jive Records) was her heart was 'completely broken' by the 9/11 attacks, that America's unified response had been 'beautiful' and all they had to do now was 'look up at the light and pray that everything's gonna work out'. That year former *NSYNC boyband fugitive turned sex-pop dazzler Justin Timberlake was still her boyfriend and soon she was insisting, two years into their relationship, she still wished to marry him, 'one day but not anytime soon' (she carried his T-shirt on tour so she could smell him) and no-sex-before-marriage was still 'definitely the right thing to do'.

Britney's highly sexualised image was, she decided, 'a beautiful thing, when I'm on stage it's time for me to express myself'. The 15lb snake she'd worn around her neck like a feather boa at that year's MTV Awards was not the suggestive perv prop it appeared but a symbol of her life as 'a jungle, really crazy, but then when we actually got [the snake] there I was like "what have I done?" It was gross! I was so scared in rehearsals I broke out in hives, seriously.'

Her life, she mused, was wonderful, feeling this was God's plan for her.

'I think in my other lifetime I had probably the worst life in the world,' she decided. "Cos I feel like this one is a breeze.'

Nine months later, Britney had split up with Justin Timberlake and was seated, alone, behind a presidential podium in a packed, lavish conference room of the Four Seasons Hotel, Mexico City. This was her first-ever press conference for the excitable Central American media, TV cameras zooming in from the back of the buzzing ballroom. At three minutes in, a thirty-something man from a Mexican TV show held his microphone to his mouth and addressed the twenty-year-old Britney Spears.

'Tomorrow in your concert,' he announced, 'would you like for Mexicans to say "Hi" to you like this?' Before the gathered press, he raised his middle finger.

The previous day, she'd been photographed through a tinted car window by the pursuing paparazzi driving away from Mexico City airport, flipping The Finger herself.

'Well, actually, what happened was,' replied Britney, calmly, 'I got off the plane and everyone was driving really recklessly and all the paparazzi almost hit our vehicle and they kept on giving out. But I love my fans here, it was the paparazzi, I was afraid we'd have a wreck. I'm human just like everybody, you know, I get mad too sometimes.'

Much muttering ensued as another Mexican TV man spoke up: 'What is the most expensive thing that you have buyed and how much did it cost?'

'Probably my house.'

TV Man: 'How much?'

'That's none of your business.'

Mexican press collective: 'Whooooh!'

A radio presenter chanced it: 'Some people say you are dating with Wade Robson, your choreographer, is it true?'

'I don't wanna talk about my personal life,' came the snap of a distressed robot under siege.

Twenty minutes later, after a series of informationally barren questions concerning Madonna (Britney would 'love to work with her') and why she didn't sing live for 95 per cent of her show ('because I'm dancing hardcore but there's a part of the show with me singing, no track at all'), Britney rose from her podium, deciding 'that was the last question' (about where music was progressing that year) and walked out to the sound of jeers, boos and discontented mumblings from three hundred unimpressed journalists. The life that been 'a breeze' less than twelve months previously was now tossing her around in a typhoon of critical bile.

Outside the emptying conference room, Britney stood in a backstage corridor, surrounded by cables and equipment, waiting to walk onto the set of a daytime Mexican TV show whose jaunty living room had been fully replicated inside the Four Seasons Hotel. Surrounded, as she always was on tour, by three door-sized bodyguards, two PRs, her personal assistant, make-up artist, hair stylist and the hotel's own security, she was cocooned inside this Circle Of Protection with her hands cradling her sobbing face. The atmosphere was grave: silence, concern, embarrassment.

'Is everyone OK?' yelped a male voice, piercing the vacuum. 'Come aaaawn, it's all so serious!'

'We'll be laughing,' added another male voice, 'when this is all over, right?'

Given an Access All Areas pass for documentary fly-on-the-wall purposes, I was watching this scene from a five metre distance, listening, writing in an unconcealed notebook when one of her three enormous bodyguards gripped my arm, roughed me along for ten metres and sent me reeling back into the conference room while shouting to hotel security, 'I don't know her!' The purple bruise on my inner arm next day, the size of a pear, was highly impressive. Britney's People were very good at their jobs.

Two years earlier, Britney had been named by *Forbes Global Business Magazine* as The Most Important Celebrity In The World (whatever that actually means), such a heady position making her the world's number one celebrity quarry. She was now subjected, post-Justin, to a relentless campaign of fallen-angel exposure by the global media (featuring paparazzi evidence if possible): she was smoking, was on a crash diet (raw vegetables, water) having gained 10–16lbs, had collapsed post-show in California and her parents had split up (all curtly denied by her PRs). The supposedly still virginal Britney was seen in lap-dancing clubs, drunk, in a store buying a book called *Satisfaction: The Art of the Female Orgasm*, was reportedly a diva-brat, ignoring fans at the opening of her NYLA restaurant in New York and again at the British premiere of her ill-received debut film *Crossroads* (not a homage, sadly, to the seventies TV soap about a Midlands motel featuring Benny the village buffoon in a beanie hat and his crush on 'Miss Diane'). Britney's self-titled third album of 2001 sold a mere 3.5 million, meagre in comparison to its predecessors, which up to then had amassed a Michael-Jackson-in-the-eighties-sized forty-five million sales. A thrilled American press then reported that Justin Timberlake had been seen publicly frolicking with Janet Jackson.

Back in the cable-bestrewn backstage corridor, Britney's eyes were now dried and dusted, her platinum blonde, double-denimed, dazzle-toothed persona fully restored, walking onto the Mexican TV set like some rebooted digital GIF beamed from a hidden screen. For the next thirty minutes she taught the presenter, a man dressed in pigtails and school uniform, how to dance just like her, played a fishing game where she pulled blue plastic gonks from a silver bucket to win the 'prize' of some Mexican dolls, and answered questions about her crazy life.

'It's crazy!'

Meanwhile, the interview I'd flown 5,500 miles to conduct was officially on hold. What was an unemployed pop scribe to do? Go on an open-top bus tour around Mexico City to contemplate the intricate, allegorical, psychedelic mosaics of the Aztecs in the fifteenth century. And to rumly ponder how it came to pass that the emblem of western culture in the twenty-first century was a holographic twenty-year-old woman hounded into insanity by an allegedly grown-up media – which sought, as its greatest prize, photographic evidence of her smoking after sex.

The following day, back at the Four Seasons, near a room now doubling as the *Pepsi Chart Show* set, I talked, while waiting for Britney's TV appearance, to her affable, southern, personal assistant Felicia, the two of us hiding from security in the space between two ten-foot stacks of chairs.

'They were runnin' us off the road,' she noted of The Finger Incident, 'runnin' us up into the kerb, they would jump out and just slam us. And what scared us so bad is we'd just talked about Princess Diana. They told us you couldn't see through the window.'

The *Crossroads* premiere no-show for fans was, she said, a farce: Britney had borrowed a half-million-dollar diamond necklace and the armed guard sent to protect it forbade her to mingle in public. 'It's never reported that way,' she frowned. 'I think sometimes someone on the inside like myself ought to sit down and write a tell-all.'

Britney was pragmatic, she added, in dealing with the brutal culture. 'People say to her, "How do you handle it when they talk about you this way, or when you have bad sites on the internet?" And she says, "I just know that goes along with the business." And it does.'

Soon, Britney returned to work, first a meet 'n' greet photo opportunity for the *Pepsi Chart Show* with, on one side, a host of Pepsi VIPs and, on the other, ten competition winners dressed up as Britney Spears. She endured the interview without a trace of irritation, either clapping her hands like an excited child or grimacing at the hopeless questions.

'What does the word "anticipating" *mean* to me? It means

you're nervous and excited about something, like waiting to go out at night.'

'Great! Great!' enthused the female presenter, with vigorous, brain-rattling nods.

We learned her favourite knickers were Skimpies, 'guy briefs, very cute', that she believed in angels, her favourite food was ice cream and her favourite colours were 'baby blue and baby pink'. And Tom Hibbert, if he had been there that day, would've punched himself in his own face and left the building six hours earlier for a flagon of finest Rioja.

The following night, at the second of her two dates at the 50,000-seater Foro Del Sol open-air stadium, the very last night of her 'Dream Within A Dream' world tour, Britney Spears' gaudy, adolescently fantastical show imploded, its star walking off after four songs with a plaintive peal of, 'I'm sorry, Mexico, I love you!' The crowd was furious, screaming 'Fraud! Fraud!' and (unfathomably) 'Coca-Cola!'

The weather was to blame; lightning from an electrical storm causing the three hundred robotic lights and pyrotechnics to malfunction, putting everyone on stage at risk. 'I'm sorry I couldn't finish the show for my fans,' announced 'Britney' in a statement. 'The Mexican fans are one of the best audiences to play for. We decided that we had no choice but to cancel the show after the storm and lightning showed no signs of clearing up.'

The next day, one of her several PRs told me she was now taking a five-month break, learning belly dancing and painting while decorating her new second home in Manhattan. Meanwhile, in the absence of any twenty-first Century Pop Star quotes, I interviewed her make-up artist instead, returning to the UK with a world-class scoop on her all-time favourite make-up brands: MAC, Clinique, Ruby & Millie Face Gloss (she 'adored the packaging') ...

Within another two years, Britney's appropriation of the sexually explicit mores of her hero, Madonna, had reached its unapologetic zenith. As the 'Onyx Hotel' Tour whip-cracked around the world, its precision choreographed moves were almost identical to Madonna's 'Girlie Show' tour of 1993: a male dancer with his head between Britney's legs, the straddling of near-naked hunks, the wearing of bras, corsets and suspenders, much all-over groping between Britney and more hunks, pelvic gyrations all over a dancer's leg/chairs/pillows, men and women fondling themselves on satin-sheathed beds, simulation of oral sex, simulation of any sex, simulation of masturbation in a rose-filled bath while singing a song called 'Touch Of My Hand'. Parents of pre-teen fans were horrified, leaving with tearful kids in tow. The show, shrieked the reviewers, was 'almost porn'. Exactly the kind of headlines, of course, the 'Onyx Hotel' Tour 2004 was designed to create.

Over the course of the previous year, we'd seen a daily, public, obsessional insight into the unravelling mind of a faltering global icon. She was very far, now, from a Bible-bothering Baptist – a 'party girl', forever smoking, drinking, swearing and kissing inappropriate men (Fred Durst, Colin Farrell, her sometime dancer Columbus Short, a married man whose wife was seven months pregnant). For a laugh, she'd stitched the word 'fuck' into her clothing and was forever spotted in tears – in church, with her mother, on TV – as she was in 2003 after queries on her break-up with Justin eighteen months previously. 'It was pretty rough,' she blinked, welling up, 'kind of weird, weird, hello, oh my goodness, can we stop?' She'd talked about smoking marijuana, 'that's enough [of a drug] for me', taking cocaine (once), and got married, drunk, in Las Vegas in January 2004 to her childhood chum Jason Alexander. Fifty-five hours later the marriage was annulled, the insanely wealthy Britney reportedly paying him off with $300,000 while she excused the escapade as 'a joke which went too far'. The following month, she was photographed carrying a book called *Listening To Prozac: The Landmark Book About Anti-Depressants and the Remaking of the Self* while swinging a goth-kitsch handbag in the shape of a coffin. By now, reportedly, she was seeing two separate psychologists.

Three years later the psychologists proved ineffective as her shaven-headed public meltdown arrived, battering an SUV with a rolled-up umbrella, now reportedly a meth-wrecked addict who began a relationship with hovering paparazzo Adnan Ghalib in December 2007.

By 2008 she'd lost custody of the two children she had with shrew-eyed hip hop opportunist Kevin Federline, was soon suicidal and hospitalised. That year, a court placed her under the temporary and later permanent conservatorship of her father James Spears alongside the spectacularly named attorney Andrew Wallet, giving them complete control of her assets. Somehow, she continued to make music; the pointedly titled album *Circus*, released in December 2008, made her the youngest female artist ever to have five albums debut at number one.

In 2011, exactly ten years after my initial, PR-bothered interview on the phone from Australia, I talked to Britney on the blower once more, the PR fortress having grown by then into a Berlin Wall of insanely controlled cobblers involving copy approval and censorship, made all the more baffling by no prospect whatsoever of anything interesting ever being said.

The questions themselves were submitted beforehand and approved (or rejected) by Britney's People (no deviation permitted), while the obviously 'dangerous' ones (i.e. instantly liftable into tabloid headlines) – about her hardly secret 2007 meltdown, or the recent death of Amy Winehouse – would be potential 'Click! Brrrrrr' situations.

Furthermore, to ensure no sneaked-in additions, we'd be accompanied on the phone by her British PR, her American PR, a manager and a lawyer. Throughout, I could hear whispering and conferring while I waited for a chink of opportunity to veer off-script without jeopardising our stop-clocked half-hour slot. None arrived, the weedily approved questions resulting in inevitably weedy replies: her current tour was 'the best I've done so far', the newly wed Prince William and Kate were 'a beautiful couple I totally respect and admire', her life so far had been 'so much fun and I genuinely have a blast, I'm a very grateful and thankful person'. A concerned male voice wondered if I could hear her properly; perhaps he thought I'd fallen asleep. Britney was possibly even more bored than I was (at least I had the adrenalised rush of panic and despair), her pre-planned answers not so much auto-pilot as human algorithm, responses not so much weedy as fifteen million dandelion puff-balls blowing their spores across a grassy wetland the size of Oklahoma. My best chance of an emotionally telling response was in the stymied magazine's suggested sisterly probe: what tricks made her feel fabulous on an insecure day? (Help!) She replied with one word, 'shopping', while more whispering skittered around the global telecom satellites. A male voice then piped with a single word. 'Chocolate,' he hushed (pronounced chak-lit), making a suggestion. And so Britney Spears, by now a 137-million album selling thirty-year-old mother of two, parroted 'Chak-lit' down the line, as twenty-five years of journalistic purpose (and occasional dignity) exploded on audible contact.

Desperation arrived and I chanced an unapproved question, reminding her of our conversation ten years previously where she'd felt her life had been 'a breeze'. Did she believe the same today?

'I think it's true,' came the steady reply. 'I still stand by that and I still believe in that.'

Silence.

I carried on, reminding her there were times things weren't so breezy.

'Y'know, I've gone through stuff but it's made me a stronger person, definitely.'

A sombre man chipped in: 'We're gonna have to wrap up . . .'

Bye, everyone!

Everyone: ' . . . .'

Click! Brrrr . . .

Staring down at my chocolate brown, antique, 1970s, dial-in-the-round phone, the sort a teenager today would think belonged to the nineteenth century, the Britney Spears of 2001 seemed an epoch away already, that year an averagely chirpy teenager, full of oh-my-gosh politeness, prone to girly giggles. By 2011 she was, reportedly, so fame, drug and culture damaged she wasn't allowed to own her own mobile phone. The following year she was hired to replace Nicole Scherzinger as a judge on the American *X Factor* alongside Simon Cowell for a reported salary of $15 million, becoming the highest-paid judge on a singing competition in television history. Still recording, touring and making guest appearances on singles, she was named by *Forbes Magazine* as the highest-grossing female artist of the year with estimated earnings of $58 million. In 2013, she began a two-year residency at Planet Hollywood in Las Vegas with the show 'Britney: Piece Of Me'. This proved so successful (and unexpectedly lucrative for the Caesars Group, which owns Planet Hollywood) in late 2014 she was given a pay rise (a reported increase of $150,000, to $475,000 per show) and booked for an additional two years.

By its close 'Piece Of Me' is expected to earn 'her' $66.5 million.

*

Our contemporary *ennertainers*' planet, meanwhile, is now a shifted tectonic pop plate away from the creative freedoms of the psychedelic *Smash Hits* days. If you asked Britney Spears, today, if she'd ever grown parsnips in a gumboot, or what colour Tuesday might be, or if she'd ever been sick all down her cleavage, you'd be frog-marched out the door by a trio of 'handlers', or cut off on the phone, before she even had the chance to gasp, with a giggle, 'excuse me!?' Then again, it's worse than that: you simply wouldn't even get the chance. At this level of twenty-first century showbiz, it's The Law.

30

THERE'S GOTTA BE A
LITTLE RAIN SOMETIME

In summer 2002, I sauntered into a publicity office in west
London to interview eighties electro-spook diva Marc Almond,
once of Soft Cell, for the *Observer* magazine's *This Much I Know*
slot, where a famous person ponders on the extracted wisdom
of their unique, perhaps even fascinating life. A pale man with
an air of haughty mistrust, Marc was in a touchy mood, so I put
him at his ease: if he wondered why I was persistently asking
'philosophical' questions it was because today's interview was a
'philosophical concept' (as opposed to endless ruminations on

his marvellous new album, etc.). He stared at me, clearly irked, and darted for the door. 'I don't do concepts!' he harrumphed, disappearing in a flouncing huff. His PR flew after him but his errant charge was gone. This single act of pop star divadom altered the course of my life forever.

That afternoon Almond had faced two publicity chores: one with me, another, alongside his Soft Cell partner Dave Ball, with a 'heritage' music magazine. The latter team arrived early: the world's chippermost lensman Tom Sheehan (already an acquaintance) and relatively-new-to-the-game journalist Simon Goddard (a total stranger). None of us, suddenly, had anything to do that sunny summer's afternoon, so we repaired to the tables outside a nearby pub, the enigmatic Goddard a funny, bright, enthusiastic, dynamically creative thirty-year-old, both gregarious and shy, a shaved head emphasising enormous, Disney-level features – striking sky-blue eyes, dramatic crow's wings eyebrows and promisingly 'Elvis' lips.

We had much in common: born in Cardiff, he grew up in Scotland where he, too, was an 'outsider' music obsessive. I'd later discover he'd bought his first full-length album while on a family holiday driving around Scotland, aged ten, in my local record shop, Perth's once-mighty Goldrush Records (and was evidently considerably less weedy than I was aged ten, purchasing *Westworld* by goth-spooks Theatre Of Hate at the age I was throwing gym breaks up a tree). We evidently liked each other's company, outstayed everyone else, had a jovial argument about whether punctuation mattered or not (writers, eh?), and stayed in touch, a flirtation detectable through the emails, especially after news arrived he'd just split up with his girlfriend. He invited me to his first book launch on 9 December 2002 where, several pints in and egged on by his rascally acquaintance Steve Diggle out of ver Buzzcocks, we had a snog-up in the Phoenix Theatre Bar in Shaftesbury

Avenue. (Robert 'Percy' Plant had been right: I *should* blame the Buzzcocks, haw haw.)

We've been together ever since, even though, at the time, we were both significantly emotionally askew. In late 2002 he was both recovering from the damage of his last long-term relationship and, aged almost thirty-one, forging a new, precarious London life as a freelance journalist and author, while I, aged thirty-seven, was going on the road for the *NME* with some grease-rock Kiwis called The Datsuns, for approximately £8.54, forging "ahead" into a professional black hole.

I had, in fact, run out of ambition already. Free falling in directionless disarray, traumatised by the collapsing magazine industry, with a dying mother, I'd buy bulk deals of skunk from a dealer who'd now become a drinking buddy, while making negligible improvements on the poverty of the late nineties. And myself and Simon found solace from all this madness in each other. We *saved* each other.

Even better, almost inevitably, Simon didn't dance – not much in public anyway – principally because he was born with a spook-foot, what they used to call a clubfoot, as Lord Byron legendarily had. Not that I noticed when I met him. I only realised the first morning he threw the covers back off my bed. (It made me smile wryly, too, to think of my mum's old mantra: 'I worried about having no shoes until I met the man with no feet . . .')

Work, suddenly, didn't hold so much appeal. I'd loved it, most of it – some of it an outrageous privilege – but it hadn't exactly brought me, you know, any security, contentment or sanity whatsoever. My main income, post-*NME*, came from *Glamour* (intermittently) and Scotland's *Sunday Herald* newspaper, now a monthly columnist penning topical musings for the Glasgow-based broadsheet's magazine, which extended over time into a weekly column and took up most of my working life. For several years I became, therefore – accidentally, and it would turn out disastrously – a regional newspaper columnist for a city I'd never lived in, published in a country I hadn't lived in for fifteen years. And this scenario I simply accepted. I had just enough work, just enough money, to stay free.

As obsession with music waned, old passions reignited for nature, art and science; constantly peering at leaves in parks with a man who might have looked like a toddler but had the old-school heart of a 1970s granddad and owned at least five meticulously illustrated guidebooks on trees – and one on fungi – to prove it. I pretty much 'dropped out', rejecting the competitive clamour, the speed and strain of the elbowing media scrum, wondered why I'd given my full adult life to this precarious, peripheral profession. I'd never been much driven by ambition anyway. Why *must* we be ambitious? And rich? Or strive to be somehow "important"? Why must we *work hard, play by the rules, do the right thing*? Instead, I was living the words to 'Leisure' by W. H. Davies, a favourite poem of my mum, who'd often pipe its most famous verse from her armchair in between puffs on a Benson & Hedges, even as she was housebound back in Perth on an oxygen mask with fag-related condition COPD (chronic obstructive pulmonary disease) and could never go for a bracing walk in a park ever again.

> *What is this life if, full of care,*
> *We have no time to stand and stare?*
> *No time to stand beneath the boughs*
> *And stare as long as sheep and cows …*

Maybe a preoccupation with the astonishment of life is the result, too, of being continuously close to death. For the last three years Mum had been increasingly ill and the doctors had told us, several times, to imminently 'expect the worst'. It takes a long time, however, to smoke yourself to death if you've the proper equipment at home: an oxygen mask from a permanent household nebuliser positioned under her nose in the spaces between the snouts and, whisking her up to her bedroom, a Stannah stairlift on which she'd perch with an enormous smile and sing the chorus of a favourite tune: 'Fly me to the mooooooooon!'

But by April 2004 she'd deteriorated severely and was taken into hospital. On the phone to a nurse I wondered: should I just come home?

'Well, if I were you,' urged the stranger's voice, 'I *would*.'

By the early noughties Mum was a reformed character. She'd developed, unfeasibly, a wry new attitude, and would announce, merrily, 'They might as well put me in the coffin with a hundred Benson & Hedges and a bottle of Grouse.' I was finally getting to know her. She was funny. We'd watch *Top Of The Pops* together and she'd prove something of a music journo herself, offering up ruthless critiques.

'I wouldnae walk five yards tae hear ye, son' (Robbie Williams).

'I've heard better on a berry field' (Ozzy and Kelly Osbourne).

'As the good Lord says, yer as good as ye think ye are' (Celine Dion).

She'd been sober for years and over a cheese scone one day I asked her what had finally made her stop drinking. There was a pause, my ears expanding into satellite dishes, anticipating the explanation I'd looked for all my life, a clue to her soul, to what psychological epiphany had finally resulted in *enough*. She replied with a single crisp word.

'Prison.'

There had been, though, between prison and 2004, one last 'hurrah'. Not only the single time in our lives we had a drink together but were comprehensively wasted together, wilfully, on the sometime worst annual day of my childhood life.

Christmas morning 2001 and I was at Mum's in Perth, just us, as it always was by then, my siblings in different towns with their own family Christmas, she still way too much of a festive liability around her grandkids (and everybody else). By then she was seventy-two years old and seemed ten years older: thin and frail, dying a grimly protracted death, smoking thirty fags a day in the grip of her lung-shredding degenerative condition. Every day she was delivered meals on wheels, which she ignored, preferring Benson & Hedges and endless cups of 'Nescaf'. She was also, though she'd never say it, dying of loneliness (and surely boredom), choosing to sleep in the tiny single bedroom because the two double rooms were so cavernously empty.

We always played a stupid game: I'd perch on her upstairs single bed where the window opened to a low-level rooftop and we'd see if we could ping our cigarette butts along the roof tiles and into the overflow gutter. Sometimes she'd wonder if I still lived 'in Hampden' (famed Scottish football stadium) when she really meant Camden, north London, where she'd visited me, just once, with Jackie, when I'd lived there with The Dancer. She'd stayed sober throughout the three-day trip and our time together was magical – giggling at a West End show, boggling on an open-top tour bus, striding through Trafalgar Square, jostling along Camden High Street through another generation of 'monsters from outer space'. But she wasn't, by then, ashamed of me anymore. 'I feel,' she wrote in her diary, of the only London experience of her life, 'like I've been round the universe.'

Back in Perth on Christmas Day 2001 I'd nipped out, as I usually did, for a pre-lunch pub hour with Ali (from The Four Of Us) and her dad. Returning that freezing winter's day I walked into the living room and her static body language told me – as it always had, as I now blurted out, aghast – 'Oh God, you've been drinking!'

She nodded to the bottle beside her feet, a large bottle of

Bailey's Irish Cream which she'd raided from my travel bags upstairs, the nearest she could get to whisky. She'd scoffed the bloody lot.

Staggeringly, though, as I scanned her face for the demonic look I'd always seen as a child, there was merely a misty reverie, the tormented psychoses alcohol had always unleashed seemingly evaporated in the last years of her life. The smile on her face was real, if bamboozled, maybe even slightly cheeky. I wasn't frightened of her anymore. Maybe she'd run out of fear herself.

There was no sign, meanwhile, of even the *suggestion* of Christmas dinner. Experience told me there was no going back so I made a first-in-a-lifetime decision: I would join her. Three months on from 9/11, six weeks on from Thailand's serenity, what harm could it possibly do? From under my bed, two bottles of more successfully hidden white wine were retrieved, alongside six ready-rolled festive spliffs, one of which I now hung out the upstairs bedroom window to smoke, remembering a lifetime's directive from The Verve's Richard 'Mashcroft' back in the 1990s: 'Sometimes, you can't go wrong with a well-placed "Fuck it".'

Back downstairs we shared our first-ever bottle of wine. I switched off the Christmas Day TV and retrieved my dad's old cassette tapes, lain dormant for years inside an antique stack system, cassettes she'd kept since his death in 1989. They were all there: classic Johnny Cash, hootenannying Jimmy Shand, easy crooning Engelbert Humperdinck ('Englehump Dinglebert!' I yelped in his memory), playing them one by one while sitting on the floor, singing in abandon, as she tapped a tartan-slippered foot, steadily smoking her beloved B&H as she surveyed the cassette-bestrewn living room carpet.

'Oh, Sylvia,' she said, blinking down at this singing, drinking, obliviously music-possessed vision, 'you're just like your father.'

Whether this was true or not, this was, without doubt, the single greatest sentence I had ever heard *anybody* say.

Soon, we'd slewed all the wine and were up for more, so I suggested the local pub, open 'til 6 p.m., nearby at the top of her street. Her tiny, white-haired frame was soon wrapped in copious layers and a cosy coat as we linked arms outside and began our treacherous ascent, edging our way up a sizeable incline sparkling with deadly black ice, equally determined that *nothing* would hold us back. Inside, I ordered her a double Grouse, the first alcoholic drink I'd ever legally bought her in my life. If we talked about much that day it's lost to the haze of the atmosphere: all I know is her Dr Jekyll didn't turn into Mr Hyde and we were amused to be in cahoots, even if I found her, at the bar, when I came back from the loo, sneaking in an extra double between rounds.

Beneath this chemically enhanced surface, though, I felt a surging undertow of melancholy, for her life's pain which I barely knew, for my dad's pain which I also barely knew, for our fractured family and her isolated existence today. In another life, I found myself thinking, she could've been Keith Richards. She was certainly, in some ways, invincible.

She took another two and a half years to finally smoke herself to death, skeletal by April 2004, in dreadful, constant pain. When I ran into the hospital ward from an overnight London train she bolted upright, threw her arms around me and through her oxygen mask attempted some kind of quip. 'I don't think I'll smoke another cigarette ever again!' She could've been one hundred years old. 'What a way,' she wheezed, struggling for air as if breathing through a thick gauze, 'to end your life.'

Days passed and she struggled on, her life force refusing to give up. I stayed overnight, attempting some sleep on a roomy chair beside her, listening to her drowning in her own lungs, the hollowed-out clatter of the death rattle, and began to weep for her lifetime's silent sorrows. She heard me, and said a single word in her woozy morphine dream-state. 'Shame.' It was she who felt sorry for me.

Another day she tapped the morphine box taped to her collarbone, this lifelong nurse, and whispered to me, 'It's not enough.' She wanted out. Wanted to be 'made comfortable'. A nurse explained there was nothing they could do – 'not,' she added, 'since Harold Shipman'.

It took her five days to die in hospital, with constant visits from us all. Some days, big brother Billy and I would sit on a bench in the forecourt of the hospital I'd been born in, with no skin, smoking our way through the trauma of watching someone die of smoking. Being seventeen years older he'd been there at the beginning of her drinking years and I could finally ask him another question I'd sought the answer to all my life: 'Why did she *start* drinking in the first place?'

'Because,' came the blunt reply, 'she could finally afford it.'

Mum surely wasn't to know, like so many others, that by the time she was addicted, she had a serious mental illness – and was often treated in the same psychiatric hospital she worked in. Once, visiting her there, where she'd been sectioned (I was perhaps thirty, in the Britpop roustabout years), she looked at me, delirious through the haze of anti-psychotic drugs, and said, 'Oh, Sylvia, your teeth are fairly coming down now!' All she could see, evidently, was a child of around seven, whose teeth had indeed taken a long time to 'come down'.

Even on her deathbed, though, there were times I didn't believe her, still didn't trust her. She said she was 'proud' of me and I was convinced this was only what she thought I needed to hear.

One morning, after we three sisters had stayed awake with her overnight, exhausted, a nurse instructed us to go home, to rest. One hour into sleep, the phone rang instructing an immediate return. When we burst into the room she was gone, Billy holding her hand. 'We're all orphans now,' said this weeping fifty-six-year-old man. She looked like a sculpture made of chalk, or an exquisitely detailed etching on parchment by a sixteenth-century Renaissance master. The kind of beautiful devastation you'd see on the cover of a Joy Division album.

The last communication we'd ever had was when I'd left earlier that morning, the sun rising after a spell of torrential rain. 'Well, you know what that means, Mum, don't you?' I whispered in her ear. 'A rainbow.' Now semi-conscious and unable to speak, she vigorously nodded. Since that day I've heard a theory: that the morphine dream at the end of life simply fills your conscience with all the colours of the rainbow. So, if we're lucky enough to have a deathbed that's where we're all going, in the end, sliding into a rainbow the size of the universe itself.

Back in London that April the World Snooker Championships had just begun and Ronnie O'Sullivan was playing. I lay on the sofa for two full weeks watching my beloved game played at its best by my snooker hero, mesmerised by its hypnotic rhythms, watching him win, thinking once again how this bewitching spectator sport was a gift from my dad, now helping me deal with the unexpected surrealism of suddenly having no parents. I felt, overnight, negligibly tiny, like an astronaut whose tether to the craft had been razored away by a meteorite blazing by, now drifting in silent space. I'd never felt so vulnerable and therefore, ironically, so childlike, in my adult life. If this was inevitable 'umbilical cord' existentialism, I wasn't expecting it: I'd been fully independent since the age of eighteen. We weren't close. Often we were estranged. But being suddenly parentless was a pummelling shock.

A new flatmate didn't help. A random stranger was now living in the King's Cross flat (my old pal had returned to his hometown), a stranger I'd foolishly picked myself because he had an amusing northern personality. He was also a self-absorbed compulsive talker, a full-time stoner and a soon-to-be-sacked social worker. Within months he was involved in a marriage (it seemed to me 'of convenience') to an ex-heroin addict, who soon moved in, their relationship founded on screaming bouts in the bedroom next door to mine. I was thirty-nine years old and living with terrifying, damaged, volatile crazyheads all over again.

Six months later I received through the post an inheritance cheque for £32,000, more money than I'd ever had in my life. It was probably the most money I'd *ever* have in my life. I put the cheque in a drawer for three months, the responsibility too huge.

On turning forty I knew: enough chaos, enough crazyheads, enough London renting insanity. Maybe this could be enough for a deposit on a place of my own. *Maybe.* I was finally contemplating the once-queasy concept of 'mortgages and fridges' (though was still some way off the pensions). But in 2005 the London housing bubble was rapidly inflating to an imminent planet-sized pop.

31

I CAN'T LIVE…

'You'll never find a place in London for that money,' scoffed yet another estate agent as I sat in yet another office with notes from a financially advising alien confirming I had £120,000 to spend on a home of my own. My parents, after everything, after they'd both gone, were now saving me on an epic scale, age forty, leaving me £32,000 – enough money for a £24,000 deposit on a home (a sum I could never have saved myself), the remaining £7,000 (after house buying fees) for renovations and household goods, as someone who did not own so much as a teaspoon, let alone a bed, a sofa, a wardrobe, a kettle or that deathly obelisk, *a fridge*.

Eventually, through the internet, I saw a flat priced £120,000 in a working-class 'parish' in north London, a one-bedroom ex-council flat in a sturdy, red-brick council block built in 1905. The interior thumbnail photos featured three ceramic ducks flying across floral wallpaper as befitted the dwelling of two pensioners in their late seventies, George and Doris, who'd lived there since the 1980s and bought the flat under Thatcher's right-to-buy scheme in 2002. (George and Doris bought it for £90,000 with a right-to-buy discount of £38,000, paying £52,000 for the flat I was about to pay £120,000 for three years later and spend all my life savings on: capitalism, eh?) The carpets were maroon and threadbare, while the bathroom featured no bath; fitted instead with a disabled person's water pump and shower tray because George could no longer step into the bath, or, the reason they were moving in the first place, climb the stairwell to the flat: 'two new knees, love'.

I visited several times, liked the old couple immensely, while the estate agents, naturally, were double-dealing crooks, a delay in accountancy information threatening to scupper the deal if I didn't purchase immediately. Impatient, they threatened to sell elsewhere. George and Doris stayed firm: 'We want Sylvie to have it.'

I moved in and burst into tears. Of relief and fear: how do I turn this shell into a home? There was nothing here except a 1980s washing machine and a cooker with a grill tray wobbling on top. I had to buy everything, including The Fridge, plus pay for full redecoration, all vitally helped by Tommy the D's best buddy from Dundee. Anth, who lived round the corner (as did Tom in his family home, one of life's outrageous coincidences), was a sometime sound engineer/musician turned professional painter and decorator, without whom I'd *still* be scrubbing carpet glue off unexpectedly discovered golden floorboards. Renovation took several months and cost £7,000: I'd spent the lot. On not only the most sensible but the most life-enhancing decision I'd ever made.

Having my own home, the home I still own to this day, is an incalculable privilege, a magical novelty which has never worn off. Simon moved in as soon as it was habitable and we've been here ever since, two freelance writers living in increasingly fragile financial circumstances. Outside the living room window there's the view of a council estate where the teenagers smoke their dope, un-hassled for 'a toke' by me, having finally given up dope forever (apart from an occasional puff with neighbour 'the D' – and for such ill-advised misdemeanours at this advanced age I *fully* blame him). Outside the kitchen and bedroom windows stretches north London's bountiful Alexandra Park, a tree-lined meadow befitting a Constable painting, which houses the Victorian heritage stunner Alexandra Palace, The People's Palace, still starring the iconic 1930s spire which sent the original signals of the fledgling BBC out across the nation (and a daily reminder of me and my mum's all-time hero who worked there in the 1950s, Sir David Attenborough).

I roar 'Thank you!' to the ceiling constantly, especially to my financially savvy dad (and to Mum for not, you know, drinking *all* the inheritance), for this gigantic posthumous gift without which I'd probably be renting in a windowless basement in Watford today, possibly even more miserable than I would've been if I'd stayed in Dundee (or possibly equally dead). All that stuff The Revolution taught me about V signs to mortgaged stability has turned out, for me, to be cobblers. Owning my own home in London is scandalously cheaper than renting and no madmen are going to wander into my living room and start blaring out Sun Ra, the ceilings aren't falling in and no one's going to have a nervous breakdown, unless it's me.

Some days, mind, I think, is this it? Will I die here? Is a one-bedroom flat on a council estate the material culmination of thirty years' work? Evidently so. I chose a precarious life, often minimally paid. All I'd ever wanted was 'freedom' and now I've all the freedom I could ever need, with no stable profession, or pension, or obvious way to fund my life for a possible further thirty years. If I'm not a bum by then, living in a leaky makeshift tarpaulin tent with my new chums under Waterloo Bridge, back on the Carlsberg Special (not bothering, anymore, with the lime). But again, I accept it. If your life is defined by the decisions you make (and it is) these decisions were mine alone.

So maybe it's just as well I never had all those children I definitely *thought* I was having ...

Simon and I had never talked about having kids. Maybe because we still felt like kids ourselves, a pair of reality-dodging romantics who'd spent all our lives in the determined avoidance of conventional responsibility. Or, at least that's how it was for me. I'd never had a trace of domestic desire, and a theory as to why: my mum had profoundly put me off. I'd been terrified, forever, of turning into her, of becoming a desperately unhappy alcoholic wife with five traumatised children and a disappointed husband. And if five kids had never made her happy then what, really, was the point? I thought Happy Families was simply what other people did. I'd never had any sense that raising kids might not only be the deepest fulfilment of your life but tremendous amounts of fun. We kids had never 'played' with our mum. Family life seemed a treacherous, tedious trap.

There were also persuasive cultural factors, being a teenager raised on eighties feminism with its central emphases on freedom, equality and choice. My freedom-seeking young self, therefore, had been free to choose fifteen years of dubious relationships with equally irresponsible men, the sort who'd struggle to keep a potted dandelion alive let alone a child, and when I finally got together with Simon (the kind of man who has, today, grown actual trees from conkers) I was thirty-seven-and-a-half. And in the summer of 2005, I fell pregnant, by accident, like a daft teenager, and everything changed. I was forty years old.

Like so many women I didn't think I wanted kids until I was having one. Until I *thought* I was having one. Abandoning reckless habits overnight was easy (booze, fags, the occasional spliff) and Simon's immediate response, as bewildered as he was excited, was to apply for his provisional driver's licence and purchase an amusing lampshade, featuring a smiley ginger cartoon cat, 'for the bairn's room' – which didn't exist, because we didn't even live together yet. Only then did I investigate the concept of pregnancy, and learned that becoming pregnant is not the same thing as 'going to have a baby'. That almost one in four pregnancies – *one in four* – ends in miscarriage for no reason whatsoever. A quarter of all human beings who might have lived, ever, have not and mothers, routinely, experience miscarriages between having children. But I didn't think The Worst, not once, perhaps testament to the evolutionary force which says 'life will prevail'.

Around eleven weeks into pregnancy, I was sent to interview the 'festive' yodelling diva Mariah Carey in her mansion in the Hollywood Hills, and on the morning of the early flight a light bleeding had begun. I was panicked, shaking, but had read this was reasonably normal and still didn't think The Worst. In the enormous atrium-sized living room of Mariah's mansion the loony-tune luvvie and I sat on two adjacent electronic massage chairs, which she temporarily switched on. Out from the chair backs shot two fist-like massage mechanisms pounding into our spines and so, for a while, I was transfixed by the sight of Mariah Carey's mythologically buoyant bare bosoms crashing into each other under her white, sleeveless vest like a pair of wriggly newborn seals. All the while I was *still* lightly bleeding into a sanitary towel, asking merry questions in this multi-million-pound showbiz paradise while thinking, 'I really *might* be having a miscarriage, right here, at this moment, on Mariah Carey's massage chair.'

I cried through all eleven hours of the overnight flight home, those gin-fuelled flight parties of the 1990s now the dewy reveries of an actual previous self. Two days later, three days before my official twelve-week all-clear, I finally had a scan, boggling at the sight of a vaginal probe, which I'd never seen before and neither had Simon, his already enormous eyes now Wagon Wheels of confusion as the probing technician scanned the screen and said, plainly, 'I can't see anything, I'm sorry.'

The word 'miscarriage' arrived like a heavyweight hook to the jawline, the filled-in future I'd so rosily fantasised spontaneously combusting in the time it took to say one word. The future disappeared like a detonated building, leaving an eerily gigantic emptiness. We walked, disbelieving, out of the Royal Free Hospital, north London, the world outside, impervious, carrying on – how dare it! – buses full of preoccupied people, destinations met, walking as if underwater back to our suddenly silly, adolescent lives. Was that, really, *it*? And then: it's my fault. My fault, my fault, *all my fault*. I'm too old already. I'm a naive, immature, feckless fool. Never planned a day in my life. Wasted years with all those losers.

The following week, nature 'took its course'. I had no clue what to expect. At home alone watching a TV documentary on, of all people, Pete Doherty, a period pain of hitherto unknown magnitude ripped through my abdomen and propelled me towards the bathroom, where what looked like purple icing pumping from an icing bag coiled into a mound of whatever it is inside you which is suddenly plunging outwards. Agony. Knuckles white, tears splashing, horrified at the contents of my own suddenly alien body. Quiet days passed, turning into weeks, and then an unexpected arrival: hope. 'At least you *can* get pregnant!' enthused everyone – friends, doctors, ourselves.

Two years passed (we were still regularly travelling away for work) and I was pregnant again, more cautious, definitely, but (again) never truly expecting The Worst. I miscarried at seven weeks (far less traumatic, at least, physically). If I was flattened, depressed, the doctors were not, I was 'older', yes, but everything was biologically 'normal'.

The hope crept back. I joined a gym, lost weight, ate fields of broccoli and at forty-four was pregnant again, ecstatic – 'someone's trying to be born!' This time, I just *knew*, everything would be OK. I miscarried at five weeks.

This time, a sustained anger, a relentless *why me?* But it's never just you, it's the little-known nature of biological humankind which makes the silence surrounding miscarriage so damagingly inhumane. We discuss abortion more readily because it's something we can politicise, distancing our emotional selves. The three-month-secret rule, albeit sensible, also compounds the silence. If you don't tell anyone you're pregnant, why would you tell anyone you're suddenly not pregnant? Friends who'd had miscarriages could talk to me openly, the majority who hadn't could not. Mothers would cringe when the subject came up, saying, 'I don't know what to say to you, Sylv.' Inside I'd shout, 'Say anything, just don't pretend this didn't happen!' But I'd say, instead, 'Och, I'm OK really.'

But was I, really? Mostly. Personally, I never felt like I lost 'a baby'. I never saw an embryo or heard a whooshing heartbeat. I felt like I'd lost a chance. Women, on the trepidatious path to parenthood, endure unimaginably worse: ten miscarriages, still-births, infant deaths, a million everyday sorrows. And for some of my friends the arrival of kids (even one) signalled the beginning of the end of their marriage.

I was never pregnant again and without money for IVF or any interest in adoption ('they' wouldn't give kids to the likes of us anyway, too financially unstable) we've simply carried on, together. It's just us now, and most days that's enough.

Once, though, I lost my mind. In 2012, my great friend Leesa, old *Smash Hits* buddy and tolerator of the 3 a.m. Oasis/Glen Campbell mid-nineties mash-ups on the Seven Sisters Road, was six months pregnant and we met one day for lunch. We'd become 'miscarriage buddies' by then; now married to old *Smash Hits* pal (and ex-*Smash Hits* ed) Gavin Reeve, she, too, had endured three miscarriages, one of which, in 2009, happened in exactly the same month as mine. It was too late for us now, I was telling her when I suddenly broke down, howling, great heaves of surging emotion driving me into the bathroom, thrashing water onto a face so burned with pain it felt (and looked) radioactive. It wasn't her pregnancy which upset me (on the contrary; at least one of us was going to have a child). I'd merely said out loud: 'It's just us now.' And that day it *wasn't* enough.

A few years on, those emotions are barely there: you find ways to accept your changing reality. And we kept the amusing cat lampshade, which lives in the kitchen of our home, a lamp which doesn't remind me of loss, it reminds me of love. We still have each other. Leesa, in the end, was the one who'd know all about loss.

Leesa and Gavin's son Spike was born on 13 September 2012. For his first birthday, they gathered old pals to celebrate for a meal in south London. Sitting next to the ever-smiling Gav, I'd never seen him so happy, *exploding* with fatherhood's joy. He'd yearned for a child, lived through the emotional crush of those three miscarriages, including twins at twelve weeks.

In a still-shocking twist of life events this was the same month that our Gav – not only a tremendous, funny, smart, fantastically creative and ludicrously handsome man but a marathon runner healthier than everyone else we knew – was diagnosed with inoperable pancreatic cancer. Over the course of exactly twelve months he underwent brutal treatments while unfeasibly inspiring all around him with his stunning levels of stoicism and relentless jokes, coining the term 'chum-o-therapy' and constantly cheering up his incalculably stunned wife, friends and family. We met several times through his last year and Gavin's spirit remained not only undimmed but astonishingly bright. I reminded him, in a Waterstone's café one day, of Spike's first birthday party, about the explosion of happiness beside me. 'Well, I am happy,' he smiled. 'I have those explosions still! I'm a happy person. I'm a positive person.'

Gav had not long become deputy editor of *Heat* magazine and in January 2014 a charity event was organised at the Hippodrome in London – 'Gav Aid', a showbiz/pop quiz (attended by generations of the old *Smash Hits* crew) which raised £30,000 for Macmillan Cancer Support. Gav was a man permanently on the verge of a quip. 'I still don't feel like a grown-up,' he announced one day, 'I've always wondered what I'll do when I'm a grown-up. At least I don't have to worry about that anymore!'

He was astoundingly pragmatic in the face of time running out, making a trip to Dundee where he'd studied art (and been far happier than me), to say goodbye to his fellow students. 'So between that and Gav Aid and all the visitors I've had,' he mused, a few days before the late spring trip, 'I'll have seen everyone I've ever known. It's amazing.'

I never heard him complain, not once. 'I've enjoyed everything I've done,' he mused over a pizza one day, a magazine man to the bone. 'Especially considering I just fell into it all, I never had a "vocation" like you. I've loved it all.' He looked across the table at Leesa and Spike. 'I've done everything I ever wanted to do.'

Abominably cruelly, he was then given false hope: the inoperable tumour, post-chemo, had become operable. If successful, it could give him, maybe, five more years. He took the opportunity, slightly risky, death-wise, though it was. I was with Leesa and Spike the day of the operation, in the Co-op, when the call came in: everything, a nurse told her, 'was fine', with a message from Gav, that he loved her. We bought food and wine, and power-walked home for a celebration. Mid-bowl of pasta, a text from Gav pinged in: the operation *hadn't* worked, the tumour was wrapped around an artery and too dangerous to move. He'd had bypass surgery instead. The young nurse who rang hadn't known the outcome, was calling with the news that the operation was over and Gav was out of the anaesthetic. It was a slow-motion moment I'll never forget. Leesa dropped the phone on her living room floor, a squall of pain, a hand flying to her mouth. He had a few months to live, through the summer.

Two weeks later, through a Facebook post after a 'perfect' moment with Spike, eating strawberries together in his play tent in the garden, Gav created the concept of the 'strawberry moment'. 'My plan is to have as many strawberry moments as possible,' he wrote on 28 July 2014. 'And I hope all of you have strawberry moments of your own. They don't have to be big things, just little moments of everyday magic that remind us that life is wonderful.' He was, at the time, deteriorating ferociously, taking four separate types of painkiller, his appetite (his 'crappetite', as he always noted, rumly) completely switched off. The Facebook quips were now about the trials of oral thrush ('nasal crabs, anyone?'), a six-foot man now weighing under nine stone. 'My weight loss is genuinely shocking,' he wrote. 'My legs look like two bits of string with knots for knees – I'm skinnier than Mo Farah. I'm Less Farah.'

That was the morning of 13 August, the last day I saw him, Simon and I visiting with a gigantic strawberry tart. The moment I saw him, I burst into tears and hugged his bony shoulders: the last time I'd seen anyone look like this was my dad in 1989, a similarly handsome, black-haired six-footer, taking his chance on his deathbed. Four weeks later, Gav celebrated Spike's second birthday and two weeks later on 28 September he finally lost his life. He was forty-four years old.

On 1 October, his buddy Jack Stephens posted on Facebook. 'This is the last text I got from Gav. As ill as he was he still managed to make me laugh out loud. Jack: "Hi Gav. So sorry to hear about your various health challenges. Let's hope those steroids kick in soon. I would willingly donate the couple of extra stone that I'm carrying at the moment." Gav: "What am I going to do with a two-stone cock in my condition?"'

Maybe it's worse, it seemed to me, for the ones who are left behind. That year I watched the heart of my capable, wise, roaringly funny friend Leesa shatter, a brick thrown through the window of her reality. One month on from Gav's 'strawberry moment' post, she posted her own thoughts, a distress signal from 'the other side' of the hell of terminal illness, a traumatic read on how 'unfair' life could be. 'This shouldn't be the way our story ends,' she wrote, contemplating their lost retirement fantasy. 'We were supposed to be in wheelchairs in Brighton hoofing each other around.' Ultimately, she was trying to find ways to accept their new reality (you have to, when there's no choice). 'I can't cry,' she concluded, 'over a life we never had.'

How could I, then, cry over a life I never had, either? Life wasn't fair, absolutely. If, after the miscarriages, my rosily filled-in future had suddenly combusted, Leesa's had been relentlessly torn down over an agonising year, one dream at a time. As the also tragically deceased *Face* journalist Gavin Hills (the one who saved my unravelling soul at Glastonbury) once wrote, in an award-winning report on some war-torn landscape of despair: 'And some people thought it was the end of the world when The Smiths split up.'

Today, myself, Simon, Leesa and Spike make the best of what's left of those ragged dreams. Spike is not only still Leesa's boisterously giggly future, but part of ours, a permanent reminder that life, ultimately, remains wonderful. A reminder that, no matter what you face, you can *still* wake up every morning and think, as Spike's seventy-eight-year-old namesake told me back in 1996, 'Thank *God*, another day!'

Some of us, after all, don't even make it past twenty-seven.

32

WHAT KIND OF …
FUCKERY IS THIS?

In January 2007, over two days in New York, the tabloid "news"papers would've paid no attention whatsoever to Amy Winehouse, her most persistently alarming behaviour then, it seemed to me, her perilous obsession with the calorie. Striding, at speed, around Manhattan and Brooklyn, her days were filled with the constant policing of her minimal food intake, giving a running commentary on the amount of fat, sugar, salt and carbohydrate of every meal she contemplated.

'It's too late to eat!' she wailed in a restaurant one night at

10 p.m. 'Maybe I'll have some mussels. Maybe I could just eat the sauce.' Another time, presented with a carton of French onion soup, she peered under the lid, declared, 'It's all full of cheese and shit,' and fished out the offending strings of fat. A bowl of clear, noodly Japanese soup on another day, meanwhile, was met with 'Happy belly!'

That month, the very month *Back To Black* finally reached number one in the UK eleven weeks after release, she was so proud of her robust physical fitness – she ran every day, was 'caning it' with sit-ups – she made me fondle her steely stomach muscles. 'And that's not even good, for me,' she chirped, bowling along Brooklyn streets, all twiglet legs, toppling beehive and Fonzie leather jacket, insisting all this effort and vigilance was for 'health reasons, it's not about weight'.

Such obsessions, though, were everyday for a twenty-three-year-old in 2007, hers a generation possessed by body image, often skewed by eating disorders, as she had been for years (both bulimic and anorexic – seemingly recovered, now, from both) remaining forensically knowledgeable about everything that invaded her body. Even if she couldn't care less when it came to the fags, the booze, the spliffs or the ink on her strikingly alabaster skin.

Amy Winehouse looked like a sailor (anchor tattoos) and talked like a sailor – 'alroight, dah'lin'!?' – an erratic, permanently distracted force-of-nature constantly tap-tap-tapping into her mobile phone while seeking out 'beers for the boys!' (her backing band, the Dap-Kings). Pinballing around pavements while I jogged after her, recorder in hand, she announced she wasn't all that arsed, particularly, about this singing lark after all.

'It's not particularly special to be able to sing,' she scoffed, her eyebrows knotting, quizzically, at my perturbed face. 'I mean, it's alright,' she reassured, 'I'm good at singing, but I'm also good at sewing, d'youknowhatImean? I thought I'd write.

You know how most people are "Dad, I wanna be a drummer" and Dad's like, "Well, son, you need something to fall back on, a trade"? I was the other way around. Music was my fallback option: if it all goes tits up, I can sing. I was never, "I wanna be famous", I was "Oh, I can sing, well, fuck it, I'm not gonna pursue it, I feel I can't write a book, so I might try to write a book", d'youknowhatImean?'

How bewilderingly bizarre. We trooped down a staircase into a junky Brooklyn basement where the Dap-Kings were parping, thrumming and snare-drum-shuffling through the album that would soon become lauded as the greatest of its era while the tomboy in our midst stuffed her hands deep inside her Fonzie jacket pockets, shuffled up to the microphone in the middle of a jostling melee of musicians and gently jigged on her pink satin ballet pumps.

'He-ee-*ee*-eeeee ... left no time to regret ... kept his *dick* wet ...'

With the opening words of the single 'Back To Black', she sounded uncannily like a vintage trumpet, forlorn and defiant. Sitting three feet away on the dusty floorboards of this makeshift rehearsal space I was transfixed, and had no idea whatsoever that this unique talent, this bawdy saloon girl with her heart pinned so freely on her stylishly battered sleeve, was in any way in any trouble. Because she wasn't. Not then. Even if she didn't, you know, eat enough and drink too much. But who didn't at twenty-three?

Amy Winehouse made me feel, perhaps for the very first time, at forty-one, *hideously middle-aged*. She thought I was ancient, I could tell (forty-one-year-olds, to twenty-three-year-olds, might as well be dead); the human embodiment of free-form jazz, she saw no kindred spirit here, only a tediously nosy adult stranger encroaching on her time with her pals. I knew nothing of the

music of her all-time hero, hip hop guru Mos Def (too left-field
for my hip hop-pretender ways). 'I first met him on the twenty-
fifth of February 2003,' she swooned, 'and you can tell it meant
absolutely nothing to me.' How odd, I ventured, that you can
remember the exact day you met Mos Def and yet you *think* you
met Mick Jagger (she did, in 2004) but were so unmoved you
can't be certain if it actually happened. 'Well, Mick Jagger is a
legend and all that,' she scoffed, unimpressed, 'but Mos Def is
a *prophet.*'

She'd squint at me with a look of borderline pity, perceiving
idiotic questions about, you know, her *incredible songs and all
that* with a curly-lipped look of both boredom and disdain. This
only made me like her even more: *this* was the rock 'n' roll spirit
missing everywhere else in the era of James Blunt, Snow Patrol
and the petulant Arctic Monkeys. Winehouse, being a geezer-
bird, was a natural-born caricature, a chaotic combination of a
young Paul Weller, a curtseying Minnie Mouse, a wolf-whistling
cockernee builder with his backside in the air and nineties
Tracey Emin plastered on TV with her finger in a splint. She'd
send herself up, tell stories proving she was 'such an idiot!', like
the one about first meeting her then-boyfriend Alex, a chef, in
the Good Mixer pub in Camden where she was always playing
pool.

'He walked in the Mixer,' she wibbled, finally sitting still
having a coffee in a Brooklyn brasserie. 'I was playing pool
and I was literally (boggled) "Fackin' 'ell." I was (fruitily) "Oh,
'allo, haven't seen you in 'ere before ..." So gorgeous! And
I had a massive bump on my head the size of a fucking golf
ball.' She fondled her forehead. 'Because the night before I
woke up in hospital about ten o'clock. I looked around and
all my best friends were there and I looked at the doctor and
was like (helplessly) "What happened to me?" and they were
like (resigned) "You had a fall." I'm like (sweetly) "Why? Was

I drunk?" and they were like (sternly) "You were *very* drunk." I'm like (relieved), "Oh, you've saved my life!" And my best friend Catriona was like this (arms folded) "Oh, what, *now* you're nice? *Now* you're not trying to hit anyone? You're all thanks to the doctor, what about me? When you were fucking swinging at *me*?" I was convinced I'd been spiked. So I got out and went back to the pub and said to the barman, "I got spiked last night, bastards! Did you see anyone funny round my drinks?" And he said, "Yeah, you! You drank about thirty Sambucas!" *Such an idiot…*'

That night, we bowled into what Winehouse called 'a proper pub', i.e. one with a pool table and a vintage jukebox, where she drank whisky shots, played pool at the speed of a young Ronnie O'Sullivan and pumped quarters into the machine, soon blaring The Specials and The Cramps. Her T-shirt was tiny, white, low-cut and sleeveless, all the better to display her tapestry of tattoos, including her *Sin City* movie-inspired woman with bare breasts.

'I'm a boy's boy,' she'd announced on the way, boyishly. 'I'm like a little boy and I like to be around boys, I don't really like girls.'

This was a classic Winehouse quip, a still upcoming musical phenomenon with zero interest in ingratiating herself to journalists, or anyone else in positions of 'authority'. In America, twenty-three-year-old women did not look like this, talk like this or feel like this, and Winehouse drew everyone's attention, especially three well-dressed, blonde, confrontationally drunk New Yorkers.

'Look, she's a lesbian,' announced one, approaching Winehouse at a table. 'The tattoo with the breasts,' she wanted to know, 'is there any significance behind that?'

'No,' replied Amy, gruffly, 'none. *Whatsoever*.'

Seemingly feeling under attack, her defence was to clatter off to the jukebox a mere foot from the girls' table and pound in the quarters, choosing early Stones, every-era Elvis, a spectrum of northern soul. An hour later, she bowled out the door, waking up next morning with a latticework of lacerations all over her forearm with no idea, whatsoever, what happened.

'I look like I've been at it with a fucking cheese grater . . .'

So whispered Amy, sidling up to me in a photographer's studio living room wondering if I'd any make-up which would cover the score marks so angrily scratched into her arm. Had she fallen over a wall?

'Probably exactly like that,' she cringed. 'I probably walked around the whole block trying to get to the hotel which is over the road. And probably fell down. I was probably outside having a fag and . . . I have no idea. I hate that. The blackouts. It's not nice to wake up in the morning and your boyfriend has to tell you exactly what you did the night before. Doesn't happen all the time but *too often*. I get wound up sometimes. Bad manners winds me up. It's not like I can't take my drink, I *can* take my drink, I'm just a really 'orrible drunk.'

When she drank heavily she'd often punch her mates and had hit Alex before. 'It's terrible, when I have one drink I'm the happiest girl in the world and then I just don't know when to stop!' Just as well she'd staggered away last night instead of punching the jeering girls. 'I am a lovely person but I thought, "They're all being horrible to me" and I'm quite an insecure person,' she mused. 'I'm like a kid, I like wide-eyed and innocent and everyone's so fucking cynical.'

That day, she looked after her own styling, hair and make-up. 'Is this for America or the UK?' she wondered. 'Well,' she announced, on hearing *The Word* magazine was *none-more* British, 'I don't know why I'm bothering trying to look nice, they know I'm ugly.'

That night we returned to the proper pub where Winehouse

sipped a Diet Coke, now banned by manager Raye from drinking tonight with two shows the following night at the Ronnie Scott's-style jazz venue Joe's Pub, her inaugural New York performance. 'It's not that easy, no,' she huffed, of enforced sobriety, twirling the straw in her pointless drink. It was here her stutter first appeared, struggling with 's', – 'asssssssociate', she was trying to say – an affliction nowhere to be heard in conversation with friends but evident in front of a recorder. A nerves thing? 'It's more excitement,' she decided, 'bit of both. I did an interview for a documentary about Dinah Washington and I love her so much the whole interview was me going "wwww … ww … www …" It's a new thing. I didn't have it when I was a kkkk … kid. Dunno.' She shrugged, uncomfortably.

Winehouse was only beginning to become the nation's favourite psychological cyclone, emotionally wide open, vulnerabilities exposed, an addictive personality prone to 'the black' (depression) which she'd treated, as a teenager, with the anti-depressant Seroxat. She'd never been, though, diagnosed with anything. 'I've periods of being so fucking happy and periods of … black, very black, and I can't explain it,' she noted, plainly. 'And alcohol doesn't help.'

In 2007, as she edged into mainstream view, the media had constantly monitored her physicality, outing her as some kind of fat traitor when she went from the normal-sized, long-haired teenager of her debut jazz album, *Frank* – 'the *spokeswoman* for curvy girls', as Winehouse scoffed – to the spindle-limbed, beehived caricature of today. She loathed the constant judgements.

'So I'm like, "I'll tell you *what*, as a spokesperson for people who don't give a *fuck*, yeah, d'you know how I lost weight?"' she fumed. 'I stopped smoking weed and I went to the gym, does that make me a bad role model? *Whatever*. It's a lose-lose situation. If you give a fuck. Which I *don't*.'

Which was all reasonably sensible until she continued.

'But I'm a drinker,' she concluded, 'I will drink rather than eat.'

Well that's no good, is it? Drinker's Rule number one: Have Your Tea. Trust me on this, I lived through the nineties.

'Well, I'd just rather have a massive meal at the beginning of the day and then drink.'

At least she was no longer a hip hop-level stoner, having long given up a '£200 a day' habit. 'Well, your tolerance goes up!' she reasoned. 'I used to smoke myself clear-headed. I used to smoke and I'd be (bawls) "Why am I so *alert*? I hate this!" So you have to smoke bush-weed, commercial stuff, rather than industrial stuff. And then I turned five and I just put the weed down.'

At this, the frenetic Amy Winehouse cackled throatily at her own joke.

That night, at Joe's Pub in downtown Manhattan, she shimmied on stage in a black, silken cocktail dress, ruched and shoulder-less in the classic doo-wop way. ''Allo,' husked Winehouse, 'I'm Ad Roc from the Beastie Boys ...' Her debut US show was a stunner, leading her band – 'gimme a chord, boys' – through the powerhouse peaks of *Back To Black*, through all those now immortal lines ('What kind of ... *fuckery* is this?' brought the house down). Somewhere out in the audience Mos Def, Jay Z and Dr John looked on approvingly. She talked constantly, sipped Amaretto sours and made New York laugh with her gags, soon singing twice as loudly and fluffing the odd intro. When she fluffed, she jabbed two fingers upright underneath her chin, pulled an imaginary trigger, sipped another sour and cracked another boy's boy gag. She was, I decided, the twenty-first century Dean Martin. Which is quite some distance from 'dead in four years, known thereafter as the twenty-first century Billie Holiday' ...

*

No one who spent time with Amy Winehouse as *Back To Black* ascended in early 2007 saw any of the madness coming: the imminent return of shady ex-boyfriend Blake Fielder-Civil, their marriage in May 2007, the full immersion into the toxic swamps of crack and smack, the violence, the blood, the self-harm, the increasing booze, the decreasing food and the tortuous decline to her tormented, dreadful death. All of which was trumpetingly reported in foot-high headlines by the now foamingly sensationalist, gleefully ambulance-chasing tabloid newspapers day after day, month after month, as up to forty paparazzi loitered permanently on her Camden doorstep, lucrative lenses hoisted at the ready, offering to buy her vodka so she'd open the front door. In 2008 *Q* magazine ran a feature on those paparazzi: us watching them watching her watching them as the tabloids waited, and doubtless wished for, the most dramatic headline of them all. Three years before the Leveson Inquiry (into the 'culture, practices and ethics' of the British Press following the News International phone hacking scandal) this was now Amy Winehouse's everyday reality as any lingering grasp on privacy fully disintegrated into a daily scandalised news bulletin over her continuing decline.

But she did not possess, to me, a scintilla of a death wish. There was no Kurt Cobain-styled 'I hate myself and I want to die', no Richey Manic-styled nihilistic despair. Back in New York, hers was the chaos which defines rock 'n' roll – an incorrigible imp, bursting with life, who spelled out the vision of her certain future with an optimistic, comic clarity.

What do you want, in the end, from music?

'I think I've got what I wanted already, pretty much,' she decided on the night with the Diet Coke. 'I've written an album I'm so proud of. I'd like to be ... *great*. My actual goal now, on paper, is ... do another two albums. Do a bunch of EPs. Bunch of covers EPs. Go and have twenty kids. And then, when I'm about sixty, "The Las Vegas Tour". I can't wait! I'll have Elton's hair, yeah, like at his fiftieth birthday. And live at the top of some casino and just come down for the show every night and they wheel me on stage. It'll be great! And my kids will be like, "Mum, you're so embarrassing . . .""

Travelling back to London I felt I hadn't really gotten to know Amy Winehouse as well as I'd wanted to. She moved so fast she was a blur, talked so fast you couldn't catch any depth, was all frantic front and dismissive, mostly, of any in-depth self-analysis (too adolescent, still). Not so different, mind, to most of us at her age, like we Stephendale Roaders ricocheting around London roaring '*carpe diem*!', celebrating the euphoria of life. At twenty-three I, too, would 'forget' to eat, blaze through boozed-up bedlam on the run from reality and shake The Specials and The Cramps from a jukebox. She, too, was A Massive Goth dressed in ghoulish black, as we all saw in the final scene of the stunning 'Back To Black' video, throwing gravel into the ground on top of her own coffin as B-Movie gothic writing spelled it out on-screen: 'R.I.P. The Heart Of Amy Winehouse'. But I hadn't come close to finding out *why* she was who she was. Or if there even *was* a why.

Back in London, out with Simon the night I flew back, still psychedelically jet-lagged, I felt agitated, disturbed, and a few drinks in, in a busy public space, an involuntary scream ripped out of my throat. He said it was like I'd been 'infected', somehow, by Winehouse. Maybe, as the Croft Original sherry ads back in the 1980s didn't say: one instinctively knows when something *isn't* right.

It was weeks later when I realised what her arm injury must have been, its two-inch-long criss-cross score marks, like a noughts and crosses grid, surely a bout of the self-harm she'd periodically succumbed to since her self-loathing teens.

I wondered what kind of psychic torment she'd been in that night, that I completely missed, alone in her New York hotel room skewed by insecurity, fallen through her memory net into the hole of a boozer's blackout, scoring large, angry lines into her skin. Maybe, beneath that towering, belligerent barnet, she wasn't so very different, after all, to the fragile, self-harming, alcoholic anorexic Richey Manic. The scores were carved along her left forearm, only a few centimetres' depth away from showing those girls who mocked her that she, too, was 4 REAL.

33

I WANNA BE A BILLIONAIRE

By summer 2007, Celebrity Culture and the great financial bubble delusion of the late twentieth/early twenty-first century had conspired to create a worldwide atmospheric fantasy, one which lifelong political theorist Paul Heaton, he of The Beautiful South and the breakfast gin 'japes' of the 1990s, would describe to me in 2008 as 'The Golden Age Of Flash – nobody cares about real things anymore'. One year before Lily Allen's fame/cash/consumerism-baiting corker 'The Fear' in 2009 ('I don't know what's right or what's real anymore,' she sang, ruefully), Paul Heaton sat in his red-bricked northern homestead becoming increasingly incensed. He was exactly the same old-school socialist he'd been when I loved The Housemartins in the mid-eighties, the lone songwriter in all his bands who ran his business affairs as an evenly split co-operative.

'People will look back at the greed, at when Blair and Brown talked about growth,' he now boiled, indignantly. 'What the fuck d'you want *growth* for? Why *more* growth? If it's not growth for your fucking tomatoes? You only want growth for your vegetable patch!' The rest of the planet, however, wasn't listening, too busy hurtling headlong into economic insanity.

By 2007, the ever-shinier world of entertainment was aggressively promoting a new glassy bauble to distract us from reality: the Celebrity Fragrance. Popular culture had now evolved into an ephemeral, pleasant waft, an aspirational deception in a hastily sculpted bottle with the name of a multi-millionaire on, whereby if you couldn't actually *become* them, you could at least, supposedly, smell like them (even if the rich, in real life, would rather douse themselves in Cillit Bang! drain un-blocker than touch these ubiquitous high street bargains). A ruse invented in 1981 by Sophia Loren (soon emulated by Liz Taylor and Joan Collins), the Celebrity Fragrance as 'revenue stream' began escalating in the early 2000s and by 2007 reached its first apex of global ubiquity (in the US alone it would account, by 2012, for a sizeable chunk of the $5.2 billion fragrance industry, a chunk mostly trousered by Beyoncé, Britney and Justin Bieber).

Into this atmosphere of consumerist illusion stepped an irresistible offer to any magazine from one of the planet's richest branded entities: Posh 'n' Becks, now more regally known as The Beckhams. Already celebrity parfum peddlers, their brand producer, Coty, was now inviting a selection of the world's media to report on the launch of their latest, an offer which involved flying first class (*first class!?*) to the Bel Air Hotel in LA (*Bel Air Hotel in LA?!?*) to interview the now globally revered Celebrity Couple. All that was required was an overwhelmingly positive story, an unapologetic 'advertorial' for the product more than any insight into the lifestyles of the rich 'n' famous. If it was already the kind of deal which rendered 'real' journalism redundant, it was made even more informationally fruitless by a series of non-negotiable caveats; in 2007, for a start, post-Rebecca Loos affair allegations, The Beckhams could no longer be exposed to journalists with a free rein.

I would be sent off for a 'face-to-face interview' which included the simultaneous faces of three other European journalists in a stop-clocked twenty-minute time slot, while all questions for the exquisitely ambrosial duo would be submitted beforehand and approved (or otherwise) by the Stalin-esque Coty bigwigs. Ten questions would be submitted, whittled by Coty to five, every one with the same theme: 'the fragrance'. After this PR-controlled lunacy, we'd be ushered into a 'cocktail party' and then served 'dinner in the presence of David and Victoria' as if they were the Sultan and Sultaness of Sultanaland.

The showbiz periodical employing me, while agreeing to 'stick to the script', suggested ways to extract a vaguely interesting personal anecdote. Something, perhaps, about their friendship with Tom Cruise and Katie Holmes (resorting to, had Katy smelt the fragrance?), plus a query on any recommended Christmas presents with a view to a sneaky, though harmless forthcoming headline: 'The Beckhams Do Your Christmas Shopping'. Even so, we had to sign a contract confirming only approved questions would be asked. So I was already in line for a Britney-style out-the-door manhandling. Help!

Still, for this level of illusional hokey we European journalists were treated like visiting dignitaries from an Arabian peninsula into a country beset by an oil drought. The British 'wing' of this fanciful farce comprised myself, delegates from the *Daily Telegraph* and the *Daily Mail*, all convening at Heathrow airport having been individually transported in the sort of sleek, black, tinted-windowed, leather-upholstered swish-mobile normally chauffeured for the likes of P. Diddy. This would be the first (and only) time I'd *ever* fly first class, the feverishly ostentatious ballyhoo funded by the evidently limitless coffers of Coty.

Giggling like twelve-year-olds, we boarded the plane and were motioned leftwards (after a noticeable double-take from the air stewards, wondering 'who?'), teetering past the paupers in business class and shown into our individual booths in the actual nose of the plane, where only five seats were available: we three liggers, the Coty PR and a thirty-something long-haired American dude who was possibly a world-renowned folk musician (and a stranger to we showbiz tarts). Settling into our humungous seats, with screens, glasses of champagne immediately bubbled into view as we inspected our already waiting, ribbon-tied silky pyjamas, toiletry-stuffed sponge bag ('in-flight amenity kit'), Japanese slippers and all-important menu.

For those of you who've never seen a first class menu (i.e. 99.9 per cent of humanity), in 2007 it included an opening page with a list of world class chefs, restaurateurs and food writers (including Michel Roux OBE and a critic from the *Financial Times*) calling themselves the British Airways Culinary Council, who met 'regularly to discuss, create and develop a range of dishes for your pleasure'. Your crew, the page bugled, 'will be delighted to prepare and serve you anything you may require at any time to suit you, nothing is too much trouble', implying they'd rustle you up an egg 'n'chips if you didn't fancy the already-offered 'Mark Edwards' foie gras and duck confit with plum wine jelly and brioche croutons', 'beef fillet with cep reduction and Anna potatoes' (sadly no 'ananas'), 'catch of the day, please ask your crew for details of today's fresh fish selection with your choice of sauce vierge or caper butter sauce', 'chocolate espresso delice with Mascarpone cream and fresh raspberries' and a cheese plate including 'Montgomery Cheddar – an award-winning straw-coloured unpasteurised cheese that is rich in flavour with a hint of fruit'. To wash it down, naturally, were all the champagnes, wines, spirits and beers on earth – which you were not encouraged to 'drink responsibly', as you were back in plebs' class – while intermittent snacks were offered including 'bacon roll', 'savoury treats', 'selection of cheese and fruit', 'sandwiches', 'patisserie' and 'Duchy of Cornwall Biscuits'. Everything was Michelin-level delicious, served on bone china with proper silverware knives and forks (because no terrorist was ever rich enough to afford first class, hem hem).

Just as I was at the 'wafer thin mint' stage of imminent gastric rupture, I dunked a Duchy of Cornwall Biscuit into a piping china cup of freshly roasted coffee as a steward stealthily walked by. 'Ooh,' he cooed camply. 'You're very brave to do that *up here*.' A demonstration, then, not only of how 'the other half' live but the world class bitchery involved.

Immediately after this gout-inducing banquet, I flicked the levers which turned the roomy seat into a fully flat bed and slept for a full six hours. Which meant, on arrival in Los Angeles at 5 p.m., I was ready to start a new day, chauffeured into the extravagantly lavish Bel Air Hotel by 7 p.m. with absolutely nothing to do, my new pals the newspaper toffs already off to their luxurious suites. And who could blame them? The Hotel Bel Air Los Angeles, once the actual home of Marilyn Monroe, was now an A-List hillside hideaway so extensively romantic its 12 acres of lavishly landscaped gardens featured a lagoon with preening swans and a stone-built lovers' bridge, while a maze of individual 'bungalow suites' spanned the grounds in the style of Old Colonial Spain. Regular celebrity guests, including Nicole Kidman and Oprah Winfrey, were now joined by our own sumptuously odorous Beckhams, not long arrived from the life in Madrid which almost scuppered their marriage, whose Coty partners were putting twenty European journalists up in Garden Suites costing $1,100 a night. For two nights. So I was almost happy to stay completely awake all night in mine.

The following afternoon we were ushered into a small conference room where a fully grown man, the Senior Vice President of Marketing for Coty, possibly on a hedge fund manager's salary, made a speech eulogising the Beckhams as 'fashion icons' before introducing their Intimately Night TV ad where Posh 'n' Becks skulked around a hotel corridor feeling each other up. We were invited to sniff the much-trumpeted fragrance on the end of some tapering sticks. His: Brut 33 from the 1970s. Hers: Charlie, for teenagers, from the 1980s.

After half an hour's more monumental flapping by several Coty executives we were split into five groups of four, my question-punting teammates now from *Joy* magazine (Germany), *Beau Monde* (Netherlands) and *Vanity Fair* (Germany), the latter an indomitable, cynical man named Jorg. A commotion erupted as we were handed our edited questions, all but the most obsequious now snipped (even the crafty Christmas gift question had been axed as controversial). 'This eez outrageous!' harrumphed Jorg, perhaps the Jeremy Paxman of German showbiz, soon grumbling to himself about how, if he had his way, he'd ask the Beckhams if they planned a then-requisite 'Hollywood sex tape'.

Finally, we were ushered into an opulent suite, all white French dressers and embroidered circle-backed stools, where The Beckhams stood to greet us one by one. 'I'm Victoria, lovely to meet you,' she piped while David offered 'How are you?' in his softly bashful way (while not remembering me as his outrageously flirting interrogator from *The Face* cover story in 2001, the tart). Victoria wore an elegant grey striped Hervé Léger 'bandage' dress, David a burgundy V-neck sweater, black Dior shirt, black tie, grey trews and shiny black shoes. We four schmucks now arranged ourselves on a single chaise longue like the condemned before 'Sir Alan' on *The Apprentice*, The Beckhams seated bolt upright on two velvet-topped chairs. Victoria sipped a glass of champagne, wondering how we were 'enjoying LA' and did we like 'the fragrances?' as lies gushed all around.

Standing like a stern head teacher in the corner by an ornate wardrobe, a Coty bigwig in a microphoned headset scowled at her clipboard ready to tick off our feeble questions one by one as we attempted to retain some dignity, and failed. The highlights from this twenty-minute farrago ran thus:

Me: *How do these fragrances reflect you as individuals and* (not on the official list but giving it a go anyway) *given the ad campaign, sexually too?*

Victoria, ignoring the attempt to glean an answer with the word 'sex' in it: 'What I think is great about the fragrances is that, you know, it's something that you can buy . . .' (snip!)

Minutes meandered by until the first German asked the difference between last year's Intimately perfume and this year's Intimately Night, which Victoria decided was 'the darker side to us, a slightly heavier fragrance would you say?'

'I agree,' agreed David, 'I think you always have to raise the bar.'

'Get you,' swooned Victoria, '"raise the bar", that's technical babe!'

Soon we learned that David Beckham sometimes trimmed his own hair and that the Beckhams' three boys used Beckham fragrance shower gels, until Jorg enquired, almost sliding with scoop-free anxiety onto the deep-pile carpet: *'When is the perfect moment to wear Intimately Night?'*

David: 'Every minute of the day.'

We lumbered on, harvesting our use-free information on how Victoria wore scent 'behind the knees' (?) until the question arrived about which scents brought back their best memories of growing up.

'I was always in football changing rooms,' offered the most fabulous, wealthy and lusted-after footballing phenomenon on earth. 'So ... Soap-on-a-Rope.'

On we cringed, soon finding out how Becks hoped for hair one day 'like George Clooney', how he and Victoria 'always find time for intimate moments, I think that's why we've been together for ten years', how their domestic life consisted of watching DVDs with the kids and a Chinese takeaway, 'with the Chinese in the actual boxes', noted Victoria, while David preferred 'In-N-Out Burger, I like Animal Style, with the cheese and the sauce'.

They'd come to America, they concluded, as the Coty Fuhrer in the corner appeared to loosen the reins slightly, not 'to be celebrities, to crack America ... Brad and Angelina are much more interesting than us', but for David 'to change the face of football in America', while Victoria was there to 'look after David, look after the children' and continue with her 'clothing line'.

On the stroke of twenty minutes they bade us farewell and Victoria waved us off with the curious wish, 'I hope you have a funny evening.'

One hour later we stymied hacks were mingling in European oneness in a spotless white marquee in the front lawn gardens of the Bel Air Hotel, sipping neon cocktails and contemplating an elegant scattering of white linen-covered tables. David and Victoria arrived, stood in front of an enormous screen embossed with their family 'crest', the dvb logo, and one by one we were photographed with the none-more-scented couple (not a single word spoken, though the smiles were wide). They took their seats at a top table as if positioned at their wedding once more, the rest of us seated approximately twenty feet away, indeed in their 'presence'. The menu lay before us on dvb-motifed dining cards:

Intimately Beckham, Thursday 2 August, 2007

Grilled Green and White Asparagus
California Morels
Orange-Vanilla Sauce
*

Achiote Glazed John Dory
Lobster Ravioli and Citrus Salad
Anise Infusion
*

Heirloom Melon Soup
Rose Petal Sorbet with Candied Violets
*

Cakebread, Napa Valley, Chardonnay 2003
Summerland Winery, Santa Barbara County, Pinot Noir 2005

And the delicately sculpted butterballs were in *the actual shape of swans*. Over dinner my new European pals surmised the most famous British couple on earth were 'very normal', 'younger' than they'd imagined and 'much less uptight', although surprised to find David 'a little sunburned'.

Around 10.30 p.m. America's new Celebrity Husband And Wife Team bid a gracious goodnight to each table, Victoria announcing 'We're going back for the boys, it's been lovely to meet you all!' And they trooped away, hand in hand, across meticulously landscaped lawns.

By the end of 2007, the overwhelmingly positive global press campaigns on the Beckhams' new fragrances had helped secure a reported $13.7 million deal to launch David's individual fragrance line in the USA. In 2008 the world's financial system finally imploded, the words 'credit crunch' and 'austerity' arrived and the concept of an extortionately lavish and editorially ludicrous press jamboree like The Beckhams In Bel Air fell into the dumper of showbiz history.

It had been the last 'hurrah'.

For several years towards the end of the noughties, I'd been made a contributing editor to a glossy UK magazine and given what's known as a 'retainer': £750 a month to not contribute to fourteen of its national competitors, both monthly and weekly. By 2011 the position was gone as crash-related cuts were announced, work for the magazine diminished (most of the features now written, for free, by the salaried editorial staff), and a freelance landscape loomed of fourteen competitors I'd never worked for before whose own cutbacks also meant little work for newly approaching freelancers. During 2011, I was no longer a columnist for the *Sunday Herald* either, 'let go' in the paper's sweeping cost-cutting cull that year, half its columnists rendered unemployed overnight. Over four months, then, in 2011, I lost 100 per cent of my guaranteed annual income and 75 per cent of my income overall. (Freelance life, from then on, would become even *more* precarious.)

But at least I still had the lavishly promotional gifts from the Coty billionaires, a pair of his 'n' hers Intimately Beckham Nights bottles, which have stood on a shelf above the cistern in the toilet of my flat ever since, and never been used, not even once. Because they are hideous.

34

I DON'T WANNA TALK . . .

In spring 2015, I sat in a hipstery Berlin restaurant with Mumford & Sons, now a generic, sombre guitar troupe having abandoned the banjo-bustin' signature sound which made them the biggest band in the world only two years before.

We were talking about contemporary culture generally that year: about how so many of the planet's best-loved musical forces had long been ideological vacuums, about how politics, protest and even general social commentary in music belonged to the radical, romantic past. The expensively educated Marcus Mumford (twenty-eight), Ben Lovett (twenty-eight), Ted Duane (thirty), and the minstrel-minded Winston Marshall (twenty-six), sometime trustafarian drop-out son of a billionaire hedge-fund titan), simply blinked at me, perplexed.

'I think it does exist, in hip hop,' maintained Winston, fifteen years after Cypress Hill's B Real told me hip hop's originally politicised belief system had been hijacked by 'attention seekin', egotistical, greedy sons of bitches'.

I mentioned John Legend's speech at that year's Oscars, where he declared 'Nina Simone said it's an artist's duty to reflect the times we live in', and still I was met with uncomprehending stares. Ben decided the word 'political' was hugely problematic. 'It's very dangerous to get up on a soap-box,' he retreated. I mentioned Noel Gallagher's recent pronouncement, about these bewildering times we live in where the radio pipes on with electro-pop pleasantries while The News booms forth fresh horrors every day about, as he noted at the time, 'people being burned in cages'. Marcus Mumford then summed up his worldview with a statement which could not have been more alien to my teenage post-punk eighties self, the sometime Smiths apostle who'd fallen on Morrissey's interviews as if holiest commandments, if he'd actually turned into a cloud of Saturnian helium.

'We're not into being influential in culture,' he concluded, evenly. 'I don't want people to listen to what I say, really. I don't think it's important. If they listen to our music, cool, but I didn't sign up to be some sort of cultural leader or inspiration or … spokesman for a generation, fuck that! I just wanna play music. And it's about as much as I'm willing to talk about, most of the time.'

It wasn't them, though, it was *me*: Mumford & Sons were merely, like all of us, a product of their time.

In the last few years there's been one, specific, shared characteristic among the public figures I've sat down with: suspicion. Not merely the general caution that's crept in since the tabloids began hijacking quotes for hollering across the internet (a ruse aggressively encouraged by magazines for years via headline-seeking briefs), but a low-level – increasingly high level – paranoia. And who can blame them?

I'd become complicit myself, as most magazines had, meeting 'the needs of the market' – a market powered by a public now addicted to insanely puerile 'scandal' and damagingly negative gossip. Which happens even when your intentions are the opposite.

A lengthy, celebratory *Q* cover story with the mighty Adele in 2011, the year her second album *21* made her the most successful artist of her generation, was gratuitously hatcheted throughout the media into tinder-dry sticks of inflammatory quotes over tax. 'I'm learning about tax at the moment with my accountant, pfffff!' she'd cackled that day in Copenhagen, hungover, sparking a Marlboro Light. 'I use the NHS, I can't use public transport anymore doing what I do, I went to state school, I'm mortified I have to pay 50 per cent! 'Cos I'd be sitting there for five hours if me appendix burst, trains are always late, most state schools are fackin' shit and I've gotta give you like four million quid, are you fackin' 'avin' a laugh? When I got my tax bill in from [debut album] *19* I was ready to go'n buy a gun and randomly open fire with my eyes closed!'

This, clearly, was cockernee Adele attempting to come to terms, in the manner of a stand-up comedian, with the sudden wealth that had arrived alongside her equally sudden household fame, and for this jesting outburst she was publicly annihilated for the first time in her career. Newspapers frothed over her 'tax gaffe' while broadsheet blogs compared her to a 'moat-friendly Tory Grandee', the most typical headline jeering, inevitably, 'But You're Rolling In It …' One website sneered, without even mentioning money, 'Fat ginger crooner Adele wants to "go and buy a gun and randomly open fire".'

In the ongoing aftermath of the Credit Crunch the public jubilantly joined in, Adele attacked all over still-burgeoning Twitter as 'ignorant', 'self-aggrandising', 'a moron', and told 'fuck you'. That July, backstage at the Wireless Festival in London's Hyde Park, I accidentally bumped into her, deep in conversation with her rave-grunge buddy Example, who I was there to meet. 'Don't talk to her about tax!' cringed Adele, as Example roared, 'Everyone hates you now!'

'I *know*,' croaked Adele and bolted out of sight.

She then stayed out of sight for years, until her stunning comeback in November 2015 when she gave, as ever, the minimum of global interviews. Fame, she told both *i-D* magazine and *Rolling Stone*, now felt 'toxic' and 'frightening'. Even in her fame-insulated reality, she added, she had recurring anxiety dreams about falling from tall buildings.

Over in America, Taylor Swift also had recurring anxiety dreams. 'I have stress dreams about paparazzi,' she told me in 2013. 'Really vivid dreams that there's people taking pictures of me while I'm sleeping. You don't ever really get used to that. Not that it isn't something I asked for, I could be singing in a cafe with no-one taking my picture, but it is odd.'

Over an enormous, shared pretzel in a cafe in L.A., she demonstrated an everyday celeb experience as she spotted, in her peripheral vision, a member of the public taking a sneaky long-range selfie. 'Whenever I go out to dinner, this is what happens ...' she whispered, holding her phone to her face, moving it minutely to the right and snapping. 'I hate that I can spot it a mile away but I can.'

She spelled out other grievances. 'What I've learned recently is,' she mused, 'if you reach a certain point in your career where it seems like things are going very well, public perception needs a "Yeah, but". Like, "Yeah, but she's been on a lotta dates apparently", "Yeah, but I hear she drinks a lot", "Yeah, but I hear she's crazy". It has a lot to do with being a woman. I resent that. I have to distance myself, the very little I'm exposed to hurts my feelings. I can't read comments underneath an article. I can't read Google alerts.' All of which became the basis for the planet-pulverising Number One single 'Shake It Off' in 2014.

In 2012, the ever-present Damon Albarn, by then pop's great polymath – Gorillaz mastermind, opera writer, world music meddler (who would prove himself *still* an arse, to the collaboratively regretful Adele in 2015) – had displayed the now customary suspicion.

'What's your angle?' he wanted to know, during a brief conversation at the annual *Q* magazine awards. 'You've been given an editorial angle, haven't you?' I really hadn't, there merely to talk cobblers about the events of the day. 'We can't be bothered to talk about anything,' came the sound of the sometime most belligerently combative voice in popular culture.

I tried some old-school comedy quips.

Is it true to say that you, Damon Albarn, might be the twenty-first century Leonardo da Vinci of pop?

'No!'

How about … The Sting of Indie?

'I'm not even going for that one!'

On one occasion I'd definitely become *one of them*, a tabloid tormentor, and it happened with an actual childhood hero. In 2012, The Blonde One Out Of Abba, Agnetha Faltskog, returned to the public domain after twenty-five years' reclusive mythology as The Garbo Of Pop.

Elegantly seated in a hotel conservatory in snowy Sweden, she was a delight: twinkly, shy, light of demeanour and charmingly open about her Garbo-echoing qualities which, she'd always felt, were exaggerated by the press. 'When I was little my mother said it was awful because when friends looked in the . . . the . . .' she explained in her broken English, miming an imaginary stroller. 'They'd look, "Oh, a little baby!" and I was (rubbing fists in her eyes) "Waaaaah!" Crying like mad. And when they had guests I was (glum face) "Ahooo, who is coming, a lot of people?" And when they left I was (beams) "Bye-bye!" And I am a little of that now. I can go into town, meet people, talk, have fun and then I like to just go back and (enormous sigh) "Aaah". Have a rest. I'm not a social person. What d'you call, when you stand with a glass of champagne, mingle? Mingle person? No. I am not a mingle person.'

When we met again as part of *Q* magazine's 'definitive' two-part interview, I had to address the difficult stuff: the stalker she'd had a secret two-year relationship with in the 1990s (a requirement specified by *Q*'s then-editor, even though her PR, the beauteous, sometime 'Susie From Creation' in my Glasgow police cell days, had explicitly asked me not to, so I circumvented around it); and the tragic circumstances surrounding the death of her mother in the 1990s, something I knew nothing about and discovered through online research.

Agnetha was strained that day, tired from endless interviews, so we swiftly addressed her turbulent romantic life, musing on the concept of regret. 'Love is very difficult, in reality, it's very very hard to find real love,' she sighed, 'but I don't want to look back and regret things, I rather live from now and forward.'

I left it there, carried on about the difficult two years where she'd lost both her mother and father. She'd never been directly quoted on her mother's death so I tentatively asked how she'd felt about it, to be met with a pained shock and a private request not to mention this in the feature. Travelling back to Britain I knew I'd compromise my journalistic instincts and respect her wishes (and respect them again here). The following day Susie rang. Agnetha was acutely upset. She'd never been directly asked about her mother's death before. She'd been awake all night, horrified this would be printed in the public domain (even though it already *was*). I wrote the feature, glossing over the details and wished, really, I hadn't known anything about it.

The day the magazine was published, Susie rang again. The Stalker Situation, never directly addressed in our conversation, was now afforded the siren-loud cover-line, 'Agnetha from Abba on surviving her stalker', while inside he was not only named but unflatteringly pictured with the inevitable caption: 'Take a chance on me?' The team around Agnetha was now attempting to keep any copies of *Q* away from her while she finished another week's promotional duties in London, otherwise she would probably 'throw in the promo towel'.

It was a miserable outcome for everyone and I was tormented for weeks. This woman I should've been thanking-for-the-music ('the myoo-zik!' as she so charmingly pronounced it) lying awake in her bed, in psychic agony, because of what pop journalism now demanded. I had made The Girl With Golden Hair *actually cry*. I had a *Smash Hits* flashback: in those carefree days all that would've been required from the best-known pop recluse in showbiz history was the quote 'I am not a mingle person'. And how we all would've laughed.

Some things, though, have never changed, only become increasingly fraught. In recent years, at the birthday party of now lifelong friend Carl Fysh, ex-keyboard player with those *Smash Hits* pineapple-posing pop scamps Brother Beyond (forever 'The 'Yond') and now a leading independent PR, another familiar figure from the 1980s shimmered into view. A glacial voice, distinctive in its sardonic Liverpudlian lilt, coolly announced: 'I remember yoooo. You're not my faaaaay-vrit.' Holly Johnson's ice-cool blue eyes steadily stared into my fully alarmed green ones as memory retrieved the *Hits*' double-page spread from 1987: 'Is This The End Of Frankie Goes To Hollywood?'

'I've waited twenty-five years to say this,' he announced, letting me know how irresponsible both I and *Smash Hits* had been, the fallout from the story causing eight months of personal, professional and litigious hell until the band finally split: a breakup which might have been inevitable but which would've had 'a softer landing' if not for the meddling *Hits*.

This was, to me, bizarre: nothing had been hidden, everyone had spoken their mind. 'You asked me over and over again if the band was finished,' he insisted. To this day the ex-members of Frankie still communicated only via solicitors, and his grievance remained steadfast: 'You people want to take some responsibility for what you write.' He had no truck with my bewildered response – 'but what I wrote was true, what else could I write!?' – and negligible mirth arose from the jocular assertion that perhaps, instead, 'I put you all out of your misery!' At least, though, by the evening's end a twinkle appeared in those pale blue eyes and the following morning an email unexpectedly pinged in: 'Holly Johnson wants to be friends on Facebook.'

But if I thought the famous folk had it in for we journalists, it was nothing on the general public . . .

35

HAS THE WORLD CHANGED...
OR HAVE I CHANGED?

New York, 2014, on-ver-road. Winsome American indie band Warpaint sounded like dreamily gauzy goths from 1982 and were, therefore, familiarly pleasing to my now prehistoric post-punk ears. We were getting along, these mostly thirty-something Californians (then anointed by the indie village as the coolest-band-in-the-world) proving themselves old-school boho hippies and agreeably more robust of opinion than previously billed.

Backstage post-show in the multi-roomed Webster Hall nightclub, we were merrily drinking when a spliff hovered into

view, which I took three puffs of despite having 'given up' weed
many years before. Immediately, I lost my mind, had learned
nothing from the nineties after all, falling down a wormhole
to a Glastonbury dance tent twenty years previously, some
yonder tantalising bassline hauling me away as if kidnapped
by swirling Dementors towards a pulverising rave-up *out there
with the general public*. Up on stage in a ballroom I'd never been
in before, a raven-haired cyber-goth was pumping brain-bleed
techno in an atmosphere so edgily druggy New Yorkers were
literally shagging on the floor. The Fear duly arrived, eyes like
revolving glass doors in the traumatised face of what surely
appeared to be a lethally dehydrated middle-aged person
who'd taken several Mitsubishi Es and hadn't had a drink of
water since 1997. I'd not only lost my mind, but all my work
companions and my iPhone containing such vital information
as where I was staying that night and the numbers of said
companions, only making it back to my hotel three hours later
with the help of a kindly Japanese tourist outside, her info-
deciphering smart phone and an unusually sympathetic New
York cabbie, while inwardly cringing, 'How could I DO this to
myself. *I'M NEARLY FIFTY!*'

Reconvening with Warpaint the following day in Philadelphia,
the girls were both sympathetic ('that cyber-goth must've been
so scary!') and gently mocking ('I've got a couple ready rolled
for you tonight!'). Two of the band, Theresa Wayman and
Emily Kokal, then both thirty-three, sat in their tour bus and
talked, for approximately seven minutes during that day's forty-
minute interview, about the most fiercely debated subject in
music that year: the hyper-sexualisation of pop music, in the
era of twerking, full nakedness, thrusting crotch shots and
permanently bouncing backsides.

Theresa mused on how so many huge artists today
compromised their more creative urges for the commercial.

'The things that get to those levels,' she decided, 'are usually compromising something, like Rihanna. She never stops working, you have to want that level of success. She naturally has an insane voice, she could've made something more subtle, more artful, but it's about the big producers and making money, running by a formula, what's popular.'

The hyper-sexualisation dismayed her. 'And it just gets worse,' she added. 'Beyoncé.' By December 2013, Beyoncé had fully reneged on her teenage template for 'appropriate dressin'' and in the explicit videos for fifth album *Beyoncé* was now fully celebrating, as she'd once described, those 'boobs hangin' all out and cleavage hangin' all out with legs and thighs hangin' all out'. Theresa carried on: 'Every song on that last album has her basically looking like a slut and she does not need to, she's gorgeous and so fucking talented. And they take it as women's liberation!'

We moved on and I thought no more about it, other than that 'slut' was a bit strong for the permanently revered Beyoncé. Then, post-show, we had a drink and a laugh once more, no mention made of any previous 'contentious' talk.

The Warpaint story was published and the internet erupted, the (mostly American) public incensed at the 'slut shaming' of Beyoncé. The demure Theresa Wayman, of all people, was accused of racist misogyny by a mob with flaming laptops and the indie village blamed me, personally, and *Q* magazine, generally, for this monstrous twisting of the truth. Journalists, they roared across social media, were scumbags.

Then came a Facebook post from Theresa herself, wishing to 'apologise with regards to the *Q* article'. She described how 'a journalist came on our bus and casually asked us what we thought about women in music', as if such a thing was sinister, claiming there were 'many long conversations behind that statement' (there weren't) 'and it's heart-breaking and painful to see it presented in such a hyperbolic and crude manner. We LOVE and ADORE Beyoncé and Rihanna, genuinely.' She echoed the public's perception. 'As we all know these days,' she surmised, 'sound bites and quotes are chosen not by their merit but by the level of sensationalism and that's exactly what happened here. Beyoncé and Rihanna are the last two women on Earth who I would ever want to disrespect or disregard.' She ended with, 'I apologize for being careless with my words. I apologize to fans of Beyoncé and Rihanna. P.S. I never said shit about twerking ... don't know how that got in there. By all means, twerk away.'

Within minutes of Theresa's apology the internet flared once more, unleashing a crackling outbreak of what was newly termed 'virtue signalling', the mostly online practice of showing the world how 'good' you are by damning the 'bad', where all levels of abuse are acceptable as long as you're on the 'right' side. In this case it was an impeccably virtuous, majority defence of the delicate indie poets from the dastardly journalist wolf. For the first time in thirty years I was comprehensively attacked, the assaults (alongside the more standard abuse – 'scurvy', 'snake', 'asshole', 'bastard', 'bottom feeder', 'female journalist who would chuck girls under a bus') including these excerpts siphoned from an online tsunami of assumption:

I find it utterly unethical and disrespectful what Q Magazine has done, they took advantage of Theresa's opinion and turned it into some 'slut shaming', hatred, racist comment.

Speaking as a former news producer for an ABC affiliate, I know first-hand there is nothing more twisted than the news and the way that these quotes are put together.

Don't worry, they hire people to make others feel bad for having opinions on social networks, this world is flawed and ruled by what is wrong with it.

It's sad that a female journalist should choose to twist words to pit successful women against each other.

Massive sensationalism caused by female-hating, male-dominated media vehicles.

And my personal favourite ...

Journalists always twist and turn shit into drama in order to sell, especially if they're new in the game.

I had to respond, also via Facebook, letting them know I'd been through the transcript and their version of events was fiction, that zero 'twisting' of any words had happened anywhere. 'I am not The Enemy, and neither are you,' I concluded. 'We live in spineless, reactionary and hideously po-faced times. The losers here, tragically, are The Sisterhood, trust between women and the oxygen of open debate. Those things are way too important to fuck with. A sad day for courage, and for the truth.'

Exactly thirty years after I shouted out of a train door window 'I'm too young for this!', I was *way too old* for social media spats with confused and fearful indie 'kids'. But all this fear, bullying and harassment is also a product of its time.

Back in 1998, the year the Manic Street Preachers released an album called *This Is My Truth, Tell Me Yours* (featuring lyrics dissecting androgyny, the Hillsborough disaster and criminal insanity), Nicky Wire mused on the potential of music to do exactly as John Legend suggested at the Oscars in 2015: reflect the times we live in.

'Our biggest record now has "libraries gave us power" as the first line,' he mused of *A Design For Life*. 'It should be all about the way you live your life, your point of view.' He mentioned the most famed work from the most cerebral music journalist of them all, Greil Marcus. 'It's the *Lipstick Traces* thing,' he noted, summing up the purpose of Marcus' masterpiece. 'All you can do is leave clues throughout history towards something better. Towards progress.'

Sixteen years later, fellow agitator Sinead O'Connor contemplated the changing purpose of musical culture. 'People's reasons for making music have changed,' she told me in 2014. 'It used to be people wanted to make music because we're all fucked up and maniacs and degenerates and there was no other way of expressing ourselves. Nowadays they don't even really care about the music, it's how they look. Now, if you get your tits out you're a maverick. The female musicians have been hoodwinked, all they're doing is looking at their tits, they're not saying anything about anything. Their audience are children and they're being raised to believe their value is in the size of their tits and how pretty you are and how many guys want you. That's the nature of female artists nowadays. It's all messed up.'

It was a rare incidence of a well-known public figure having a strident opinion about anything, the infinite freedom of our digital age having become, ironically, a simultaneous opportunity for infinite suffocation, the most colossal public arena mankind has ever invented now so often running on fear: of public humiliation, of ruinous tabloid headlines, of having the 'wrong' opinion, of ludicrously disproportionate scandal and the platoons of Twitter trolls on constant trawl for the sackable offence. Which makes the very culture it serves to create and reflect significantly poorer: artists cowed, ideas suppressed, opinions unexpressed. With very few, as the hapless dudes from Milli Vanilli once had it, 'laughings' anywhere to be seen.

In 2014, rock 'n' roll cartoon believers Noel Fielding and Serge From Kasabian also drubbed our conservative times.

'I won't expose any bands,' said thirty-three-year-old Serge, 'but there's nothing more depressing than seeing a band come off stage at a festival, go backstage and just flip their laptop open, at online shopping. And eBay. And having – no shit, I've seen it – chicken and broccoli after a gig. I'm thinking, "Are you not gonna have a drink now? Cause some carnage?" And they're (pats stomach) "Naw mate, I've gotta watch the weight." Fuck that, you don't deserve to be doing this job!'

'I'm ancient now,' declared Noel, at forty-one. 'I was brought up in the seventies and eighties, my parents were brought up in the sixties and everything was insane. The children's programmes were insane, the music was insane, the clothes were insane, the colours were insane. Now you see these [indie] boys dressed at Top Shop and you're *fucking hell*. You're not gonna get a band like Slade again, working-class boys in red fucking trousers and mirrors on their top hats. Noddy Holder, he's like an apparition from the future! Where's that gone, that glam-rock fun thing? I sound like an old man ranting but there's a generation who've had no links to psychedelic *anything*.'

Me, I'm even more ancient than Noel, and the other Noel, all hoary old bastards now as lumberingly past it, no doubt, in the eyes of the young as Led bleedin' Zeppelin were to me aged eighteen, in 1983, with my towering, toppling Smiths quiff and *incredibly dangerous* Alien Sex Fiend T-shirt.

In October 2014, twenty-three-year-old Ed Sheeran sat in a swanky, wood-lacquered trailer outside the *X Factor* studios, north London, and felt even sorrier for me than Kylie had twelve years earlier. With a lacerating hangover, he was no overly groomed pop hologram, nor a paranoiac without opinions, smoking roll-up tobacco while contemplating the values of his generation. Beneath his casually tousled carrot-top there lurked a ruthless marketing mind, a shrewd analyst obsessed with sales, iTunes charts and global demographics. To be any other way, he was telling me, was a mug's game.

'The industry has changed so much,' he noted, nonchalantly puffing away. 'Back in the day managers were crooks, record labels took 50 per cent, whereas now people are savvy. When I signed my deal my manager, who used to work at Atlantic, said, "I know the fucking deal you gave to James Blunt last week so you'll give Ed exactly the same deal because I know you can." Whereas back in the day it was, "Record deal! Cool! Sign, done, hits, where's the money!?" Now, everyone's cautious.'

Signed in 2011, the sometime dreadlocked homeless busker had now bought three properties on the advice of sometime nineties drum 'n' bass madman Goldie.

'I met Goldie when I was seventeen at some industry event,' he explained, 'kept in touch and as soon as stuff started to go well he rang me up and goes (giving Goldie, from the Black Country, the voice of a cartoon cockney) "Buy a fackin' 'aahs! Don't be a cunt, buy an 'aaahs!" Literally. Probably the same advice Adele was given. I feel like the older generation are passing on their advice to us.'

All his peers and friends were similar: focused, in control, obsessed with business analysis.

'I know it's not very artistic, being into the way things work,' he noted. 'But I wanna know the numbers. We're all like that. Taylor Swift knows everything about everything. She texted me today with predictions for UK and US sales. I'm sure there are musicians out there who do not give a fuck about what they sell or figures, or stats ... nah! No one's like that! Maybe that's what they wanna make you *think* they're like.'

He was now laughing at my distraught face.

'Pop stars nowadays are just more sensible,' he smiled,

reassuringly, as I heard an echo in my mind of Noel Gallagher's indignation in 2001 – 'it's all up its own fucking arse, man!' – well over a decade before Britain's latest biggest pop star would sound like a finance-advising CEO with three paid-off mortgages by the age of twenty-three. 'Because it doesn't last as long,' he carried on. 'It's: do your time, earn your money, buy some property and when it all goes to shit you've got something to fall back on. Whereas your generation, a lot of people just lived for the day.'

'You see the nineties generation on TV in *The Big Reunion*,' he reasoned, musing on the reality show featuring mainstream nineties pop tarts of a later *Hits* era than my own, almost all of whom became bankrupt, burnt out, inter-band enemies or fame-damaged rehab survivors. 'I mean they definitely lived it, I've met them and they've come out with a load of stories! So I hope to come out with as many stories and to have lived it as well. But with three houses. We've learnt.'

You're making my generation look like a right bunch of schmucks ...

'But at least your generation cared!' he guffawed, as I gathered up my belongings, talking to him that day for *Q*, the lone music magazine I now worked for, off back to my one tiny home, while Three Homes Sheeran stepped onto the *X Factor* stage, played the exquisite 'Thinking Out Loud' to 7.69 million people and went to number one the following morning.

Which was absolutely as it should be, because Ed Sheeran is a strikingly talented young man. And his best mate Taylor Swift is not only the greatest songwriter in pop today but a byword for industry power. The kids are *still* alright. They're just *absolutely nothing like the olden days kids*. Which is exactly as it's always been, forever. Whether we old bastards like it or not.

In September 2015, after sixty years in physically printed form, the *NME* finally lost its monetary worth and became a free-sheet, with all the advertorial compromise that entails, now as risk averse a corporate concern as any other. Rihanna smouldered from its cover, the interview inside bereft of a single joke, her often dubious contribution to popular culture gone inevitably unchallenged. Music journalism's agonisingly slow death is now even more protracted than my mother's. Three decades on from arriving at *Smash Hits* – smelling, I've been told, 'of talc' – there's no surprise everything is unrecognisable. Thirty years is an actual epoch.

But I could never have foreseen how music journalism would simply become obsolete. How mistrusted we would become. How the magazines would disappear one by one and we'd lose our natural habitat, now standing like the polar bear on a tiny wedge of melting ice in the Fox's Glacier Mint ads of the bygone twentieth century. How we'd all be amateur music journalists now, mostly unpaid (bloggers, commentators, reviewers, recommenders), how so many creative people would also lose their monetary worth and how all the music, from all time, would become freely available, everywhere, forever. Which is partly the reason why, as Mogwai's Stuart Braithwaite first suspected back in 2001, music as a cultural force is no longer a way of life.

The new heroes of the young, meanwhile, arrive every day in random chaos from a shape-shifting cloud in infinity; the YouTubers, an ever-increasing flow of DIY communicators turning journalistic discovery into a search for a tadpole in the Pacific Ocean, in a leaky dingy, with a stick and a piece of string. Today, the global big-gun book publishers (who are following the corporate sponsors) save their biggest advances for the ghost-written autobiographies of the Vloggers, gamers and schemers who no one under twenty-one, rightly, knows anything about.

If the world should be different by now, it's not the world I'd imagined in other ways, believing the silvery future of the twenty-first century would be an infinitely more compassionate place – a kinder, fairer, more equal, tolerant, giving, sharing, sustainably balanced pale blue dot suspended in outer space. A world where we'd given up the idea of killing other people in the name of power, or ideology, or land, or resource, and found a much better idea for our daily ride around the sun than Money Runs The Show. I thought, by now, we'd be living the post-punk utopian dream and *actually saved the world.* Those teenage dreams really *were* so hard to beat.

There's been staggering progress of course: we lived in actual Medieval Times, once, *for one thousand years.* The world we're still confronted with, though – beaming out from the screens of our spectacular technological achievements – appears a more self-possessed, greedy, divisive, violent, volatile world than ever. Our genes have remained selfish, our primary value the acquisition of stuff, our media often mean, our lives run by corrupt corporations populated by human automatons where ever more laughable Orwellian doublespeak erupts in ever more ludicrous forms.

We no longer, my friends in corporate places tell me, have customer 'complaints', we have 'expressions of dissatisfaction that are triaged by the first line of defence, before a warm handoff is given to the appropriate dissatisfaction area'. Which sounds, frankly, like someone taking the piss in a perv parlour.

There have, though, been some recent twitches of change: the return of an increasingly ideological young, furious political street protest across the erupting planet and dissenting voices, *finally*, in America at least (from Superbowl to Grammies to the Oscars) taking a highly-visible, vocal risk in popular entertainment.

I hear, too, 'post capitalism' is on its way. We're going to live, seemingly, in a new age of sharing, evolved from the information democracy and our new world of free stuff, where worker drones are no longer necessary, nor the 'needs' of any market. Sounds like a revolution to me. Due, apparently, 2075. So I'm *still* planning to live forever – to 110, at least. Because as Patrick Hernandez always promised back in 1979, 'it's good to BE alive ... to BE alive ... to BE ALIVE' (deedle-eedle-ee!)

In late 2014, an email pinged in wondering if I'd like to talk to the greatest hero I've ever had, more influential and inspirational than all the other lifelong personal greats, more so than Hibbs, Peelie, Madonna, Johnny Cash or Spike Milligan: me 'n' my mum's all-time hero since the early 1970s, David Attenborough Himself. On contact with the email opening on my mobile phone, girly-sap tears sprang down my cheeks, standing outside the home my parents had given me the opportunity to buy. A few hundred yards upwards through Alexandra Park beamed the spire of Alexandra Palace, where Attenborough had worked in the 1950s, ten years before he introduced snooker to the BBC, and then to me and my dad's life. A few days later, the very morning after my friend Gavin's funeral, his hand was outstretched to shake mine – David Attenborough, *Sir*, not only our Greatest Living Briton but possibly the planet's best-loved public figure. And the expression on his insanely familiar eighty-eight-year-old face could only be described as *thunderingly bored*.

We were in a frostily glassed meeting room of TV production house Atlantic in west London, where he'd been cooped for days on a promotional conveyor belt and had clearly had enough, another day perched like a hoop-twirling seal before an endless procession of agenda-driven journalists no doubt seeking, as ever, some BBC-bothering headline. Seated opposite him was an un-introduced man silently taking notes, ready to spring should an unwanted query arise. Our eighteen-minute conversation began awkwardly, simple queries specifically requested by the *Big Issue* (that day's employer) on what motivated him at eighty-eight met with a few terse words – 'I'm just very lucky that they still want me to do anything,' averred the most respected broadcaster in TV history – followed by silence and a disconcerting stare from those bogglingly sky-blue eyes. Didn't he ever think, though (as the *Big Issue* also wanted to know) when he was, say, drenched on a speeding dinghy contemplating low-flying geese overhead, why didn't I just do the voice-over from my comfy couch in Richmond? He now addressed me as a fool.

'But making films is *fun*,' he dismissed. 'It's a team business and most of the team are old friends, it's great.'

Silence. The Stare. Next question ...

I attempted to cheer him up: had he ever fancied a trip on the International Space Station?

'I'd be *bored stiff*,' he scoffed, finally bolting into life. 'Yes! There's nothing to do. There's no animals. There's nothing new to see, I'd much rather go to the Barrier Reef. And on the Space Station you can't escape. You're there for years! It takes you forever to get there and once you get there it's all black. And you're weightless, that must be extremely boring.'

Encouraged, I now contemplated Professor Stephen Hawking's assertion, that for mankind to survive into the next millennium we must colonise other planets ('escape beyond our fragile planet'). The great pragmatist here on Earth was having none of it.

'For humans?' he withered. 'Planets take *decades* to reach. *This* is where we are! Good heavens, we need to sort out what we've got! There is *everything* here that we need if we behave in the proper way.'

As our eighteen minutes began speedily running out, thirty years after I'd begun seeking, fruitlessly, The Meaning Of Life from a procession of fame-damaged creatives, I finally had the opportunity to ask a public figure who might *actually have a clue*.

'You've spent your whole life showing us how life on earth works,' I ventured hopefully. 'As a non-religious man, have you any theories as to why? Why, you know, ALL THIS?'

'I have *no* idea why,' came the breezy, crushing reply from the man who'd studied the origins of life forever. 'Science needs *how* questions. *Why* questions are for philosophers, not scientists.'

So all of this ... all of life ever, IS just a random, scientific accident?

'Yes, I find that plausible,' he nodded, serenely, before a magnificent, broadcast-level, DNA-stirring soliloquy from the most trusted voice on earth. '*If*, as astronomers tell us, there are an *infinite* number of galaxies with an *infinite* variety of conditions then it's not surprising that there should be *one*, in all that, which would actually *syoot* the kind of life which has evolved on earth. Yes. It's perfectly sensible.'

I blinked at him, transfixed, thinking this must finally be The Answer: IT IS ALL MADNESS AND NO ONE KNOWS ANYTHING ABOUT ANYTHING.

So it's all just ... chaos?

He blinked back at me. 'But it isn't chaos,' he announced, in his coolly matter-of-fact way. As the man opposite us declared 'Time's up' and David Attenborough rose to leave. I suspect, if he'd completed his answer to the most important question there has surely ever been, he would've said something like this: 'It isn't chaos, because it's perfect. The natural world is perfect.' And he'd be right. Other than natural disasters (which are still natural) it's only we humans who create the chaos. And there wouldn't *be* any of that chaos if we *behaved in the proper way*.

The day I met my all-time hero, I'd brought along the last gift I'd ever given my mum, reclaimed after she died: a copy of Attenborough's autobiography *Life On Air*. 'I'll sign it,' he nodded, meticulously writing his name, 'David Attenborough' – no Sir, no fuss, no flash – as I babbled about Mum, the seventies and 'our' shows, about *Pot Black*, Dad and 'our' sport. And finally, for the first time that day he beamed, with his explosively familiar, skew-toothed smile. 'Well,' he twinkled, 'how *wonderful.*'

In summer 2015, I found myself lying on patio paving stones behind a lemon-bordered cottage on the isle of Arran, west Scotland, at midnight, with Simon, staring straight up into infinity, goggling at the busting, cloudy glitterings of the unknowable vastness of our very own Milky Way. A shooting star – psssssssst! – flared into view, a silvery-golden streak, that most sure of cosmic arrows, tapering across and downwards towards oblivion. The International Space Station, containing earthly humans (though none called David Attenborough), steadily sailed its silent path through a sprinkling of the 400 billion stars across 120,000 light years of the only galaxy we will ever call home.

This time, unlike in Jamaica exactly twenty years previously, no hallucinogenic drugs had been smoked and I knew exactly where the reality was and which way up the world worked. What's it all about? No one knows, not even David Attenborough, other than the permanently staggering fact: against every conceivable and inconceivable odd, *you got to be alive.* And know about it. Unlike if you'd been born a different collection of atoms and become, say, the two millionth identical red brick on a Wimpey estate in Tyneside. It is a *privilege* to be a human being. It might not seem so, sometimes, when we see humanity's horrors played out daily on our 24 hour news, but it *is.* And there wouldn't be any of *those* horrors, either, if we *behaved in the proper way.*

That week on Arran there was a huge joint fiftieth birthday celebration for my oldest friends and everyone was there, still, like they'd always been and always will be until we're all punting off into The Dumper of humanity itself: The Four Of Us, Rimmy, Sandra, an almost complete 'shifty lot', partners, school friends, the parents who were still alive, brothers, sisters, cousins, toddlers, teenagers, new best friends alongside oldest best friends, an eighty-strong extended family, dancing, laughing, drinking, crying, cackling, falling over and linking arms at the end of a shoreside party as the roar of 'Loch Lomond' erupted – while the universe overhead, no doubt, couldn't have cared less about any of us.

What's it all about?

Maybe it's exactly as Diana Ross, of all people, told me it was so simply twenty-eight years before: Good friends and family. Going for a picnic. Going on a long walk. Relationships. Dancing or reading a good book. Watching a daffodil grow. Maybe even some champagne on a *very* special occasion, like this one. I was still, as I had been as a child, a *monumental* sap. (Maybe most of us, deep down, are.) That night, I kept thinking it, and saying it, over and over again: 'I feel *privileged*.' I was earning less money, by then, than I'd earned in the *Smash Hits* staff years thirty years before. Significantly less than I would earn as a twenty-year-old manning the checkout in a branch of Lidl today. I'd be heading home to find out if this book I'd written was deemed printable or not. And then I'd have to start, professionally, all over again. With no clue how anyone does this. Where the conclusion could not be more uncertain. Just like so many of us in the creatively confounding era of the early twenty-first century. Some days I'm terrified – of losing my home, of approaching true poverty, of outright destitution in old age (if I even get there). But life, ultimately, remains wonderful, still gives to us all those moments of everyday magic – as Gavin reminded us two weeks before he died. And as the newly-winged Clarence Odbody wrote in a copy of *Tom Sawyer* in my favourite-ever film, the sap's perennial, *It's A Wonderful Life*: 'No man is a failure who has friends.' (The film where we all get to see, of course, just how many lives a single human being will never know they saved.)

Even if we are all living, now, in the gin-slewed, crook-run, neon-lit pleasuredomes of Pottersville.

Meanwhile, we've got a planet to sort out *today*. And these things, as ever, will be up to the new generation. So *go on* Ver Kids. Whether a disco dreamer with your gym breeks up a tree, a bronchial spliff-head housed in a derelict building, or a startled romantic striving in your dream profession (and if so, be very careful what you've wished for): find your own ways to start *your* version of The Revolution.

Ways to burn away the bollocks.

To celebrate the euphoria of life.

Before you, too, go to hospital for a very long time. i.e. forever.

GOODBYE YELLOW BRICK ROAD

Magazines we have loved in my journalistic lifetime, in Britain alone, now decomposing in The Dumper ...

Raw. . . Record Mirror ... No.1 ... Mizz ... Blue Jeans ... Patches ... Jackie ... My Guy ... Just 17 ... Big ... TV Hits ... Ikon ... Select ... SKY ... The Hit ... Vox ... Sounds ... Frank ... City Limits ... Honey ... The Face ... Modern Review ... Encore ... Hip-Hop Connection ... Spare Rib ... Melody Maker ... Muzik ... Ministry ... Deluxe ... Bang ... Smash Hits ... Arena ... Punch ... Neon ... Maxim ... The Word ... Easy Living ... More ... The Fly ... Nuts ... Loaded ... (the spirit of) NME ... FMH ... Zoo . . . .
....
....
.... (Space to write the names of the next lot, as they come in. Hours of fun guaranteed!)

ACKNOWLEDGEMENTS

The 'Blimey, I've Written A Book About My Stupid Life And I'm Not Even Famous (It's A Rum Do And No Mistake)' Department Presents ...

JINGS! A GIGANTIC THUMBS ALOFT TO ...

BACKSTAGE 'WINGS': Kevin 'Agent P' Pocklington, Jenny Brown Associates (for having The Faith) and the team at Sphere, Little Brown; Antonia 'An Editor Writes' Hodgson (for the guidance, encouragement and Pub Enthusiasm); organisational titan Rhiannon Smith (much better than Rihanna) and nerve-steadying PR guru Stephanie Melrose (*much* better than Kate Moss).

SWINGORILLIANT: Tom Hibbert (blub!), Steve Bush, Barry 'Banzai' McIlheney, Vici MacDonald, Jaqui Doyle, Chris 'The Toff' Heath, William 'Sir Trilliam' Shaw, Derrin Schlesinger, Lola Borg, Sue Miles, Paul Rider, Julian Barton, Leesa Daniels, Gavin Reeve (talk about swizzed, mate), Reg 'Reg' Snipton, Mike 'Soapy' Soutar, Uncle Disgusting, Old Rope and everyone else at *Smash Hits* 1986–1994. Wibble.

MADFERRIT: Steve Sutherland, Stuart Bailie, Ted Kessler,

James Oldham, Simon Williams, Andy Capper, Alex Needham, Johnny Dee, Kathy Ball, Barbara Ellen, Dele Fadele, Ben 'Bono's Pal' Knowles, Kevin Westenberg, Steve Double and all the nice ones at the *NME*. Special Paul Weller-style 'shout to the top' to Paul McNamee at ver *Big Issue*.

IT'S GURREAT BEING A GIRL: the acutely fabulous *Glamour* magazine trio Jo Elvin, James Williams and Helen Placito (for the colossal generosity).

HOARY OLD BLOKE'S MAGAZINE: Chris Catchpole, Matt Mason, Niall Doherty, Dave Everley, 'Filthy' Phil Alexander (you're not getting two, Kessler) and all the pavement partiers every year at the *Q* magazine awards.

SWIZZLE! (mags too good for The Man): Craig McLean, Johnny Davies and Richard Benson at *The Face*; Mark Ellen and David Hepworth at *The Word*. *Weep*.

THE SHOW MUST GO ON: the foxy 'ladies' and alleged gents of Public Relations; Terri Hall, Gillian Porter, Sophie Williams, Carl Fysh, Polly Birkbeck, Paddy Davis, Susie Ember, Shane O'Neill, Andy Prevezer, Murray Chalmers, Barbara 'BC' Charone, Amanda Freeman, Tony Linkin, Jamie Woolgar, Simon Hargreaves, Steve Phillips, Graham Hill, John Yates. And Anton 'Pimpernel' Brookes.

MY SHOWBIZ CHUMS HEM HEM: Liam 'n' Noel Gallagher (for permission to relive September 12th 2001), Kylie Minogue (for the sheets), Holly Johnson (for singing 'The Power Of Love' down the phone to Leesa) and Marc Almond (for being a massive diva).

RUMBLED! THE PHOTOGRAPHIC EVIDENCE: Ali, Sand, Trish, with special thanks to proper photographer Rachael Wright for the image on page 411 (and Jack Stephens for permission to use Gavin Reeve-Daniels' spectacular joke).

OLD CODGERS CORNER (you're all still there, it's a miracle, sorry about being a bit mental that time, and all the other times): Jackie McDonald, The Four of Us (Alison Doyle, Evelyn Hocking, Jill Henry), Rimmy, Sandra Milne, The London Four of Us (Patricia Darvell, Gillian Best, Sian Pattenden), the mysterious 'M', Anth 'Broon' and Tom 'Tommy the D' Doyle (the dealer I never wanted ... only joking, m'lud!!).

THE ONE AND THE GUY: Monsieur Simon Goddard (half man, half compass). For the damp shoulder, the infinite jokes, the dedicated (ruthless) red pen and not so much the constant support as the permanent Life Scaffold (and you ain't even got the legs for it, 'haw' 'haw'). Your spirit is inspirational, and I love you. 'So do I, mate,': Boris Becker.

LYRIC CREDITS

'E.S.T. (Trip To The Moon)': Alien Sex Fiend, Cherry Red Songs, 1984. By John Freshwater, David James, Chris Wade, Nicholas Ian Wade.

'Good Life': Inner City, Sony/ATV Music Publishing LLC, 1988. By Roy Holman, Shanna Jackson and Kevin Saunderson.

'Yes, We Have No Bananas': Billy Jones, Shapiro Bernstein and Co, 1923. By Irving Conn and Frank Silver.

'Stayin' Alive': Bee Gees, Warner/Chappell Music Inc., Universal Music Publishing Group, 1977. By Barry Gibb, Maurice Gibb, Robin Gibb.

'Song For Guy': Elton John, Sony/ATV Music Publishing LLC, 1978. By Elton John.

'Rose Garden': Lynn Anderson, Sony/ATV Music Publishing LLC, 1970. By Joe South.

'5:15': The Who, Universal Music Publishing Group, 1973. By Peter Townshend.

'Born to Be Alive': Patrick Hernandez, Low Spirit Music Publishing, 1978. By Patrick Hernandez.

'Shirt of Blue': The Men They Couldn't Hang, 1986. By Stefan Cush, Shanne Bradley, Jon Odgers, Phil Odgers and Paul Simmonds.

'It's a Small World': Walt Disney Music Publishing Group, 1962. By Richard Sherman and Robert Sherman.

'I Owe You Nothing': Bros, Warner/Chappell Music Inc., 1987. By Nicky Graham and Tom Watkins.

'Loaded': Primal Scream, Sony/ATV Music Publishing LLC, Universal Music Publishing Group, 1990. By Bobby Gillespie, Andrew Innes and Robert Young.

'Song 2': Blur, Sony/ATV Music Publishing LLC, Warner/Chappell Music Inc., 1997. Damon Albarn, Graham Coxon, Alex James and Dave Rowntree.

'Small Black Flowers That Grow in the Sky': Manic Street Preachers, Sony/ATV Music Publishing LLC, 1996. By James Bradfield, Richey Edwards, Sean Moore and Nicky Wire.

'Supersonic': Oasis, Sony/ATV Music Publishing LLC, 1994. By Noel Gallagher.

'Digsy's Dinner': Oasis, Sony/ATV Music Publishing LLC, 1994. By Noel Gallagher.

'Champagne Supernova': Oasis, Sony/ATV Music Publishing LLC, 1995. By Noel Gallagher.

'Slide Away': Oasis, Sony/ATV Music Publishing LLC, 1994. By Noel Gallagher.

'Kuff Dam': Happy Mondays, Warner/Chappell Music Inc., Universal Music Publishing Group, 1987. By Paul Davis, Mark Day, Paul Ryder, Shaun Ryder and Gary Whelan.

'Make the World Go Away': Sydney Devine, Sony/ATV Music Publishing, 1963. By Hank Cochran.

'Stand by Your Man': Tammy Wynette, Sony/ATV Music Publishing, 1968. By Billy Sherrill and Tammy Wynette

'One Day at a Time': Cristy Lane, Sony/ATV Music Publishing, Universal Music Publishing Group, 1974. By Kris Kristofferson and Marijohn Wilkin.

'Release the Bats': The Birthday Party, Songs of Windswept Pacific, 1980. By Nick Cave and Mick Harvey.

'We Live As We Dream, Alone': Gang of Four, Bug Music

Limited, 1982. By Andrew Gill and Jon King.

'Rapper's Delight': Sugarhill Gang, Warner/Chappell Music Inc., 1979. By Bernard Edwards and Nile Rodgers.

'A Man': Cypress Hill, Universal Music Publishing Group, 2000. By Lance Correa, Jeremy Fleener, Louis Freese, Senen Reyes and Andy Zambrano.

'My Name Is': Eminem, BMG Rights Management US LLC, 1999. By Marshall Mathers, Andre Young and Labi Siffre.

'Back to Black': Amy Winehouse, Sony/ATV Music Publishing, BMG Rights Management US LLC, 2007. By Amy Winehouse and Mark Ronson.